THE HEROIC COUPLET

THE
HEROIC
COUPLET

William Bowman Piper

THE PRESS OF
CASE WESTERN RESERVE UNIVERSITY
Cleveland & London
1969

To the memory of my great teacher,
Ruth Wallerstein

PREFACE

The first of the two main parts of this book, "A Brief History," explains itself; but the second, "Essays and Illustrations," requires a few preliminary remarks.

Each of the forty-eight separate sections of "Essays and Illustrations," as I originally composed them, contained, in addition to a critical essay on one of the couplet poets, an illustrative selection of that poet's work. This complete system was judged, however, to involve the publication of too much poetry that was already widely available and to present too great an expense to the publisher. And, although I regret losing the chance to represent the whole heroic couplet tradition that "Essays and Illustrations" was originally intended to afford, I have been obliged to cut it down. As things now stand, there are essays on twenty-five poets — and these, naturally, the most famous and the most accomplished ones — which lack any illustrative accompaniment. Thus, the reader, in order to realize the complete design of "Essays and Illustrations," must read through it within easy reach of the works of these twenty-five poets. I have indicated convenient texts of these works in footnotes to the separate essays.

The poetic illustrations which, because they are relatively inaccessible, are still represented in "Essays and Illustrations" have generally been derived from their best early versions. Except for a few minor changes, such as the replacement of the old long *s* and the regularization of *u* and *v*, this poetry appears in its original form. Several of the illustrations have been augmented with the Latin or French verse from which they were translated, each example of this analogous material immediately following its English counterpart. In composing this element of my book and, indeed, in determining on all my poetic quotations, I have depended on the work of previous editors: on Hebel's *Drayton*, for example, on Grierson's *Donne*, and on Pope's *Sheffield*. I have always tried, however, to arrive

[vii]

at texts which, despite the slight alterations required for convenience of reading, still represent the poetry as the poets, editors, amanuenses, and printers presented it to their contemporaries.

Every one of the essays in "Essays and Illustrations" refers precisely and extensively to the relevant illustrative poetry and can be understood only in connection with that poetry. These references should be clear. (It may be well, however, to point out that I have indicated shorthand and other approximate quotations with single quotation marks: thus, I refer to the echo in this Ovidian pentameter, "*carmina — qui placeo, protinus ipsa placet,*" in the following way: '*placeo–placet.*') I hope that the reader will often be inclined to follow up these references. My guiding purpose in "Essays and Illustrations" and, indeed, throughout *The Heroic Couplet*, has been to induce readers of English to consider — or to consider in more detail — the styles and the expressive powers of our one great tradition of public poetry.

In composing this book I have incurred many debts: one to the editors of *Modern Philology*, who have permitted me to use my article, "The Inception of the Closed Heroic Couplet." I should also like to acknowledge the interest and the forbearance of my students, one of whom told me that he began, after taking a course of mine, to dream in heroic couplets. Several of these students, especially Mrs. Jessie Waters, in her work on Sheffield's *Essay upon Satire*, Mr. Jerome Bednarski, in his paper on Dryden's dramatic prologues, and Mrs. Nancy Lampl, in her essay on Pope's *Epilogue to the Satires*, have contributed to this book in particular and describable ways. And Mrs. Carol Lovejoy, on a visit to the British Museum, kindly verified some of my illustrative texts. I am also indebted to Mrs. Esther Scheps and Miss Delia Burke, who gave me valuable editorial assistance, and to Miss Sidonie Smith, who compiled the index. My greatest and most various debts, however, are those I owe to my colleagues, especially Professors Charles Reeves, Edward Knox, Michael Sundell, W. Speed Hill, Walter Scheps, and Christopher Q. Drummond. Mr. Drummond has, indeed, been my guide, philosopher, and friend throughout virtually every stage of my work. Finally, I must acknowledge my wife, Katharine Welles Piper, who was also Miss Wallerstein's student in poetry and metrics, and who gave up her own career as an English scholar to help me face the problems and the frustrations of mine.

CONTENTS

A BRIEF HISTORY

I

※※※※※※※※※※※※※※※※

INTRODUCTION

Since the decasyllabic line is the traditional heroic line of English poetry, every English decasyllabic couplet is a heroic couplet. Thus a history of this form must acknowledge poetic practice beginning gloriously with the great decasyllabic couplet poems of Chaucer [1] and running up to the present day. This vast sweep of time, however, falls naturally into three nearly equal periods, only the second of which offers significant rewards to historical study.

In the first period, which runs from about 1385 to 1585, there is only one great practitioner of the form, Chaucer himself. A study of this period of couplet history can merely acknowledge a number — and a surprisingly small number — of Chaucerian imitations. There is *The Troy Book*, which Lydgate composed in roughly decasyllabic couplets in the generation after Chaucer, for example. Then, two or three generations later, there are a few couplet works from the Scottish Chaucerians. The most famous of these, significantly, Gavin Douglas's translation of Vergil's *Aeneid*, is historically important chiefly in the foundation of English blank verse.[2] In the middle of the sixteenth century, John Dolman composed a decasyllabic-couplet account of Hastings which he contributed to *A Mirror for Magistrates*, and the editor of the *Mirror*, William Baldwin, also used this form for his complaint, "The Funerals of King Edward VI." Finally, there is Edmund Spenser's *Mother Hubberd's Tale*, with which, except for some old-fashioned poems in the next few decades, this meager tradition comes to an end. We have then in the two hundred years after Chaucer almost no original heroic couplet composition at all and none, including Spenser's interesting poem, that either escapes the influence or approaches the art of the great innovator of the

---

[1] The beginnings may actually be traced back before Chaucer: the coupled lines of *Gamelyn* (ca. 1350), for example, are inclined to be decasyllabic.

[2] See Howard Baker, *Induction to Tragedy* (New York, 1965), pp. 68–75, who describes Surrey's dependence on Douglas in making his blank verse translation of *Aeneid*.

[3]

form. To acknowledge Chaucer's style and to recognize the degree of its continuance in Spenser, which I have done in my essays on these poets, sufficiently accounts for the form up to 1585.

There are two other aspects of the early heroic couplet besides its style which, since all three would be sharply changed after 1585, ought also to be emphasized. First, its use was confined almost completely to long narratives — due no doubt to the influence of Chaucer: even Spenser's satiric allegory and Baldwin's elegiac complaint were cast as long narrative poems. Second, it was a rather unfashionable form of poetry partly, at least, because Chaucer used it chiefly for comedy. His rhyme royal, which Gascoigne described as "fittest for grave discourse," [3] was much the more popular and the more respectable form. Both Gascoigne and Puttenham, for example, speak of the Chaucerian couplet condescendingly as "but riding ryme" and agree that its chief use is for "a merie tale." [4] So much then for the early heroic couplet.

The history of the heroic couplet since the romantic poets degraded and rejected it is even less interesting than that of the early period; our age has no Chaucer. The dramatic but unhappy destruction of the great couplet tradition I have sufficiently recognized in my essays on Byron and Keats. Since their time there have been only isolated outcroppings of heroic couplet practice, some of which, like Browning's "My Last Duchess" and Arnold's "The Tomb," are hardly recognizable as heroic couplet poems at all. Once the tradition of this most confining and most demanding of English poetic mediums had failed, its use, even by poets who came to require its qualities and effects, became virtually impossible.

This history of the heroic couplet, then, is the history of those years from around 1585 to 1785 during which the form reveals a living and developing tradition. Virtually every English poet of this period, including Shakespeare and Milton, used it for some of his poetry, and it was the staple of most poets, especially, of course, after 1660. But long before then it was the favorite measure not only of Waller and Denham, but of Donne, who wrote nearly as much of his poetry in it as in all other measures combined, and of Ben Jonson, who explicitly distinguished it from all others.[5] The history of this long and extensive poetic practice is, however, simpler and clearer than one might expect. This is

---

[3] *Elizabethan Critical Essays*, ed. G. Gregory Smith (Oxford, 1904), I, 54.
[4] Ibid., I, 56; II, 64.
[5] *Ben Jonson's Conversations with Drummond of Hawthornden*, ed. R. F. Patterson (London, 1923), pp. 1–2.

so because it is chiefly the history of one triumphant adaptation of the form, an adaptation which, for convenience, we may call the *closed couplet*.

The closed couplet evolved by and large from the efforts of many Elizabethan poets (among them Christopher Marlowe, Sir John Harington, Michael Drayton, Thomas Heywood, Joseph Hall, and, of course, Donne and Jonson) to reproduce in English the effects of the Latin elegiac distich, especially as it had been employed by Ovid in his *Amores* and *Heroides* and by Martial in his *Epigrammaton*. The English form in which they all found, almost simultaneously as it seems, that these Latin effects could be transported was the old and thitherto rather unfashionable decasyllabic couplet; [6] hence its sudden transformation and popularity at the turn of the sixteenth century. Its continued popularity, however, can only be explained by describing the remarkable developments the English made in this elegiac adaptation.

I will attempt in the next chapter to furnish a general description of the closed couplet and, in the chapters following, to describe the stages of its development and to survey the variety of its poetic uses.

---

[6] Nicholas Grimald freakishly preceded these poets in the distich-couplet transference; he published several such exercises, drawn from the Renaissance Latin of Theodore de Beza, in Tottel's *Miscellany* of 1557.

II

⚞⚞⚞⚞⚞⚞⚞⚞⚞⚞⚞⚞⚞

THE NATURE OF THE
CLOSED HEROIC COUPLET

1. THE INDIVIDUAL COUPLET

Because of its long and varied use, the closed heroic couplet took many different shapes, but in every one we can discern several points of general similarity. Let us begin by considering two of these: first, the couplet's normal metrical organization and, second, its characteristic rhetoric.

Its persistent closure is only one aspect of the normal metrical organization of the closed couplet. This pause, which divides each couplet from the next, is, indeed, only the strongest in a regular hierarchy of metrical pauses. John Dennis, the eighteenth-century critic, described this hierarchy as follows: "The Pause at the End of a Verse [that is, at the end of the first line] ought to be greater than any Pause that may precede it in the same Verse [that is, the mid-line pause], and the Pause at the End of a Couplet ought to be greater than that which is at the End of the first Verse." [1] Dennis is here describing more than a hundred years of closed-couplet practice during which this tripartite hierarchy of pauses had been observed. Ben Jonson, speaking with the conciseness of a poet, had recognized it early in the seventeenth century when he called couplets "the bravest sort of verses, especially when they are broken, like Hexameters." [2] And we can find this hierarchy of pauses exemplified in Marlowe's translation of Ovid's *Amores*, a work done well before the end of the sixteenth century.

Consider, for instance, this passage from Marlowe's translation:

> *Cypassis* that a thousand wayes trimst haire,
> Worthy to keembe none but a Goddesse faire,

---

[1] *The Critical Works*, ed. E. N. Hooker (Baltimore, 1943), II, 328.
[2] *Ben Jonson's Conversations with Drummond of Hawthornden*, ed. R. F. Patterson (London, 1923), pp. 1–2.

> Our pleasant scapes shew thee no clowne to be,
> Apt to thy mistrisse, but more apt to me.
> Who that our bodies were comprest bewrayde?
> Whence knowes Corinna that with thee I playde?

One especially feels the formal regularity of the pauses in the fourth line of this passage with its antithetical balance and its emphatic use of repetition and alliteration. But the rule, as Dennis has formulated it, is pretty well observed throughout. The first couplet contains the speaker's address to Cypassis, its two lines defining the two parallel adjectival elements by which his address is developed, and the third couplet defines the question of the discovery of their love-making, each of its two line ends punctuating one aspect of this question. One also notices the importance of the mid-line pause, especially in the second line (between "keembe" and "none") and in the third (between "scapes" and "shew"). Marlowe must count on our getting these pauses right, although he may not have indicated them adequately, or risk our losing his meaning.

Now consider this passage by Dennis's young contemporary, Alexander Pope:

> Where-e're you walk, cool Gales shall fan the Glade,
> Trees, where you sit, shall crowd into a Shade,
> Where-e're you tread, the blushing Flow'rs shall rise,
> And all things flourish where you turn your Eyes.

Pope has, of course, indicated the tertiary, that is, the mid-line, pause with absolute precision; it is so sharply marked after the fourth syllable of each of the first three lines, indeed, that Pope's shifting it to the fifth syllable in the fourth line helps him assert this line's climactic force. We might also notice, in connection with this and the other formal pauses of the closed couplet, the youthful virtuoso's handling of his four "where" clauses, each of which fills up one half of one of the four lines and, by its placing, helps Pope variously to assert and, indeed, exalt his half-lines, lines, and couplets.

This hierarchy of pauses of the closed couplet defines a system of speech which has four segments or, more precisely, a system of two segments within two segments. The two major segments, that is, the lines, are precisely equal in length and thus exactly balanced. However, because the second rhymes and thus closes more emphatically, it naturally receives a greater emphasis. The second half of each line is also commonly more emphatic than the first half, but for a different reason, namely, the prevailing iambic movement of the line. If the mid-line pause should come after the fifth syllable, that is, at the syllabic center of the line, there would be three metrical stresses in the second half-line to only two in the first half-line. Notice, for example, how the exactly central mid-line pause in this line from the passage just above, "And all things flourish where you turn your Eyes," allows Pope to focus a metrical stress on the merely logical term "where" and thus drive home this climactic one of his four parallel "where" clauses. A closed-couplet poet had the normal option of pausing after a sixth syllable, of course, and thus giving greater scope and, ordinarily, greater force to the first half of a line. But the pause after four syllables, which early critics of the heroic line felt to be the most correct mid-line pause,[3] naturally augments the second half-line. Abstractly speaking, then, the second line of a closed couplet is essentially climactic and the second half of each line prevailingly so. We must, however, set against this tendency the exact syllabic equivalence of the two lines; the approximate equivalence to one another of the two half-lines in every line; and the flexibility, based on its metrical imbalance, of each line. The closed couplet thus offered a poet a variety of ways of achieving statements that could be, on the one hand, sharply defined and firmly balanced and, on the other hand, gracefully modulated and subtly tipped.

Even considering the pauses and the segments of the closed couplet in this abstract fashion, we can recognize its built-in qualities of flexibility and variety. It imposed, nevertheless, severe limitations on a poet: he had to articulate his poem in speech systems of twenty, ten, and roughly five syllables, and continuously to observe a strong prompting not only to a balance within these systems but to a texture of balances within balances. Good poets, however, found ways of observing these limitations — thus receiving their expressive benefits — and at the same time of modifying them. Listed below, in descending order of the strength of the pause at the ends of their first lines, are five nonconsecutive couplets from Pope's *Windsor Forest*:

> 1. Here in full Light the russet Plains extend;
>   There wrapt in Clouds the blueish Hills ascend.
> 2. Here waving Groves a checquer'd Scene display,
>   And part admit and part exclude the Day.
> 3. The Groves of *Eden,* vanish'd now so long,
>   Live in Description, and look green in Song.

[3] See, for example, *Elizabethan Critical Essays*, ed. G. Gregory Smith (Oxford, 1904), II, 75.

4. There, interspers'd in Lawns and opening Glades,
    Thin Trees arise that shun each others Shades.
5. Let *India* boast her Plants, nor envy we
    The weeping Amber or the balmy Tree.

By examining the extremes at either end of this list, we can discover the flexibility, the dynamic resolution between regularity and freedom, which came to be an essential quality of the closed couplet.

Each line of our first couplet, to begin at that extreme, defines a complete thought, a complete main clause, so that the first-line pause may seem equivalent in weight to the couplet pause. But the obvious connection between these two lines, namely, their extensive syntactic parallelism and their rhetorical opposition— "Light" against "Clouds" and "Plains" against "Hills" — binds them into a unit so that, despite their grammatical equivalency, the couplet pause is finally stronger than that at the end of the first line. One might notice other strongly divided couplets such as this, "Rich industry sits smiling on the Plains, / And Peace and Plenty tell, a STUART reigns," whose syntactically separate lines share a causal or inferential unity; or this, "The Fox obscene to gaping Tombs retires, / And savage Howlings fill the sacred Quires," whose lines are joined by a chronological flow — the second giving us something that would follow the first in time.

Our fifth couplet above, to take the other extreme, reveals an enjambed first line, the line end separating the subject and verb, "envy we," from the compound direct object, "Amber or . . . Tree," which is necessary to the meaning. The first line has, nevertheless, some stability, some integrity: it defines an opposition between India's boast and our possible envy; its end is dramatized with a kind of inversion; and the word on which it ends is both a syntactically important word, the subject of a clause, and one capable of a firm rhyme. The second line strengthens the first line's integrity, moreover, by achieving its own in the form of a perfectly balanced compound object. One might also note such couplets as this, "But see the Man who spacious Regions gave / A Waste for Beasts, himself deny'd a Grave," whose enjambed first line gains stability by inversion of the verb, which is a potentially strong rhyme word, by inclusion of the subject, verb, and object of that clause which overflows it, and by a double pattern of assonance; or one might consider this, "Short is his Joy! he feels the fiery Wound, / Flutters in Blood, and panting beats the ground," the stability of whose first line is assured by an apparent syntactic stop, an appearance the next line will, of course, modify by the alliterating "f" sounds and by the neatness of the parallel verbs defined in the concluding line.

It should be clear even from so sketchy a set of examples and analyses as these that the closed couplet, as English poets came to use it, was a highly and variously dynamic measure. No first line in the couplets above — or, generally speaking, in any closed-couplet poetry — is so stiff in its definitive pause but that it also shows some forward impulse, some thrust toward a connection with the larger unit of utterance, and, on the other hand, none is so enjambed but that it shows some definitive integrity, some significant degree of closure. And what is true of the pauses at the ends of first lines is similarly true of those at the mid-lines and those at the ends of couplets.

The closed couplet is recognizable not only from this flexible observance of a hierarchy of definitive pauses, but also from a characteristic kind of rhetoric. Three major practices of this rhetoric, as George Williamson has pointed out, are inversion, parallelism, and antithesis.[4] Such practices quite naturally accompany the regular organization of pauses and segments we have just been describing: inversion allows a couplet poet to assert his pauses, his points of closure; parallelism allows him to make emphatic use of the equal metrical segments, that is, of the couplets, lines, and half-lines, he is asserting by inversion and by other means; and antithesis allows him to benefit from the fact that the equal line and half-line segments come in pairs. So sharply defined a system of pairs as the closed couplet provided virtually forced poetic utterance, Professor Williamson has suggested, into patterns of antithesis.[5]

To exemplify these three characteristic rhetorical practices, consider the following passage of Pope's *Windsor Forest*, a passage to which we will be referring for examples throughout this chapter:

The Groves of *Eden*, vanish'd now so long,
Live in Description, and look green in Song:
These, were my Breast inspir'd with equal Flame,
Like them in Beauty, should be like in Fame.   10
Here Hills and Vales, the Woodland and the Plain,
Here Earth and Water seem to strive again,
Not *Chaos*-like together crush'd and bruis'd,
But as the World, harmoniously confus'd:
Where Order in Variety we see,   15
And where, tho' all things differ, all agree.

---

[4] "The Rhetorical Pattern of Neo-Classical Wit," *MP*, xxxiii (1935), 62.
[5] Ibid., esp. pp. 62–65 and 75–81.

Here waving Groves a checquer'd Scene display,
And part admit and part exclude the Day;
As some coy Nymph her Lover's warm Address
Nor quite indulges, nor can quite repress.　　　　　　　20
There, interspers'd in Lawns and opening Glades,
Thin Trees arise that shun each others Shades.
Here in full Light the russet Plains extend;
There wrapt in Clouds the blueish Hills ascend:
Ev'n the wild Heath displays her Purple Dies,　　　　25
And 'midst the Desart fruitful Fields arise,
That crown'd with tufted Trees and springing Corn,
Like verdant Isles the sable Waste adorn.
Let *India* boast her Plants, nor envy we
The weeping Amber or the balmy Tree,　　　　　　　30
While by our Oaks the precious Loads are born,
And Realms commanded which those Trees adorn.

It will be noticed that this passage contains every couplet in the catalogue with which we exemplified the range of the individual closed couplet's metrical dynamics. Now, however, let us turn to closed-couplet rhetoric.

The inversion of a verb and its object or, more precisely, the suspension of a verb to the line end strengthens line 17 of this passage, a first line. Lines 15, 23, 24, and 26 are strengthened by the suspension to their ends of combined subjects and verbs — a less obtrusive form of inversion, and a whole clause is suspended to the end of line 16. Elsewhere in this passage one finds inversions which bridge pauses at the end of first lines. By filling out line 7 with the adjectival phrase, "vanish'd now so long," for instance, Pope was able to begin line 8, the second line of this couplet, with the verb "Live," thus tying these two lines together and, with the same stroke, emphasizing the syntactic backbone of the clause they define. We may note, by the way, that the verb coordinate to "Live," namely, "look," enjoys an alliterative and a caesural emphasis so that the couplet does not tail away. Another couplet (ll. 19–20) is unified by a similar suspension of its verb to the second line; while in the next couplet following, the poet's filling his first line with a participial phrase allowed him to withhold a whole main clause until his second line. Finally, the couplet at lines 27–28 opens with the subject of the single clause it defines and closes — after a participial phrase which fills out the first line, a prepositional phrase which fills the first half of the second line, and the modified direct object — with the verb. Thus does Pope and thus do closed-couplet poets in general use inversion to assert and, indeed, to dramatize the metrical pauses and segments of their poetry.

The passage we have drawn from Pope's youthful work is as rich in examples of parallelism as it is in inversions. Line 8, for instance, defines two parallel predicates, and line 10, two parallel "like" phrases. In both these cases the mid-line pause separates the pair and thus punctuates the parallel relationship. Lines 25 and 26 give us two lines in parallel, each line defining a co-ordinate clause, and lines 7–10 define two parallel couplets, the first describing Eden's literary perpetuity and the second that of Windsor Forest. Lines 17–20 similarly define parallel couplets, the second one in this case holding an item which is analogous to that held in the first, the adolescent poet here describing a likeness between Windsor's "waving Groves" and the conduct of "some coy Nymph." Their point of likeness is underscored by the parallel form of their second lines: just as the waving groves partly admit and partly exclude the sunlight, so does a coy nymph partly allow and partly deny "her Lover's warm Address." The second lines of the parallel couplets on Eden and Windsor (ll. 7–10), each of which also defines a parallel, are richer and more complex in their effect. The second line of the Eden couplet holds a compound predicate which gives us merely a twofold assurance of Eden's literary continuance; that of the Windsor couplet, one of whose parallel phrases is governed by the subjunctive "should be," presents us with a hopeful equivalency between Windsor's actually similar beauty and her possibly similar continuance. Thus Pope uses subsidiary parallels here, both to underscore his parallel between Eden and Windsor and to define its limits.

This passage from *Windsor Forest* is, of course, a texture of parallel and antithetical statements. Antithesis is probably best understood as a special form of parallelism: a form which, first, is limited to two separate items, and which, second, points out differences or oppositions rather than likenesses or agreements. Any vivid paralleling of just two items carries an antithetical flavor, as in this line from Pope's *Essay on Man*, "To low ambition and the pride of Kings," whose parallel substantives are held apart by their apparently — but not certainly — antithetical modifications. The parallel between Eden and Windsor, as we have just seen, asserts one point of certain likeness and one of possible difference. The parallel lines that make up a couplet on Windsor's light and shade (ll. 23–24) are also rhetorically ambivalent. We can derive from these coupled lines, on the one hand, the impression of two sharply opposed images or, on the other, the impression of one single system of sylvan chiaroscuro; the sharply separated lines underscore the impression of two images in opposition, their rhyming unity that of one harmonious system. The "Here waving Groves" couplet similarly opposes the "There . . . thin Trees" couplet, but in this case, obviously enough, rhyme works on the side of opposition rather than on the side of unity. This system is, of course, smudged by the intervening "coy Nymph" couplet — not ruinously so, however, because of the power of the couplet to encapsulate such digressive matter.

Our passage is as rich in line-defined antitheses as it is in the more largely articulated ones. We have already noticed lines 18 and 20, which define antithetical verbs, that is, opposing actions, and the partially antithetical "like" phrases in line 10. We might also notice line 15, which defines antithetical substantives, line 16, which defines antithetical clauses, and line 25, which defines antithetical substantive phrases. Each of these three line patterns is modified by syntactic inequities which I will discuss in the next few pages, but their condition of rhetorical opposition, which is heightened by a mid-line pause in every case, is perfectly clear.

We recognized in discussing the normal pauses of the closed couplet a persistent flexing of these pauses, a scale of varieties and modifications, which created a dynamic tension within each couplet between its general metrical pattern and the particular movement of its speech. Inversion, parallelism, and antithesis are naturally involved in this closed-couplet dynamics. A catalogue of these and some other important speech elements, suggesting the extent to which each fits or opposes the meter (suggesting, that is, the part each plays in this dynamics), will allow us to conclude our description of the closed couplet as a single, isolated entity. This closed-couplet dynamics, to give it a general description, involves the simultaneous poetic maintenance of stability and movement, unity and diversity, and, to use Pope's words, order and variety.

Rhyme, to begin with this most simple speech element in closed-couplet production, is a device for asserting stability and unity. Rhyme words used in closed-couplet composition are strong both in sense and sound. Approximately nine-tenths of them are either substantives or verbals, and the remainder are adjectival or adverbial modifiers — generally significant ones. In our quotation from *Windsor Forest*, for instance, twelve of the twenty-six rhyme words are verbals, ten of them

regular verbs; twelve are substantives; and two are adverbs. Such pro-
portions run fairly constant throughout closed-couplet history. Rhyme
words are also typically either words of one syllable, or two-syllable iam-
bic words only the second syllables of which rhyme. The one-syllable
words are more common. There are fifteen one-syllable rhyme words to
eleven iambic rhyme words in our quotation, but in the "whirring Pheas-
ant" passage from the same poem (ll. 111–18) the ratio is seven to
one, and in the passage on Windsor's fishing (ll. 135–46) it is eleven to
one. Pope seldom used words of more syllables for his rhymes — except
for special effects. Other closed-couplet poets were less careful in this
respect: in the first two hundred lines of Dryden's *Absalom and Achito-
phel*, for instance, "liberty" (rhyming with "free"), "Qualifi'd," "Ene-
mies" (rhyming with "wise"), "Multitude," "Consequence," and "An-
archy" (rhyming with "free") are used as rhyme words. But as a rule,
Dryden and all closed-couplet poets confined their rhymes, first, to
nouns and verbs and, second, to one-syllable, or two-syllable iambic,
words to make their rhymes. The result is, of course, a strong emphasis
on the end of the couplet, and, once we are into a closed-couplet poem,
a secondary emphasis on the end of the first line — together with the in-
dications of closure and segmentation that these emphases bring. Thus
rhyme enforces the primary and the secondary pauses of the closed-cou-
plet hierarchy.

Inversion, unlike rhyme, has an ambivalent effect on the regular
closed-couplet hierarchy of pauses. This practice commonly strengthens
a stronger pause, the couplet or the first-line pause, and modifies one or
more of the weaker pauses. In the line, "Here waving Groves a chec-
quer'd Scene display," the shifting of the verb to the end of the line en-
forces the line end and, of course, increases the integrity of the line while
compressing the mid-line pause: we are drawn from "Groves" rapidly
or, at least, with a sense of suspended expectation by our desire for a
verb, and the verb, when it finally comes, gives us a strong sense of ful-
fillment and completeness. The removal of the verb "adorn" to the end
of the *couplet* which its subject opens (ll. 27–28) has a corresponding
effect: it exalts the couplet close at the expense of the pause at the end
of the first line and at the expense of both mid-line pauses. The effect of
the inversion of the combined subject and verb with the prepositional
phrase in the line, "Here in full Light the russet Plains extend," is simi-
lar to, although less obtrusive than, that of inversions which separate
verbs from their subjects. This inversion of word groups, as a study of
the half-line inversions in lines 7–8, 13–14, and 19–20 of *Windsor For-*

est and of essentially full-line inversions in lines 9–10 and 21–22 will suggest, can modify the hierarchy of closed-couplet pauses in many different ways.

The operation of inversion on closed-couplet patterning is, however, more complex and more subtle than I have yet indicated. An inversion does truly draw us to its conclusion, but it also makes us aware of the inverted elements, as maneuverable segments of speech, and of the points at which these segments can be broken and joined. Thus when the breaks by which an inversion is made correspond with metrical breaks, with mid-line or with line-end pauses — and this is the normal way of closed-couplet inversions — they intensify the pauses. In the line, "Here waving Groves a checquer'd Scene display," then, we are both drawn through the gap after "Groves" where "display" ought ordinarily to be and, at the same time, made vividly conscious of this gap — doubly conscious, of course, because Pope's prevailing practice has prepared us for a pause in some such mid-line position as this which the inversion makes. Inversion then, as Alexander Allison puts it, "both creates a medial caesura and strengthens the final period." [6]

Rhetorical balances of parallel and antithetical elements also have ambivalent and, indeed, complex effects on the unity and order of the closed couplet. A balance integrates and stabilizes any metrical unit it spans. Such lines as "Live in Description, and look green in Song" and "Like them in Beauty, should be like in Fame" obviously hold together in part because of their balance — a balance which is underscored in the first of them by alliteration and in the second by the repetition of the word "like." Lines whose balance is augmented by inversion, such as "And part admit and part exclude the Day" or "And where, 'tho all things differ, all agree," are naturally even more strongly unified. But where we find textures of balances, as in lines 15–16 and lines 25–26 of *Windsor Forest*, we also have textures of unity and diversity. The couplet, "Where Order in Variety we see, / And where, 'tho all things differ, all agree," is obviously made of two separate and, indeed, syntactically coordinate systems, each one unified by its own meter and rhetoric. On the other hand, there is also a couplet unity here, a climactic movement from a less profound, a more tentative, utterance of Pope's theme to a more profound and absolute utterance of it: the first line articulates this theme, the vision of *concors discordia rerum*, by balancing a direct object ("Order") against the object of a preposition ("Variety") and closing on our vision of the situation; the second, from which the intrusive

---

[6] *Toward an Augustan Poetic* (Lexington, Ky., 1962), pp. 78–80.

and unnecessary insistence on our vision has been stripped, balances order and variety (with significantly reversed placing) in two complete clauses, closing climactically on the prevailing harmony in this scene and, as we connect this couplet with that above it, in the world at large. Thus rhetorical parallels and balances, variously comprehending and refining other parallels and balances, allow the poet to accommodate varieties in the details of his utterance and yet to integrate them in its larger unities.

Individual rhetorical balances can also be given a metrically oblique articulation and thus modify the order and stability of individual closed couplets. The last two couplets of our quotation from *Windsor Forest* give separate instances of this. In lines 29–30 the speaker gives two parallel commands, let India boast and let us not envy, the first of which fills six syllables and the second, fourteen. The main rhetorical pivot comes then at the mid-line pause in the first line rather than at the normally stronger pause, that is, that at the end of the first line — thus establishing a brief tension between metrical and rhetorical promptings. Similar to this in style is this couplet from *Absalom and Achitophel*, "For Laws are onely made to Punish those / Who serve the King and to protect his foes," in which the first of the two balancing infinitive phrases overflows the first line, and in which the rhetorical pivot, consequently, coincides with the mid-line pause of the second line. Similarly oblique is this couplet from Sir John Denham, the first virtuoso of the closed couplet: "No unexpected inundations spoyl / The mowers hopes, nor mock the plowmans toyl." Such oblique articulation of rhetorical parallels and antitheses has many varieties. In lines 31–32 of *Windsor Forest*, for instance, Pope has placed one of two parallel clauses in the second half of his couplet's first line and the other in the first half of its second line.

Closed-couplet poets commonly countered such rhetorical obliqueness with some special assertion of couplet stability and balance. In the first example above, Pope stabilized the second line by using it to define parallel direct objects, each of which, furthermore, is preceded by a two-syllable adjective. Or consider the opening couplet of Pope's *Essay on Man*: "Awake my St. John! Leave all meaner things/To low ambition and the pride of Kings." The second line of this oblique couplet, which we previously cited in another connection, is unified by its ironical paralleling of low ambition and kingly pride, a system which that kind of inversion called chiasmus intensifies; thus unified, it stiffens retrospectively, as it were, the pause at the end of the first line so that the closed-couplet hierarchy of pauses is indicated here even in the presence of a first-line enjambment. Denham, in the couplet of his which we have just quoted, assured the impression of order with alliteration and the precise balancing of his parallel predicates. The second line of the oblique couplet at lines 31–32 of *Windsor Forest*, finally, is strengthened by the inversion of a verb to the line end. At any rate, we *may* take this verb, "adorn," to be inverted; doing so would make "which" the subject of this clause that fills the last half of the line and "Trees" the object, and would require us to apply the clause to "Loads" in the line above. Actually, we may also consider this clause to be normal in word order; this would reverse subject and object and require us to apply the clause to "Realms" in the first half of this line. Such an ambiguity of dependency may be rather too subtle, too clever, to augment the widely public effect Pope was striving for in this poem, but it suggests the wonderful facility with which a closed-couplet poet could maneuver his words and phrases and thus modulate his utterance.

The divisions and the connections of syntax, like these different rhetorical patterns, sometimes strengthen and sometimes weaken the abstract metrical organization of the closed couplet. A complete clause, like a complete rhetorical balance, unifies the span of syllables it covers, and so, to a less extent, does a phrase. And these syntactic units can, like the rhetorical patterns, be drawn to various lengths. In our quotation from *Windsor Forest*, for example, we find single clauses filling out half-lines (ll. 16, 22, 29, 32), lines (ll. 9, 15, 23, 24, 25, 26), a line and one-half (ll. 29–30), and full couplets (ll. 7–8, 11–12, 19–20, 27–28). And we find different kinds of phrases filling out half-lines (ll. 7, 10, 14, 23, 24) and full lines (ll. 13, 21). Every couplet is, obviously, a texture of such elements in various patterns. In such a couplet as this, "There, interspers'd in Lawns and opening Glades, / Thin trees arise that shun each others Shades," the syntactic and metrical organization are nearly identical — although not perfectly so, since the last half-line defines a subordinate clause. The syntax and meter reinforce one another quite strongly throughout this passage and, indeed, in closed-couplet poetry in general. But Dryden had been able to engage in a much greater range of syntactic movement and still keep up the form, and Pope would broaden his range as he matured. Consider, for instance, this couplet drawn from Dryden's *Absalom and Achitophel* — "When Nature prompted, and no law deny'd / Promiscuous use of Concubine and Bride"; and this from Pope's *Epistle to Dr. Arbuthnot* — "The things, we know, are neither rich nor rare, / But wonder how the Devil they got there." But even our quotation from the youthful Pope shows a wide variety of syntactic systems: the couplet at lines 13–14 defines two antithetical phrases; that at lines 27–28 defines a single adjectival clause, a highly inverted one enriched with a line of participial-adjectival modification and with a half-line of prepositional-adverbial modification; and that at lines 31–32 defines an adverbial complex made up of three clauses, one of them dependent on the other two, and an adverbial phrase. Although the syntax of every couplet in this passage conforms to closed-couplet metrical conventions to a high degree — so much so that the passage as a whole seems mannered and showy — no two couplets have the same syntactic paradigm.

Syntax in closed-couplet poetry normally coincides with rhetoric just as it does with meter. The antithetical expansion of Windsor's sylvan complexity (ll. 13–14), "Not . . . / But," for instance, is defined in two participial phrases, each of which fills one line; thus it receives both syntactic and metrical emphasis. The antithetical actions of the groves (l. 18) and the coy nymph (l. 20), again, are both articulated as compound verbs — each compound being line-defined and caesurally punctuated. The balancing of sunlit plains and cloudy hills in lines 23–24 is similarly illuminated by both metrical and syntactic paralleling: each of these line-defined items is an independent clause in active voice — both of them composed of virtually equivalent adjectives, subjects, and verbs which fill up the last six syllables of the two lines, and of similar, although not perfectly similar, systems of modification which in both cases cover the first four syllables.

Often, however, the syntax reinforces the rhetoric in couplets whose rhetoric runs oblique to the meter. This is true of every example we gave above of oblique couplets. We may once again recall this couplet, "Awake my St. John! Leave all meaner things / To low ambition and the pride of Kings," in which two parallel commands, one covering five syllables, the other, fifteen, are composed in two main clauses, each in the imperative mood. Syntax can also run counter to the rhetoric, in which cases, however, it commonly reinforces the meter. In the line, "And 'midst the Desart fruitful Fields arise," for instance, a rhetorical balance between waste land and fertile land, a pattern which is composed in one line-defined clause, is slanted by the first member's being the object of a prepositional phrase and the second, the subject of the whole clause. The second member is actually compounded of the subject and a modifier which is virtually necessary to the line's antithetical force, and this smudges the utterance. Other and more perfectly achieved cases in which progressive syntax slants a rhetorical balance can be found in lines 15, 16, and 25 of our quotation — all of these being lines we have already discussed. By comparing these, each of which is differently slanted, of course, with lines in which syntax and rhetoric and meter reinforce each other — lines 8, 20, and 27, for instance — and again with lines and couplets in which syntactic and rhetorical corresponden-cies counter the meter — lines 29–30 and 31–32, for instance — one may get a sense of the vast range of choices a poet enjoyed in his efforts to achieve that dynamic maintenance of the conflicting tendencies to-ward order and variety, toward stability and movement, that each indi-vidual closed couplet required.

2. SUPRACOUPLET COMPOSITION

This dynamics prevailed in the larger elements of closed-couplet po-etry too. The couplet pause, while always formally observed, was subject to modification, just like the pause at the end of the first line and the mid-line pause. It was, indeed, the dynamic handling of couplet closure, that is, the yoking together of highly individuated couplets into highly in-tegrated paragraphs, a practice whose development we will study in the historical section of this book, that made possible Dryden's and Pope's employment of the closed couplet to articulate their own and their age's most vital and most controversial problems.

This larger dynamics, this unity of several sharply individuated cou-plets in one sweep of poetic discourse, is extremely various both in kind and in degree. The differences in kind of Pope's closed-couplet para-graphs from Dryden's and the differences of Churchill's and Johnson's from those of Dryden and Pope and from those of one another will emerge most naturally and precisely as our history unfolds. The differ-ences in degree, however, we can conveniently take up here — starting with the minimal degree of paragraph unity. Consider, for instance, this catalogue of fish from *Windsor Forest*:

Our plenteous Streams a various Race supply;
The bright-ey'd Perch with Fins of *Tyrian* Dye,
The silver Eel, in shining Volumes roll'd,
The yellow Carp, in Scales bedrop'd with Gold,
Swift Trouts, diversify'd with Crimson Stains,   145
And Pykes, the Tyrants of the watry Plains.

The first line states a general truth, that there are many types of fish in Windsor's streams, and the catalogue proves this, one fish and one line at a time. Each item, each line, is slightly different from the others, and the lines forming each couplet pair are more similar to one another than to any other. In the last couplet, for instance, both the trouts and the pikes are named in the first iambic foot — whereas Pope took two feet to name each fish in the other three lines. On the other hand, the trout line is developed by means of a participle and its adverbial modification, that on pikes with an ennobling appositive and its adjectival modification; the participle following trouts, again, covers four syllables, the appositive following pikes, three. Even in such mannered lines as these, then, close attention reveals Pope varying the elements of his poetry, not only to accommodate individual differences in the details of his subject matter, but also to achieve something of a supracouplet movement and climax. These five lines are, nevertheless, oppressively alike. More oppressive still, the pauses between them are of identical rhetorical weight — thus reducing even the abstract, mechanical variety between the first-line pause and the couplet pause. We might compare with this stiffly articulated catalogue of fish the catalogue of human senses in the *Essay on Man* (I, 193–204), by which Pope will demonstrate the sufficiency of our senses to our situation; or the catalogue of attitudes in which he will catch Atticus in his *Epistle to Dr. Arbuthnot* (ll. 193–214); or the catalogue of qualities which Dryden attributed to Achitophel in the sweeping sentence with which he opened his portrait of that great rebel (*Absalom and Achitophel*, ll. 150–62). The range of single couplets and the variety of their interconnections correspond with and augment the impression of a precise grasp on details and a vivid sense of discursive purpose that radiate from these examples of mature, masterly closed-couplet composition. In contrast, the obtrusive formal repetitiveness of the youthful Pope's fish catalogue reveals the generality of his grasp on its details and the conventionality of his discursive intentions.

No passage in *Windsor Forest* has the force, the point, or the density of such paragraph systems as those Dryden had composed in his maturity or as Pope would compose in his. But the "Order in Variety" passage, whose individual couplets we have already examined, is more richly and variously composed than the catalogue of fish. Its first two couplets are unified in the task of exalting Windsor for its beauty; the next three define this beauty in general; and the next six particularize this beauty in three separate capsules, respectively, three, one, and two couplets long. The last two couplets of our quotation open, at least, with an implied comparison between Windsor's trees and India's, a comparison whose purpose seems to have been to eulogize Windsor for being English. However, despite these interrelationships, which are luminously clear at least until the last two couplets, the passage is essentially a series, a string, of pretty things rather than a unified system of thought. The larger unity has been subordinated, indeed, not only to that of the separate groups of couplets that I have acknowledged, but to the separate couplets making up these groups. Take, for instance, the three-couplet explanation of Windsor's beauty, which is the most tightly composed supracouplet system in the passage (ll. 11–16). Although it defines only one complete sentence, both the first and second couplets *seem* completely to round out the thought: the first defines the main clause, apparently a completed utterance; the second defines a participial appendage, once again apparently closing the statement; then the third adds on a somewhat imprecisely connected pair of "where" elements. This short-windedness, this timidity in yoking the couplets together, this politeness that never asks a reader to stretch his mind beyond the couplet immediately before him even in supracouplet utterance, is the rule throughout this passage. Notice, for example, the pair of two-couplet sets at the end of the passage. Both define a main clause and thus, apparently, a complete thought in the first couplet and then add on some subordinate material in the second. Thus this passage allows a complete stop at the end of every couplet.

The shorter "whirring Pheasant" passage from this same poem is somewhat more dynamically organized:

See! from the Brake the whirring Pheasant springs,
And mounts exulting on triumphant Wings;
Short is his Joy! he feels the fiery Wound,
Flutters in Blood, and panting beats the Ground.
Ah! what avail his glossie, varying Dyes,   115
His Purple Crest, and Scarlet-circled Eyes,
The vivid Green his shining Plumes unfold;
His painted Wings, and Breast that flames with Gold?

The first two couplets, although strongly end-stopped, show considerable internal movement, especially the second, which gives a strikingly oblique exposition of the break between the bird's joyful vitality and his being shot and which, in its expanded second half, follows the bird in its fall. The last two couplets define another Popean catalogue, but the subjection of every item in it to the exclamation with which it opens gives it a movement and a coherence that were missing in the catalogue of fish. We might also notice the grace and flow Pope has given this list of pheasant splendors by articulating two of its members, those in line 117, with a syntactic slant — the "Green" being the object of the unfolding "Plumes." We might notice, finally, the climactic force of the last line: it depends on the inversion which allowed Pope to end on the splendid word "Gold"; on the six-syllable second half, into which Pope was able to wedge an ennobling clause of modification for the concluding item, "Breast," rather than the normal adjective-noun combination; and, of course, on the poetic splendor of this concluding clause.

Pope came to compose much denser and much more forceful couplet paragraphs than any of these from *Windsor Forest*, as the unfolding of this history will demonstrate. And Dryden, in rather a different way, composed even larger supracouplet systems than Pope. We may better suggest the pervasiveness of this achievement of a dynamic supracouplet composition, however, by considering a passage of verse from a closed-couplet poet both earlier than these masters and much less accomplished than they, namely, Lucius Cary, Lord Falkland. In writing the following lines, excerpted from Falkland's complimentary poem on George Sandys's *Paraphrase upon the Psalms*, the poet was undoubtedly remembering the Ovidian love elegies which many of his contemporaries had been turning out and thinking of those profane poems in comparison with this religious exercise of Sandys:

Those who make wit their Curse, who spend their Brain,   105
Their Time, and Art, in looser Verse, to gain
Damnation and a Mistres; till they see
How Constant that is, how Inconstant she;
May from this great Example learne to sway
The Parts th' are Blest-with, some more Blessed way.   110

Only the pause at the end of the third couplet, marking the end of the single sentence which spans all three, is a full stop. But the pause at the end of the second couplet is also quite strong: its close separates a two-couplet system of subordinate matter from the predicate of the main clause, and its second line defines an antithesis that brings this subordinate matter to a climactic conclusion. The first couplet too, despite its syntactic thrust into the second, maintains some integrity — from the strong rhyme, from the apparent inversion of "to gain" to complete this rhyme, and from the fact that "to gain" governs the two terms, "Damnation" and "Mistres," whose development exactly fills and thus defines the second couplet. Even the first line, whose incompleteness draws us into the passage's extensive span of thought, enjoys some stability; a stability derived, first, from the importance of its concluding word "Brain" and from the potential strength of this word as a rhyme; second, from the paralleling of the second and incomplete "who" clause with the first —

each of them presenting us in this line with subject, verb, and an object modified by "their"; and, finally, from Falkland's establishment of the integrity of his first lines or, more precisely, of the hierarchy of closed-couplet pauses in the lines and couplets preceding this relatively enjambed line and in those following it.

In discussing Falkland's handling of the pauses in this passage we have naturally referred to the movement of its thought and to the syntactic and rhetorical practices by which Falkland controlled that movement. Now let us look at these practices directly. We may notice, first, that the syntactic backbone of the one sentence that fills these three couplets, "Those . . . May . . . learne to sway," has been variously suspended so as to receive the metrical emphasis it needed to clarify its progress and its interconnections. We may also notice Falkland's dynamic handling of the parallel "who" clauses: the first is wedged into a half-line, by which means the poet renders his own opinion of the amorous use of poetry with a terseness whose finality cannot be missed; the second fills the rest of the first couplet and all of the second, by which means the poet asserts his responsiveness, his totality of awareness, his willingness to allow whatever scope is necessary to comprehend the nature and the results of this vicious use. This combination of firmness and comprehensiveness gives Falkland's judgment, that is, his condemnation of the amorous uses of poetry, tremendous force. Falkland's use of antithesis is similarly flexible. There is, first of all, the short, half-line opposition between "wit" and "Curse," a terse, inarguable assertion of an impropriety. Then there is the weighted, the shocking, "Damnation and a Mistres" — an equation of seemingly antithetical terms — which itself required the refinement, the clarification, of the line-defined antithesis, "How Constant that is, how Inconstant she," to fulfill itself as an element of rational argument. And, finally, there is the climactic, line-strengthened balance between a man's parts and his use of them, underscored by the echoing terms "Blest" and "Blessed"; a system whose slanted syntax — that is, its playing off of a direct object (with modifiers) against an adverb (with modifiers) — ties it into the line above and, indeed, into the whole three-couplet system.

3. THE CLOSED COUPLET AS A MEDIUM FOR PUBLIC DISCOURSE

The closed couplet, as it came to be produced in this dynamic fashion, was primarily a medium for public discourse — rather than a medium for dramatic effects, say, or for those of meditation. Its persistent order allowed a poet to define issues, to balance arguments, and, in the process, to give the impression of a clear and balanced mind. Its interior flexibility and its exterior movement allowed him, on the one hand, to respond to the details, to the individual aspects and elements, of his discourse and, on the other, to extend his attention so as to comprehend the full range of its complexities; and, correspondingly, to give the impression of a responsive and comprehensive mind. Such a medium, then, wonderfully satisfied the vital need of the seventeenth and eighteenth centuries to formulate public statements and to carry on public discussion. A poet, by making use of this medium, could project through a speaker of apparent sense and probity the great issues of his day in the fullness of their complications and thus impress with a tremendously persuasive force his judgment of these issues on the audience of those who were vitally concerned with them.

The examples of closed-couplet practice we have been examining do not, admittedly, suggest a speaker and his audience very strongly. And we will come upon other poems in our examination of closed-couplet history in which the sense of a speaker and his correspondents is faint or, better perhaps, abstract. But the great and central achievements in closed-couplet literature from its very beginnings are, nevertheless, articulations of public communication — of personal conversation, polite address, or political oratory. This speech tone was persistently present in those Latin poems of Ovid and Martial with whose English translations and adaptations our history begins. And it rings out, with many varieties, of course, in the closed-couplet poetry of Donne, Jonson, Dryden, Rochester, Pope, and Churchill, as the history to which we shall soon turn will show. Virtually all the major closed-couplet poetry depends on the poet's articulating this most strict and artificial metrical arrangement, with its characteristically artificial rhetoric, in such a way as to create the impression of some kind of a public voice and, beyond this, of a significant public milieu.

Pope will strike typically the tone of elegant conversation and create an atmosphere of polite society. Great poems of his maturity will open with such couplets as these: "Who shall decide when Doctors disagree, / And soundest Casuists doubt, like you and me"; "Nothing so true as what you once let fall, / 'Most Women have no Characters at all.'" Dryden typically will strike an oratorical note and address an essentially political audience. We can observe him perfecting it for the great poems of his maturity in his theatrical prologues and epilogues — those usually mocking speeches of an actor to his and the poet's audience — which open with such couplets as these: "Almighty critiques! whom our *Indians* here / Worship, just as they do the Devil — for fear"; "Thus have my Spouse and I inform'd the Nation, / And led you all the way to Reformation." The varieties of public tones with which the closed couplet could be infused and the development of an individual tone by each of our two greatest closed-couplet poets will emerge in the course of this history.

III

𝓧𝓧𝓧𝓧𝓧𝓧𝓧𝓧𝓧𝓧𝓧𝓧𝓧𝓧𝓧

THE INCEPTION OF THE CLOSED HEROIC COUPLET

1. THE ENGLISH MEASURE

By the end of the sixteenth century English poets had established the nature of the English heroic line and demonstrated its central importance to their poetic needs, and although many English critics yearned for some exact transference into English metrical practice of classical measures and chiefly, of course, of the classical heroic line, they all knew what the poets had done. "The meeter of ten sillables," wrote George Puttenham, "is very stately and Heroical, and must have his *Cesure* fall upon the fourth sillable." [1] These two principles, that the English heroic line should number ten syllables and that it should have a regular mid-line pause, George Gascoigne had expressed earlier (in 1575) in *Certayne Notes of Instruction*,[2] and he had put them rather strictly into practice in his own blank-verse satire, *The Steele Glas*. Both Puttenham and Gascoigne described the verse of *The Canterbury Tales* as "but riding rhyme," apparently, as Puttenham explains it, because Chaucer was careless about the caesura.[3] Since the verse of the *Tales* lacked this metrical dignity, it was only good "for a merie tale." [4] Thus both of those pauses which would become the secondary and the tertiary ones in the closed-couplet hierarchy were explicitly imposed on the heroic line some years before the closed-couplet revolution.

Early in the next century the poet Samuel Daniel asserted the pre-eminence of this bipartite ten-syllable line, calling it not heroic, but "the plaine ancient verse, consisting of ten sillables or five feete" and, again,

---

[1] *The Arte of English Poesie* (1589), in *Elizabethan Critical Essays*, ed. G. Gregory Smith (Oxford, 1904), II, 63, 64, and esp. 75.

[2] *Essays*, I, 54.

[3] *Essays*, I, 56; II, 79.

[4] *Essays*, I, 56; II, 64.

"our old accustomed measure of five feet." [5] One notices, not only Daniel's insistence on the wide recognition and use of this line, but his confidence that it scans as five feet. Puttenham had denied the importance of feet in English verse partly, it seems, to harden the distinction between it and classical verse — which was measured in feet, of course.[6] To Puttenham and, for that matter, to Sidney too, number was the key to English meter.[7] On the other hand, both these critics make significant allowance of English poetic feet — Puttenham by speaking of two-syllable "portions" within the larger units and Sidney by remarking that English verse takes "some regarde of the accent." [8]

Gascoigne actually settled this matter before Sidney and Puttenham expressed themselves on it by insisting on the virtually complete dependence of English poets on "a foote of two sillables, wherof the first is depressed or made short, and the second is elevate or made long." [9] This is, of course, the English iambic foot, the basic foot of what Roger Ascham called the *carmen Iambicum* and into which, as he asserted in 1570, English verse naturally tended to fall.[10] Thomas Campion, who wrote at the end of the century, agreed completely with Ascham and Gascoigne: "*Iambics* . . . fall out so naturally in our toong," Campion asserted, "that . . . our owne writers . . unawares hit oftentimes upon the true *Iambic* numbers, but always ayme at them as far as their eare without the guidance of arte can attain unto." [11]

Campion, furthermore, although he was one of those who desired as near a transference of classical measures into English as seemed possible, realized that the line of five iambic feet was the heroic, the staple, measure of English poetry — so much so that he took elaborate pains to equate it with the heroic line of classical poetry, that is, the dactylic hexameter.[12] He used this "old accustomed measure of five feet" as a substitute for the dactylic hexameter when he attempted — with remarkable academic success — to achieve a form of elegiac distich in English verse. Here, for instance, is the model elegy he composed:

Constant to none, but ever false to me,
    Traiter still to love through thy faint desires,

---

[5] *A Defence of Ryme* (1603), in *Essays*, II, 376–77.
[6] *Essays*, II, 70.
[7] *An Apologie for Poetrie* (ca. 1583), in *Essays*, I, 204.
[8] *Essays*, II, 70; I, 204.
[9] *Essays*, I, 49–50.
[10] *The Scholemaster* (1570), in *Essays*, I, 30–31.
[11] *Observations in the Art of English Poesie* (1602), in *Essays*, II, 333.
[12] *Essays*, II, 334.

Not hope of pittie now nor vaine redresse
   Turns my griefs to teares and renu'd laments.
Too well thy empty vowes and hollow thoughts   5
   Witness both thy wrongs and remorseles hart.
Rue not my sorrow, but blush at my name;
   Let thy bloudy cheeks guilty thoughts betray.
My flames did truly burne, thine made a shew,
   As fires painted are which no heate retayne   10
Or as the glossy *Pirop* faines to blaze,
   But toucht cold appeares, and an earthy stone.
True cullours deck thy cheeks, false foiles thy brest,
   Frailer then thy light beawty is thy minde.
None canst thou long refuse, nor long affect,   15
   But turn'st feare with hopes, sorrow with delight,
Delaying, and deluding ev'ry way
   Those whose eyes are once with thy beawty chain'd.
Thrice happy man that entring first thy love
   Can so guide the straight raynes of his desires,   20
That both he can regard thee and refraine:
   If grac't, firme he stands, if not, easely falls.

Campion, following Martial and the Renaissance Latin epigrammatists, also wrote model epigrams in this form.[13] In both these cases, he has approximated in his second line the second (pentameter) line of the Latin elegiac distich, whose paradigm is $- \smile \smile - - \smile \smile - \| - \smile \smile - \smile \smile -$, with a similarly stiff English line, whose paradigm is $- \smile - - \smile - \| - \smile - \smile -$ (substituting trochees for dactyls). This line, like its Latin analogue, amounts to an elaborate metrical brake and assures a poetic progress in completely decisive two-line clicks, a progress, that is, which precisely imitates that of its Latin model. However, Campion has made the first line of this form not an English equivalent of the Latin hexameter, but a perfectly regular iambic pentameter. Campion, despite his classical leanings, would have no doubt agreed with Ben Jonson when that much better classical scholar and much greater English poet said that "Abram Francis in his English Hexameters was a foole." [14]

    The iambic pentameter line with a regular mid-line pause was, then, completely established as the staple of English versification by the time

---

[13] *Essays*, II, 345–46.
[14] *Ben Jonson's Conversations with Drummond of Hawthornden*, ed. R. F. Patterson (London, 1923), p. 6.

the history of the English closed couplet began. It had also been subjected, as a number of recent critics have shown,[15] to an extensive process of refinement. The imposition of iambic movement on the English decasyllable, which becomes clearly noticeable in the work of Surrey around 1550 and was explicitly advocated and practiced by Gascoigne around 1575,[16] had become, by 1585 or 1590, broadly absorbed in English poetic practice.[17] English poets had worked out the problem this iambic imposition forced on them, that central problem in all metrical composition of resolving the contrary requirements of meter and speech, and created a wonderfully resilient and versatile poetic measure. The way was then prepared for the achievements of Shakespeare and Milton in blank verse and for the closed-couplet revolution in rhyme.

That this iambic pentameter line should be defined by rhyme and worked into rhyming stanzas, the contrary arguments and examples of Campion notwithstanding, was another principle widely accepted by the Elizabethans. Sidney asserted that "the chief life" of contemporary poetry "stands in rime." [18] Daniel, who looked back over many of the great Elizabethan achievements in poetic drama, admitted the propriety of blank verse to that form of composition, but he argued the necessity of rhyme in other poetry. His essay on English prosody was, of course, named "A Defence of Ryme." [19] And Campion, whose attack on rhyme Daniel was answering in this essay, was himself a great and persistent rhymester. Puttenham, who had insisted on the importance of rhyme in English poetic composition long before the debate between these two poets, apparently thought of it as a substitute for the patterns of feet in classical measures: [20] just as the pattern $- \smile \smile - -$ concluded each classical hexameter, and the pattern $- \smile \smile - \smile \smile -$ concluded each classical pentameter, so the "Gothic" chime of final syllables might bind and define the numbers of the individual English verses. Jonson, in his

---

[15] Notably John Thompson, *The Founding of English Metre* (London, 1961); Howard Baker, "The Formation of the Heroic Medium," in his *Induction to Tragedy* (New York, 1965), pp. 48–105; and Yvor Winters, "The Audible Reading of Poetry," in *The Structure of Verse*, ed. Harvey Gross (New York, 1966), pp. 131–49.

[16] *Essays*, I, 49–51.

[17] See Thompson, pp. 2–3, and James G. Southworth, *Verses of Cadence* (Oxford, 1954), p. 46, on the emergence of self-conscious iambic measurement in English poetry.

[18] *Essays*, I, 204.

[19] *Essays*, II, 382.

[20] *Essays*, II, 80.

"Fit of Rime against Rime," similarly describes the device as binding and cramping the verse, of "Propping Verse, for feare of falling / To the ground" and, more technically, of providing the only "ceasure" for verses in the "Vulgar Languages." [21]

Actually, the use of rhyme to define lines and, of course, couplets endowed the body of the English decasyllabic line with a rhythmic freedom and flexibility lacking in the classical pentameter line. For a kind of negative exemplification of this we may recall the English elegiac distichs of Thomas Campion, every second line of which, as we have already noticed, the poet composed as an elegant system of metrical brakes, a practice which diminished the responsiveness of the line and halted the movement of the thought. Rhyme, which furnishes a one-syllable metrical brake, allowed English poets to define their materials as neatly and precisely as the Latin poets had done with the elaborate metrical mechanics of the elegiac distich and yet permitted them to retain the flexibility of their lines and couplets. This flexibility allowed English poets, first, to bend their lines and couplets in response to the individual qualities of their subject matter in its details and, second, to weld their lines and couplets into larger, more comprehensive spans. Thus rhyme made it possible for English poets to turn the closed couplet, which would begin as an imitation of a narrowly neat and pretty Latin form, into an instrument of major poetic utterance. Rhyme made it possible, that is, for English poets to develop the closed couplet into a device by which their most vital and their most complex issues could be submitted to the scrutiny of sense and reason.

Jonson saw that rhyming the English heroic line in couplets was "the bravest sort" of rhyming.[22] But others did not. Gascoigne and Puttenham, for instance, treated the many choices of rhyming stanzas with fine impartiality,[23] and Daniel explicitly preferred some form of "alternate or cross rhymes" — the kind of rhyming he himself practiced, of course.[24] We may infer from their poetry that Wyatt, Surrey, Sidney, Spenser, and all the sonneteers would have agreed with Daniel. One reason for this, which Daniel has given, is the monotony "of couplets used in long and continued Poemes,"[25] and if one considers the kind of couplets that had

---

21 *Ben Jonson*, ed. C. H. Herford and Percy and Evelyn Simpson (Oxford, 1947), VIII, 183–84.

22 *Conversations*, pp.1–2.

23 *Essays*, I, 54–56; II, 86–95.

24 *Essays*, II, 382–83.

25 *Essays*, II, 382.

prevailed in English practice up to 1590 and which continued in use into the seventeenth century, namely, the early English couplets used by Lydgate, Baldwin, Spenser, and Breton "in [their] long and continued Poemes," one can sympathize with Daniel's feelings. Writing his "Defence of Ryme" in 1603, he did not take into sufficient account the elegiac innovation in couplet composition which had already led Donne and Jonson to produce some brilliantly short and pithy poems. What Daniel saw, apparently, was two centuries of medieval couplet practice, all of it, a Renaissance poet might feel, badly in need of the energy, flexibility, and raciness which, of course, numbers of Daniel's contemporaries were beginning to infuse into this unfashionable old form.

Here, for example, is a passage of predominately medieval couplet writing employed for what would have been called "complaint." [26] In it the author, Nicholas Breton, presents Machiavelli as giving advice to his son:

Come hether *son*, & learn thy fathers lore,	
It is not now as it hath beene before,	
For in my youth would no man reade to me	
That now in age I can deliver thee,	
If thou wilt be a man of much esteeme,	5
Be not the same what ever so thou seem,	
Speak faire to al, be gentle, curteous, kind,	
But let the World know nothing of thy minde,	
Let slip no time may be for thine availe,	
Nor trust no friend, for faith begins to faile:	10
Refuse no gift to fill thy coffers full,	
The wisest poore man passeth for a gull.	
Be temperate in affect, sober in talke,	
And often make a solitarie walke,	
Tickle conceits, commit to memorie	15
For written lines may ly in jeopardie.	
Affect no follies, do no quarrels move,	
And if thou love thy selfe, fall not in love,	
Have eare for all men, conferre with few,	
And count faire words to be but as a dew.	20

---

[26] See John Peter, *Complaint and Satire in Early English Literature* (Oxford, 1956), for a distinction between complaint and satire which illuminates my distinction between the early English couplet, one of the normal media for complaint, and the new elegiac couplet, the one great medium for satire.

These verses, to use J. V. Cunningham's words, consist of "a sequence in serial order of sententiae, maxims, proverbs, or propositions of a similar kind, usually one to a line [ll. 9, 10, 14, 19, 20], sometimes two [ll. 13, 17], and occasionally a single sententia over two lines [ll. 5–6, 7–8, 15–16]," and constitute "a cumulative experience of serious insistence." [27] This poetry depends for its tone on the metrical stiffness of its individual couplets and, indeed, of its individual lines. Its stiffness, which had been prescribed by Gascoigne,[28] gives it the effect of a strictly one-way communication whose truths are perfectly determined; of a speaker, to put its effect another way, who has reached a perfection of wisdom and is no longer responsive to — no longer dependent on — experience, who is not open to new arguments or new impressions.

Medieval couplets, as this passage shows, are stiff throughout, but not regular in their stiffness. One almost as often finds heavy stops at the ends of first lines, for instance, as at the ends of couplets (ll. 1, 7, 9, 11, 17, 19). Again, one finds incidental mid-line pauses of great weight (ll. 7, 17) and, on the other hand, many lines with virtually none at all (ll. 3, 5, 8, 16). Despite the occasional heavy caesuras, the line is the prevailing unit of this poetic measure, and, as our quotation suggests, poems composed in it jog on in statements indiscriminately one or two and, sometimes, three or four lines long. It is no wonder, then, that Daniel found this measure monotonous; no wonder, furthermore, that it was only one of several rhyming systems in use around 1603 when Daniel wrote his "Defence."

Let us sum up. By the last ten or fifteen years of the sixteenth century, the time at which the new elegiac couplet was to burst into English poetry, the English heroic line had been established as the staple measure of verse; it was already a highly refined measure, although it would become still more refined in the years to come; it was generally rhymed in nondramatic poetry, but usually not in the form of couplets.

2. THE LATIN MOLD

Between 1585 and 1600 several English poets discovered the affinity between their own rhyming heroic couplet and the Latin elegiac distich, chiefly as it was practiced by Ovid and Martial, which was to lead them, first, to transform the couplet and, eventually, to alter the course of Eng-

---

[27] "Lyric Style in the 1590's," in *The Problem of Style,* ed. J. V. Cunningham (New York, 1966), p. 163.
[28] *Essays,* I, 56.

lish poetry.[29] To understand the affinity they discovered and the transformation they achieved, we must understand the Latin elegiac distich.[30]

Ovid's own description of this form, itself an example of it, will allow us to begin:

> *Sex mihi surgat opus numeris in quinque residat:*
> *ferrea cum vestris bella valete modis!*

or, as Marlowe translated it:

> Let my first verse be sixe, my last five feete,
> Farewell sterne warre, for blunter poets meete.

The elegiac distich, then, as Ovid says, is a pair of lines, the first six feet long and the second five. Its metrical paradigm is,

$$- \smile \smile - \smile \smile - \smile \smile - \smile \smile - \smile \smile - -$$
$$- \smile \smile - \smile \smile - \; || \; - \smile \smile - \smile \smile - \; .$$

It is a measure, to notice Ovid's second line above, fit not for war, fit not, that is, for utterance of the first importance, but fit, as Ovid said in the lines just before these, for the talk of love. Martial would come later to show that it was also fit for brief and pointed satiric address.[31] We might also notice the implication, strongly present in the balancing verbs "*surgat*" and "*residat*," that this two-line measure is strongly end-stopped.

Its distinguishing feature is its second line, which is the pentameter. This line is composed of two exactly equal metrical halves and divided in the middle. In our example, the pentameter scans,

> *fērrĕă cūm vēstrīs || bēllă vălētĕ mŏdīs.*

The first two feet in the first half of this line are subject to spondaic substitution — as in the second foot of our example, but the second half

[29] That the closed heroic couplet derived from the Latin elegiac distich has been acknowledged in general for a long time: see, for example, Ruth Wallerstein, "The Development of the Rhetoric and Metre of the Heroic Couplet," *PMLA*, L (1935), 166–67.

[30] I have depended for my understanding of this measure as a metrical entity on a number of classical metrists: among them, Maurice Platnauer, *Latin Elegiac Verse* (Cambridge, 1951); and W. R. Hardie, "The Elegiac Couplet," in his *Res Metrica* (Oxford, 1920), pp. 49–55.

[31] Martial was preceded by Catullus in using the elegiac distich for satiric epigrams — as was Ovid, indeed, in using it for love poetry. For a history of this form and a description of its various uses see Archibald Day, *The Origins of Latin Love-Elegy* (Oxford, 1938).

must always run $-\,\smile\,\smile\,-\,-\,\smile\,\smile\,-$. The mid-line pause, moreover, always comes at a word end and is thus always prominent. This line then is strongly balanced and sharply defined.

The first line of the distich, the hexameter, conforms to the classical heroic line that was used in unbroken series by Vergil and Lucretius and Juvenal in their variously major utterances. It is composed of four dactylic feet, all of which are subject to spondaic substitution (note the fourth foot in our example), and a concluding pattern of two feet, the first of which is almost always a dactyl and the second, always a spondee. This more subtle way of signalling the line end is, however, stiffened in elegiac poetry by the strictly demarcated pentameter line. The mid-line caesura of the hexameter, which is achieved by a word's ending inside a metrical foot, is flexible although the third foot is commonly its place. When this break comes immediately after the long syllable of the third foot, which occurs ninety percent of the time in Ovid's elegiac writing,[32] the first half of the hexameter approximates the halves of the pentameter in meter. Such is the case with our example above which scans $-\,\smile\,\smile\,-\,\smile\,\smile\,-\,\|\,\smile\,\smile\,-\,-\,-\,\smile\,\smile\,-\,-$. This caesural practice naturally strengthens the impression of sharp definitions and persistent balance. Metrically speaking, then, the Latin elegiac distich presents us with a regular hierarchy of pauses — the strongest at the close of the distich, the next strongest at the end of the first line, the third strongest at the midpoints of the two lines — and with a system of utterance whose prevailing unit is made of two segments each of which is subdivided into two.[33]

To observe its nature in concrete detail, let us consider the following passage taken from Ovid's *Amores*:

vivet Maeonides, Tenedos dum stabit et Ide,
    dum rapidas Simois in mare volvet aquas;   *10*
vivet et Ascraeus, dum mustis uva tumebit,
    dum cadet incurva falce resecta Ceres.

---

[32] Platnauer, pp. 9–10.

[33] Platnauer has implicitly acknowledged this regular hierarchy of pauses: remarking at different points in his book, first, that it is Ovid's virtually unbroken rule to achieve a caesura in the third foot of his hexameter (pp. 6–10) and the virtual obligation of all elegists to observe "the main caesura" of the pentameter (pp. 13–14), second, that "the most frequent sense-pause in the elegiac couplet is that between the hexameter and the pentameter" (p. 25), and, third, that elegiac poets "nearly always complete the sentence, or the clause, at the end of the pentameter" (p. 27).

Battiades semper toto cantabitur orbe;
  quamvis ingenio non valet, arte valet.
nulla Sophocleo veniet iactura cothurno;   *15*
  cum sole et luna, semper Aratus erit;
dum fallax servus, durus pater, inproba lena
  vivent et meretrix blanda, Menandros erit;
Ennius arte carens animosique Accius oris
  casurum nullo tempore nomen habent.   *20*

.   .   .   .

Ergo, cum silices, cum dens patientis aratri
  depereant aevo, carmina morte carent.
cedant carminibus reges regumque triumphi,
  cedat et auriferi ripa benigna Tagi!
vilia miretur vulgus; mihi flavus Apollo   *35*
  pocula Castalia plena ministret aqua,
sustineamque coma metuentem frigora myrtum,
  atque ita sollicito multus amante legar!

The editorial punctuation of this passage makes the hierarchy of pauses
we have been discovering clear enough. We may also notice, to augment
our sense of it, that the caesura comes after the first syllable of the third
foot in every hexameter so that the first half of every one is metrically
equivalent to the pentameter half-line.

It is evident from this passage, moreover, that the secondary and ter-
tiary pauses are subject to modification in their strength although the
primary pause, that is, the close of the distich, is not. The pauses at the
ends of hexameter lines 17, 31, and 35, for instance, are all subjected to
the pressure of syntactic thrust. Line 31 must thrust on in order for *"si-
lices"* and *"dens patientis aratri"* to reach their governing verb, *"deper-
eant."* And the thrust at line 35 is greater still, since one clause is con-
cluded with the first half of the hexameter line, and the subject of the
second, *"Apollo,"* stands alone. This line is not simply abandoned, how-
ever, for, besides its metrical stability, it contains a sharp rhetorical an-
tithesis, between *"vulgus"* and *"mihi"* — an antithesis which Apollo's
action, as described in the pentameter line, will explain. In turning to the
rhetoric of these lines, we will be able to define their interior dynamics
more precisely. For the present, let us say that Ovid handles the interior
pauses of his distichs very flexibly and their closes very stiffly. The only
distich close which is not absolute, that at line 36, closes a complete, in-
dependent clause and could have ended on a full stop without confusion:

the next distich following defines its own syntactically independent matter — two line-defined co-ordinate clauses.

Let us consider the presence in this passage of those three rhetorical practices, inversion, balance, and parallelism, which we have described as common elements in the English closed couplet. The inflection of Latin allowed Ovid greater opportunities for inversion, for the emphatic placing of words, than English poets could enjoy. The Roman poet often removed nouns and verbs to line ends and, less strikingly, to caesural breaks, and thus naturally heightened the metrical force of his form. Verbs are significantly shifted, for instance, to the ends of lines 11, 16, 18, and 38, in the passage above, and nouns to the ends of lines 12, 14, and 36. The whole Menander distich is yoked together by the fact that its short main clause has been suspended until the very end of its pentameter (ll. 17–18).

The practice of balance is also a persistent element in Ovid's style. Sometimes the poet places two substantives which are in syntactic agreement on opposite sides of a caesura: there are "*ingenio . . . arte*" in line 14, for instance, and "*aevo . . . morte*" in line 32. This practice English poets would, of course, be able to copy, but they could not duplicate an even more common Ovidian practice, the balancing of syntactically agreeing nouns and adjectives. In our passage there are "*rapidas . . . aquas*" (l. 10); "*Sophocleo . . . cothurno*" (l. 15); "*meretrix blanda*" (l. 18); and the doubled set, "*casurum nullo tempore nomen*," whose pattern has been dramatized by chiasmic placing. Similarly complex in its balance is the line, "*pocula Castalia plena ministret aqua*," in which "*pocula*" is modified by "*plena*" and in which "*Castalia*" modifies "*aqua*." Because of its persistence and because it is merely a syntactical, rather than a substantial, balance, this practice adds to the mannered effect of Ovid's style.

Another common practice of Ovid, one which English poets could capture, is his production of parallels. In the passage above, for instance, half-lines define the parallel halves of a compound subject, Ennius and Accius, together with the modifiers of each (l. 19), and in another line (l. 31) they define the two halves of a compound subject of a dependent clause, "*silices*" and "*dens*," together with the repeated term "*cum*" which underscores this parallel. Whole lines, again, define parallel statements on the immortality of Sophocles and Aratus (ll. 15–16) and, elsewhere (ll. 33–34), the two parallel statements on things that must give way to poetry. Complete distichs, finally, define parallel assertions of the poetic immortality of Maeonides (ll. 9–10), Ascraeus (ll. 11–12), and Battiades (ll. 13–14).

It may be noticed that the first two of these three distichs are strictly parallel, the movement and syntax of the second, "*vivet . . . dum . . . / dum*," perfectly reflecting those elements of the first, but that the third, the one on Battiades, is completely different in its internal order. This shift from a strict repetition to a completely unique order recalls Yvor Winters's statement on the English closed couplet, that it is extremely flexible because of its seeming inflexibility.[34] Once the poet, Ovid in this case, has established his pattern, he can vary its elements widely to accommodate the special qualities of each detail of his discourse and still maintain these elements in his larger poetic order. Thus the distich on Battiades fulfills its place in this larger scheme — being a further case of poetic immortality — while, at the same time, defining a special statement on Battiades: we know that Battiades will endure as long as the great processes of life and nature which he sang about endure, simply because he belongs to the sharply defined catalogue whose first two members have been presented to us in this way; in addition, we are told something particular about Battiades himself, that he excelled in art although not in invention. Ovid has formed his distich on Menander even more in accordance with the details of that writer's achievement. In both these cases the poet is informing us with his pattern itself, now that it is firmly established, as well as with the words he puts into it.

The distich between these on Battiades and Menander reveals a different but similar benefit Ovid could derive from his established parallel order. The appearance of Sophocles in its first line, which places him with the three preceding poets who were similarly set in the first lines of their distichs, declares his participation in the category of poetic immortality, and the appearance of Aratus in the second line, which gives him a metrical dignity similar to Sophocles, also draws him into the plan. The most obvious benefit here, although Ovid has been able to give us some special information about each of these poets in working out this new departure in his form — that Sophocles was a tragedian, for instance — is the gain in compression. After turning the next distich to an extensive discovery of the immortality of Menander, he will achieve another compressed distich, that coupling Ennius and Accius, a distich which is differently articulated from this on Sophocles and Aratus. Throughout this catalogue, then, Ovid derives a general expressive value from his form which he variously refines in producing its individual elements.

---

[34] "The Heroic Couplet and Its Recent Rivals," in his *In Defense of Reason* (Denver, 1943), pp. 141–42.

In recognizing some of the freedoms Ovid's strict patterning of his distichs allowed him and some of his manipulations, we have verged on another aspect of his practice, its pervasive achievement of a dynamics between its meter and its language. Let me insist, even at the danger of being repetitious, that this dynamics is almost completely confined to the distichs individually; the pentameter, that elaborate metrical brake, makes their closes virtually absolute, the meaning of each one residing inside its own confines. Within separate distichs, however, we find a considerable variety of movement, a wide range of rhythms. Sometimes a complete balance, both elements of it, will be wedged in a half-line (l. 14); sometimes the two elements of a balance will be divided unevenly, one element cut off in a half-line and the other draped over three halves, as in lines 35–36 of our passage. In this latter distich we might notice further varieties of ordering: first, the tightly joined terms of an opposition, "*mihi*" and "*vulgus*," are different in syntax; second, they are at opposite ends of their governing statements — by which chiasmic ordering Ovid has heightened his antithesis; third, the extensive development of the "*mihi*" element has led Ovid to compose an enjambed first line. One finds other enjambed first lines in this passage too (ll. 17, 19, 31), each of which makes a modification in the normal hierarchy of distich pauses.

The danger in all these distichs whose first lines are enjambed is that of an internal failure of pattern. There is in all three cases, however — as in all cases of Ovidian enjambment — a strong countering force by which the integrity of the first line and the balance of the distich are preserved. Ovid has stiffened one of these first lines, for instance, by using it to define the two halves of a compound subject, emphasizing this by repeating the logical term "*cum*" that governs their clause (l. 31); he has preserved another in a similar way (l. 19). And the first line of the Menander distich defines three (of four) parallel subjects, each of them modified by its own single adjective. Moreover, the break between the first and second coincides with the caesura, and that between the second and third coincides with the commencement of the – ‿ ‿ – – tag by which the hexameter line defines itself, so that the segments of matter in the line stiffen its form. In two of these three distichs whose first line is enjambed (ll. 17–18, 31–32), again, Ovid has practiced an inversion, putting off crucial terms to the end of the distich and thus reasserting his measure. All three of these enjambed first lines, finally, enjoy the hexameter close of one dactyl and a spondee and the persistent metrical stiffness of the pentameter. By thus playing on the different elements of his art, its rhetoric, syntax, and meter, Ovid achieved a dynamics between thrust and stasis within his individual distichs.

Marlowe, as his translation of this passage from Ovid will show, achieved a remarkable duplication of this model:

Homer shall live while *Tenedos* stands and *Ide*,
Or into Sea swift *Simois* doth slide.   10
Ascraeus lives, while grapes with new wine swell,
Or men with crooked Sickles corne downe fell.
The world shall of *Callimachus* ever speake,
His Arte excelld, although his witte was weake.
For ever lasts high *Sophocles* proud vaine,   15
With Sunne and Moone *Aratus* shall remaine.
While bond-men cheate, fathers hard, bawds whorish,
And strumpets flatter, shall *Menander* flourish.
Rude *Ennius*, and *Plautus* full of witt,
Are both in fames eternall legend writt.   20

.   .   .   .

Therefore when Flint and Iron weare away,
Verse is immortall, and shall nere decay.
To verse let Kings give place, and Kingly showes,
And bankes ore which gold-bearing *Tagus* flowes.
Let base conceipted witts admire vilde things,   35
Faire *Phoebus* lead me to the Muses springs.
About my head be quivering mirtle wound,
And in sad lovers heads let me be found.

Marlowe has brought ten closed Latin distichs into ten exactly corre-
sponding closed English couplets, and this couplet-by-distich transference
is the virtually unbroken rule of his whole translation of *Amores*. Mar-
lowe has often caught the internal movement of his model too: he gave
line definition to the two "while" clauses in our first couplet, exactly cap-
turing Ovid's organization of the two corresponding "*dum*" clauses; the
same thing is true in the second couplet; and his "With Sunne and
Moone *Aratus* shall remaine," again, duplicates even the word order and
the caesura of Ovid's "*cum sole et luna, semper Aratus erit*" — only sub-
stituting "shall remain" for "*semper . . . erit.*"
    But this remarkable degree of duplication must not blind us to the
differences between Marlowe and his model, to the adjustments he has
had to make. Marlowe, for instance, has not only reproduced Ovid's
practice of placing his verbs at the ends of lines (ll. 11, 16, 20, 38), but
he has engaged in this practice often when Ovid did not (ll. 10, 12, 13,
34, 37) — to the point of monotony, it should be admitted. Ovid had

ended on a noun in every one of these cases. Marlowe was forced to narrow his use of inversion in this way, obviously enough, by the lack of inflections. Deprived of the freedom to disperse nouns and adjectives that Ovid enjoyed, the English poet had either to shift his verbs or to give up the neat, emphatic closure Ovid got by inversion, that is, by the suspension of important terms to the ends of his lines. Marlowe's adjustment, one in which he would be followed by Sandys and Waller and, indeed, the whole closed-couplet tradition, makes for a less variously elegant but more emphatic verse utterance.

Marlowe also modified some of the balances of his model, as our example suggests. The witty effect Ovid got by cramming "*non valet . . . valet*" into one half of a pentameter line Marlowe sacrificed, as the exigencies of English prompted, for a whole balanced line with caesural definition: "His Arte excelld, although his witte was weake." The same tendency is evident in Marlowe's more broadly articulated "To verse let Kings give place, and Kingly showes." This tendency toward a simpler and stiffer practice is even clearer in whole couplets: Marlowe has turned two of Ovid's dynamically unbalanced distichs, for instance, namely, those at lines 31–32 and 35–36, into perfectly balanced couplets, making the breaks at the ends of their first lines, rather than the weaker caesural pauses, coincide with the major pivots in their rhetoric. And yet again: where Ovid had handled two parallel statements in quite different ways — in terms of both their syntax and their organization — "*sustineamque coma metuentem frigora myrtum, / atque ita sollicito multus amante legar*," Marlowe lined everything up, "About my head be quivering mirtle wound, / And in sad lovers heads let me be found." The 'head–heads' pattern, which the syntax and the placing emphasize, is, of course, Marlowe's addition; the propriety of its wit is questionable.

In Marlowe's defense it must be said, first, that the lack of inflection in English forced him to simplify Ovid's rhetorical patterns and, second, that he found the cue for his adjustments in Ovid himself. We may recall, for instance, the stiffness of the parallels in the first two Ovidian distichs, a stiffness Marlowe perfectly observed in his translation, and Ovid's fairly common practice of placing his verbs at the ends of lines. We may even find in Ovid's 'valet–valet' and 'reges–regumque' repetitions a sanction for Marlowe's creation of the 'head–heads' repetition we have just observed. Marlowe followed his model precisely where he could, and, where he could not, he substituted practices he had found elsewhere in his model.

One last point before we leave this comparison. The elegiac distich gave Ovid the choice of as many as seventeen syllables in his first line and up to fourteen in his second; Marlowe, of course, was confined to ten and ten. The English poet compensated for his fewer syllables chiefly in two ways. First of all, he made use of English's many monosyllables: in the first few lines of our comparative passages, for instance, he substituted "stands," "swift," "slide," "lives," "wine," "swell," and "fell," respectively, for *"stabit," "rapidas," "volvet," "vivet," "mustis," "tumebit,"* and *"cadet."* Later poets, having turned away from the problems of strict translation, would bring Latinate polysyllables into the English couplet, the polysyllables they had learned from such Latin poets as Ovid, of course. Hence the combined smoothness and bite of such couplets as these: *"True Wit* is *Nature* to Advantage drest, / What oft was *Thought,* but ne'er so well Exprest," and "Great Wits are sure to Madness near ally'd, / And thin partitions do their bounds divide." One notices in the last line above the monumental grace given the chiefly English diction of "great," "wits," "madness," and "thin" by the Latinate "partitions."

Another practice of Marlowe's for realizing about thirty syllables of Latin in twenty syllables of English, one which Dryden and especially Pope would accept, was the Elizabethan's use of zeugma. In each of our first two couplets above, for instance, Marlowe makes one "while" do the work Ovid did by repeating *"dum."* More striking than this, in lines 33–34 Ovid's two verbs *"cedant . . . / cedat"* are telescoped into one, "let . . . give place," thus gaining Marlowe a little elbowroom in his second line. A timid beginning, no doubt, but it would lead in time to such passages as this:

> Say what the use, were finer optics giv'n,
> T' inspect a mite, not comprehend the heav'n?
> Or touch, if tremblingly alive all o'er,
> To smart and agonize at ev'ry pore?
> Or quick effluvia darting thro' the brain,
> Die of a rose in aromatic pain?

These practices by which Marlowe transferred Ovid's *Amores* into his own *Elegies* helped lay the foundation on which the closed couplet would develop. Here, all at once, we have its basic form: the hierarchy of pauses; the rhetorical practices of inversion, balance, and parallelism; and the impulse, implicit in such meter and rhetoric, toward regularity and neatness, toward conciseness and compression of statement.

To recognize another major impulse that Marlowe and his English colleagues in the distich-couplet transference derived from the Latin form, that is, the impulse to articulate couplet poetry as some kind of direct public address, we must turn to another of them, Ben Jonson, and, more specifically, to Jonson's transference into English couplets of some elegiac distichs of the great classical epigrammatist, Martial. Here is Martial addressing a mimic poet:

Scribebamus epos; coepisti scribere: cessi,
  aemula ne starent carmina nostra tuis.
transtulit ad tragicos se nostra Thalia cothurnos:
  aptasti longum tu quoque syrma tibi.
fila lyrae movi Calabris exculta Camenis: 5
  plectra rapis nobis, ambitiose, nova.
audemus saturas: Lucilius esse laboras.
  ludo levis elegos: tu quoque ludis idem.
quid minus esse potest? epigrammata fingere coepi:
  hinc etiam petitur iam mea palma tibi.   10
elige quid nolis (quis enim pudor omnia velle?)
  et si quid non vis, Tucca, relinque mihi.

This poem is beautifully composed. The first distich, especially the first line with its compressed discovery of response and counterresponse, prepares us for the speaker's mock-desperate effort to outstrip the claims of his emulous rival; the three following distichs define the aspects of this effort, the elements of this process of creation and mimicry; the next-to-last distich gives us the end of this process — the end being exactly like the beginning with the rival still sticking to the speaker; and the last one, in which the rival is addressed by name, gives the speaker's despairing plea — *you* go first and just leave me anything you don't want.

The outside distichs, although they abide by the rules of the form, are extremely talky: the first, whose first line holds three segments of utterance and is relatively enjambed, is headlong in movement, and the last, with its breaks for a general opinion and for a naming of the rival, is conversationally erratic. The three interior distichs are much stiffer. The first and second of them each define one step in the process of imitation, tragedy and ode, each hexameter defining the speaker's effort and each pentameter, the response of his rival; this stiffness and this repetitiveness of formal definition underscore the absurdly mechanical motivation in the rival. Martial has compressed two steps of the process into the third, the hexameter giving us the two rivals' two-part effort toward satire, the pentameter, that toward elegy — thus presenting us with an example of the condensation allowed by a strict observance of the form similar to the one we noticed in our Ovidian passage. This denser distich is also stiff, of course, perfectly correspondent, in fact, to the two distichs above; the caesuras do exactly the same definitive job in this distich that the first line breaks did in those two. At the same time, the intensely talky quality of the poem, so strongly asserted in the exterior distichs, is kept up in all three of these distichs too. Every one of them has an I–you form of utterance, for instance; in line 6, moreover, the speaker name-calls his rival, "*ambitiose*," and in line 4 one catches the note of scornful parody in the speaker's tone, that is, we hear him mimic his rival's claim. The whole poem is, thus, pervaded with the speaker's exasperated and incredulous voice.

About half of Martial's epigrams are in elegiac distichs; and virtually all of these are, on the one hand, organized to enjoy the emphases and definitions of the form and, on the other, projected as fluent, racy conversation. The speaker's tone of voice is clear, and the personalities of his targets, who are usually named, are vividly defined. Hoyt Hudson has said of Martial's epigrams that they "are always written to be heard." [35] Martial himself spoke of them as having tongues and of their speaking up for themselves. He also insisted that they constituted epistles. [36] And the epistle was commonly held by Latin poets to be the most conversational form of writing, being, as Wesley Trimpi has shown, one of the four genres of "*sermo* or the conversational style." [37] We may notice here that three of these four classical genres of the conversational or plain style, namely, the epistle, the epigram, and the satire, would come into England after 1590 almost always in some form of the closed heroic couplet. We may suggest the importance of Martial's epigrams to this transference by further recognizing that English satires of this period, which we will study in some detail later on, have been described as little more than strings of epigrams in the style of Martial. [38]

To examine the nature of Martial's influence in particular, let us consider Ben Jonson's virtual translation of the poem we have just studied in his epigram "To a Weak Gamester in Poetry":

[35] *The Epigram in the English Renaissance* (Princeton, 1947), p. 17.

[36] *Epigrammaton*, II, "Val. Martialis Deciano Suo Sal." in the Loeb Edition, ed. W. C. A. Ker (New York, 1919), I, 109.

[37] *Ben Jonson's Poems: A Study of the Plain Style* (Stanford, 1962), pp. 6–8.

[38] Morse Allen, *The Satire of John Marston* (Columbus, 1920), p. 84.

I cannot for the stage a *Drama* lay,
   Tragick, or *Comick*; but thou writ'st the play.
I leave thee there, and giving way, entend
   An *Epick* poeme; thou hast the same end.   10
I modestly quit that, and thinke to write,
   Next morne, an *Ode*: Thou mak'st a song ere night.
I passe to *Elegies*; Thou meet'st me there:
   To *Satyres*; and thou dost pursue me. Where,
Where shall I scape thee? in an *Epigramme*?   15
   O, (thou cry'st out) that is thy proper game.

Jonson, like Martial, gives a full unit to each of his first three examples of imitation, although changing around the imitated genres, and compresses two examples in the next, giving a line to each of these. Jonson also gets Martial's sense of the mechanical regularity of the rival's responsive activities, but in his own way: each of our first three couplets pivots at the midpoint of its second line, rather than at the formally stronger pause at the end of the first line. Other practices of Jonson modify the couplet even more. The first lines of the first three couplets are all relatively enjambed, for instance, and the closing line of the fourth, which breaks into three segments, is quite strongly enjambed, making, of course, an enjambed couplet. The chance for condensation allowed by our first three couplets Jonson has, formally speaking, *more* than taken, completing the thought of his fourth couplet not in the ten syllables of its second line, but in nine syllables, and he has then practiced the enjambment, "Where, / Where," by which he dramatizes his recognition of the rival's unshakable persistence. This enjambed, three-part second line we may compare to a metrically correspondent line in Martial, the Latin poet's very first line. With it Martial precipitated a situation which then proceeded unchanged; his poem was thus a satiric elaboration of a stable condition. Jonson's powerfully broken couplet pattern is dramatic rather than satirically detached: his speaker comes suddenly in mid-career to discover the horrible unshakableness of the rival, to make the discovery, that is, with which Martial opened his poem.

    The point is that Jonson, even when prompted by the sharply closed distich and the sharply indicated detachment of Martial, followed the natural curve of his awareness and abided by the natural shape of his thought, rather than a strictly epigrammatic form of organization and its correspondent indications of epigrammatic poise. Jonson, then, has not translated Martial as Marlowe had Ovid; he has tried, rather, for a compromise between his model's impression of a witty, detached address and his own impulse toward an utterance more dramatic. One may doubt that he has achieved a perfect amalgamation of the two attitudes. The three couplets which precede his dramatic intensification of utterance are not only stiff, but similarly stiff — although unbalanced in their stiffness — and thus strongly indicative of a totally comprehended situation, of a situation, that is, which can give rise to no new discoveries.

For a more faithful, a less creative, rendering of Martial's epigrams in English couplets one might refer to Sir John Harington's "Epigram on Paulus" and his "Epigram to a Cuckold"[39] and compare them to their models in Martial. Harington, it will be seen, has also striven for Martial's conversational tone and has only fallen short of Martial, indeed, by failing to reproduce his epigrammatic terseness and polish.

This pointed conversational tone, which English epigrammatists found in Martial and which, after 1585, they attempted commonly to fit into English closed couplets, is also strongly evident, if not quite so persistently so, in Ovid's elegiac poems, especially in his *Amores*. Professor Trimpi has suggested that the elegy was "traditionally associated with the middle style or *genus floridum*."[40] Ovid's elegiac *Heroides*, which is comprised of letters from heroic lovers, most of them the letters of ladies heroically addicted to love, could very well be called "florid." But they are epistles, thus enjoying a link to the conversational or plain style, and they are epistles, moreover, of some directness and particularity of address. And the sense of personal address in *Amores*, a more influential work than *Heroides* on most of the inaugurators of the closed couplet, is various, persistent, and quite compelling.

One of these elegiac poems, in which the lover addresses the door-keeper of his beloved's house, begins:

> *Ianitor — indignum! — dura religate catena,*
> * difficilem moto cardine pande forem!*
> *quod precor, exiguum est — aditu fac ianua parvo*
> * obliquum capiat semiadaperta latus.*

In other poems from *Amores*, the lover pointedly and conversationally addresses his mistress, Corinna (I, xiv; II, vii; III, xi, b); Corinna's servants, Nape (I, xi) and Cypassis (II, viii) — the latter of whom he also

---

[39] Pp. 177–78 and 179 in this book.
[40] Trimpi, pp. 228–29.

addresses as a mistress; and a friend, Graecinus (II, x). In some poems, he addresses first one person and then another (II, xvii; III, viii); in others he reports earlier conversations (I, viii; I, xiv). In this passage addressed to his fellow poet Macer, for instance, we hear the lover describe some talk between his mistress and himself:

> *Carmen ad iratum dum tu perducis Achillen*
>   *primaque iuratis induis arma viris,*
> *nos, Macer, ignava Veneris cessamus in umbra,*
>   *et tener ausuros grandia frangit Amor.*
> *saepe meae "tandem" dixi "discede" puellae —*
>   *in gremio sedit protinus illa meo.*
> *saepe "pudet!" dixi — lacrimis vix illa retentis*
>   *"me miseram! iam te" dixit "amare pudet?"*
> *inplicuitque suos circum mea colla lacertos*
>   *et, quae me perdunt, oscula mille dedit.*

Ovid, moreover, has a general sense of his audience throughout *Amores*:

> *Hoc quoque conposui Paelignis natus aquosis,*
>   *ille ego nequitiae Naso poeta meae.*
> *hoc quoque iussit Amor — procul hinc, procul este, severae!*
>   *non estis teneris apta theatra modis.*
> *me legat in sponsi facie non frigida virgo,*
>   *et rudis ignoto tactus amore puer;*
> *atque aliquis iuvenum quo nunc ego saucius arcu*
>   *agnoscat flammae conscia signa suae,*
> *miratusque diu "quo" dicat "ab indice doctus*
>   *conposuit casus iste poeta meos?"*

The poet-lover of *Amores*, then, speaks to other lovers whom he persistently takes into account as his proper audience, and he makes throughout its course a variety of more pointed, more positively conversational addresses.

Thus English poets who turned the Latin elegiac distichs of Ovid and Martial into closed English couplets coped, in both cases, not only with the metrical and rhetorical problems this transference involved but with the further problem of producing a conversational tone, a tone of personal address. Marlowe, as a brief recollection of our example of his work will show, did not measure up very well to this further aspect of his Latin model. His English, indeed, is often bad and sometimes incomprehensible. Jonson, who rewrote the poem from which our exemplary passage comes, took it, as his chief job, to repair the bad English. The distich Marlowe had rendered, "While bond-men cheate, fathers hard, / bawds whorish, / And strumpets flatter, shall *Menander* flourish," for instance, Jonson rewrote, "Whil'st slaves be false, fathers hard, and bawdes be whorish, / Whil'st harlots flatter, shall *Menander* flourish." Still artificial, no doubt, but the parallels have been straightened out so that we may find it speakable — spoken, indeed, since this appears in Jonson's play *Poetaster*.[41] Jonson improved the crabbed Marlovian line on Sophocles, again, to read, "No losse shall come to *Sophocles* proud vaine." To make the English flow more clearly and forcefully in the channels of speech, Jonson sacrificed one of Marlowe's neatest effects: Marlowe's couplet, "The world shall of *Callimachus* ever speake, / His Arte excelled, although his witte was weake," becomes in Jonson, "*Callimachus*, though in invention lowe, / Shall still be sung: since he in art doth flowe." Obviously enough, Jonson is further here from Waller and from Pope than Marlowe was. A major problem for Pope, as this may suggest, would be to reconcile Marlowe's epigrammatic balances and closures with Jonson's flow of good conversational English.

This revolutionary intercourse between the Latin elegiac distich and the English heroic couplet, which resulted in the English closed couplet, persisted almost as long as the closed couplet did. As the illustrations in this book declare, translations, adaptations, and imitations of Ovid, Martial, and other elegiac poets, among them the Renaissance Latinists, make a sizable fraction of the total couplet output right on to William Cowper, who made virtually couplet-for-distich translations of six out of seven of the youthful Milton's Latin elegies. Jonson, Drayton, and Donne all imitated Ovidian elegies; Donne, moreover, wrote one poem, "Sapho to Philaenis," and Drayton a whole series, *England's Heroical Epistles*, in close imitation of *Heroides*. Dryden, Rochester, and Oldham all translated elegies out of *Amores*; Dryden also translated a couple of epistles from *Heroides*, and Rochester mocked this form in his "Very Heroical Epistle." William Walsh, still later, wrote several rather anemic Ovidian elegies, and his youthful friend Pope translated one of the *Heroides*, "Sapho to Phaon," and imitated the form in his *Eloisa to Abelard*. Martial received almost as persistent an attention from English couplet poets as Ovid: early in the development of the form, for instance, Cowley and Herrick followed Harington and Jonson in making

---

[41] *Ben Jonson*, IV, 207–8.

virtually couplet-for-distich transcriptions of individual epigrams, and Joseph Hall and John Marston tailored a wealth of Martial's material to fit their closed-couplet satires. Pope was translating and imitating Martial at the turn of the seventeenth century; and Samuel Johnson, later still, turned fragments of Martial's epigrams into English heroic lines. Johnson also wrote some couplet poems which are reminiscent of Martial's epigrammatic style and others that resemble Ovid's elegies.

Thus even as the English closed couplet developed and as it extended itself to subjects far beyond the scope of the Latin form, it still kept a lively commerce with this classical predecessor.[42] And what English poets first learned about couplet writing from translating and imitating this form — namely, the hierarchy of pauses, the metrical definition of such rhetorical uses as inversion, parallelism, and balance, and the conversational tone — remained a central part of closed-couplet practice until the closed couplet was abandoned in the nineteenth century.

---

[42] George P. Shannon, "Nicholas Grimald's Heroic Couplet and the Latin Elegiac Distich," *PMLA*, xlv (1930), 542, has asserted that there was "no cessation of elegiac influence throughout the neoclassic period."

IV

EARLY DEVELOPMENTS

We may simplify our study of the heroic couplet during the years roughly from 1595 to 1645 by distinguishing three quite different productions of the form: the early English couplet; the new elegiac adaptation which we have called the closed couplet; and the enjambed romance couplet.

The first of these I will not treat in any further detail. Suffice it to say that it continues to crop up right to the end of our history, sometimes as the main form in old-fashioned poems like Drayton's *Moon Calf* and quite often as patches in works whose chief metrical mode is different. Weak poets, like George Wither, and poets who were devoted to a kind of medieval didacticism, like Donne in his *Anniversaries*, fell into it quite naturally. But the youthful Joseph Hall in his self-consciously classical satires, *Virgidemiarum*, also exhibits patches of this stiffer, simpler, more assertive measure — especially when he is echoing satiric formulations of Chaucer or Spenser.

The new elegiac couplet, that which was to develop into the poetic mode of Dryden and Pope and Johnson, we must continue to study in detail, first by recognizing three separate lines in its development. These are: (1) the satiric style, whose greatest exponent was Donne; (2) the style of Ben Jonson and his tribe; and (3) the abstract or amateur style, that practiced with some differences by George Sandys, Sir John Beaumont, and Lord Falkland, which led immediately to Waller and Denham. Each of these three lines will require its own discussion.

Before turning to them, however, I should like to consider and put out of our way the third kind of couplet production, that exasperating abuse of the form which I have called the romance couplet.

1. THE ROMANCE COUPLET

This kind of couplet writing seems to have been chiefly inaugurated by Christopher Marlowe in his tremendously popular romance *Hero and*

Leander. He was much the most restrained of all those poets whose use of this practice we will examine here and exemplify in this book at large,[1] but the others merely outdistanced him, as will come out, on the path he first trod. The prevalence of this adaptation of our form was explicitly recognized by George Saintsbury, who had a weakness for it; but he has given it an excessively broad name, merely "the enjambed decasyllabic couplet." Saintsbury perfectly understood that it was a meter for long poetical romances, however, and has taken the time to give special praise to William Chamberlayne's *Pharonnida*,[2] a poem whose verse we will soon consider. Other examples of its use occur in Drayton's *The Man in the Moon* and Marmion's *Cupid and Psyche*; in Thomas Moore's *Lalla Rookh*, Leigh Hunt's *The Story of Rimini*, and John Keats's *Endymion*.

As this little list may suggest, the romance couplet was most widely used, first, at the time when the new closed couplet was being vigorously achieved and, second, at the time when it was being vigorously discarded. The reason for these curiously divided outcroppings of this kind of couplet should become clear as we examine its nature and its expressive qualities. It may be worth noticing beforehand that Marlowe and Drayton practiced both this and the new closed form; that they worked with this, moreover, after working with the closed form; that Keats, on the other hand, went from an early use of this form, in *Endymion*, to an attempt at the closed form, later, in *Lamia*; and that several other poets, among them Wither and Byron, also made extensive attempts at both.

Let us begin our study of the romance couplet with two examples. The first, drawn from Drayton's *The Man in the Moon*, is the beginning of a long, involved description of Phoebe's mantle:

Now here, now there, now up and downe that flew,
Of sundry Coloures, wherein you might view
A Sea, that somewhat straitned by the Land,
Two furious Tydes raise their ambitious Hand,   150
One 'gainst the other, warring in their Pride,
Like two fond Worldlings that themselves devide
For some slight Trifle, opposite in all,
Till both together ruined, they fall.
Some comming in, some out againe doe goe,   155

---

[1] George Saintsbury, *A History of English Prosody* (London, 1908), II, 97, describes *Hero and Leander* as the "instigator" of this kind of couplet production.
[2] Ibid., II, 119–21.

And the same way, and the same Winde doth blowe,
Both Sayles their course each labouring to prefer,
By th' Hand of eithers helpfull Marriner:
Outragious Tempest, Shipwracks over-spread
All the rude NEPTUNE, whilst that pale-fac'd dread   160
Ceaseth the Ship-boy, that his strength doth put
The Ancored Cable presently to cut.
All above Boord, the sturdy EOLOUS casts
Into the wide Seas, whilst on Planks and Masts
Some say to swim: and there you might behold,   165
Whilst the rude Waters enviously did scold,
Others upon a Promontory hie,
Thrusting his Blue top through the bluer Skie,
Looking upon those lost upon the Seas,
Like Worldly Rich men that doe sit at ease,   170
Whilst in this vayne World others live in strife,
Warring with sorrow every-where so rife:
And oft amongst the Monsters of the Maine,
Their horrid Foreheads through the Billows straine,
Into the vast Aire driving on their Brests,   175
The troubled Water, that so ill disgests
Their sway, that it them enviously assailes,
Hanging with white Jawes on their Marble Scales.

The second, drawn from Chamberlayne's *Pharonnida*, comes in the middle of a long, involved description of the view from Pharonnida's palace:

We turn to view the stately Hils, that fence
The other side oth' happy Isle, from whence
All that delight or profit could invent   165
For rural pleasures was for prospect sent.
    As Nature strove for something uncouth in
So fair a dress, the struggling streams are seen,
With a loud murmure rowling 'mongst the high
And rugged clefts, one place presents the eye   170
With barren rudeness, whilst a neighbouring field
Sits cloathd in all the bounteous spring could yield,
Here lovely Landskips, where thou mightst behold,
When first the Infant Morning did unfold
The Dayes bright Curtains, in a spacious Green,   175
Which Natures curious Art had spread between

Two bushy Thickets, that on either hand,
Did like the Fringe of the fair Mantle stand,
A timerous herd of grasing Deer, and by
Them in a shady Grove, through which the eye   180
Could hardly pierce, a wel-built Lodge, from whence
The watchful Keepers careful diligence,
Secures their private walks, from hence to look
On a deep Valley, where a silver Brook,
Doth in a soft and busie murmure slide   185
Betwixt two Hils, whose shadows strove to hide
The liquid wealth, they were made fruitful by,
From ful discoveries of the distant eye.

The romance couplet, as these examples of it should suggest, is an exact perversion of the closed couplet; not merely a careless loosening of its proper emphases and definitions but, to repeat, a perversion. The poet practicing this form abuses the means by which closed-couplet poetry gains force and lucidity — its rhymes, its system of pauses, and its definitive segments — in order to achieve exactly opposite effects, dreaminess and mysterious suggestiveness.

Its practitioners make extensive use of adjectives and adverbs for their rhymes and sometimes even of conjunctions and prepositions. Chamberlayne, for instance, focusses this special emphasis not on "cliffs" or "hills," not on "pierce" or "strove," but on the accidental attributes of these terms, and, again, not on "Art" or "deer" or "wealth," but on the terms that indicate merely something of their linkages and relationships. One notices in our *Pharonnida* passage, to be more precise, that rhyme gives "high" a false superiority to its syntactic parallel, "rugged" (ll. 169–70); that rhyme presses "between" forward into a falsely adverbial eminence, making "Two bushy Thickets" seem briefly to be the object of "behold" — we have been waiting for its object for three full lines; that the real objects of "behold," "herd" (of deer) and "Lodge," are tucked away still further along in two different first lines, although not in anything like a parallel fashion, in two first lines whose rhyme words are "by" and "whence" (ll. 173–81); but there is no end to a catalogue of the confusions in emphasis that such rhyming brings.

The metrical segments, the line and couplet units, of poetry that rhymes in this way naturally reveal a corresponding confusion in definition. In the *Pharonnida* passage, again, line definition commends to the reader's attention as units of poetic utterance such groupings of words as "And rugged clefts, one place presents the eye," "A timerous herd of grasing Deer, and by," and "Could hardly pierce, a wel-built Lodge, from whence" — every one of which, insofar as it carries any meaning at all, suggests a meaning that runs counter to that which the poem's syntax must require. Or consider, in the passage from *The Man in the Moon*, the simile which likens contrary tides to a couple of fighters (ll. 150 ff.): we may take it to cover three lines or, since the preceding metaphorical treatment of the tides has been drifting toward this simile, five lines, but not two or four or six. It thus resists couplet definition and, obviously enough, requires us either to suspend the couplet's force — which is persistently indicated by the rhymes, of course — or to lose its meaning. But this is nothing to such couplet patterns as these which Chamberlayne offers us: "The Dayes bright Curtains, in a spacious Green, / Which Nature's curious Art had spread between"; "As Nature strove for something uncouth in / So fair a dress, the struggling streams are seen."

Again, consider lines 155–63 in the Drayton passage: we have here the worst of both closed and enjambed composition, that is, the artifices of closure coupled with the confusions of enjambment. Drayton has used three "do" expletives and two verb inversions to stiffen his lines and couplets, but he still does not make it clear what exactly his mariners or his ship boy is about. Chamberlayne has also coupled the confusions of enjambment with the artifices of closure on occasion; note, for instance, the stiffening inversion in the line, "Did like the Fringe of the fair Mantle stand," which is one of those lines separating the verb "behold" from its objects. Such artificial practices, which are defensible only as a means to order and clarity, make the confusions in *The Man in the Moon* and *Pharonnida* more intense.

The point is, of course, that when such elements of order and lucidity as the couplet furnishes are abused they have the opposite of their natural effect; that is, they become elements of confusion and obfuscation. They actually lead a reader astray, pressing on him as major terms those which are really ancillary, pressing upon him as units of utterance sets of words that make no sense at all or a different sense from what he will work out in other ways. Narration and description that would be simply muddy in prose become beautifully incomprehensible when composed in such measures as these of Drayton and Chamberlayne. Thus the intense confusion which Saintsbury noticed, in his empirical way, to be always attendant on the enjambed romance couplet is not merely a case of its strangely persistent ill luck, as Saintsbury seemed to think;[3] this confu-

---

[3] Ibid., II, 119–21.

sion is its very essence and, as Chamberlayne and Drayton would surely insist, its glory.

To insist on its essential confusion is not to deny that this kind of couplet has an expressive value, but rather to begin defining it. To carry this definition further, let us view more broadly Drayton's description of Phoebe's mantle. This exercise runs on for some forty lines beyond what I have just quoted — and in the same way, that is, giving descriptions within descriptions within descriptions, none of them clear and none related back to the mantle. If *we* attempt to relate these secondary and tertiary images back to it, all we can imagine is that it is full of business. Drayton makes no mention of the disposition of its images, and gives no sense of its threads or its weaving. More significant still, many of the images, that of "the two fond Worldlings," for example, and that of the "Worldly Rich men," being merely similes, have no place on the mantle at all — if, that is, we pause to think about it. But, in fact, this mantle is not an object for the reader's contemplation; it is, rather, an excuse for the poet's expansive fancy. The more the poet loads it with details, the less substantial it grows.

Marlowe's description of the pavement of Venus's temple in *Hero and Leander*, although quite restrained in its formulations, has rather the same expressive effect. Its long catalogue of the images one might see in this pavement, although each one is given some metrical definition and, thus, some clarity in itself, distracts us from the pavement just as the fuzzy images of Drayton distract us from Phoebe's mantle. Consider this couplet, for instance: "Blood-quaffing Mars heaving the iron net, / Which limping Vulcan and his Cyclops set." Neither line of it hints at any connection between its imagery and the pavement: there is no mortar and no mosaic about it. Neither of its lines, furthermore, defines an image that might possibly be realized in that way. "Blood-quaffing" in the first line is a purely literary modification; Mars would hardly be shown quaffing blood while caught in Vulcan's net. And in the second line we are given a flashback that turns the whole thing into a narrative, into an action that obviously cannot be caught in stone. Thus Marlowe, even while using his couplets to define and clarify the individual items of his own fancy, inaugurated that romantic irresponsibility of descriptive reference and that fluidity of descriptive expansion which led to Phoebe's dissolving mantle and Pharonnida's dissolving landscape.

The practitioners of the romance couplet make no more effort to define an audience than they do to define their fancies. Their expressive design, insofar as we may accuse them of any public intention, is to reduce the members of any audience whatsoever to the same dreamy state, to the same abandonment of common sense and common judgment, to the same dependency on the vagaries of fancy that apparently possessed them. In this cultivated rejection of common intelligence, in this refusal to discriminate between the different elements of their discourse or the different attitudes of an audience, this poetry is, to reassert the point, the opposite of poetry in closed couplets. If one responds to it, as Saintsbury did, one "floats . . . with such pleasant aimlessness, and in such agreeable country."[4] One of the entranced reader's impressions, to expand on this description, is that he floats forever, since the utterance that flows so thoughtlessly through its rhyming closes has no proper end. This impression is enhanced, of course, by the virtual interminableness of these poems. Another of his impressions is that this pleasant country is no land that ever was — certainly not seventeenth-century England whose bitter problems in politics and society demanded close study and terse, pointed discussion.

The popularity in the early seventeenth century of this perversion of the closed couplet and of the romances that flowed through it is easily explained: escape. An age whose practical concerns required such intense and continuous force of mind, an age that made so strong a commitment to public issues, an age, finally, whose vital tone is best suggested by its coming to choose the closed couplet as the major agency for its poetic expression naturally would take respite in the dreamy, fanciful irrelevancies of romance, in the vacations from public discussion and public duty that *Cupid and Psyche*, *The Man in the Moon*, and *Pharonnida* provided. The popularity of the romance couplet in the early nineteenth century is also easily explained. This form allowed Hunt and Moore and Keats to make the strongest possible rejection of the eighteenth-century closed-couplet sensibility, to articulate a polar opposition to the closed couplet and its implications. The romance couplet, by its very nature, rejects the common sense, that is, the dependence on widely shared experience, widely discussed opinion, and widely communicable understanding, which radiates from the poetry of Dryden and Pope.

2. Early Closed-Couplet Achievements

The closed couplet was being widely employed and significantly refined during the first wave of enjambed-couplet romances, furnishing a powerful poetic force to which, as we have suggested, they were merely the

---

[4] Ibid., II, 121.

reaction. Two of these employments, moreover, the Jonsonian couplet and the satiric couplet, resulted in some poetry of the highest quality.

Each of them can be accounted for in general by reference to another Latin influence working in combination with that derived from the elegiac distich. The second influence one can perceive in Jonson's couplet verse is that of Horace, precisely, the Horatian *Sermones* and *Epistulae*, and that of the classical *sermo* or conversational style in general.[5] The second influence on the satiric couplet is that of Latin satire, chiefly as practiced by Juvenal and Persius.[6] Juvenal's and Persius's satiric poems, like the *Sermones* and *Epistulae* of Horace, were, of course, in classical hexameters, blank verses which had no regular multiline units and thus a great tolerance of enjambment, so that both Jonson and the satirists derived from this poetry the sanction for more flowing measures than the elegiac distich indicated. But the Horatian style was a style of talk, sensible and quiet, easy without being careless, terse without being crabbed; whereas the satiric style, especially that of Juvenal, was exalted, oratorical, impulsively flowing from one great blast into the next. The couplet style of Jonson, then, represents a compromise between the neat couplet promptings of the elegiac distich, especially as practiced by Martial, and the Horatian conversational style; that of the satirists, a compromise between the epigrammatic promptings of Martial and the noble satiric fury of Juvenal — and, of course, the crabbed satiric spleen of Persius.

These compromises cannot be very well pinpointed, however, at least not in metrical analysis. The Latin hexameter hardly ever influenced the English heroic line in a demonstrable one-for-one fashion except as it played its part in the elegiac distich. The purely hexameter Latin poetry had no proper metrical correspondent in English poetry, despite tremendous efforts of Elizabethan metrists. We can merely suggest, then, that the Horatian poems prompted such a conversational loosening of the closed-couplet style as we find it in Jonson and that the grander, more egocentric poems of Persius and Juvenal prompted such interruptions and overflowings of it as we find, say, in the satires of John Marston.[7]

---

[5] This influence on Jonson's style has recently been described by Wesley Trimpi, *Ben Jonson's Poems* (Stanford, 1962).

[6] Morse Allen, *The Satire of John Marston* (Columbus, 1920); and John Peter, *Complaint and Satire in Early English Literature* (Oxford, 1956), esp. pp. 116–22.

[7] We can refine a little upon this description of the influence on the satirists of Juvenal and of Persius: from Juvenal they would chiefly have drawn the sanction for long periods and a swelling overflow of the metrical definitions; from Persius, the sanction for brief, witty, and obscure interpolations — as a comparison of the first satire of each of these Latin poets with that of the other will show.

Let us, then, consider directly each of the two English styles.

The satiric style came to hand the earlier of the two, its most brilliant productions, the youthful satires of Hall, Marston, and Donne, having been composed, indeed, before 1600.

We may begin our study of it by considering Marston's adaptation of this one distich epigram of Martial:

> *Carmina Paulus emit, recitat sua carmina Paulus.*
> *nam quod emas possis iure vocare tuum.*

One notes that Martial has made significant use of the normal distich pauses, fitting Paulus's two-part action of purchase and recitation in the caesurally defined two parts of his hexameter and the rationale for this action in his pentameter. One notes, secondly, the *"Carmina Paulus"* repetition in the hexameter, a repetition that gains emphasis from its placing and that gives emphasis to the identity between the songs Paulus buys and those he claims, and the '*emit–emas*' repetition by which Martial underscores the relevance of the pentameter's general statement to the particular situation enunciated in the hexameter.

Marston expanded on this little piece of wit in the second of his *Certain Satires* as follows:

> Who would once dreame that that same Elegie,
> That faire fram'd peece of sweetest Poesie,
> Which *Muto* put betwixt his Mistris paps,
> (When he (quick-witted) call'd her *Cruell chaps*,
> And told her, there she might his dolors read   45
> Which she, oh she, upon his hart had spread)
> Was penn'd by *Roscio* the Tragedian.
> Yet *Muto*, like a good *Vulcanian*,
> An honest Cuckold, calls the bastard sonne,
> And brags of that which others for him done.   50
> *Satyre thou lyest, for that same Elegie*
> *Is* Mutos *owne, his owne deere Poesie*:
> Why tis his owne, and deare, for he did pay
> Ten crownes for it, as I heard *Roscius* say.

This passage runs to three supracouplet sentences, the first and longest ending at the end of a first line, rather than with a couplet. On the other hand, it is riddled with metrically fragmentary interjections, "quick-witted," "oh she," "like a good Vulcanian," by which the poet stuffs his utterance with incidental bits of wit, learning, and special emphasis. Marston thus weakens the couplet pattern both within and without, making his meaning inaccessible except to the *aficionados* in satire, like himself, and thus obviously narrowing his implied audience to this indefatigably witty few. We understand, as part of the product of our reading, that only those who catch the scorn in "quick-witted," the witty allusiveness in "Vulcanian," the 'deere–deare' word play, and who can follow the long, imprecisely defined flow of the attack in general are welcome to the pleasures of this satire. The introduction of "Roscius the Tragedian," by which Marston seems to be indicating a specific person, and his use of words like "paps" and "bastard" similarly confine his audience; only the young blades, who know or know how to feign knowing who this Roscius is and who take the public use of such shocking terms in stride, can be imagined to be this speaker's satiric correspondents.

The close of this passage, which suggests that the speaker frequents the spots where poets meet and gossip, clinches the impression of the speaker as a member of a clique of wits — especially since it introduces a doubt: one wonders, although Marston may not have meant him to, how good the word of Roscius is. That is to say, one senses an in joke, a jibe that depends on specific knowledge about Roscius which the speaker does not divulge. The reader finishes the passage, then, not knowing whether two attacks have been made, one on Muto and one on Roscius, or only one. If there are two, we cannot know for sure what either attack amounts to, but we do know that the *cognoscenti* know. Marston's most reliable achievement in such poetry as this, then, is the creation of cliquishness, of that exclusive clubbiness of the young intellectuals. To manage it, of course, he has sacrificed major elements of poetic art, its meters and its meanings.

Donne did much better than Marston as a satirist, but in much the same way. To demonstrate this, let us consider a rather long passage from the opening of his "Satire II":

Sir; though (I thanke God for it) I do hate
Perfectly all this towne, yet there's one state
In all ill things so excellently best,
That hate, toward them, breeds pitty towards the rest.
Though Poëtry indeed be such a sinne   5
As I thinke that brings dearths, and Spaniards in,
Though like the Pestilence and old fashion'd love,
Ridlingly it catch men; and doth remove
Never, till it be sterv'd out; yet their state
Is poore, disarm'd, like Papists, not worth hate.   10

One, (like a wretch, which at Barre judg'd as dead,
Yet prompts him which stands next, and cannot reade,
And saves his life) gives ideot actors meanes
(Starving himselfe) to live by his labor'd sceanes;
As in some Organ, Puppits dance above   15
And bellows pant below, which them do move.
One would move Love by rithmes; but witchcrafts charms
Bring not now their old feares, nor their old harmes:
Rammes, and slings now are seely battery,
Pistolets are the best Artillerie.   20
And they who write to Lords, rewards to get,
Are they not like singers at doores for meat?
And they who write, because all write, have still
That excuse for writing, and for writing ill;
But hee is worst, who (beggarly) doth chaw   25
Others wits fruits, and in his ravenous maw
Rankly digested, doth those things out-spue,
As his owne things; and they are his owne, 'tis true,
For if one eate my meate, though it be knowne
The meate was mine, th' excrement is his owne: 30
But these do mee no harme, nor they which use
To out-doe Dildoes, and out-usure Jewes;
To out-drinke the sea, to out-sweare the Letanie;
Who with sinnes all kindes as familiar bee
As confessors; and for whose sinfull sake,   35
Schoolemen new tenements in hell must make:
Whose strange sinnes, Canonists could hardly tell
In which Commandements large receit they dwell.
But these punish themselves; the insolence
Of Coscus onely breeds my just offence,   40
Whom time (which rots all, and makes botches poxe,
And plodding on, must make a calfe an oxe)
Hath made a Lawyer, which was (alas) of late
But a scarce Poët; jollier of this state,
Then are new benefic'd ministers, he throwes   45
Like nets, or lime-twigs, wheresoever he goes,
His title of Barrister, on every wench,
And wooes in language of the Pleas, and Bench.

We find here the same stringing of epigrams which characterizes Mar-
ston's satire and which, indeed, Morse Allen describes as typical of Ren-

aissance satiric practice: [8] epigrams, for instance, on dramatic poets (ll. 11–16), amorous poets (ll. 17–20), courtly poets (ll. 21–22), and thievish poets (ll. 25–30). We find also the same tremendously extended thrust of thought. The hierarchy of ills that the speaker commends to us in the first four lines of this passage it takes him over forty lines to resolve; we must maintain our attention through a great catalogue of minor poetic vices which, the speaker finally admits, "do mee no harme" (l. 31) and then through a sketchy extension of this catalogue (ll. 31–39) before we reach the poet, Coscus, whom he hates so much that he only pities all these others. On the other hand, this passage is riddled with witty, learned, and exclamatory expletives, again like that from Marston: "I thanke God for it," "like Papists," "beggarly," "'tis true," and "alas," for instance.

These practices, the demanding thrust of the thought and incidental interpolations of wit and learning, naturally define an audience rather similar to that which we discovered for Marston's satires. Donne's wit is, actually, much wider ranging, much more pointed in its articulation, in short, much more demanding than Marston's. One must have immediate access to the laws governing benefit of clergy, to the mysteries of courtly love, and to the ritual of confession; he must recognize the fashionable prejudices against Spaniards, Papists, and Schoolmen; he must be able to cope with military, musical, religious, legal, and digestive figures of speech and to unravel puns like "Pistolets" — all this if he would include himself in this speaker's audience. He must, furthermore, have the brass to absorb such harsh, smart terms as "Papists," "excrement," "Dildoes," and "poxe" without suffering the shock that would, among other things, cause him to lose touch with Donne's complex of satiric meanings. As we read the poem, we infer the addressees, the correspondents, who can cope with such problems successfully, and thus imagine an extremely narrow audience — a few of the wittiest and most elegantly cynical young fellows at the Inns of Court, to be particular. [9] Donne thus suggests the audience to his satiric talk, although it is much the same as Marston's audience, much more densely and precisely.

Donne is also much more persistently aware of this audience. Notice, for instance, his immediate insistence on an addressee in the "Sir" with which his poem opens. More important, Donne's English always smacks

---

[8] Allen, p. 84.

[9] George Hemphill, "Dryden's Heroic Line," *PMLA*, LXXII (1957), 878, suggests that Donne's satiric style projects the impression "of a man speaking in a small group of old and intimate friends."

of talk — even if it is the snappy talk bandied between unbearably clever young dandies. Marston suspended his utterance over numbers of couplets, thus giving it the unmistakable flavor of oratory — an oratorical flavor that ill suits the indications of close confidence with a narrow group of understanders suggested by other aspects of his style. Donne, on the other hand, although he sometimes suspends his main point, as in our passage, communicates every step of the way: every one of the six subordinate epigrams which precede the turn to Coscus, for example, makes telling sense — at least for those who understand benefit of clergy, who hold a prejudice against Spaniards, and can sift the wit in "Pistolets."

In working out these elements in the movement of his satiric discourse, Donne made a far greater use and a far more illuminating use of the couplet's definitive and emphatic qualities than Marson did. He used couplets and sets of couplets to define separate epigrams (ll. 11–16, 17–20, 21–23), a practice which naturally helped him indicate their parallel relationship to one another and, thus, their unity as a single catalogue of the secondary poetic offenses. He also used couplets to define separate figures of speech (ll. 15–16, 19–20), and he defined rhetorical antitheses both with single lines (l. 15) and with single couplets (ll. 19–20) — although commonly in a syntactically slanted and metrically crabbed manner. However, Donne has used the couplet only incidentally. He often enjambs first lines (ll. 1, 5, 13, 15, etc.) and, quite often, couplet stops (ll. 2, 8, 26, 34); he often concludes major segments of thought at mid-lines (ll. 2, 8, 9, 17, 28); and, finally, there are the metrically fragmentary interpolations — solicitous, witty, exclamatory — which pervade and obstruct the metrical flow (ll. 1, 8, 10, 25, 28, 43). Marston seldom ended anything in as little as a couplet; but Donne composed in segments shorter than, equal to, or longer than the couplet as his satiric perceptions prompted him. The expressive result of this is, of course, to suggest his responsiveness to the facts of his experience and to the flow of his wit. Marston seems to be a man who is driven by an unquenchable annoyance, one whose reference to his satiric targets is imprecise because it is secondary. But Donne's satiric utterance is always referential, always relevant.

Donne seems arrogant, not because he is too selfishly devoted to his own satiric perceptions to concern himself with an audience, but because he is too willing to confine his full satiric impact to an audience which extensively shares his feelings and knowledge along with his intellectual penetration and range, with an audience, that is to say, which excludes us. He will not take the trouble to simplify his satiric address, to line up the elements of his discourse in unmistakably lucid order, to emphasize and define their connections so that society in general can absorb his complaints — any more than he would cut out his witty, but generally incomprehensible, interpolations. Donne will not deign to be smoothly correct, that is to say, he will not deign to be widely courteous, in enunciating his satire. The difference between Donne and Pope, between whom an affinity has been widely recognized,[10] is chiefly this of their relative degrees of metrical correctness and social courtesy.

To discuss the similarities and the differences between these two great satirists, let us consider Pope's redaction of lines 5–10 from Donne's "Satire II," which we have just quoted above:

> I grant that Poetry's a crying sin;
> It brought (no doubt) th' *Excise* and *Army* in:
> Catch'd like the plague, or love, the Lord knows how,
> But that the cure is starving, all allow.
> Yet like the Papists is the Poets state,
> Poor and disarm'd, and hardly worth your hate.

We have in this passage, which strictly observes the proprieties of closed-couplet composition, at least as strong a conversational address as we found in the freer utterance of Donne. Its strong conversational flavor combined with the correctness, the grace, and the lucidity of its movement, however, implies a much broader audience than that implicitly created by Donne's satiric practice, an audience to whose ranks all ladies and gentlemen of good sense, good education, and good breeding belong. We might notice particularly Pope's handling of Donne's anti-Catholic appeal. Donne's interpolation of two words, three syllables, "like Papists," Pope has expanded to a couplet. With this expansion Pope, first of all, makes the figurative relationship of poets and papists luminously clear — articulating it with the combined emphases of meter, of caesurally defined balance, and of alliteration: thus does metrical correctness become social courtesy. This expansion allows Pope, secondly, to suggest a modification of the prejudice, a polite limitation of its scope and expression, so that no lady or gentleman of even the most delicate religious sensibilities need be offended by it. Pope's social courtesy or, to put it another way, his ambition for broad social attention has caused

---

[10] Ian Jack, "Pope and 'the Weighty Bullion of Dr. Donne's Satires,'" *PMLA*, LXVI (1951), 1009–22; and F. R. Leavis, *Revaluation* (London, 1949), esp. p. 33.

him in this case to dilute Donne's satiric formulation. But in his own work the Augustan poet would achieve addresses in which he could combine a perfect politeness with a perfect assertion of his satiric perceptions.

English closed-couplet satire did not, however, develop in a continuous line from Donne to Pope. Indeed, Renaissance satiric practice was essentially cut off before 1600. The general example of Donne, his witty style as it infuses all his works, persisted as an influence in English poetry at least through the Augustan age. But there are only isolated outcroppings — in Wither's tedious *Abuses Stript and Whipt* of 1613, for example, and in Cleveland's politically turned satires of the 1640's — of the satiric couplet as Donne and Marston had practiced it.

The Jonsonian couplet appeared a few years later in English literature than the satiric couplet, but, partly because of Jonson's long poetic labors and the profound consistency of his ideals, it lasted somewhat longer — right up to the Civil War in fact. This style was also practiced by many of the sons of Ben, most successfully by Thomas Carew; and we may possibly detect its influence in the stricter, narrower couplet practice of the Falkland circle, especially in Lord Falkland's own thoughtful and carefully argued poems. Jonson's tremendous personal prestige and his strong preference for the couplet may have been chiefly responsible, indeed, for establishing it as the staple measure of English nondramatic poetry even though his own style of couplet production finally lost out.

We can approach this style by comparing with it a poem by Jonson which, while sharing many of its qualities, is stanzaic. The first stanza of this poem, entitled simply "An Ode," runs:

> High-spirited friend,
> I send nor Balmes, nor Cor'sives to your wound,
> Your fate hath found
> A gentler, and more agile hand, to tend
> The Cure of that, which is but corporall,   5
> And doubtfull Dayes (which were nam'd *Criticall,*)
> Have made their fairest flight,
> And now are out of sight.
> Yet doth some wholsome Physick for the mind,
> Wrapt in this paper lie,   10
> Which in the taking if you mis-apply,
> You are unkind.

The progress of the thought in this stanza rather closely follows the lines and the rhyme-indicated systems of lines: for instance, its first short line defines the addressee, its last short line, a complete statement of conclusion; rhyming lines 7 and 8, again, both three feet long, define the two parallel elements of the predicate whose subject (with its modification) fills line 6. Thought and meter then rather extensively cohere in this stanza, but they do so because in this case, as it seems, Jonson has found a kind of metrical glove for his thoughts, a system whose unique variety of lines and rhymes closely fits the flow of his argument.

Even here, however, the thought actually dominates the metrical form and overrides it when it must do so to maintain its shape. The first four lines of the stanza, for instance, which make a system of interlocking rhymes, suffer a relatively strong enjambment, and the next two, which form a decasyllabic couplet, split apart, the first defining the object of the verb "tend" in the line above it and the second defining the nominative "Dayes" (with its modification) which governs the predicate that fills the two lines following it. The progress of Jonson's thought is so clear that he can articulate an apparent rhetorical parallel in these two lines — each one defining a substantive with a "which" clause of modification — without endangering it. The paralleling of these lines, reinforced, of course, with rhyme, actually ties together, then, not the two lines of the couplet, but the first five lines of the stanza, which are concluded by the couplet's first line, and the next three lines of the stanza, which open with the couplet's second line. With this practice Jonson has heightened the chronological and causal connection between the material defined in his first five lines and that closed off in the next three.

If we turn from this stanza to an example of Jonson's couplet writing, the last six lines of "To Heaven," a passage which asserts a similar system of antitheses and distinctions, we will see a remarkable stylistic similarity:

> I feele my griefes too, and there scarce is ground,
>   Upon my flesh t' inflict another wound.
> Yet dare I not complaine, or wish for death
>   With holy PAUL, lest it be thought the breath
> Of discontent; or that these prayers bee
>   For wearinesse of life, not love of thee.

In both the stanzaic and the couplet passages, the voice of sense and reason is directed toward the correspondent who can most properly consider its argument. In both cases the shape of the argument has required a significant divergence from the shape of the metrical form, a divergence we can understand as emphasizing the absolute reasonableness of the utterance. In both cases, on the other hand, details of the argument have been defined and related together by a selective use of the available formal definitions and interrelations. The difference between the two passages is one of degree: there is a somewhat greater congruence between meter and argument in "An Ode." This poem is slightly less dynamic, slightly closer to the early English plain style of stiffly uttered wisdom, than the other — quite properly, of course.[11] But in both passages a reasonable man addresses himself to correspondents for whom his reasons and his reasons alone, as it were, must be enough.

When Jonson lapsed from this kind of poetic practice in his couplet writing, when he lapsed, that is, from this metrical asymmetry, by which he normally asserted his subordination of all other considerations to those of sense and reason, he lost his force. In this epigram "To King James," for instance, Jonson briefly forecasts the supine courtliness of Edmund Waller:

How, best of Kings, do'st thou a scepter beare!
  How, best of *Poets*, do'st thou laurell weare!
But two things, rare, the FATES had in their store,
  And gave thee both, to shew they could no more.
For such a *Poet*, while thy dayes were greene,   5
  Thou wert, as chiefe of them are said t'have beene.
And such a Prince thou art, wee daily see,
  As chiefe of those still promise they will bee.
Whom should my *Muse* then flie to, but the best
  Of Kings for grace; of *Poets* for my Test?   10

The metrical equation drawn in the first couplet between James as a king and James as a poet is too strict, too perfect to represent any such equivalency one might find in life. Jonson, we see, has suspended his judgment, his awareness of the actual evidence and the true inferences; he has dwindled into an uncomfortable courtier. The meager variety in the third and fourth couplets, which carry on the equation between James as a poet and as a king, suggests an awkwardness in the attitude rather than a restraint of reason.

---

[11] On the early English plain style see J. V. Cunningham, "Lyric Style in the 1590's," in *The Problem of Style*, ed. J. V. Cunningham (New York, 1966), pp. 168–71; also Trimpi, pp. 115–19.

With this failure of his characteristic mode of utterance we may balance his beautiful poem on the death of his first son:

Farewell, thou child of my right hand, and joy;
    My sinne was too much hope of thee, lov'd boy,
Seven yeeres tho' wert lent to me, and I thee pay,
    Exacted by thy fate, on the just day.
O, could I loose all father, now. For why   5
    Will man lament the state he should envie?
To have so soone scap'd worlds, and fleshes rage,
    And, if no other miserie, yet age?
Rest in soft peace, and, ask'd, say here doth lye
    BEN. JONSON his best piece of *poetrie.*   10
For whose sake, hence-forth, all his vowes be such,
    As what he loves may never like too much.

The mechanical structure of the couplet, generally speaking, can suggest a formal, arbitrarily organized condition of life, or, rather, it can underscore the particular indications of such a condition as given in any particular poem. In the case of this poem, we may think of this mechanical system of meter as suggesting the ceremonies surrounding grief — the Roman ceremonies of parting in the *"ave atque vale"* echo in the first line and the Christian ceremonies in the reference to "My sinne" and in the idea of death as a debt we owe for the loan of life. If so, the thrust through the first line's normal caesural point, that made by the integrated expression, "thou child of my right hand," and the imbalance in the second couplet, whose thought pivots at the midpoint in its first line, may be thought to assert the poet's personal, unconforming grief — that dreadful individuality of emotion which the whole system of European ceremony is required to keep in public bounds.

The poem is, of course, not so simple as this. For example, the word "boy" is an ejaculation full of personal feeling, an ejaculation to which rhyme gives a powerful emphasis, while being, at the same time, the term with which the couplet, which I have suggested as a symbol for the mechanical ceremonies of mourning, is completed. Thus the stiffness of the first couplet — its heavy pauses after each of its lines and the heavy stroke on its rhyme — may be differently understood, that is, as an underscoring for the stiffness, the recalcitrance, of Jonson's grief. The total expressive force of this couplet is clear, however, although its elements seem too complex, too tightly composed, to be resolved; it throbs with the stress between Jonson's grief and his effort to enunciate some grounds for composure and resignation.

The working of the third couplet may be easier to explain. Here Jonson's reasonings clearly bend the mechanical form of his measure, the heavy pause which marks the shift from an assertion to its explanation coming after the eighth syllable of the first line. The fourth couplet, too, with its three parallel objects and its one major modification, seems to have been bent to endure the shape of Jonson's thoughts. We may thus be inclined to see in the flexible projection of these couplets the suggestion that Jonson's understanding is bringing his grief under control. But since the last couplet of the poem draws a lesson on the excess of grief and love which clearly depends on all the earlier couplets, their metrical imbalance seems hardly reducible to any expressive equation. The overflowing question in lines 5 and 6, for instance, has surely a strong tinge of intellectual desperation; the attitude it suggests as the only sensible one seems hardly to have been achieved.

Only in the last line of the poem, in which meter and meaning concur to make a clearly didactic point, can we confidently describe the precise sentiment of the speaker, the precise expressive value of the poet's metrical practice. But the persistent impression of a complex and powerful struggle between Jonson's mind and heart has, nevertheless, clearly depended on his flexible, unbalanced handling of his couplets: technically speaking, on such things as his common use of a misplaced or equivocal caesura (ll. 1, 2, 5, 8) and, on the other hand, his common dependence on a heavy caesural pause, rather than a first-line pause, to serve as the major pivot of his couplets (ll. 3, 5, 9). Jonson's addressing himself to his son augments the impression of this struggle, of course, since we may think of the son's presence either under the aspect of his Christian immortality or as a sign of the poet's merely personal refusal to accept the son's mortal withdrawal.

Jonson, as these examples may suggest, did not feel bound to achieve a persistent closed-couplet utterance, although he made extensive incidental uses of the couplet's definitive and emphatic qualities. The poem on his first son is an excellent example of his practice of "caesural variation," which Professor Trimpi pointed out, and also of his use of the strong caesura by which one often finds, to use Professor Trimpi's words again, "the caesural unit's cutting across the rhythmical unit." [12] In Jonson's longer poems one often finds enjambed couplets — couplets that flow together in what J. V. Cunningham has described as a noticeably unnoticeable way.[13] Since the persistent cause of these fundamental modifications in couplet flow is the shape and flow of reasonable

---

[12] Trimpi, pp. 124–26 and 131–32.
[13] Cunningham, pp. 169–71.

argument — of antitheses, equations, distinctions, evidence, inferences — Jonson's couplet poetry emanates as a discourse of reason. The shape of reason, Jonson's couplet practice persistently implies, is more important than the shape of the couplet. And since the shape of the couplet is quite forceful in his practice, although only incidentally forceful, the force of reason comes out very strongly indeed.

Because Jonson achieved a persistent conversational, discursive tone in his couplets, they seem to suggest not the disembodied voice of reason, but a reasonable talker. And since Jonson commonly focussed his couplet poems at a person or an audience capable of judging their arguments, they create, further, the illusion of a company of reasonable people, a speaker and various correspondents who embrace reason and good sense as the compelling grounds of their society and of their vital choices.

Carew, Herrick, and other members of the tribe of Ben maintained this style of couplet he had inaugurated, subordinating the mechanics of the form to the flow of sense and argument, and infusing that flow with the accents of public conversation. Contemporaries of Jonson too achieved poems in this style; there are, for example, the elegies with which Drayton addressed friends toward the end of his life and the verse epistles of Donne. We might mention in particular, however, Carew's fine poem to Jonson, in which the younger man commends to father Ben himself a draught of his own potation, imploring him to practice the same reasonable judgment, the same good sense, in regard to his plays that he had himself commended to so many others. But there is no continuance in the use of the couplet to create a climate of unhampered conversational reasoning after the disappearance of the tribe of Ben. When this subordination of mechanical form to the flow of mind that Jonson had achieved escaped the scrutiny of public conversation — that is, when the poet came to settle for a fit audience though few — and when it also escaped the definitions of rhyme, it became, as Professor Trimpi has suggested, the metrical manner of *Paradise Lost*;[14] in the process, of course, it also escaped the bounds of our history.

Most of the age following Jonson, however, agreed with him that couplets were the bravest sort of verses, but its poets were unable to emulate him in his flexible and reasonable handling of them. Englishmen after 1640 required a greater fixity, a stricter adherence to unquestioned principles than Jonson's reasonable utterance could project. They practiced

---

[14] Trimpi, pp. 129–31.

a more strictly closed form of couplet, projected more stiffly held opinions — opinions rather than reasons — and addressed a narrower society than the company of reasonable men one joins in the tribe of Ben. Something of Jonson's reasonableness and something of his feeling for spoken English persist in the form — most apparent in the poems of Dryden. A connection between Jonson's and Dryden's couplet prologues, for instance, has been explicitly noticed.[15] But Dryden wrote his prologues in the closed couplets he had learned to write from other poets than Jonson.

3. THE CLOSED-COUPLET DESCENT

We must now consider the work of these other poets from whom Dryden would learn to write closed couplets and to whose work he and Pope would refer for a continuous poetic tradition. Waller and Denham are, of course, the most famous of them. But there are other poets too who helped establish the tradition of the strictly closed couplet, poets, indeed, from whom Waller and Denham learned. The most important of these are George Sandys, Sir John Beaumont, and Lucius Cary, Lord Falkland.

One is tempted to describe these closed-couplet pioneers as a poetic circle.[16] Certainly Sandys and Waller were friends of Falkland, and both belonged to the informal society of wits and scholars that collected at Falkland's home, Great Tew, during the 1630's; the younger Denham also had connections there. Sir John Beaumont has no possible connection with this society, since he died in 1627, but he and its oldest member, Sandys, were both friends of Michael Drayton, and he shared with virtually all of them an acquaintance with Ben Jonson. Lord Falkland, who was the center of this society, no doubt learned much about couplet writing from Sandys, whose complete *Metamorphosis* appeared when Falkland was barely sixteen — several years, of course, before the gathering of the Great Tew society. On the other hand, Sandys's turning from Ovid to religious models during the 1630's, a change the serious-minded Falkland praised in his commendatory poems to Sandys's sacred works, indicates a counterinfluence too. Waller, who wrote a closed-couplet poem,"On the Danger his Majesty Escaped at St. Andrews," to commemorate an event of 1623 and who was still turning them out in the 1680's, no doubt influenced and was influenced by both Sandys and

---

[15] Reuben Brower, *Alexander Pope* (Oxford, 1959), p. 4.
[16] This paragraph is chiefly based on Kurt Weber, *Lucius Cary, Second Viscount Falkland* (New York, 1940), esp. pp. 82–130.

Falkland. Denham, the youngest of these poets, had a rather slight connection with the Great Tew society, it seems, but he did know Waller's poetry before it was published, and he has lavishly praised Waller in his own poem, *Cooper's Hill*. From this passage and from several addresses and allusions passed back and forth among these poets, we can infer a rather lively conversation on the correctness and the uses of closed-couplet poetry amidst the comforts of Falkland's hospitality. It is, however, probably more important than these exchanges on the couplet — exchanges whose details we can never recapture — that all these poets were aristocrats or closely joined to the aristocracy, that all were men of means and leisure, more or less, that all, including the fairly prolific Sandys, were what we might call literary amateurs. This fact does much to explain the particular type of concern they all felt toward the problems of poetry and toward their favorite poetic form.

The concern of these pioneers in closed-couplet composition was, generally speaking, abstract, that is, a concern with the form itself. Sandys, whose versification in his *Metamorphosis* we shall soon consider, was chiefly a translator. In this he was following poets like Marlowe, Thomas Heywood, Nicholas Grimald, and Sir John Harington, who had first imposed the practice of the Latin elegiac distich on the English couplet. Like them, his chief problem was the formal, abstract one of metrical transference — his substance having been fixed once he picked his Latin poem. This poem, Ovid's *Metamorphoses*, is in hexameters, not in distichs, but its many balanced and parallel lines and its tendency to line closure strongly recall Ovid's earlier work in the distich. Thus Sandys's task as a couplet writer was quite similar to Marlowe's and Grimald's and Heywood's — a task in formal adjustment. The best work of Beaumont and Falkland was abstract in a different way; Beaumont's poem "To his late Majesty, concerning the True Form of English Poetry" and Falkland's commendations to different ones of Sandys's religious translations all consider the nature, the dignity, and the use of the couplet poetry *in* couplet poetry, thus providing at one and the same time, abstract literary discussions and concrete literary examples. Denham, whose work we will also discuss in this chapter, was essentially a closed-couplet virtuoso, and Waller, with whom our next chapter will be concerned, seems to have been chiefly proud of his efforts to remedy the "want of smoothness" in English poetry.[17]

Let us begin with George Sandys, who was the oldest of these amateur poets. Here, for example, is an excerpt from Polyphemus's amorous ad-

---

[17] John Aubrey, *Brief Lives*, ed. Oliver Dick (London, 1950), p. 308.

dress to Galatea, first, as it appears in Book XIII of Ovid's *Metamorphoses* and, then, in Sandys's translation:

Candidior folio nivei Galatea ligustri,
floridior pratis, longa procerior alno, 790
splendidior vitro, tenero lascivior haedo,
levior adsiduo detritis aequore conchis,
solibus hibernis, aestiva gratior umbra,
nobilior pomis, platano conspectior alta,
lucidior glacie, matura dulcior uva, 795
mollior et cygni plumis et lacte coacto.

O *Galatea*, more then lilly-white,
More fresh then flowrie meads, then glasse more bright, 990
Higher then Alder trees, then kids more blithe,
Smoother then shels whereon the surges drive,
More wisht then winters Sun, or Summers aire,
More sweet then grapes, then apples farre more rare,
Clearer then Ice, more seemely then tall Planes 995
Softer then tender curds, or downe of Swans.

In all but one of these lines, after the first line of introduction, Sandys achieves almost perfect equivalencies of the line-defined Ovidian balances. In every case but one, two of Ovid's balanced substantives with their modifiers come over into similarly balanced patterns in Sandys's translation. His one failure is the "*adsiduo . . . aequore*" balance which Latin inflection allowed Ovid in line 792; Sandys had to give up this balance for a slanted pattern, his line 992. In the other six lines of this passage, however, Sandys has been able to duplicate Ovidian hexameter balances in his own balanced pentameters.

In translating two Ovidian lines a bit further on (ll. 1007–8), Sandys achieved a nicely patterned couplet, turning "*non tantum cervo claris latratibus acto, / verum etiam ventu volucrique fugacior aura*" into "More speedie then the hound-pursued Hind / Or Chaced clouds, or then the flying wind." Sandys, again, has lost an Ovidian balance, the "*cervo . . . acto*" balance of noun and agreeing adjective in the first line; but, by governing "Hind" in his first line and "clouds" in his second with the same phrase, "More speedie then," and by representing this phrase in the second line by the word "then" — by this timid use of zeugma — he has united three parallel nouns in a well-knit closed-couplet pattern, instead of the pattern of two isolated lines in parallel he inherited from Ovid. This is not a persistent or even a very common achievement in Sandys's translation, however. One finds another at lines 1039–40, where the two isolated lines of Ovid, "*Iam modo caeruleo nitidum caput exere ponto, / iam, Galatea, veni, nec munera despice nostra,*" whose separate but parallel commands are asserted by the repetition of "*iam,*" become in Sandys, "Come *Galatea,* from the surges rise, / Bright as the Morning; nor our gifts despise." Unfortunately, the Latinate placing of "Bright as the morning" and the inversion of the verbs in both lines make this a very stiff, unnatural English utterance. The truth is that Sandys seldom pairs off Ovid's lines into acceptable English couplets even at points of transition, where the couplet's capacity for comprehending more complex syntactic systems than individual lines and for defining major poetic closes would have been most serviceable.

To conclude our description of Sandys, consider the following example of his translation, which contains in fairly representative proportions his achievements in couplet composition and his failures — this another excerpt from Polyphemus's address to Galatea:

Sunt mihi, pars montis, vivo pendentia saxo   *810*
antra, quibus nec sol medio sentitur in aestu,
nec sentitur hiems; sunt poma gravantia ramos,
sunt auro similes longis in vitibus uvae
sunt et purpureae: tibi et has servamus et illas.
ipsa tuis manibus silvestri nata sub umbra   *815*
mollia fraga leges, ipsa autumnalia corna
prunaque non solum nigro liventia suco,
verum etiam generosa novasque imitantia ceras.

For I have caves within the living stone;
To Summers heat, and Winters cold unknowne;
Trees charg'd with apples; spreading vines that hold
A purple grape, and grapes resembling gold.
For thee I these preserve, affected Maid.   1015
Thou strawberries shalt gather in the shade,
Autumnal cornels, plummes with azure rind,
And wax-like yellow of a generous kind.

Ovid has draped his balance between summer and winter over his second and third lines above; Sandys, by the use of zeugma, has wedged it into his second line. Again, Ovid strung out three parallel "*sunt*" clauses, putting one each into the third, fourth, and fifth lines above; whereas Sandys has fit the three into a couplet (ll. 1013–14), achieving once again the incidental couplet unit we observed just above. The very next couplet to this, however, breaks down: its first line comes to a complete stop, in accordance with the prompting in Ovid (l. 814), and its second line contains the subject and verb that govern the whole next couplet.

The two lines of this fragmented couplet, like every single line in the passage, even including the first line of its one achieved couplet (l. 1013), have some integrity, and every line has some obvious metrical and rhetorical grace. Sandys has stiffened Ovid's moderately flexible hexameter movement, obviously at the prompting of his own rhymes, making, however, not so much a system of static, end-stopped couplets — as Marlowe did in translating Ovid's *Amores* — but a system of generally graceful, though largely static, end-stopped lines, a system that now and then follows the prompting of its rhymes strongly enough to form incidental couplets. Sandys's chief achievement, then, as this passage should suggest, is the formulation of individual decasyllabic lines — virtually all adaptations of Ovidian hexameter patterns — which are capable of playing graceful parts in true couplet composition, lines which are often strengthened by zeugma and inversion and which often give significant, even elegant, definition to rhetorical balances and parallels. If by "versifier" Dryden meant "maker of lines" — and he should have, of course — he was remarkably just when he praised Sandys as "the best versifier of the last age." [18]

It may illuminate Sandys's achievement and, on the other hand, the great work that was yet to be done to consider Polyphemus's self-description as it was conceived by Ovid, then as it was translated by Sandys, and, finally, by Dryden. Here is the Ovid:

> *Certe ego me novi liquidaeque in imagine vidi*　　　　　840
> *nuper aquae, placuitque mihi mea forma videnti.*
> *adspice, sim quantus: non est hoc corpore maior*
> *Iuppiter in caelo, nam vos narrare soletis*
> *nescio quem regnare Iovem; coma plurima torvos*
> *prominet in vultus, umerosque, et lucus, obumbrat;*　　　845
> *nec mea quod rigidis horrent densissima saetis*
> *corpora, turpe puta: turpis sine frondibus arbor,*
> *turpis equus, nisi colla iubae flaventia velent;*
> *pluma tegit volucres, ovibus sua lana decori est:*
> *barba viros hirtaeque decent in corpore saetae.*　　　　850

---

[18] *Essays of John Dryden*, ed. W. P. Ker (Oxford, 1900), II, 247.

unum est in media lumen mihi fronte, sed instar
ingentis clipei. quid? non haec omnia magnus
Sol videt e caelo? Soli tamen unicus orbis.

Here is the Sandys:

I knowe my selfe; my image in the brooke
I lately saw, and therein pleasure tooke.
Behold, how great! Not *Jupiter* above
(For much you talke I knowe not of what *Jove*)
Is larger siz'd: curles, on my browes displaid,   1045
Affright; and like a grove my shoulders shade.
Nor let it your esteeme of me impaire,
That all my bodie bristles with thick haire.
Trees without leaves, and horses without maines,
Are sights unseemely: grasse adornes the plaines,   1050
Wooll sheepe, and feathers fowle. A manly face
A beard becomes: the skin rough bristles grace.
Amid my fore-head shines one onely light;
Round, like a mighty shield, and cleere of sight.
The Sunne all objects sees beneath the skie: 1055
And yet behold, the Sunne hath but one eye.

Here is the Dryden:

Come, Galatea, come, and view my face;
I late beheld it in the wat'ry glass,
And found it lovelier than I fear'd it was.
Survey my tow'ring stature, and my size:
Not Jove, the Jove you dream that rules the skies,   150
Bears such a bulk, or is so largely spread.
My locks, the plenteous harvest of my head,
Hang o'er my manly face; and, dangling down,
As with a shady grove my shoulders crown.
Nor think, because my limbs and body bear   155
A thickset underwood of bristling hair,
My shape deform'd: what fouler sight can be
Than the bald branches of a leafless tree?
Foul is the steed, without a flowing mane;
And birds, without their feathers, and their train.   160
Wool decks the sheep; and man receives a grace
From bushy limbs, and from a bearded face.

My forehead with a single eye is fill'd,
Round as a ball, and ample as a shield.
The glorious lamp of heav'n, the radiant sun,   165
Is Nature's eye; and she's content with one.

Sandys, in trying to reflect the flexible hexameter movement of his model, has lost his own proper movement, has neglected the grotesque charm of his model, and has wandered once or twice into virtual nonsense. The absurd and yet touching hopefulness with which Polyphemus recommends his looks and the humor of the figures to which he must resort in order to achieve this recommendation Sandys has almost entirely lost. Dryden, on the other hand, has marvellously reproduced these Ovidian qualities right from the start: "I . . . found it [his face] lovelier than I fear'd it was." He has done so, moreover, while turning Ovid's flexible but lucid hexameter movement into a lucid and yet flexible couplet movement of his own, with oblique single couplets, yoked pairs of couplets, enjambed first and second lines — all kept within the bounds of good English and orderly meter. The couplet pause, for instance, which sets off the bitter truth, "My shape deform'd," from Polyphemus's hopeful effort to redeem the particular deformity of his bristling body, perfectly hits off the ambivalence of Ovid's conception. Dryden's addition of "bald," again, by which his Polyphemus attempts to humanize the tree and thus validate his use of it as a figure for himself, corresponds to and even enriches his model. The youthful Pope, who also translated this Ovidian passage, imposed upon it his more stringent measure, which is stricter in its implied scrutiny and narrower in its implied sympathy, squeezing out Polyphemus's monstrous charm and leaving only his monstrous absurdity. But then, the broad movement of Ovid's verse in this passage and its grotesque humor were better suited to Dryden's style, and Dryden made his translation, moreover, when he was at the height of his powers.

Dryden was able to advance on Sandys to the extent that this comparison suggests in part because of his greater poetic talent, of course, but also in part because of the refinements other poets had made in their common poetic medium. Among these poets were Sir John Beaumont and Lord Falkland, both of whom achieved something of the pervasive closed-couplet composition which Sandys did not. Falkland, as we have seen, composed in paragraphs of closed couplets. Beaumont published a couplet imitation of Ovid's *Metamorphoses* early in his life, *The Metamorphosis of Tobacco* (1602), which, at the very most, hints at the substantial Ovidian imitation later achieved by Sandys, but he wrote a number of poems toward the end of his life which reveal an advance toward the closed-couplet paragraph. To discover his achievement, which was both earlier and more modest than Falkland's, let us consider the style of his best and most famous poem, "Concerning the True Form of Poetry." First, this:

In ev'ry Language now in Europe spoke   35
By Nations which the Roman Empire broke,
The rellish of the Muse consists in rime,
One verse must meete another like a chime.
Our Saxon shortnesse hath peculiar grace
In choice of words, fit for the ending place,   40
Which leave impression in the mind as well
As closing sounds, of some delightfull bell:

The first couplet of this passage has too weak a close, despite the strong 'spoke–broke' rhyme, to declare a dominant pattern. The third line, to continue, is too strongly integrated by syntax and by the 'rellish–rime' alliteration to allow it to play a properly subordinate place in the second couplet: once again, then, no real couplet pattern. The lack of significant caesural definition further stiffens the individual lines of these two couplets, giving them the monolithic solidity one often finds in the lines of early English couplets, so that the passage seems at first to be a system of lines. But the next couplet, whose second line depends syntactically on its first, is sufficiently unified to suggest the longer, more complex measure as the primary shape of the utterance, especially since the first line, although it holds subject, verb, and object, is strongly enjambed. The trochaic inversion of the third foot in the second line suggests a caesura and thus gives the couplet a valuable cadence, a cadence that is reminiscent of the last half-line of the elegiac distich. The next couplet, which sets off an analogy, defining each half of it with a complete line, also declares the couplet to be this poem's primary unit of measure. However, the mid-line pause, that third in the hierarchy of formal closed-couplet pauses, is weak or, rather, unused in this couplet as it is, indeed, throughout the passage.

In the following quotation from the same poem, however, in which the poet prescribes some of the conditions of good verse, we find significant use of all the closed couplet's formal pauses:

Pure phrase, fit Epithets, a sober care
Of Metaphors, descriptions cleare, yet rare,

Similitudes contracted smooth and round,
Not vext by learning, but with Nature crown'd.
Strong figures drawne from deepe inventions springs,   55
Consisting lesse in words, and more in things:
A language not affecting ancient times,
Nor Latine shreds, by which the Pedant climes.

The first and third couplets open with an adjective-noun compound, the second and fourth with a noun alone: this may suggest a budding sensitivity to supracouplet composition. But, except for this, the passage falls into four sharply individuated units, four parallel assertions in the catalogue of Beaumont's prescription. Inside the separate couplets, however, there is quite a lot of business. There is, first, the dynamic enjambment of the first couplet's first line and its flexible treatment of its four rhetorically parallel elements. We might also notice the sharp antitheses defined in the second lines of the second and third couplets and the enforcement gained in both with the mid-line pause. Then the final couplet condenses the second of the parallel negatives with which it explains the right kind of poetic language — the two being set off from one another by the first-line pause — so that the poet can close his couplet on a refinement, "by which the Pedant climes," and give his poem an incidental satiric enrichment. This passage, then, although it is stiff overall, is a stiff passage of individually flexible couplets.

The immediately following eight lines, on which the poem concludes, show signs of still larger, more flexible, and more variously expressive systems of closed-couplet verse.

A noble subject which the mind may lift
To easie use of that peculiar gift,   60
Which Poets in their raptures hold most deare,
When actions by the lively sound appeare.
Give me such helpes, I never will despaire,
But that our heads which sucke the freezing aire,
As well as hotter braines, may verse adorne,   65
And be their wonder, as we were their scorne.

Here, briefly, we have two sets of two couplets each: the first of them suffers a decline, a trailing off in its syntax and its meaning; but the second, with its dynamic deployment of the 'freezing–hotter' antithesis, its suspension until the first and second lines of its *second* couplet of the two verbs governed by "heads," and the vividly balanced antithesis of its last line, brings the poem to a splendidly climactic conclusion. Beaumont is here on the edge of the dynamically articulated closed-couplet paragraph.

Falkland and Denham were the first poets, however, to compose consistently in closed-couplet paragraphs; they were the first, that is, to observe and yet refine the couplet stop so that their poems could enjoy both its lucid definitions and, at the same time, a persistently integrated reach of thought beyond its bounds. At his brief best the earlier of these, Falkland, produced the finest closed-couplet poetry before Dryden. We have already examined a few lines from his best poem, his "Commendation of Sandys's *Paraphrase upon the Psalms.*"[19] The combination of stability and flow, of definition and expansiveness, with which this poem considers the question of poetry's human value has more metrical range and reliability, more expressive density and force, than Denham's one significant poem, *Cooper's Hill.* But in this famous poem Denham also achieved coherent closed-couplet paragraphs and something of a complete poetic movement — if not a coherent poetic structure or meaning.

The first lines of this poem, whose importance in English literary history George Williamson has indicated,[20] show something of this larger achievement:

Sure there are Poets which did never dream
Upon *Parnassus*, nor did tast the stream
Of *Helicon*, we therefore may suppose
Those made not Poets, but the Poets those.
And as Courts make not Kings, but Kings the Court,   5
So where the Muses & their train resort,
Parnassus stands; if I can be to thee
A Poet, thou *Parnassus* art to me.
Nor wonder, if (advantag'd in my flight,
By taking wing from thy auspicious height)   10
Through untrac't ways, and aery paths I fly,
More boundless in my Fancy than my eie:
My eye, which swift as thought contracts the space
That lies between, and first salutes the place
Crown'd with that sacred pile, so vast, so high,   15
That whether 'tis a part of Earth, or sky,
Uncertain seems, and may be thought a proud
Aspiring mountain, or descending cloud,

---

[19] See pp. 279–81 of this book for a long quotation from this poem.
[20] "The Rhetorical Pattern of Neo-Classical Wit," *MP*, xxxiii (1935), 55–81.

Pauls, the late theme of such a Muse whose flight
Has bravely reach't and soar'd above thy height.   20

One notices in the first eight lines the metrically oblique deployment of parallels (ll. 1–3, 7–8), the first of which required an enjambed couplet, and, as a counter to this, the line-bound antitheses in lines 4 and 5, each of them strengthened by inversion. The rhetorical reflection of these two lines, the one of the other, may be seen to enforce the "And" which connects them and tie together the first four and the second four lines into an eight-line system. One notices, again, the argumentative texture of these lines — whose movement is indicated by such logical terms as "therefore," "as," and "so" — which will come often to accompany the organizing of closed couplets into larger systems. One may look back to Falkland or ahead to Dryden for other examples. The whole passage is variously unified, of course: the verb "wonder," which governs the passage from line 9 onwards, for instance, depends on lines 7 and 8 for its subject. More striking is the span of thought which leads from "my eie," whose repetition ties the four lines it closes to the eight lines it introduces, on to "the place," which is the object of the eye's action, and then down, through four lines modifying "the place," to its appositive, "*Pauls*." One notices throughout the passage, finally, parallels and balances, some of them line- and couplet-defined, some at dynamic variance with these metrical units.

One may complain that this great sweep of utterance encloses too little meaning, that the reasonings and modifications have too little representative force, that it is, in short, a virtuoso performance. One may complain, moreover, that the poet overreaches himself; that he has not perfectly defined his opening reasonings; again, that he has held off the revelation of "the place" for too long; and that the climactic force placed on this revelation is excessive. But as an example of the closed-couplet paragraph's capacity to define the stages of an extensive argument, this passage and, indeed, *Cooper's Hill* entire proved an extremely valuable and influential poem.

The most famous four lines of this poem were also of tremendous exemplary value, although in a rather different way. The second couplet of this address to the Thames,

> O could I flow like thee, and make thy stream
> My great example, as it is my theme!
> Though deep, yet clear, though gentle, yet not dull,
> Strong without rage, without ore-flowing full,

which has been extensively discussed and praised by Earl Wasserman,[21] is quite remarkable: being, on the one hand, worthless as literature and, on the other, invaluable as a literary discovery.[22] The figure it develops is easy and therefore vulgar; it is a cliché — in the same way that the expression "Danish assignment" as a description for the role of Hamlet is a cliché — whether it was often uttered before or not.[23] Half the terms used to develop this figure, moreover, "gentle," "dull," "strong," and "rage," are too vague, too abstract, to enrich or enliven it. The movement of the couplet, finally, is labored and flat, depending essentially on a seesaw between abstract adjectives and abstract oppositions to them.

But in this couplet Denham has demonstrated the tremendous discursive density and coherency of the closed couplet, its capacity to crystallize, to stabilize statements whose elements present an explosive diversity. He has found in the closed couplet a means for doubly, for quadruply, binding into one lucid and orderly system a remarkable wealth of life's and nature's variety and complexity. He has, in short, discovered the remarkable degree to which the closed couplet can endure and articulate for public understanding the vision of the world as a *concors discordia rerum*.[24] Denham knew this old figure, of course; he explicitly discussed a view in *Cooper's Hill* (ll. 197–228) as an example of it. But he had no poetic experience, no imaginative awareness of any important living or natural composition so explosively unified that its discussion required this powerful poetic engine, this wonderful medium for giving the most harmonious articulation to the most discordant conditions, which he had stumbled onto.

But Alexander Pope — for he is the chief beneficiary of this discovery, as Dryden is of Denham's advances in multicouplet structuring —

---

[21] *The Subtler Language* (Baltimore, 1959), pp. 82–85.

[22] It is interesting to compare these lines to those by William Cartwright, a son of Ben, which appeared in 1638 in a poem, "In Memory of the most worthy Benjamin Jonson":

> But thou still put'st true passions on; dost write
> With the same courage that tried captains fight;
> Giv'st the right blush and color unto things,
> Low without creeping, high without loss of wings;
> Smooth, yet not weak, and by thorough care,
> Big without swelling, without painting faire.

[23] I have drawn this description of cliché from W. K. Wimsatt, Jr., "Poetic Diction: Wordsworth and Coleridge," in *Literary Criticism*, co-author Cleanth Brooks (New York, 1957), pp. 354–60.

[24] See Wasserman, esp. pp. 53–72 and 81–85, on *concors discordia rerum* as it dwells in the couplet practice of Denham — and, incidentally, for much higher praise of Denham's poetic achievement than I have been willing to give.

would need it badly and use it to its limits. He would pack it with discordancies, for example, when he came to sum up the hideously ambivalent Sporus, who had "Beauty that shocks you, parts that none will trust, / Wit that can creep, and pride that licks the dust"; again, when he contemplated the ambitions and the destinies of coquettes — "A Fop their Passion, but their Prize a Sot; / Alive, ridiculous, and dead, forgot!"; and, most of all, when he confronted his own dreadful opposition to the society with which he was inescapably concerned and to which he inescapably belonged:

> Who starved a Sister, who forswore a Debt,
> I never named; the Town's enquiring yet.
> The pois'ning Dame — *Fr.* You mean — *P.* I don't *Fr.* You do!
> *P.* See now I keep the Secret, and not you!

In the conversational exchange between Pope and a friend that fills the third line of this passage, Pope has strained the harmonizing power of his couplet to the limit and, by this means, crystallized his and his friend's explosive discordancy. Once again, it was Denham who made the purely abstract discovery that put these remarkably elegant compositions of life's rudest and most unseemly contradictions within Pope's reach.

Denham's *Cooper's Hill*, then, like the best verse of Sandys, Beaumont, and Falkland, is essentially abstract: chiefly distinguished not as poetry but as a set of poetic examples.

A further sign and a further aspect of the abstract nature of all this poetry is furnished by its mode of address, by its feeling for its audience. Sandys addressed nobody or, equally good, everybody — in pursuance of his model, of course. Ovid's *Metamorphoses*, a much grander poem than his *Amores*, as its continuous flow of hexameter lines indicates, gives up the pointedness and pungency of address we noticed in his earlier, plainer work. Thus the translator could turn *Metamorphoses* into elegant and musical verses, ignoring the question of their conversational or oratorical bite. Beaumont made a quite perfunctory address to King James in his best and most ambitious poem, and Falkland, a similarly unpointed address of congratulation in the best of his. Denham, in our two quotations from *Cooper's Hill*, addresses, respectively, the hill and the River Thames.

This freedom from the pressure of particular or urgent material, in the first place, and from the pressure of a particular audience of interlocutors, in the second, allowed these poets to give their full attention to the refinement of the metrical instrument, to the achievement of such well-wrought couplets as Beaumont and Denham explicitly praise. The examples of Ben Jonson and John Donne in their asymmetrical couplet productions and of Ovid and Martial in their Latin distichs obviously prompted these poets to bring their poems within the range of the spoken language. But these essentially amateur poets freed themselves from the more pressing aspects of poetic composition and attended, rather, to what Beaumont called "The solid joining of the perfect frame, / So that no curious finger there can find / The former chinks, or nails that fastly bind." It is sufficient praise to say that each of them helped to make this "perfect frame" a reality.

V

THE HEROIC
COUPLET OF WALLER

Although Edmund Waller made a unique advance on the amateur poets, an advance we must soon discuss, he wrote several couplet poems of the same abstract, neatly polished kind. One example is "The Story of Phoebus and Daphne, Applied," versions of which, significantly, occur in both Latin and English. Here is the English version of this little exercise in comparative literature:

> *Thirsis* a youth of the inspired train,
> Faire *Sacharissa* lov'd, but lov'd in vain;
> Like *Phoebus* sung, the no less amorous boy;
> Like *Daphne*, she as lovely, and as coy;
> With numbers, he the flying Nymph pursues,   5
> With numbers, such as *Phoebus* selfe might use;
> Such is the chase, when Love and Fancy leads
> O're craggy mountains, and through flowry meads;
> Invok'd to testifie the lovers care,
> Or forme some image of his cruell Faire: 10
> Urg'd with his fury like a wounded Deer
> O're these hee fled, and now approching neer,
> Had reach'd the Nymph with his harmonious lay,
> Whom all his charmes would not incline to stay.
> Yet what hee sung in his immortall straine,   15
> Though unsuccesfull, was not sung in vaine,
> All but the Nymph that should redress his wrong,
> Attend his passion, and approve his song.
>   Like *Phoebus* thus acquiring unsought praise,
>   He catch'd at love, and fill'd his arme with bayes.   20

This poem strongly recalls *Metamorphoses* or, better, Sandys's translation of it — both in its mythical materials and in its abstractness of address. Waller, like Sandys, is here free to practice a rather more mellifluous and easy movement than in those poems in which he tried to cope with real feelings or, at least, to address particular people. "Craggy mountains," "inspired train," "amorous boy," and "cruell Faire" will be difficult to assimilate in poems on any immediately pressing subject; again, such expressions as "Like *Daphne,* she" or "*Phoebus* selfe" and such a line as "Faire *Sacharissa* lov'd, but lov'd in vain" will hardly work in poems of pointed, conversational address.

Waller's longer poem, *The Battle of the Summer Isles,* from Canto I of which the following lines are taken, furnishes another case of Waller's abstract closed-couplet practice.

Bermudas wall'd with rocks, who does not know,	5
That happy Island where huge Lemmons grow,	
And Orange trees, which golden fruit doe beare,	
Th' *Hesperian* garden boasts of none so faire.	
There shining Pearl, Corall, and many a pound	
On the rich shore of Amber-greece is found:	10
The lofty Cedar, which to heaven aspires,	
The Prince of trees, is fuell for their fires:	
The smoak by which their loaded spits doe turn,	
For incense might on sacred Altars burn;	
Their private roofs on odorous timber born,	15
Such as might Palaces for Kings adorn:	
The sweet palmetta's a new *Bacchus* yield	
With leaves as ample as the broadest shield;	
Under the shadow of whose friendly boughs	
They sit carousing where their liquor grows:	20
Figs there unplanted through the fields doe grow,	
Such as fierce *Cato* did the Romans show,	
With the rare fruit inviting them to spoil	
Carthage, the Mistress of so rich a soil:	
The naked rocks are not unfruitfull there,	25
But at some constant seasons every yeare	
Their barren tops with luscious food abound,	
And with the eggs of various fowles are crown'd:	
Tobacco is the worst of things which they	
To English landlords as their tribute pay:	30
Such is the mould, that the blessed tenant feeds	
On pretious fruits, and payes his rent in weeds.	

We may notice here the same sort of catalogue of slightly fabulous pretties we studied in our quotation from Sandys. The difference, generally speaking, is that Waller defines his things not in smoothly composed lines, as Sandys did, but in smoothly composed couplets. There are, for example, whole couplets given over to Bermudian cedars (ll. 11–12), smoke (ll. 13–14), and roofs (ll. 15–16), and, not only this, but several two-couplet systems — one on figs (ll. 21–24), for instance, and one on tobacco (ll. 29–32). We might also notice the single dynamic couplet, one quite reminiscent of Sandys, into which Waller has fit three pretty things, pearl, coral, and ambergris (ll. 9–10). Then there are the fairly common balances (ll. 12, 25, 27, 32) and the profusion of inversions (ll. 5, 7, 10, 11, 13, 14, 15, 16, etc.), both of which strengthen and illuminate the separate metrical units in which they occur. All in all, the passage clicks along in neatly composed and neatly defined couplets, occasionally pausing heavily at a first line and occasionally extending on to a double couplet. This expansion of Sandys's effects to the bounds of the couplet as his general practice is Waller's contribution to the development of our form as a purely metrical device: this is Waller's famous "sweetness," as Denham's rhetorical dynamics is his famous "strength."

Waller's fame and his importance depend, actually, on a rather different accomplishment, on one, however, to which this "sweetness" is highly relevant. Waller was the first poet to find a specific and a broadly interesting application for the closed couplet's poetic elements — that is, for its hierarchy of pauses, its characteristic rhetoric, and its typical mode of pointed, conversational address — which his predecessors and his friends had been establishing. Waller, of course, applied the closed couplet to a concern which has been characterized as "purely polite," that is, to the presentation of elegant social flattery.[1] This employment of the form, an employment to which Waller found he could turn all its qualities, although ignoble in itself, had tremendously important consequences for the Augustan poets, especially for Alexander Pope.

In order to consider this application of the closed couplet, consider the two poems below. This one, "On the Misreport of her being Painted," comes early in Waller's career:

As when a sort of Wolves infest the night
With their wilde howlings at fair *Cynthia*'s light;
The noise may chase sweet slumber from our eyes,

---

[1] Alexander Allison, *Toward an Augustan Poetic* (Lexington, Ky., 1962), p. 26.

But never reach the Mistress of the skyes:
So with the news of *Sacharissa*'s wrongs,   5
Her vexed servants blame those envious tongues;
Call love to witness that no painted fire
Can scorch men so, or kindle such desire;
While unconcerned she seems mov'd no more
With this new malice, then our loves before: 10
But from the height of her great minde looks down
On both our passions without smile or frown;
So little care of what is done below
Hath the bright Dame, whom heav'n affecteth so;
Paints her 'tis true, with the same hand which spreads   15
Like glorious colours through the flowry meads,
When lavish Nature with her best attire
Cloaths the gay Spring, the season of desire.
Paints her 'tis true, and does her cheek adorn
With the same art wherewith she paints the morn,   20
With the same art, wherewith she guildeth so
Those painted clouds which forme *Thaumantia*'s bow.

This one, "Of Tea, Commended by her Majesty," comes very late:

Venus her myrtle, *Phoebus* has his bays;
Tea both excels, which she vouchsafes to praise.
The best of Queens, and best of herbs, we owe
To that bold nation, which the way did show
To the fair region, where the sun does rise;   5
Whose rich productions we so justly prize.
The Muse's friend, Tea, does our fancy aid;
Repress those vapors which the head invade;
And keeps that palace of the soul serene,
Fit, on her birth-day, to salute the Queen.   10

Both of these poems are, obviously enough, exercises in flattery. The
early one praises an earthly goddess, first, for her composure in the face
of reports that she paints and, second, for her natural beauty; the late
one praises the queen as one of the two richest gifts — the other being
tea — which Portugal has made to English social life. In both situations,
then, Waller flatters the object of his attention by gracefully exalting her
in her social milieu — the milieu furnished by gossip in the early poem
and by royalty in the late one. The early poem, in which the poet strikes

a pose of romantic adoration, is no doubt a bit overblown. Waller failed, for one thing, to strengthen its lines and couplets with that texture of inversions which makes the late one so neat and spruce in its flattery — perhaps fearing that so artificial a device would compromise his sincerity. Despite this, these poems are remarkably similar in style, as they are in basic motivation. Dr. Johnson's remark that Waller did not advance as he grew older seems remarkably just.[2]

Both of these poems, first of all, make extensive use of the pauses and the rhetorical definition which are inherent to the closed couplet. Lines 8 and 19 of the early poem, for instance, define parallel elements, and a caesura separates the two elements in each case; the two lines of its second couplet, again, set off the two sides of an antithesis; and each of the two succeeding couplets, later on in this same poem (ll. 9–12), holds one side of an antithesis, an antithesis which is completely defined by the two of them together. Emphatic placing of the logical terms throughout this poem — note "As," "So," and "While" at the beginnings of lines 1, 5, and 9 — and its use of strong rhymes strengthen these metrically defined parallels and balances. Flattery must, of course, be luminously clear to be effective.

The late poem makes use of the same devices. We might notice, by the way, that it uses the expletive "do" three times to only once in the early poem, smoothness being as important to the elegant flatterer as clarity — and more important than terseness. We might also observe the neat balances in lines 1 and 3; the use of the first couplet's pauses to heighten the comparison between Venus and Phoebus, on the one hand, and tea, on the other; and the balance in the sixth line between the "rich productions" and the esteem in which they are held — a balance maintained, despite the slanted syntax, by caesural definition, by the alliterating "pr" sounds, and by the insistent "justly." We might also recognize the phony parallel between "bold nation" and "fair region" in lines 4 and 5, a mistake in phrasing and in metrical placing which neither the syntax nor the meaning — and not even the couplet break — can entirely correct.

Both poems vary and qualify their neatness with considerable intracouplet dynamics. Several couplets in the early poem (ll. 7–8, 9–10, 13–14) and in the late one (ll. 3–4, 7–8), for example, have relatively enjambed first lines. The fourth couplet of the early poem makes an especially nice use of such an enjambment: the thought thrusts quite

---

[2] "Edmund Waller," in *Lives of the Poets,* in *Works* (Troy, N. Y., 1903), VIII, 163–64.

strongly into the second line, since the first line gives us only the subject of a clause; but the second line, which gains emphasis from this thrust, absorbs it by defining a compound predicate whose elements perfectly fit the meter. We may complain that the other couplets in this poem which receive the emphasis of a first-line enjambment conclude lamely: both its fifth and sixth couplets, for instance, close with prepositional phrases and with phrases, moreover, that modify adverbs in their first lines. We will discuss this emphasis on modification later. For now, we can at least allow that these couplets are both neatly and flexibly composed, and that similar ones in the late poem, especially its fourth couplet, which benefits from the poet's use of inversions, are rung off quite smartly.

Waller does not achieve significant supracouplet patterns in either poem; or, more precisely, he confines himself in both to incidental quasi stanzas of double couplets. The fourth and eighth lines from the end of our early example, for instance, both begin, "Paints her, 'tis true," thus asserting two parallel systems of two couplets each as the climax of this poem. The opening twelve lines of the poem, moreover, although they are spanned by one complete sentence, fall into three strongly marked four-line units — an "As" element, a "So," and a "While." Between these three double-couplet systems and the last two comes a single couplet of transition — a bridge of sorts between Cynthia's composure in the face of the false charge against her and Waller's flattering assertion of the truth.

The "Tea" poem is more nicely drawn: it consists of an introductory couplet, which makes the connection between tea and the queen that occasions the flattery to follow; and two double-couplet systems of development, the first of which flatters the queen by telling where tea comes from and the second of which tells how tea helps one assume the attitude of flattery. The first couplet of the first of these is relatively enjambed, its second couplet, which modifies the empty term "way" (unfortunately not a rhyme word), being obviously necessary for us to understand the nature of that "way." The second system is also tied together, since each of its first three lines defines one part of the triply compounded predicate which is governed by "The Muse's friend, Tea" with which the system opens.

The most striking evidence of this stanzaic tendency in Waller's couplet composition is furnished by his most successful couplet poem, "A Panegyric to My Lord Protector." This poem has been composed and, indeed, spaced throughout in double-couplet systems of utterance. With only one exception, each of these forty-seven systems ends on a full stop, and, since most of them define a complete sentence, the first-couplet stop is reduced in importance — as in this case:

> Fame, swifter than your winged navy, flies
> Through every land that near the ocean lies,
> Sounding your name, and telling dreadful news
> To all that piracy and rapine use.

We have thus an arbitrary extension of the hierarchy of pauses; a new distinction between odd and even couplet stops for which the measure itself gives no sanction; a stiffening of the metrical texture, of the machinery of his verse, which Waller voluntarily assumed. We may suggest that this extra stiffness reinforces Waller's social attitude. For one thing, it expresses an intention to be unnaturally elegant, to be more graceful in the articulation of his flattering addresses than the unvarnished particulars of any situation should allow. For another, it assures an easy absorption, a communication in easy, rounded installments, of his flattery.

There is another factor in Waller's couplet production, besides this peculiar stanzaic tendency, which gives his couplets their special quality and, as it seems to me, especially befits them for their use as the purveyors of flattery: this is Waller's tendency to conclude the units of his couplet poetry — its couplets and double couplets — with matter of modification. We have noticed already that the fifth and sixth couplets of our early example give the emphasis of a first-line enjambment to their second lines and that those lines hold adverbial modification. The second line of the first couplet, similarly, defines two adverbial phrases. The first couplet of our late example, again, closes with an adjectival clause. This tendency to end on modification is more persistent still in Waller's double couplets, as that one we have quoted from "A Panegyric" may suggest. The first such system in our late poem, for instance, ends with a full couplet modifying the empty term "way" in its first couplet (ll. 3–6), and the second double couplet, which concludes the poem, has as its last line the adjective "Fit" and this adjective's modifiers. In the early poem, the third double-couplet system, which closes the opening sentence, ends with a full line of adverbial matter, and the last double couplet of the poem ends with a couplet composed of "With," "wherewith," and "which" elements hooked together in a descending scale of syntactic importance.

We may look on this persistent tendency of Waller to close the units of his thoughts with modification — and his tendency to the closed double couplet, as well — as evidence of his metrical short-windedness, agreeing with Ruth Wallerstein that he is stopped "by sheer pause for intellectual breath." [3] But we may also see in this practice a calculated — or possibly instinctive — desire to focus his metrical climaxes on qualities rather than substances, to place his emphases not on the realities of life, but on its ceremonial outside, on its show, and further, perhaps, courteously to avert his gaze at the close of each flattering period, to practice an ingratiating trailing away at the nadir of each bow.

At all events, this and Waller's other special adaptation of the closed couplet, that is, his composing of double couplets, both reinforce his chief poetic intention, the intention, that is, to be polite. Thus the Augustans, who credited Waller, as F. R. Leavis notes, with establishing "a verse-mode . . . polite . . . [and] intimately related to manners and a social code," [4] were perfectly right. Waller, as Dr. Leavis recognizes, achieved "a correctness . . . in his numbers which is inseparable from a concept of 'Good Form.' " [5] We may say, indeed, that he achieved an excessive correctness of versification to express an excessive politeness of address.

It is this application of a polite utterance to polite occasions, this linkage of means and meanings — as confined and meager as the entire poetic result may seem to us — that gives Waller his special place in our history. Other poets around his time, Jonson in his "Epigram to King James," for instance, and Cowley in several poems, approached this identity between the closed couplet and social flattery. But Waller achieved it in many poems over many years. In doing so, he suggested only one aspect, and that an ignoble one, in the whole range of social discourse. But Pope and other eighteenth-century poets, whose work began with politeness, found in Waller the key to their deeper and more various poetic ambitions.

---

[3] "The Development of the Rhetoric and Metre of the Heroic Couplet," *PMLA*, L (1935), 201–2.

[4] *Revaluation* (London, 1949), p. 30.

[5] Ibid., p. 112.

VI

✯✯✯✯✯✯✯✯✯✯✯✯✯✯

THE POLITICAL COUPLET

Until 1630 or so the several strands of the closed couplet — the Jonsonian couplet, the satiric couplet (which actually faded away rather early), and the abstract couplet — developed separately to a great extent, in separate poems and in separate poets. But contemporaries, of course, did not think of these strands in the schematic way that I have described them. Ben Jonson, for example, commended Donne's satires to Lucy, Countess of Bedford, and sent Donne a copy of his own *Epigrammes*.[1] And Lord Falkland, again, considered himself a son of Ben.[2] The separate strands of closed-couplet development, moreover, were sometimes woven together, and they were sometimes qualified by returns to the firmly closed, elegiac couplets of Marlowe and Harington and even to the stiffly composed medieval couplets of Baldwin and Spenser. One finds virtually all these strands somewhere in the poems of John Donne, Abraham Cowley, and Michael Drayton. Take, for example, this passage from Drayton's "Elegy to Master William Jeffreys":

But soft my Muse, and make a little stay,
Surely thou art not rightly in thy way,
To my good *Jeffrayes* was not I about   45
To write, and see, I suddainely am out,
This is pure *Satire*, that thou speak'st, and I
Was first in hand to write an Elegie.
To tell my countreys shame I not delight,
But doe bemoane't I am no *Democrite*:   50
O God, though Vertue mightily doe grieve
For all this world, yet will I not beleeve
But that shees faire and lovely, and that she

---

[1] *Ben Jonson*, ed. C. H. Herford and Percy and Evelyn Simpson (Oxford, 1947), VIII, 60–61 and 62.

[2] Three of Falkland's extant poems are addressed "To my Father Jonson."

So to the period of the world shall be;
Else had she beene forsaken (sure) of all,   55
For that so many sundry mischiefes fall
Upon her dayly, and so many take
Armes up against her, as it well might make
Her to forsake her nature, and behind,
To leave no step for future time to find.   60

Drayton explicitly recognizes the presence of two conflicting modes, but the lines which recognize this conflict recall the movement of yet another, that of Ben Jonson, and the flat utterance of universal dismay in the lines following echoes the style of the medieval complaint. Donne's "First Anniversary" also reveals a mixture of styles, especially those of medieval complaint and Renaissance satire, and Thomas Carew's "Spring," a mixture of medieval and Jonsonian styles.

During the thirties, as we have recognized, a persistently closed couplet, a neat and elegant form, began to evolve from this variety of styles, a form which Waller was able to apply with considerable contemporary effect to the problems of polite, social discourse. But the tremendous political upheavals which began to shake England around 1640 diverted the closed couplet from the social situation, for which it seemed to have been tailored, and directed it to the broader realm of politics. And it was as a political instrument, in the hands of such poets as John Cleveland, Andrew Marvell, John Oldham, and chiefly, of course, John Dryden, that it was to be most vitally employed for the next fifty years.

This was, of course, the time in England during which modern politics — that is to say, the practice of national compromise and adjustment, the practice by which national factions could oppose one another without killing one another, the practice by which one faction could lose national power without its leaders being executed for treason — was miraculously attained. We may suggest the nature of the time by recognizing that it produced Charles II, whose greatness lay in his laziness and moderation, and George Savile, Marquis of Halifax, whose greatest boast was that he was a trimmer, or, again, by recalling that its first bloody chapter closed with the execution of Charles I and that its last, almost bloodless one closed with the dismissal of James II. The closed couplet came very soon to stand at the center of this leading national concern; it is the metrical form in which poets chiefly defined and argued the issues and that which chiefly illuminates the progress of events and the tenor of the times. Its development through these years from 1640 to

1680, which led to the great political poems of Dryden, reflects this diversion from the portrayal of social discourse which was becoming and, once the political upheavals were absorbed, would yet become its primary use.

The political modification of the closed couplet began with a series of political satires by the royalist John Cleveland, the most famous of which is *The Rebel Scot* of 1644, and with Abraham Cowley's *The Puritan and the Papist* of 1643. Cleveland turned the definitions, balances, and emphases of the couplet against the Scots in such attacks as this: "But that there's charm in verse, I would not quote / The name of Scot without an antidote." We can sense Cleveland's awareness of the form's expressive use by noticing his willingness to repeat himself — "charm . . . antidote" — to get the force of its rhyme and its definition. To study his practice in some detail, let us consider this passage:

He, that saw Hell in his melancholy dream
And in the twilight of his fancy's theme,
Scared from his sins, repented in a fright,
Had he viewed Scotland, had turned proselyte.   60
A land where one may pray with cursed intent,
O, may they never suffer banishment!
Had Cain been Scot, God would have changed his doom;
Not forced him wander but confined him home!
Like Jews they spread and as infection fly,   65
As if the Devil had ubiquity.
Hence 'tis they live at rovers and defy
This or that place, rags of geography.
They're citizens of the world; they're all in all;
Scotland's a nation epidemical.   70

One notices, once again, Cleveland's willingness to repeat — "dream . . . fancy's theme" and "Scared . . . in a fright" — to derive the couplet's emphatic snap. There is a broader repetitiveness here too: Cleveland takes three different ways to say that Scotland is a dreadful place, once in the first two couplets above, again in the third, and yet again in the fourth, and three different ways to remark that the Scots are a widely wandering tribe, once each in the fifth, the sixth, and the seventh couplets. The shortness of Cleveland's satiric breath which this shows, the compulsive going over and over of his feelings, obviously bespeaks a burning, an unqualified rage. This is, of course, not political, but factional poetry.

One notices, as a further sign of this, the learned language with its pedantic connotations, "proselyte," "ubiquity," and "epidemical," by which, like the Renaissance satirists, Cleveland makes an exclusive appeal to those with his education and his frame of reference, and the learned figures — to the Bible, to religious practices and rituals, to medicine — which add to the appeal of snobbery the appeal of ancient prejudices. Elsewhere in this poem, by the way, Cleveland has followed the Renaissance satirists in his use of insulting figures, likening the Scots to wolves (l. 40), to ostriches (l. 78), to leeches (l. 85), and to devil's food (ll. 122–26). The following passage further exemplifies his reversion to this style:

> Come, keen *Iambics*, with your badger's feet
> And badger-like bite until your teeth do meet.
> Help, ye tart satirists, to imp my rage
> With all the scorpions that should whip this age.

One might notice the syntactic confusion over the word "bite" — which seems at first to be a noun, parallel to "feet" — a confusion strongly reminiscent of Marston. Cleveland is also like Marston in the Thresitical tone of his utterance. The difference is, of course, that instead of indulging himself only, as Marston does, Cleveland indulges his whole party, his whole political faction.

For Cleveland, the closed couplet was chiefly a stinging or, to use his word, a biting instrument: it gave an edge to the different aspects of his ire. Cowley, his contemporary in political satire, has made a richer, a more extensive use of the form in articulating his satire, as this passage addressed to the Puritans shows:

Power of dispensing *Oaths*, the *Papists* claime;
Case hath got leave *o' God*, to doe the same.   50
For you doe hate all *swearing* so, that when
You have sworne an *Oath*, ye *breake* it streight agen.
A Curse upon you! which hurts most these Nations,
Cavaliers swearing, or your *Protestations*?
Nay, though *Oaths* by you be so much abhorr'd,   55
Ye allow *God damne me* in the *Puritan Lord*.
  They keepe the *Bible* from *Lay-men*, but ye
Avoid this, for ye have no *Laytie*.
They in a forraigne, and unknowne *tongue* pray,
You in an unknowne *sence* your prayers say: 60

So that this difference 'twixt ye does ensue,
Fooles understand not *them,* nor *Wise men you.*

Here we have a whole string of couplet-heightened antitheses and
distinctions — balances defined by the two lines of a couplet (ll. 49–50,
55–56, 57–58, 59–60), for instance, and by the two halves of a line
(ll. 54, 62) — by which the poet tips the scales of his judgment again and
again against the Puritans. Although the passage at large is stiff and its
movement from couplet to couplet quite jerky, one finds considerable
intracouplet flexibility: a major rhetorical pivot after a first line's fourth
foot, for instance, by which the poet gives an explanation more elbow-
room (ll. 51–52) or this same metrical practice again (ll. 57–58) by
which he depresses his satiric scale against the Puritans, rhyming them
into the focus of his disapprobation. Of course, the metrical lameness of
this latter couplet's second line and the weakness of its 'ye / *Laytie*'
rhyme reduces the effect.

The chief deficiency of Cowley's poem, however, is its lack of a supra-
couplet movement, of a more comprehensive span of thought, a span of
evidence and relationship that would give his individual satiric balances
the strength of an argumentative context, a rational ground. Cowley,
here, just goes along touching off his target in couplet after couplet after
couplet. His separate thrusts are better controlled than those of Cleve-
land and his tone is one of judgment rather than of bias, but the effect is
equally absolute, equally inflexible. The impression of responsiveness,
that is, of a sensitivity to the full range of the arguments in their details,
and the impression of comprehensiveness, that is, of a grasp on the rea-
sons which support each and all of the opposing factions — those impres-
sions which would make the speaker's address political and not merely
factional — hardly emerge any more from *The Puritan and the Papist,*
then, than they do from *The Rebel Scot.*

Both of these poets tried spasmodically for that broader sweep of ut-
terance by which they could comprehend their topics fully enough to
give their own positions some force of argument. One might study Cow-
ley's extensive play on the words "reserved" and "reservation" (ll. 33–48),
for instance, by which he has tried to turn out all sides of the political
opposition before him. And there are Cleveland's brief periodic suspen-
sions, such as that in the first two couplets of the passage quoted above
and this:

The Indian, that Heaven did forswear
Because he heard some Spaniards were there,

> Had he but known what Scots in Hell had been,
> He would *Erasmus*-like have hung between.

But the enrichment of the prejudice against the Scots with a prejudice against the Spaniards and the learned reference to Erasmus — those elements which the longer span of utterance have allowed him to include in his attack — can hardly be thought to incur a decent political climate.

Before 1660 the general practice of a long span of thought realized in closed couplets, the general practice, that is, which would allow Dryden to give politics a poetic form, had been achieved only in nonpolitical poems, notably in Denham's meditative virtuoso piece, *Cooper's Hill*, and in Cowley's biblical epic, *Davideis*. Denham's achievement we have sufficiently exemplified. To account for Cowley's, consider the following passage, an invocation from very near the opening of his epic:

> Thou, who didst *Davids* royal stem adorn,
> And gav'st him *birth* from whom thy self was't *born*.
> Who didst in *Triumph* at *Deaths Court* appear,   15
> And slew'st him with thy *Nails*, thy *Cross* and *Spear*,
> Whilst *Hells* black *Tyrant* trembled to behold,
> The glorious light he forfeited of old,
> Who Heav'ns *glad burden* now, and justest pride,
> Sit'st high enthron'd next thy great *Fathers* side,   20
> (Where hallowed Flames help to adorn that Head
> Which once the *blushing Thorns* environed,
> Till crimson drops of precious *blood* hung down
> Like *Rubies* to enrich thine *humble Crown*.)
> Ev'en *Thou* my breast with such blest rage inspire,   25
> As mov'd the tuneful strings of *Davids Lyre*,
> Guid my bold steps with thine old *trav'elling Flame*,
> In these untrodden paths to *Sacred Fame*;
> Lo, with *pure hands* thy heav'enly *Fires* to take,
> My well-chang'd *Muse* I a chast *Vestal* make!   30
> From earths vain joys, and loves soft witchcraft free,
> I consecrate my *Magdalene* to Thee!

This was meant to be one complete sentence, one integrated thrust of thought, and it is, except possibly for the break at line 28 and the shift in the next four lines from the poet's request to the exalted Christ — a request phrased in the imperative mood — to a description of the poet's own attitude and intentions.

It would be easy enough for us to point out flaws in the meter and diction of this passage, but we should still recognize its artfulness as a system of closed couplets. Its opening two words, the first preparing for the imperative verbs with which the thought will be concluded and the second introducing the adjectival material that will suspend this conclusion, make a clear and proper attack on this ambitious metrical scheme. The pointed parallelism of the first two couplets, again, each one defining a single "who" clause with a compound predicate and each one giving the same emphatic placing to the two verbs, both asserts the couplet as a persistent unit of statement and carries us on into the passage. The expansion of the second of these "who" clauses through another couplet and the expansion of the third and last such clause with an oblique, double-couplet parenthesis continue the dynamic mode. Every couplet and almost every one of the normal set of closed-couplet pauses define and illuminate this complex of descriptive and vocative material, but none of them blocks us from the request, the imperative verbs, that Cowley has promised us. The two couplets which contain the fulfillment of this promise are also artfully handled: the first couplet, for instance, opens emphatically by repeating the term "Thou" with which the poet first asserted this promise, and the two imperative verbs by which he makes it good receive valuable metrical emphasis, the first being inverted to the end of the first couplet's first line, the second opening the second couplet. This couplet does tail off, and it is followed by the disruptive indicative material already mentioned (how easy, it seems, to have gone on, "Behold my hands, etc."). Nevertheless, Cowley has achieved with considerable skill both a grand heroic sweep of utterance and, at the same time, an illumination of the individual heroic details.

Several poets between Cowley and Dryden made interesting political uses of the couplet and enriched it as a political medium. Their individual contributions, which I have discussed in my separate essays on their poetry, can be generally described. There is John Oldham, who achieved an extended oratorical sweep in his *Satires on the Jesuits*; John Caryll, in whose *Naboth's Vineyard* one finds characters drawn into political dialogue, political narrative, and a palpable biblical-English political allegory — all, of course, significant to *Absalom and Achitophel*; and Andrew Marvell, who infused his political satires with meditative resonance, with a sense of the ideals against which practical politics worked out its devious way.

Finally, there is Dryden, who wrote a fine political poem in 1660, *Astraea Redux*, and then refined and extended his style over the next twenty years so that, when the dangerous political turbulence sparked by the Popish Plot made necessary an appeal to national moderation, to a broadly addressed English consensus, to the spirit of national solidarity and national compromise, when, that is to say, the times required a great political poem, he was ready.

VII

✦✦✦✦✦✦✦✦✦✦✦✦✦✦✦✦

THE HEROIC
COUPLET OF DRYDEN

1. DRYDEN'S METRICAL DYNAMICS

In the first of the two major sections of his poem "To the Memory of Mr. Oldham," Dryden examines the affinities between himself and the much younger man whose death he is mourning:

Farewel, too little and too lately known,
Whom I began to think and call my own;
For sure our Souls were near ally'd; and thine
Cast in the same Poetick mould with mine.
One common Note on either Lyre did strike,   5
And Knaves and Fools we both abhorr'd alike:
To the same Goal did both our Studies drive,
The last set out the soonest did arrive.
Thus *Nisus* fell upon the slippery place,
While his young Friend perform'd and won the Race.   10

Dryden here defines, one couplet at a time, his and Oldham's similarity in "Poetick mould," their similarly satiric "Note," and their similar literary "Goal," and he concludes with the contention, tactfully phrased in the figure of a race and illuminated by an allusion to the famous footrace in Vergil's *Aeneid*, that Oldham was the better satiric poet, the winner of this race in which they had both participated. The details of the allusion to Vergil and the subliminal sense one may have of this race between an older and a younger man as a race not to literary achievement but to death may diffuse this contention, but Dryden has defined the racing figure as the goal of their "Studies" and thus tied it and its allusive expansion to his and Oldham's poetic efforts so carefully that his having made this apparently exaggerated claim for his young colleague is unmistakably clear.

[99]

Dryden drives home this judgment of Oldham's superiority by reasserting it in the first couplet of the second major section of the poem:

O early ripe! to thy abundant store
What could advancing Age have added more?
It might (what Nature never gives the young)
Have taught the numbers of thy native Tongue.
But Satyr needs not those, and Wit will shine   15
Through the harsh cadence of a rugged line.
A noble Error, and but seldom made,
When Poets are by too much force betray'd.
Thy generous fruits, though gather'd ere their prime
Still shew'd a quickness; and maturing time   20
But mellows what we write to the dull sweets of Rhyme.

This whole section is obviously devoted to establishing the validity of Dryden's praise. The poet immediately faces its apparent excess, turning the seemingly rhetorical question defined in its first couplet into a real question and, indeed, the vital question of the next three couplets.

Dryden faces this question, typically, by making an admission, by refining upon his praise of Oldham: the youthful poet's satires *are* metrically rough. Evidently this admission, like that with which *Absalom and Achitophel* opens, confronts the strongest point against Dryden's position: if he can blunt it, he will have established Oldham's pre-eminence as a satiric poet. He manages this by a further refinement, this time sharpening not his description of Oldham, but of poetic satire, the endeavor for which he has praised Oldham. This feeling for poetic modification, this dedication to intellectual refinement and precision, was established in the opening couplet of the poem, indeed, in the opening line — with Dryden's admission of his slight and brief acquaintance with Oldham, and its presence was reinforced by the care Dryden showed in ticking off the points of likeness between himself and the younger poet and in defining the point of difference between them. If one compares Dryden's poetic conduct with John Milton's on the similar situation which underlies "Lycidas," he may see the truly classical address of Dryden — his economy of means, his sharpness of focus, the absolute lucidity and relevance of his utterance. Dryden, then, defends his praise of Oldham by refining our sense of its elements. Having admitted that age might have improved Oldham's meter, he insists in one couplet that satiric poetry, for which he praised Oldham, does not depend on smooth meter for its effect and in the next couplet that this seeming error of metrical roughness is actually the outward sign of a rare satiric virtue, intellectual force, a virtue which, as he will recognize in the triplet immediately following, his own mature and mellow satires are without. In the triplet, then, Dryden returns to the comparison between Oldham and himself, or, more precisely, between Oldham's tart satire and his own, which age has made sweetly dull, and thus clinches his praise of this Marcellus of English poetry.

The affixing of laurel on the stricken Oldham's brows, then, with which the poem ends —

Once more, hail and farewel! farewel, thou young,
But ah too short, *Marcellus* of our Tongue;
Thy Brows with Ivy, and with Laurels bound;
But Fate and gloomy Night encompass thee around —   25

is not, as was Milton's praise of the peerless young poet Edward King, merely figurative, merely ceremonial. Dryden has compared the rough young satirist with his sternest competition in the race for the laurel, that is, of course, himself, and considered the strongest argument against his claim, that is, his metrical roughness. And he has thus established Oldham pre-eminent. The conclusion of this poem is a just and necessary inference from the argument preceding it.

We have seen in passing how the achievement of this argument depended on Dryden's making the elements of his analysis perfectly clear and perfectly emphatic, that is, on his use of the closed couplet. The first line's comprehensive definition of the degree of acquaintance between the two poets, by which Dryden established his probity and his refinement of intellect; the second and third couplets, in each of which he defined one aspect of his and Oldham's similarity and, hence, of their rivalry; the fourth couplet, a transitional one, whose first line generalizes their similarity and whose second modifies it with a point of difference, Oldham's superiority; and the fifth couplet, in which Dryden defined the allusion by which he developed and insisted on this point of difference — in these couplets and throughout the poem, closed-couplet punctuation allowed Dryden to define the elements of the argument and to establish the mental quality of its proponent. But the achievement of this argument also depended on the contrary handling of the couplets through which it was drawn, that is, on Dryden's weaving these closed couplets together into larger units, on his gathering them all — and especially those of the truly dialectic second section — into a single indissoluble statement. Too heavy a pause after the couplet defining the rhetorical question with which the second section opened, for instance, would have given the impression of Dryden as excessive and merely eulogistic; too heavy a pause after the next couplet, again, would have established the commonly held view he was opposing, that Oldham was, after all, a rough sort of poet. It is this dependence of his persuasive effect on larger unities of utterance than the single couplet that chiefly validates Mark Van Doren's insistence that it is fatal for Dryden to lack drive.[1] Dryden has achieved this drive through his highly individuated couplets, yoking them into great movements of verse, not for the sake of drive and movement, themselves, but for the sake of his argument.

Dryden's handling of his syntax is one aspect of this necessary drive. The second major section of the Oldham poem, to continue briefly with that, falls, despite its heavy punctuation, into only three sentence units: the one-couplet question, a triply compounded sentence of modification that covers the next three couplets, and a one-sentence conclusion in the triplet. Moreover, the pronoun "It," which opens the second sentence, referring back to "Age" in the one before, ties these two sentences firmly together. The third sentence, that defined by the triplet, is tied into this whole eleven-line thrust of argument in a rather different way. The words, "Thy gen'rous Fruits," with which it opens recall the "ripe . . . store" metaphor of the opening line of the section, thus by its figurative consonance defining the extremities of this section and assuring us that what was opened with the fruit figure is now being concluded. Within the three-couplet middle sentence of this section, we might notice, besides this long span of thought itself, another syntactical way by which Dryden ties his couplets together. Consider the phrase "and but seldom made": when related backwards, it suggests that the error of roughness was seldom made by Oldham; when related forwards, that so splendid an error is seldom reached in the world of poetry; in both cases, it strengthens, first, Dryden's assertion of Oldham's excellence and, second, the interconnection of the argument by which he establishes this assertion.

Dryden's achievement in "To the Memory of Mr. Oldham," then, depends on both the integrity of the separate couplets and on their interconnections, that is, on the dynamics between definition and movement in his closed-couplet production, the dynamics which closed-couplet poets had been striving for since Marlowe made his couplet-for-distich translation of Ovid's *Amores*.

---

[1] *John Dryden* (New York, 1946), p. 112.

Dryden accomplished this dynamics, in "To the Memory of Mr. Oldham" and in his mature poetry generally, first of all, by digesting the devices of earlier closed-couplet poets, especially Falkland, Denham, and Cowley. In this little poem of his, for instance, we find a variety of established practices: periodic inversion (ll. 5, 7, 11–12, 13, 18, 24), syntactic extension (ll. 1–4, 13–18, 19–21), oblique disposition of rhetoric (ll. 3–4, 15–16, 22–23), and progressive or slanted syntax (ll. 6, 8, 14, 21) — all of which augment that dynamics which consists both in observing the regularity and stability of the couplet and in shaping it, inside and out, to fit the particular details and relationships of different topics.

Dryden came, of course, to use these basic devices of couplet dynamics with greater force and greater subtlety than his predecessors. One may remember, for instance, the great sweep of verse which opens *Religio Laici*, a passage whose interconnections Rachel Trickett has delineated,[2] or this, the opening ten lines of *Absalom and Achitophel*:

In pious times, e'er Priest-craft did begin,
Before *Polygamy* was made a sin;
When man, on many, multiply'd his kind,
E'r one to one was, cursedly, confin'd:
When Nature prompted, and no law deny'd   5
Promiscuous use of Concubine and Bride;
Then *Israel's* Monarch, after Heaven's own heart,
His vigorous warmth did, variously, impart
To Wives and Slaves: And, wide as his Command,
Scatter'd his Maker's Image through the Land.   10

This poem's first three couplets define a "When" complex, which begins as an appeal to the good old days but develops into a universally conditional statement; it describes, of course, the condition of natural piety as a man might understand it. The next two couplets describe the proper response to such a condition, the proper life in such natural and blessed conditions — the life of Charles II, that is. To begin understanding the art with which Dryden has unified this passage, we may notice the strategic placing of the key logical terms, "When" at the beginnings of the second and third couplets and "Then" at the beginning of the fourth; the enjambment of the third couplet's first line which emphasizes the couplet break and thus helps punctuate the whole three-couplet

---

[2] "The Idiom of Augustan Poetry," in *Poetry: Form and Structure*, ed. Francis Murphy (Boston, 1964), pp. 117–18.

"When" system; and the much more dramatic enjambment of the fourth couplet by which the two-couplet "Then" complex is yoked into one glorious action and the whole sentence brought to a climactic close.

Dryden augmented such basic devices of couplet dynamics as these with many others. For one thing, he often extended a single figure of speech, such as the food figure in the "Prologue to *All for Love*" (ll. 31–40), the trial figure in that play's "Epilogue" (ll. 1–6 and 18–27), and the fruits figure in "To the Memory of Mr. Oldham" (ll. 11–21). The allegory in *Absalom and Achitophel*, in *The Hind and the Panther*, and in *MacFlecknoe* are all, among other things, large-scale versions of this figurative unification.

Dryden also unified long spans of thought by playing on words. The complexities and progressions of meaning which arise, for instance, from such repeated terms as "civil" ("Prologue to *Don Sebastian*," ll. 9, 12), "treason" (*Absalom and Achitophel*, II, 434, 445, 459, 485, 497), and "play" ("Prologue to *Aureng-Zebe*," ll. 4, 24, 35, 40) integrate the supra-couplet systems they appear in. Dryden has an especially emphatic way of handling this device: the placing of a word that appeared somewhat less prominently in one couplet at the very beginning of the next. The term "thoughtless" is used in this way to yoke together two couplets in *MacFlecknoe* (ll. 26–27), and "rhyme," to unify two in the second part of *Absalom and Achitophel* (ll. 485–86). In the early lines of *Absalom and Achitophel*, one finds "God" (ll. 48–49) and "plot" (ll. 83–84) similarly employed, and there is, finally, the term "wit" in the following lines —

> He sought the Storms; but, for a Calm unfit,
> Would Steer too nigh the Sands, to boast his wit.
> Great Wits are sure to Madness near ally'd
> And thin Partitions do their Bounds divide —

by which Dryden unifies his admission of Shaftesbury's wit with a general statement on wit which taints it. It will be noticed that this practice of beginning a couplet with a repeated term allows Dryden to make both a strong couplet stop and a strong bicouplet connection at once.

Still another of Dryden's many devices for the dynamic maintenance of definition and movement that his persuasive intentions required is his employment of ambivalent syntactic connections. For instance, the last half of the line that immediately precedes the Shaftesbury material quoted just above, "when the waves went high," can be understood to modify "danger" in the first half of that line or "sought" in the next line — that is, of course, in the next couplet. We have already noticed the similar syntactical ambivalence of the phrase "and but seldom made" in "To the Memory of Mr. Oldham." We might also notice the ambivalence of "wide as his Command" in the opening lines of *Absalom and Achitophel*, a phrase which can modify "impart" in the line above it or "Scatter'd" in the line below; the phrase, "and many winged wounds," from the famous opening of *The Hind and the Panther*, which can be understood as the object of the preposition "with" in the line above, or of the verb "Aim'd" in the line below; and, finally, the adjectival complex, "Round as a globe, and liquor'd ev'ry chink, / Goodly and great" in the second part of *Absalom and Achitophel* (ll. 461–62), which can modify the "rolling . . . Og" immediately preceding or the sailing Og which immediately follows. Such ambivalences of syntax allow Dryden to tie couplets together, it should be noticed, without equivocating his meanings. Sometimes, as in the case of the phrase "and but seldom made" from "Oldham," an ambivalently applicable phrase will suggest two clearly separable meanings, both of which fit Dryden's argument; more often the same understanding will fit both applications, so that such a phrase indicates a powerful syntactic movement, a richly woven coherency.

With all these devices Dryden was able to unify great webs of argument — forestalling his readers' judgment of Oldham's poetic power, Charles's sex life, and, indeed, every public question he raised until he had delineated the evidence necessary to establish the position he was arguing.

The persuasive effect of these dynamic webs of utterance can be described in general. They allowed Dryden to absorb and to extend the impressions projected by almost all closed-couplet poetry, balance of mind, clarity of vision, and detachment of judgment. Dryden's dynamically articulated couplet paragraphs and poems project the presence of these valuable qualities of mind even when he is attacking questions whose elements and relationships are too complex to be comprehended in single couplets or in double-couplet capsules. Dryden's dynamic style allowed him, moreover, to augment this basic set of closed-couplet impressions with others equally valuable to his persuasive intentions; these impressions, which are virtually unique to Dryden in English political poetry, are, broadly speaking, those of intellectual refinement and intellectual comprehensiveness.

The impression of intellectual refinement Dryden achieved by weaving into his long spans of argument a variety of modifications, some of them defined within the bounds of individual couplets, some of them stretching over several. The second line of "Oldham," for example, modifies the addressee of the first line and refines our understanding of the friendship between him and the speaker, vividly articulating the difference between the spiritual depth of this friendship and its pitifully brief extent in time. The argument for Oldham's satiric pre-eminence, again, as we have already seen, is a texture of such refinements. Dryden achieved extremely delicate modifications such as that in the second half of the line, "What faults he had (and who from faults is free?)," and, on the other hand, such sharp reversals of meaning as in the second half of this one: "And never broke the Sabbath, but for Gain" — the famous whiplash effect. Notice the same range of modification in this pair of examples — here articulated in the second full line of each couplet: "The bristl'd *Baptist Boar*, impure as He, / (But whitn'd with the foam of sanctity)"; "About thy boat the little fishes throng, / As at the morning toast that floats along." In the first of these, Dryden's modification merely adds a crowning satiric touch to his already satiric attack; in the second, it turns gross flattery into gross contempt. The rabble passage from *Absalom and Achitophel*, which we will soon examine, is a great system of modification: its first sentence being augmented with seven lines in apposition to "The *Jews*," the whole devoted to extending and refining our sense of them; its second sentence being similarly enriched by six lines of adjectival modification in the form of "who" clauses.

The great sentence which opens the portrait of Achitophel is also an exercise in this practice of refinement:

Of these the false *Achitophel* was first: 150
A Name to all succeeding Ages Curst.
For close Designs, and crooked Counsels fit,
Sagacious, Bold, and Turbulent of wit:
Restless, unfixt in Principles and Place;
In Power unpleas'd, impatient of Disgrace.   155
A fiery Soul, which working out its way,
Fretted the Pigmy Body to decay:
And o'r inform'd the Tenement of Clay.
A daring Pilot in extremity;
Pleas'd with the Danger, when the Waves went high   160
He sought the Storms; but, for a Calm unfit,
Would Steer too nigh the Sands, to boast his Wit.

Dryden taints Achitophel's name, his soul, his body, and his gifts by mingling adjectival and appositive material in this sweeping system of assertions and refinements.[3] Dryden's treatment of King Charles's sorrows as an exile (*Astraea Redux*, ll. 71–92) furnishes an early example of his practice of supracouplet modification; he does not know, he says, whether to "regret or bless" these sorrows and then explains, telling how Charles had preserved his honor in defeat and had learned valuable lessons from the exile that followed. Dryden's exposition of the Panther's mixture of vices and virtues from *The Hind and the Panther* (I, 327–46), with its subtle tone of sympathetic condescension, furnishes a late example. As these three passages taken together may suggest, this practice was a persistent and a developing element of Dryden's art.

The tendency toward a supracouplet comprehensiveness of statement, to turn to this second major effect of Dryden's dynamically extended couplets, also shows up as early as *Astraea Redux*. Its opening nine couplets, for instance, cast at a comprehensive description of the English body politic, pointing out the young and the old, the commons and the nobles, the victims and their oppressors. Dryden worked the impression of a comprehensive grasp of his material more economically and more deeply into his description of the rabble in *Absalom*, giving both their political and religious conduct, both their general nature and their particular applications of it. The portrait of Achitophel also depends for its total effect on this impression. We may notice first that Dryden uses single lines throughout this passage to indicate a comprehensive awareness, encompassing the great rebel in various opposite aspects: "In Power unpleas'd, impatient of disgrace"; "In friendship false, implacable in hate"; "Bankrupt of Life, yet Prodigal of Ease." In the larger spans of this portrait, likewise, he describes the good side and the bad of Achitophel's great wit; his private, as well as his public, life; and his good offices, as well as his evil practices.

Dryden's weaving of general principles into the Achitophel portrait — as into the great spans of his poetic discourse generally — augments this impression of his comprehensiveness of understanding. Especially

---

[3] It may be worthwhile to point out the large-scale syntactic ambivalence of lines 151–62. To describe it a little too simply, the three appositives, "Name," "Soul," and "Pilot," along with their adjectival embellishments, can be thought to relate to "*Achitophel*" in line 150 or to "He" in line 161; the reader as he goes along feels them all to relate back to "*Achitophel*" and then at line 161 consciously recognizes the forward connection of "Pilot" and senses a web of more extensive connections.

telling in the case of Achitophel is the pronouncement, "Great Wits are sure to Madness near ally'd," which absorbs as a particular example Dryden's preceding admission of Achitophel's wit — thus countering that admission — and then serves as a principle for Dryden's discussion in the following lines of Achitophel's personal conduct. The poet's many-faceted presentation of a topic, his capacity to comprehend the extremes of each facet as he presents it, and the vastness of his vision, which radiates from his power to square his topic in the course of presenting it against great principles of human life — all of which are exemplified by the portrait of Achitophel — were accessible to Dryden because of his command of a dynamic supracouplet movement and organization.

Such impressions as these of refinement and comprehensiveness give Dryden's judgments — of Oldham, of the rabble, of Achitophel — tremendous persuasive force; one who has comprehended these subjects as completely as Dryden has done and dedicated himself this deeply to a perfect refinement of statement in describing them must be fair and just and wise in his judgments. This persuasive effect, to repeat, depends on the drive of Dryden's closed-couplet production, on its power to keep us from resting at any point along the way toward Dryden's final equation, on its power to make us continue from one aspect of Dryden's vast overview to the next, and on our thus absorbing in one comprehensive pattern the elements of his perfectly defined and perfectly interrelated understanding.

2. Dryden's Development

Perfecting this great medium of persuasion was not the work of a day, as anyone can see who compares the mature "Oldham" to the adolescent "Elegy to Lord Hastings" or who compares two passages on the rabble, one from a work of Dryden's early maturity, *Astraea Redux*, and one from *Absalom and Achitophel,* composed twenty years later. To make this second comparison, consider, first, the rabble passage from *Astraea Redux*:

Nor could our Nobles hope their bold Attempt
Who ruin'd Crowns would Coronets exempt:
For when by their designing Leaders taught
To strike at Pow'r which for themselves they sought,
The Vulgar gull'd into Rebellion, arm'd,
Their blood to action by the Prize was warm'd;
The Sacred Purple then and Scarlet Gown,   35
Like sanguine Dye to Elephants was shown.

Thus when the bold *Typhoeus* scal'd the Sky,
And forc'd great *Jove* from his own Heaven to fly,
(What King, what Crown from Treasons reach is free,
If *Jove* and *Heaven* can violated be?)   40
The lesser Gods that shar'd his prosp'rous State
All suffer'd in the Exil'd Thund'rer's Fate.
The Rabble now such Freedom did enjoy,
As Winds at Sea that use it to destroy:
Blind as the *Cyclops*, and as wild as he,   45
They own'd a lawless salvage Libertie,
Like that our painted Ancestours so priz'd
Ere Empire's Arts their Breasts had Civiliz'd.

The first two couplets of this passage form a hazy transition in which the rabble are only vaguely and peripherally indicated as "their." Then, after they are named as "The Vulgar" in the next couplet, a couplet devoted to describing them, the passage slides into two artful but digressive analogies: the first of these is confined to one couplet or, rather, to the second line of one couplet, but the second covers three. The next three couplets, the last of the passage, strike the topic, finally, with concentrated force. These couplets are quite good, although the third is diluted rather than intensified by its rather pedantic figure; but they do not seem to climax a unified system of satiric attack. The problem is not merely the secondary relevance of so much of the material, but the heavy pauses that separate and encapsulate its elements. The heavy pauses at lines 34 and 42, neither of which is bridged by syntactic reference, by a point of logical progression, or by any figurative correspondency, divide Dryden's attack on the rabble into three random shots, the first of which is imperfectly directed and the second of which is essentially irrelevant.

The rabble passage from *Absalom and Achitophel*, on the other hand, opens on target and continues so throughout, making one relentless satiric barrage:

The *Jews*, a Headstrong, Moody, Murmuring race,   45
As ever try'd th' extent and stretch of grace;
God's pamper'd People, whom, debauch'd with ease,
No King could govern, nor no God could please;
(Gods they had tri'd of every shape and size
That God-smiths could produce or Priests devise:)   50
These *Adam*-wits, too fortunately free,
Began to dream they wanted liberty;

And when no rule, no president was found
Of men, by Laws less circumscrib'd and bound,
They led their wild desires to Woods and Caves;   55
And thought that all but Savages were Slaves.
They who when *Saul* was dead, without a blow,
Made foolish *Ishbosheth* the Crown forgo;
Who banisht *David* did from *Hebron* bring,
And, with a General shout, proclaim'd him King: 60
Those very *Jewes*, who, at their very best,
Their Humour more than Loyalty exprest,
Now wondred why, so long, they had obey'd
An Idoll Monarch which their hands had made:
Thought they might ruine him they could create;   65
Or melt him to that Golden Calf, a State.

The single couplet of transition which precedes this passage, "But Life can never be sincerely blest: / Heaven punishes the bad, and proves the best," forces the reader to infer that what follows will be a trial to the established national order and a threat to national peace — thus putting him into exactly the right frame of mind to absorb Dryden's opinion of the rabble.

The passage itself flows forth in two major sweeps of utterance, each taking up one complete sentence: the first, a compound-complex sentence, whose scope is defined in the line "No King could govern, nor no God could please," is chiefly devoted to the political and the religious sentiments of the rabble in general; the second, a complex sentence with a compound predicate, turns toward the rabble's particular applications and, climactically, the particular application of this moment. The combination of a general religious and political judgment in the first sentence makes us sense a religious — that is, of course, an irreligious — relevance to the mainly political actions pointed out in the second. It was Dryden's power over supracouplet organization that allowed him to weave the rabble's irreligion into the first sentence and thus to intensify his condemnation of their present political activity: their attack on David he has made to seem an attack on God as well.

We have recognized the one strong pause in this passage, that at line 56 between its two sentences. This pause was necessary to define the more general description from the more narrow and immediate one and thus to assert the elements and the relationships of this complicated system. The pause also allowed Dryden to give the powerful satiric formulation with which he concluded his first sentence, "And thought that all but Savages were Slaves," a ringing emphasis. This strong pause cements the 'Savages–Slaves' antithesis, which the slanted syntax of the line — necessary, of course, to integrate it with the sentence to which it furnishes a climax — would otherwise diminish. But since Dryden's persuasive intentions required him to present the rabble's general nature and their particular activity in one unified system of description, he had to find ways of bridging this necessary pause, and he found several. The "They" opening of the first couplet after this pause recalls the "They" which opened the preceding couplet and, of course, "The *Jews*" to which both of these pronouns refer. The immediate continuation of this couplet, again, with "who when" assures us of considerable syntactical scope in what follows and thus augments our impetus into this second sentence of the passage. There is, finally, a narrative or chronological strand that bridges the pause between these two long sentences and pulls them together: it is most clearly asserted, in the first sentence, with the verb of the first main clause, "began," and with the conjunction "when," which introduces the second, and, in the second sentence, with the sharply delineated step-by-step description of the rabble's conduct on the death of Saul and with the emphatically placed adverb "Now." Dryden, then, has drawn the benefits of clarity and emphasis from the one major pause in this passage and still managed to bridge it and to integrate the two elements of his discourse that it punctuates. Thus when we reach the last line of the passage, "Or melt him to that Golden Calf, a State," we can absorb its rich allusive mixture of religious and political indictment as truly and totally relevant to a description of the rabble.

Dryden used eleven line-strengthening inversions in the earlier passage on the rabble and only five in the later one, or, to extend this statistic, he used twenty-four such formal props in the first forty-eight lines of *Astraea Redux* and only sixteen in the first sixty-six lines of *Absalom and Achitophel*. Early on, Dryden needed such inversions, quite abstractly, to help him hold his lines and couplets together — just as Beethoven, according to Tovey, needed rhythmic figures to unify his earlier compositions; but in such later poems as *Absalom and Achitophel*, inversion is quite often an expressive device. The doubled inversion, for instance, in the isolated couplet, "But since like slaves his bed they did ascend, / No true succession could their seed attend," gives this utterance of the principle on which Dryden based his rejection of Monmouth great force and dignity: a dignity which depends, obviously, on Dryden's not having overused periodic inversions before, especially on his not having overused them merely to prop up weak lines or couplets.

The dignity of this couplet also depends on its heavy closure. And, as in the case of inversion, the expressive weight of closure varies inversely with its use. In the first thirty-three couplets of *Absalom and Achitophel*, only one of which is enjambed (ll. 7–8), there are only two pauses (ll. 42, 44) as heavy as this one at line 16 — although there are several equally heavy punctuation marks. We have noticed another similarly expressive use of heavy closure in the passage on the rabble from *Absalom and Achitophel*, that one in the middle of the passage. Heavy closure, then, like inversion, became for the mature Dryden, not an automatic answer to formal slippage, but a selective element in his poetic expression. His ability to keep up the integrity of his individual couplets without the mechanical use of inversion or heavy closure, moreover, augments the dynamic movement of his poetry whose crucial relevance to his persuasive intentions we have already discussed.

3. DRYDEN'S POLITICAL ADDRESS

Dryden's mature couplet practice, of which "Oldham" and *Absalom* have furnished us examples, was a means of public persuasion, primarily of political persuasion.[4] It was a means, that is to say, of coping with public questions and public factions, of defining and choosing between alternatives in national judgment and national conduct. Again and again in his mature poetry, Dryden argued the great public issues of his day — the uses and extent of royal power, the relationship between religious belief and national loyalty, the relative merits and the relative rights of Charles II and James II and of their foes — and faced the parties whom these issues divided — the king and the Commons, the Anglicans, Catholics, and Presbyterians, the Whigs and the Tories. His persistent problem — in such occasional poems as *Astraea Redux* and *Britannia Rediviva*, in such religious poems as *Religio Laici* and *The Hind and the Panther*, and in such satires as *Absalom and Achitophel* and *The Medal* — was that of uniting behind his and his party's position as large a segment of the English body politic as possible.

Even the nonpolitical poems, such as the dramatic prologues and the personal addresses, reveal a political mode of thought and address and, quite often, a political message as well. One thinks, for instance, of the address "To my Honour'd Friend, Dr. Charleton," a poem whose politi-

---

[4] The political nature of Dryden's poetry has been recognized by several scholars and critics, most emphatically by E. N. Hooker, "Dryden and the Atoms of Epicurus," *ELH*, XXIV (1957), 177–90.

cal implications Earl Wasserman has brought to light,[5] or the "Prologue to *Don Sebastian*," that manly address of the cast laureate to all of his victorious opponents. All of Dryden's dramatic prologues and epilogues are political in tone. They are pervaded, first of all, by political figures of speech, with references to kings and parliaments, to civil wars, jury trials, and a variety of national and international differences. More important, every one of them, as in the case of political oratory, emanates from a platform. In each of them we catch the raised and ringing voice of a man who speaks to a multitude, and sense, moreover, the inarticulate but lively and factious multitude addressed — the bustle, the rowdiness, and the diversity of Dryden's audience. Dryden persistently suggests the two great parties in the theater, the dramatic company and its audience, and variously indicates their points of possible discord and agreement. He often recognizes factions inside each of these two parties as well: dividing the audience sometimes, for instance, into poets, fops, and fools ("Prologue to *All for Love*," ll. 1–30), into men and women ("Epilogue to *Marriage A-La-Mode*"), and into young women and old women ("Epilogue to *All for Love*," ll. 20–31). In these poems, as in most of his mature poetry, once again, Dryden faced the problem of persuading as broad a spectrum of public opinion as he could — in the prologues, of course, it was primarily persuasion to watch the plays with sympathy.

The oratorical tone, on which depended the achievement of this persuasion in his own time and the impression of this persuasion in later times, is actually a composite of many tones. Its basic forensic breadth, its power as an address to all the gentlemen of England, depends on a note of heroic exaltation, which Dryden learned in part from Cowley, and on a noble detachment, which he found in Denham. We might think, for example, of David's closing speech in *Absalom and Achitophel*, of the exalted opening of *Religio Laici*, or of the mock-heroic tone of *MacFlecknoe* entire. Dryden's debt to Cowley's *Davideis* in this latter poem has long been acknowledged.[6] Dryden, however, often qualified this resounding and heroic mode of address. The prologues and epilogues, for instance, modulate between entreaty, apology, command, courtliness, and mockery — each one reflecting the fluid conditions of its utterance, that is, of course, the shifting susceptibilities and moods Dryden could expect in his audience. To extend our sense of the range in

[5] "Dryden: 'Epistle to Charleton,'" in *The Subtler Language* (Baltimore, 1959), pp. 15–33.

[6] See, for example, Van Doren, esp. pp. 19–21.

Dryden's address, we may recall some of the varieties of Dryden's mockery: those cases, for instance, in which he asks his audience to join him on the grounds of their modernity in laughter at earlier ages, or on the grounds of their patriotism in laughter at the French, or on the grounds of their common sense in laughter at themselves. The nondramatic poems often verge upon a conversational mode of address and thus play on social and personal biases for their persuasive effect. There is, for instance, the talk between the panther, "The Lady of the spotted-muff," and the hind (*Hind and Panther*, II, and III, 1–426). There is also the portrait of Zimri (*Absalom*, ll. 544–68), in which Dryden comes close to the purely social address of Pope — as one can see by comparing this portrait of human shiftiness with Pope's portrait of the amphibious Sporus. Finally, we can recall the wonderfully insinuating opening of *Absalom and Achitophel*, which was quoted earlier in this chapter. It is an exaltation of barbershop humor, in which Dryden turns Charles's miscellaneous lechery into a kind of democratic generosity. This range and flexibility in his address allowed Dryden to appeal to various aspects of his audience and to ingratiate himself with its different parties of opinion and sensibility.

Dryden's audience naturally varied in accordance with changing times and circumstances. Not only did the audience to a printed poem differ from that which attended a play, but an Oxford play would be differently attended from one in London. Each of Dryden's poems, correspondingly, implies a different audience in a different mood from every other. He addressed a fairly homogeneous group, nevertheless, as his basic and persistent correspondent, a group whose nature we can catch quite clearly in the opening lines of *Absalom and Achitophel*. This passage, to which we have just referred, makes confident appeals — albeit implicit ones — to certain prejudices. Indeed, Dryden depends heavily on these prejudices in the weaving of his persuasive web: on a prejudice against the clergy in the first couplet, on one against matrimony in the second, and on a general bias in favor of masculine license throughout. As his reliance on such prejudices makes clear, Dryden chiefly addressed himself to an audience of men — an obvious focus for political address in the seventeenth century.

The audience generally implied as the correspondent to Dryden's political utterance, to speak more precisely, is that of sensible, everyday Englishmen.[7] It is richly implied by Dryden's various evocations of such

---

[7] George Hemphill, "Dryden's Heroic Line," *PMLA*, LXXII (1957), 878, describes Dryden's poetic style as projecting as its speaker "a man talking to men . . . in courtly, public, full-dress manners."

prejudices as these I have just mentioned. Others, whose persistent presence as an implicit common ground of Dryden's poetry augments our sense of this audience, are those against the Jews, the Dutch, the French, the last century, the Papists, and, of course, women. Dryden broadened his address to include the ladies in his playhouse prologues and epilogues, but never at the sacrifice of his appeals to essentially masculine sensibilities. The point of these appeals, like those to more respectable English masculine feelings, was to create as rich a web of common agreement as possible and thus to enlist the sympathy of English masculine opinion as variously as possible. The more points of agreement, rational and irrational, Dryden could remind the different factions of and the more he could soften and de-emphasize their differences, the more of their individual members he could win over to his views of these differences. In working out this pattern of persuasive appeals, of course, he has defined the audience, the milieu of his political utterance, creating thus not only a discourse but the situation in which it lives.

Dryden's persistent appeal to the body of enfranchised Englishmen and his consequent creation of this body as a part of his political poetry are cemented by the profoundly English ring of his language, by the sense it gives us of revealing, in Gerard Manley Hopkins's words, "the naked thew and sinew of the English language." [8] This impression, which pervades Dryden's mature poetry, can best be illustrated, perhaps, by Dryden's general statements, such as "All human things are subject to decay"; "Heaven punishes the bad and proves the best"; and "Great Wits are sure to Madness near ally'd." Notice the homely "sure" in the last of these statements. Such general pronouncements, which pervade Dryden's mature couplet poetry, the poet has articulated with an almost proverbial force, endowing them, as it were, with the accumulated wisdom of the English people. Such statements as these or, rather, the generally native English ring of Dryden's verse, which they exemplify, makes a kind of persistent prejudicial appeal, an appeal, that is, to the mere Englishness of his audience and, thus, clinches the impression of an audience of Englishmen as the proper and continuous correspondent to his discourse.

Again and again in Dryden's great poems, the speaker copes with a seriously and dangerously divisive question, and, while comprehending both sides of it and acknowledging in extensive detail the opinions and arguments of both parties, maintains a position based on balanced consideration and detached judgment which ordinary Englishmen of good sense and good heart must respect and, indeed, embrace.

---

[8] *A Hopkins Reader*, ed. John Pick (New York, 1953), p. 164.

These poems open brilliantly. They do so, often, because Dryden immediately confronts his strongest opposition, as in the "Prologue to *Don Sebastian*," or admits the greatest weakness of his own position, as in the "Prologue to *Aureng-Zebe*," "To the Memory of Mr. Oldham," and *Absalom and Achitophel*. Dryden's opening of this last poem with the king's lechery was a stroke of genius — but only because Dryden had the poetry to turn it, at least for gentlemen of worldly wisdom, into a point of amused admiration. In all these instances, as we may describe it, Dryden opens by admitting a major modification to himself as a judge or to his judgment and then refines away that modification, thus establishing himself or his view with tremendously persuasive force. If the rhyming dramatist insists on the dramatic limitations of rhyme, as Dryden does in his "Prologue to *Aureng-Zebe*," his judgment of this rhyming play can surely be trusted; likewise, if he recognizes the failures of Charles, whose cause he champions, his judgment of Charles can surely be trusted: so run the persuasive implications of Dryden's openings.

Dryden's poems close tentatively just as, in the preface to *Absalom and Achitophel*, he explained that they should. Tomorrow will bring new challenges to the sensitivity and scope of the political mind. Moreover, once the issues, as they stand today, have been comprehended and defined, the decision is best left to "all right thinking people." Thus a Dryden prologue simply gives way to the play which follows, commending it to its audience's good sense and good nature. *Absalom and Achitophel* ends with the rebels still at large, and *MacFlecknoe* closes with the new king of dullness comfortably occupying his throne. This tentativeness in closing his poems, like the direct grip on the issues with which they open, is an aspect of the tact and art which allowed Dryden, in facing the political stresses of his own most factious time, to crystallize in his poetry the stress, the flux, the mixture of sense and prejudice, and the agony of choice men suffer whenever they turn their minds and their voices to politics.

4. DRYDEN'S LATER POETRY

After 1688, political utterance became virtually impossible for our language's greatest political poet, as he himself acknowledged in 1690 in his "Prologue to *Don Sebastian*." The work of his last years, chiefly translation, lies outside the vital center of his art. But he brought to it the same powers and spirit that had guided him before. In his translation of Chaucer's "Nun's Priest's Tale," we can see the old master responding to Chaucer's literary promptings, much as he had to the political attributes of Charles and Monmouth, comprehending them and absorbing them in his own poetic style.

To particularize Dryden's wonderfully politic reconciliation of Chaucer's medieval poem to his own skeptical and contentious time, consider, first, this passage of "The Nun's Priest's Tale":

Thre large sowes / hadde she and namo   4020
Thre kyn / and eek a sheep / that highte Malle
Ful sooty was hire bour / and eek hire halle
In which she eet ful many a sklendre meel
Of poynaunt sauce / hir neded never a deel
No deyntee morsel / passed thurgh hir throte   4025
Hir diete / was acordant to hir cote
Repleccioun / ne made hire nevere syk
Attempree diete / was al hir phisyk
And excercise / and hertes suffisaunce
The goute / lette hire no thyng for to daunce   4030
Napoplexie / shente nat hir heed.

Now here is Dryden's translation of it from "The Cock and the Fox":

The Cattel in her Homestead were three Sows,
An Ewe call'd Mally; and three brinded Cows.
Her Parlor-Window stuck with Herbs around   15
Of sav'ry Smell; and Rushes strew'd the Ground.
A Maple-Dresser, in her Hall she had,
On which full many a slender Meal she made:
For no delicious Morsel pass'd her Throat;
According to her Cloth she cut her Coat: 20
No paynant Sawce she knew, no costly Treat,
Her Hunger gave a Relish to her Meat;
A sparing Diet did her Health assure;
Or sick, a Pepper-Posset was her Cure.
Before the Day was done her Work she sped,   25
And never went by Candle-light to bed:
With Exercise she sweat ill Humors out,
Her Dancing was not hinder'd by the Gout.
Her Poverty was glad; her Heart content,
Nor knew she what the Spleen or Vapors meant.   30

One notices that Dryden has moved a dresser in to bridge and unify his account of the widow's living quarters with his discussion of her diet; that he has added the relish, hunger, to balance her lack of a real sauce; that he has balanced the assertion of her generally good health with an account of her sicknesses; and, finally, that he has concluded his treatment of her with a couplet of general summary. He has transformed Chaucer's vivid and selective details into a unified and comprehensive exposition of the widow at bed and board, in satiety and hunger, in sickness and health — thus allowing himself to make a general judgment of her whole way of life: "Her Poverty was glad; her Heart content, / Nor knew she what the Spleen or Vapors meant." Chaucer would have questioned the need to judge this widow, but he must have admired, first, the skill with which Dryden has validated his judgment and, second, the extent to which he has preserved his model's intention — the providing of Chaunticleer's grand and noble bearing with a vivid contrast — while achieving his own.

VIII

✦✦✦✦✦✦✦✦✦✦✦✦✦✦✦

FROM DRYDEN TO POPE

The time between the Glorious Revolution in 1688, which demonstrated the universal establishment of politics in English national life, and the death of Queen Anne in 1714, after which the Tories finally lost out and the Whigs began their long ascendency, was a time of adjustment for both the English people and English poetry. At the close of this era the social situation had succeeded the political as the center of English life, and the closed couplet, which had been molded in the various societies of Donne, Jonson, and Waller to portray varieties of social discourse and then recast by the various national factions to portray varieties of political opinion, was recast again. It had been bent out of its normal shape to allow Dryden to encounter and define the vital concerns of his age; now it was bent back, allowing Pope to encounter and define the vital concerns of his.

One can observe a transformation of the political couplet of Dryden into the social couplet of Pope by referring to a number of occasional poems written by Matthew Prior.[1] First comes the Drydenesque "Advice to the Painter" of 1685; then the poem "Presented to the King" of 1696; then the "Prologue spoken before the Queen" of 1704; and, finally, the "Epilogue to *Phaedra*" of 1707. In these poems, which I consider in detail in my essay on Prior, one observes a shift from the bitter urgency of political strife, during which even such a rebel as the "King of Lyme" can shake national confidence, to the ceremonial calm of polite addresses to settled royalty, whose very health and life are becoming matters of merely complimentary concern; and on to a racier, more incisive social utterance, in which kings and queens are merely details. With this

---

[1] In *The Literary Works*, ed. H. Bunker Wright and Monroe K. Spears (Oxford, 1959), 2 vols.

modulation we come to the very edge of Pope's description of Hampton Court, where "Thou, Great *Anna*! whom three Realms obey, / Dost sometimes Counsel take — and sometimes *Tea*."

The poems of Addison, who was several years younger than Prior, vividly illuminate the new social sensibility. His *Letter from Italy* and his *Campaign*, although both consider topics of substantial political importance, are nevertheless simply poems of compliment — the first a compliment to England, the second, to the Duke of Marlborough. Under the spell of the Addisonian heroic, Marlborough's profoundly important military actions become a form of pageant and Marlborough's personal conduct, a demonstration of his honor. Consider these lines, for instance:

While MARLBRÔ lives *Britannia*'s stars dispense   165
A friendly light, and shine in innocence.
Plunging thro' seas of blood his fiery steed
Where-e'er his friends retire, or foes succeed;
Those he supports, these drives to sudden flight,
And turns the various fortune of the fight.   170
     Forbear, great man, renown'd in arms, forbear
To brave the thickest terrors of the war,
Nor hazard thus, confus'd in crouds of foes,
Britannia's safety, and the world's repose;
Let nations anxious for thy life abate   175
This scorn of danger, and contempt of fate:
Thou livest not for thy self; thy Queen demands
Conquest and peace from thy victorious hands;
Kingdoms and empires in thy fortune join,
And *Europe*'s destiny depends on thine.   180

Marlborough's heroic action is merely a public display, a ceremonial parade, of bravery: his balancing actions of support and attack are graceful turns in the attitude, in the pose; his parallel "scorn of danger, and contempt of fate," suggestions of his admirably composed cast of countenance. The passage, as Rachel Trickett has said of a similar one from the same poem, "reads like a poetic version of some grand-style historical painting," [2] that is, like another set of Wallerian instructions to the painter: Marlborough, wearing his honors, astride his horse, is placed against a background of red paint and martially busy distances. We must read the poem in this fashion or recognize the probability that those

---

[2] "The Idiom of Augustan Poetry," in *Poetry: Form and Structure*, ed. Francis Murphy (Boston, 1964), p. 116.

"seas of blood" would simply extinguish Marlborough's "fiery steed." We must do so, again, to accept those red seas as a background to this parade of individual honor.

It is, of course, this neglect of war's personal horror and its variously dreadful consequences, this perfect reduction of it to one aspect of social display, that makes the Addisonian heroic, although poetically negligible, historically significant. For Addison and for his time, every human action, even war, was an aspect of social life. Pope, who shared Addison's social sensibility, had a clearer and a deeper understanding of society and of life; he would transform social events — such as card games, for example — into wars, rather than turning war into a social event, and, equally important, he would make the ladies and gentlemen converse and not merely promenade. But Addison's more crude and shallow poetic formulations exhibit the tenor of the times he and Pope inhabited.

We must not think of Prior and Addison as reviving a languishing mode of expression, however, for the closed couplet had been used to formulate social communications and thus to create the illusion of society all through the great political age of Dryden. Waller went on in his flattering way up into the 1680's. One of his most attractive poems is that addressed to Charles II in 1661 on the king's improvements of St. James's Park; one of his most famous poems, "Instructions to a Painter," dates from 1666; and the poem on tea, which we have studied, was occasioned by Queen Catherine's birthday in 1683. Moreover, Waller was followed by a little band of polite poets, the most important, historically speaking, being George Granville, Lord Lansdowne, who, according to Dr. Johnson, copied all of Waller's faults and very little more,[3] and William Walsh. Both of these men knew the young Pope, and Walsh, who was called "the best critic of our nation" by Dryden,[4] advised the youthful genius to strive for correctness and looked over his verses to make sure he had achieved it.[5] Indeed, the line to Pope, metrically speaking, leads from Waller through Granville and Walsh.[6] The ex-

---

[3] "George Granville," in *Lives of the Poets*, in *Works* (Troy, N. Y., 1903), IX, 319.

[4] *Essays*, ed. W. P. Ker (Oxford, 1960), II, 244.

[5] Joseph Spence, *Observations and Anecdotes*, ed. James Osborn (Oxford, 1966), pp. 31–32.

[6] That Pope derived his metrical style primarily from Waller and Walsh has been at least partially recognized: see, for example, Reuben Brower, *Alexander Pope* (Oxford, 1959), pp. 12–13; and Mark Van Doren, *John Dryden* (New York, 1946), p. 258. Van Doren remarks that Pope did not really draw his style from Dryden, "but from the smooth equable tradition of Sandys and Waller."

ample of Dryden, which would have drawn Pope out of the center of his age, he absorbed only by degrees.

Another social strain, articulated in closed couplets, runs through the age of Dryden, that of social satire, which was practiced by John Wilmot, Earl of Rochester, and John Sheffield, eventually Duke of Buckinghamshire. Rochester seems to have looked back to the satiric practice of Donne, with its implications of clique and coterie, for his inspiration. In his satiric portrait "My Lord All-Pride," for instance, he echoed some unpleasant lines of Donne's "Satire II." Rochester, however, for all his carelessness, writes much rounder couplets than Donne, achieves a more broadly communicable utterance, and, correspondingly, suggests a broader audience. We can indicate the difference between these poets rather neatly by comparing the unpleasant passages mentioned just above. Here are first the Donne passage and then the Rochester:

But hee is worst, who (beggarly) doth chaw   25
Others wits fruits, and in his ravenous maw
Rankly digested, doth those things out-spue,
As his own Things; and they are his owne, 'tis true,
For if one eat my meat, though it be knowne
The meate was mine, th' excrement is his owne.   30

And with his *Arme,* and *Head,* his *Brain*'s so weak,
That his starved fancy, is compell'd to take,
Among the *Excrements* of others wit,
To make a stinking *Meal* of what they shit.   10
So *Swine,* for nasty *Meat,* the *Dunghil* run,
And toss their gruntling *Snowts* up when they've done.

The Donne passage is more trenchant, more intensely reasoned, and more demanding; the Rochester, more accessible to general attention, more showy. Donne describes a three-stage process, the eating of fruit, the imperfect digestion of it, and its violent ejection (apparently as vomit). None of these stages is line- or couplet-defined, so that one must scrutinize the logical progression of the process itself to understand the statement. Moreover, Donne has wedged in modifiers, "beggarly," "ravenous," and "Rankly," whose satiric enrichments one must absorb in course. Donne sums up the process or, rather, the plagiarist's claim which follows it with a point of reason which fills two and one-half lines, and not a couplet, although he closes on a brilliant line-defined antithesis.

Rochester gives only one step in the process of plagiarism, that of eating, and he makes this, somewhat improperly, an eating of excrement — not of fruit, as in Donne. The Rochester figure, then, is not as natural, not as vividly perceived an image as Donne's, but it is wonderfully nasty as a public display of the plagiarist. Rochester found it so effective, indeed, that he repeated it and then repeated it again, the third time visualizing the plagiarist as a hog. His double emphasis on "shit," that gotten by rhyming it and by balancing it with *"Meal"* (a balance that is diffused, however, by the adjective "stinking"), is primarily a matter of social bravado, but it does make clear Rochester's judgment of the plagiarist's appetite. If we accept his judgment, we will find his public display of the plagiarist extremely effective. Its repetitiousness, the metrical punctuation of its repeated action, especially the couplet break that separates the simple statement of the figure from the hoggish enrichment of it, the generally emphatic metrical definition of its thought, and the emphasis of rhyme broaden the circle of understanders of Rochester's attack — quite far enough so that his circle includes many members of society who will be offended by his language.

Pope revised Donne's passage as follows:

> Wretched indeed! but far more wretched yet
> Is he who makes his meal on others wit:
> 'Tis changed no doubt from what it was before,
> His rank digestion makes it wit no more:
> Sense, past thro' him, no longer is the same,
> For food digested takes another name.

Rochester clearly enough marks a halfway point between Donne, who simply excluded society at large from his satire, and Pope, who politely invited society at large to consider every step, every term, and every figure in his.

To suggest the affinity between Rochester and Pope on a broader scale, we may notice that Rochester's "Satire against Mankind" addresses almost exactly the same audience as Pope's *Essay on Man*, that Rochester counters the attitudes of vanity and skepticism, much as Pope does those of pride and reason in the *Essay*, and that Rochester endures an interruption by a speaker of conventional feelings much as Pope will do in many of his later essays and epistles. We might also notice that both Rochester and Pope in their universal considerations of humankind depend on ordinary sense experience as the basis of their judgments and that they take as a chief duty the reduction of human pride. Turning to other poems by Rochester — to "A Very Heroical Epistle," the "Prologue spoken at Whitehall," and the "Letter from Artemisa to Cloe," for instance — we may acknowledge the range and pointedness of his social address. In each of these poems Rochester has defined a narrow mode of social address and, in developing it, suggested a much broader perimeter of social attention — much as Pope will do in his *Epistle to Dr. Arbuthnot*, in his "Epistle II. To a Lady," and, indeed, in all his epistolary poems.

Sheffield, in his most famous poem, his "Essay upon Satire," is at least as close to Pope as Rochester is.[7] He makes the same kind of appeal to an educated class, to all gentlemen of educated good sense, that Pope will address, for instance, in his *Essay on Criticism*. Sheffield precedes Pope, again, in the explicit dislike of pedants, of specialists, and in the insistence on public elegance and grace. He handles the couplet, correspondingly, in a fashion both conversationally easy and, at the same time, epigrammatic — always in range of the bon mot that describes a peak in polite discourse. In describing ancient satirists, for instance, Sheffield writes:

> Some did all folly with just sharpness blame,
> Whilst others laugh'd and scorn'd 'em into shame.
> But of these two the last succeeded best,
> As men aim rightest when they shoot in jest.

One notices here the sharpness of the closure; its use in the first couplet to define an opposition and in the second, an analogy; its combination of conversational ease and epigrammatic finality. In the last line, especially, we find a precision of figurative definition articulated with a conversational easiness which will characterize Pope throughout his career. The figure of the hunt, especially of a gentlemen's hunt, augments the achievement of elegant precision as it will do when it is produced, marvellously extended and refined, at the opening of Pope's *Essay on Man*.

---

[7] Dryden's collaboration in the *Essay*, which has long been acknowledged [see, for example, Johnson's *Lives*, in *Works*, IX, 216; and George Noyes and Herman Mead, *"An Essay upon Satyr," University of California Publications in English*, VII, 3 (1939–50), pp. 139–56], does not alter my point, since the poem is consonant with the generally social tone of Sheffield's style. The tactful and politic Dryden, who may have added more than Noyes and Mead allow, especially to the figurative pungency of the poem, simply caught and augmented the style as Sheffield had inaugurated it. Dryden clearly understood the essentially social quality of Buckingham's (that is, Zimri's) public conduct; he might surely have seen Shaftesbury both as a political figure and, when prompted by Sheffield, as a social figure.

A comparison of Sheffield with Dryden will also illuminate this minor poet's social deployment of the couplet. We may particularly compare his portrait of Shaftesbury [8] with the Achitophel portrait of Shaftesbury by Dryden. Sheffield's portrait is composed of short, epigrammatic periods each of which indicates a witty judgment, a laugh at Shaftesbury's expense — rather than Dryden's great sweep of evidence and his single profoundly articulated condemnation. Sheffield forces us to recognize not the national danger posed by this wily, ambitious politician, but the follies, the absurd incongruities of bearing, which compromise his social respectability. The incongruity between Shaftesbury's physical weakness and his mental force makes Sheffield exclaim, "What gravity can hold from laughing out." This couplet-defined assertion of Shaftesbury's ambivalence of character and the demeaning figure comparing Shaftesbury to a dog bring us remarkably close to Pope's portrait of Sporus. Dryden, we may remember, likened Shaftesbury to a dangerous pilot, a giant, and a demi-Satan. Here is Sheffield's dog figure:

> Will any Dog, that has his Teeth and Stones,
> Refin'dly leave his Bitches and his Bones,
> To turn a Wheel, and bark to be employ'd,
> While *Venus* is by Rival Dogs enjoy'd?
> Yet this vain man, to get a Statesman's Name,
> Forfeits his Friends, his Freedom, and his Fame.

The vignette of the dog, defined in two couplets whose subordinate pauses variously illuminate its elements and clarify their relationships, is, in the third couplet, focussed by way of satiric distinction on Shaftesbury. This merely "vain man," who wishes for a "Name," that is, of course, for social exaltation, is thus held up for social ridicule: he lacks even a dog's awareness of his own true interests. Thus does the social satirist dispose of the man Dryden recognized and attacked as a threat to the peace of all England.

The problem of Alexander Pope or, better perhaps, his opportunity was to combine the satiric force of Rochester and Sheffield with the polite correctness of Waller and Walsh: to combine, that is, a sharpness of attack with a courtesy of address. Pope began his career under the influence of Walsh, striving for correctness of meter and its concomitant politeness of address in the *Pastorals* and *Windsor Forest*. Their lucidity of

---

[8] Pp. 324–25 in this book.

statement, their elegance of utterance, their calculated short-windedness, and the accompanying simplicity of their thought all assure their making an ingratiating public appearance. But the adolescent genius had the tangier form of social address before him too — in the persons of William Wycherly, whose couplets he corrected as Walsh corrected his,[9] and John Sheffield, then Duke of Buckinghamshire, whose posthumous poems, in 1723, Pope would edit. It is to the development of Pope's style, to his achievement and then his refinement of this combination of the socially polite and the socially satiric strains of closed-couplet composition, that we must now turn our attention.

[9] *The Correspondence of Alexander Pope*, ed. George Sherburn (Oxford, 1956), I, 1–25.

IX

★★★★★★★★★★★★★★★★

THE HEROIC
COUPLET OF POPE

1. POPE'S CORRECTNESS

Here are two couplets of Pope's early poem, *Windsor Forest:*

> The Groves of *Eden*, vanish'd now so long,
> Live in Description, and look green in Song:
> *These*, were my Breast inspir'd with equal Flame,
> Like them in Beauty, should be like in Fame.

And here are the two couplets of Waller's "On St. James's Park," from which Pope's two couplets derived:

> Of the first Paradise there's nothing found;
> Plants set by Heav'n are vanished, and the ground;
> Yet the description lasts; who knows the fate
> Of lines that shall this Paradise relate? [1]

Pope's verses are not perfect, of course: "so long," although not purely an expletive, hardly required the emphatic end place of its line; "Song" and "Flame," again, are merely conventional terms; and the passage in general is a little mannered, a little stiff in its precision. But it is, nevertheless, beautifully composed. Waller had resorted to four short-winded statements, only the very briefest of which is in decent English, to achieve an imperfect definition of the complex parallel between Eden and a modern garden. He smudged the relationship between them, more-over, first, by reaching his rhetorical pivot only at the midpoint of his

---

[1] Pope had as an added model the tightly organized couplet from *Cooper's Hill* in which Denham, addressing the first builder of Windsor Castle, compared his unknown origins and his lasting honor with those of Homer: "Like him in birth, thou should'st be like in fame, / As thine his fate, if mine had been his Flame."

third line and, second, by shifting at this misplaced pivot from a statement to a question. One can only guess, finally, that Waller hopes his lines will give St. James's Park the literary immortality he has recognized in Eden. The youthful Pope, on the other hand, composed his pair of gardens in a pair of metrically equivalent syntactic thrusts, which allowed him, on the one hand, to underscore his hope for a final equivalency between them and, on the other, to define their present complexity of likenesses and differences.

Pope began his career, as this comparison shows, achieving with remarkable skill that emphatic combination of rhetoric and meter, called "correctness" by the Augustans, which his model, Edmund Waller, and his older friend, William Walsh, strove for, and which Walsh commended to him as the major concern of English letters. Pope's achievement was to extend this correctness of couplet composition so that he could turn the couplet from the elegant flatteries and imitations to which Waller and Walsh and he himself as a youth had been confined and focus it on the vital concerns of his life and his age.

We might particularize the correctness with which Pope began by considering this line-defined catalogue of desolations from *Windsor Forest*, which he wrote in his teens:

The Fields are ravish'd from th' industrious Swains,   65
From Men their Cities, and from Gods their Fanes:
The levell'd Towns with Weeds lie cover'd o'er,
The hollow Winds thro' naked Temples roar;
Round broken Columns clasping Ivy twin'd;
O'er Heaps of Ruin stalk'd the stately Hind;   70
The Fox obscene to gaping Tombs retires,
And savage Howlings fill the sacred Quires.

These lines, as stiffly closed and pointedly paralleled as they are, are not mechanically repetitious — as are similarly line-defined passages of description in Sandys and Waller. The corresponding items in lines 67 and 68, for instance, have been inverted, and, in the following couplet, the likeness of the two lines has been eased by the suspending of the second line's verb to the line end. One also notices the syntactic thrust within the first, the introductory, couplet, and the climactic force of the last, a couplet whose two line-defined items of description, fox and howlings, enjoy a causal connection. One might also study the line-defined catalogue of fish in this same poem (ll. 141–46) or, better still, compare it with the charmingly overflowing catalogue of fish in Ben Jonson's "To

Penshurst" (ll. 31–38). Such a comparison, however, must not, while illuminating the stiffness of Pope's early correctness, blind us to the fact that this passage, like the catalogue of desolations, has elements of variety and flexibility.

Pope's couplets in *An Essay on Criticism* are somewhat more flexible. They are also more strongly tied together in extracouplet patterns of thought. Of course, the couplets of *Windsor Forest* were tied together, as in the passage on the forest's beautiful variety (ll. 11–28), for instance, but not as significantly unified as most of the verse paragraphs in the *Essay*. Consider, for instance, this paragraph which develops the theme of man's intellectual limitations:

Nature to all things fix'd the Limits fit,
And wisely curb'd proud Man's pretending Wit:
As on the *Land* while *here* the *Ocean* gains,
In *other Parts* it leaves wide sandy Plains;   55
Thus in the *Soul* while *Memory* prevails,
The solid Pow'r of *Understanding* fails;
Where Beams of warm *Imagination* play,
The *Memory*'s soft Figures melt away.
One *Science* only will one *Genius* fit;   60
So *vast* is Art, so *narrow* Human Wit;
Not only bounded to *peculiar Arts*,
But oft in *those*, confin'd to *single Parts*.
Like Kings we lose the Conquests gain'd before,
By vain Ambition still to make them more: 65
Each might his *sev'ral Province* well command,
Wou'd all but *stoop* to what they *understand*.

The limitations of the individual human mind, after being generally stated in the first couplet, are demonstrated in two separate aspects: the first, that only one of a mind's several powers can be exercised at a time (ll. 54–59); the second, that a mind can encompass only a fraction of the total expanse of the humanly knowable (ll. 60–67). The couplets developing this system of exposition are, unluckily, stiffly closed, and their closure blurs the passage as a whole. If, for instance, the three couplets that describe the shifting powers of the mind had been bound together into one syntactic system — instead of being composed as three closed-couplet capsules, the pivotal pause between this aspect of the theme and the other would have been heightened, and each of the two more sharply outlined. Such a definition seems especially desirable since these two aspects of man's limited intelligence have not been bridged by a transition and since they have not been presented in the parallel form that might have asserted their actually parallel relationship — the first being introduced figuratively ("As on the *Land*") and the second directly ("One *Science* only"). Pope here is guilty to a smaller degree of Waller's besetting sin, that is, of writing with an imperfect overview of his material, and his reader must work to get clear on the pattern of his thoughts. Such a difficulty as Pope has left his reader, we may notice in passing, diminishes one major illusion of the *Essay*, the illusion of polite, conversational discourse. More on this point later. The passage is easier to follow, however, than it would have been if the order of its two major aspects were reversed: to introduce the first in a direct way and then, without a transition, to give a figurative representation of the second would smudge the passage impossibly. In preserving the outline of his argument, then, the youthful Pope shows some sensitivity to the problem of clarity in the supracouplet reaches of his thought. The famous 'Alps–learning' simile in this same early poem (ll. 219–32) further exemplifies this point.

Leaping forward about twenty years to the *Essay on Man*, we find in the mature Pope's supracouplet composition a remarkable new fluency and coherence. In this paragraph from it, for example, Pope develops a rather complex argument, first, that Heaven hides the future from all creatures and, second, that this is a good thing:

Heav'n from all creatures hides the book of Fate,
All but the page prescrib'd, their present state;
From brutes what men, from men what spirits know:
Or who could suffer Being here below?   80
The lamb thy riot dooms to bleed to-day,
Had he thy Reason, would he skip and play?
Pleas'd to the last, he crops the flow'ry food,
And licks the hand just rais'd to shed his blood.
Oh blindness to the future! kindly giv'n,   85
That each may fill the circle mark'd by Heav'n;
Who sees with equal eye, as God of all,
A hero perish, or a sparrow fall,
Atoms or systems into ruin hurl'd,
And now a bubble burst, and now a world.   90

In working out this argument, Pope has raised as many separate items of evidence as he did in describing the past desolation of Windsor Forest —

a passage we looked at above; but in the *Essay* he is able to manipulate the formal segments and pauses that had stiffened that earlier utterance. Two of his cases here, the blind lamb and its equally blind butcher, Pope has yoked together in a two-couplet vignette; then, after a transitional couplet which augments the theme of the creatures' blindness with that of divine kindliness, a couplet that is syntactically tied strongly to the rest of the passage, comes a set of six more cases or, rather, a set of three opposing pairs — all these metrically defined. It may indicate the rhetorical density of this passage to remark that it gives us along with the richness of detail we found in the desolation passage from *Windsor Forest* a broad two-part organization of the paragraph similar to that on man's intellectual limitations from *An Essay on Criticism* — with a fluency and coherence lacking in the former, and a clarity lacking in the latter. We may notice especially the climactic last line of this passage. By using it to balance "bubble" and "world," two examples of divine contemplation, whose disparity in size and substance explains our sense of them and whose likeness in shape and destiny explains God's, Pope has clinched his exposition of the difference between the apprehension of the creatures and that of their creator. By tying this balance into the four-line clause whose syntactic governor is the creator and into the six-line sentence which asserts the actual governance of the creator, Pope has allowed us briefly to see our situation from the vantage of divinity and thus to recognize the comprehensiveness and kindliness of the divine apprehension.

To conclude our survey of Pope's development of his metrical and rhetorical correctness, consider this passage from the first dialogue of his very late poem *Epilogue to the Satires*, describing the difference in Pope's eyes and in the eyes of the world between virtue and vice:

Let modest *Foster*, if he will, excell
Ten Metropolitans in preaching well;
A simple Quaker, or a Quaker's Wife,
Out-do *Landaffe*, in Doctrine — yea, in Life;
Let humble A L L E N, with an aukward Shame,   135
Do good by stealth, and blush to find it Fame.
Virtue may chuse the high or low Degree,
'Tis just alike to Virtue, and to me;
Dwell in a Monk, or light upon a King,
She's still the same, belov'd, contented thing.   140
Vice is undone, if she forgets her Birth,

And stoops from Angels to the Dregs of Earth:
But 'tis the *Fall* degrades her to a Whore;
Let *Greatness* own her, and she's mean no more:
Her Birth, her Beauty, Crowds and Courts confess,   145
Chaste Matrons praise her, and grave Bishops bless:
In golden Chains the willing World she draws,
And hers the Gospel is, and hers the Laws:
Mounts the Tribunal, lifts her scarlet head,
And sees pale Virtue carted in her stead!   150

We may notice, first, that Pope achieves here the same fluency and, indeed, the same combination of richly textured details and bipartite organization that we found in our quotation from *An Essay on Man*; and that he does so with the same closed-couplet correctness, the same perfect lucidity, and over a significantly greater span of utterance — ten couplets as opposed to seven. We might mention in connection with the lengths of the discursive spans, moreover, that we have not given the whole paragraph from the *Epilogue* as we did from the *Essay*.

Our quotation also shows an increase in discursive range: its first section, that on virtue, is developed in a highly informal, a talky, tone and by means of particular cases; its second section, that on vice, which counters the two couplets of generalized statement on virtue's integrity of nature (couplets of a more elevated tone than those preceding), presents in swelling and heroic cadences a pageant, a parade, of vice in social triumph. Our quotation closes by fitting virtue into this parade and thus unifying in one couplet, in one image, the contrasted topics of the whole passage. We know fully, although Pope has touched the different elements of his contrast in quite different ways, the relative positions in the eyes of society and in the poet's eyes of virtue and of vice. Consequently, we know both the contrasting natures of virtue and vice and the contrasting ethical standards of the poet and society.

So vividly and so centrally has Pope focussed his art in the *Epilogue* that he can depict his age — in the form of a normal and thus representative gentleman — advising him to go back to the more generalized and less vitally contested topics of his earlier work: "Alas! Alas! pray end what you began, / And write next winter more *Essays on Man*." Thus Pope has augmented the correctness with which his career began so as to give the lucid and pointed definitions which that correctness allowed to the most vexed and the most emotionally explosive concerns of his age — definitions more lucid and pointed, apparently, than his age could abide.

Pope's mature couplet style is characterized by a new density and a new flexibility in his individual couplets as much as by his increased power to enunciate couplet paragraphs. There are in Pope's mature verse, for instance, double antitheses within single lines: "Now high, now low, now Master up, now Miss"; "Wit that can creep, and Pride that licks the dust." Pope occasionally extended this doubling, this condensation of his rhetoric, over a whole couplet: "A Fop their Passion, but their Prize a Sot, / Alive, ridiculous, and dead, forgot!" But more often he played denser systems of rhetoric against more fluent ones — as in this couplet, for instance: "Eye Nature's walks, shoot Folly as it flies, / / And catch the manners living as they rise." Here, as one moves from a line that defines two parallel predicates to one that holds a third, one feels a lift and a freedom, a sense of the poet's power to respond to his material — without surrendering to it — by either condensing or expanding his utterance. There is also the reverse movement — "Is there a Parson, much be-mus'd in Beer, / A maudlin Poetess, a ryming Peer" — in which we see the poet take advantage of the syntactic terms and broad assertion of a relationship in his first line to double the weight of the second.

Pope augmented this impression of flexibility and movement with a wide range of oblique couplets, among which are these: "Then turn repentant, and his God adores / With the same spirit that he drinks and whores"; and "Thou gav'st that Ripeness, which so soon began, / And ceas'd so soon, he ne'er was Boy, nor Man." In the second of these oblique couplets one notices an antithesis between "began" and "ceas'd" which spans the line break. Such couplets are commonly integrated in larger sweeps of utterance so that none, by standing alone, weakens the impression of balance on which Pope's effects significantly depend. Take, for instance, the combined obliqueness and periodicity in the two-couplet description of the crone's last act (*Moral Essays*, I, 238–41) or, again, the striking obliqueness in the second couplet of the following passage, by which Pope particularized the difficulty of ascertaining a man's ruling passion:

> When Cataline by rapine swell'd his store,
> When Caesar made a noble dame a whore,
> In this the Lust, in that the Avarice
> Were means, not ends: Ambition was the vice.

Pope gets the impression of a balanced, perfectly controlled movement of thought in this single syntactic system with the vivid paralleling of Cataline and Caesar in his first couplet, and, at the same time, enjoys the emphasis his judgment of Cataline and Caesar receives by being wedged into the last half-line of his second couplet.

As this passage should suggest, one must study the individual couplets of Pope's mature poetry in their contexts to catch their full force and radiance — and sometimes, indeed, simply to understand them. The last couplet in the passage above, for instance, makes sense only when we know what its pronouns, "this" and "that," refer to, and it carries its full weight as an example of the difficulty in determining a man's true motives only when we consider it, first, in its paragraph (*Moral Essay*, I, 210–21) and, second, as an element in Pope's total awareness of the complexity of human motivation — an awareness which permeates virtually all of this essay.

This enrichment of Pope's couplet correctness, this weaving of closed couplets into more and more complex discursive webs, depended, first, on his extension of traditional couplet practices, chiefly those of parallelism and antithesis. The passages we have already examined, with their varieties of series and contrasts, sufficiently exemplify this point. The enrichment of Pope's couplet practice also depended, however, on a number of other devices. One of these is the extension of syntax, the extension of single sentences and clauses, to cover more than one couplet. Our quotations also exemplify this to some extent. But to recognize the reaches to which Pope could carry a single sentence, we should recollect the famous portrait of Atticus (*Arbuthnot*, ll. 193–214), a piece Pope tinkered with for many years. The first of its two sentences, which runs on for twenty-one of its twenty-two lines, accommodates, first, a variety of descriptive expansions — verbal, adjectival, and appositive — and, second, an interior expansion of its 'were–be' predication by a highly developed 'should' element. The representation of all this matter, the wedging of it, into the second half of the line — "Who but must laugh, if such a man there be?" — brings a remarkable sense of unity and focus to the indictment enunciated in this line's first half, a sense of unity which is heightened by the next line, the last of the passage — "Who would not weep, if Atticus were he?" — which exactly reverses the emotion with which we were just directed to view the whole system. The unity and compactness Pope imposed on his complex indictment of Atticus by weaving its many aspects into a single sentence thus allowed him to turn it this way and that, to toss it up and down, as though he were playing with a ball.

The equally famous portrait of Sporus (*Arbuthnot*, ll. 305–33) also enjoys an extensive syntactic binding, since much of it must be felt either to stand in apposition to "Bug" and "painted child" or to modify these terms. It is also unified by a kind of figurative web. "Bug," for instance, was a modification of "butterfly" in the preceding couplet, and is carried into the next with the term "buzzing"; the spaniel's failure to bite its game in the next couplet, again, connects it to the untasting bee above; and the spaniel's empty smiling is reflected later in the shallow, dimpling stream and later still in the hollow puppet. The term "Amphibious," to give further exemplification of this figurative web, catches the earlier "seesaw" descriptions of Sporus as well as the "familiar toad" earlier still in the passage and, augmented by these affinities, catches the reptilian cherub further on. Thus the discrete figures with which Pope described Sporus in one sharply defined couplet and couplet segment after the other blend together, cohere, and make one overwhelming impression: no matter how you look at him, the passage implies, Sporus is always the same shocking composite of external charm and inner corruption.

Pope found many other ways besides these of drawing his sharply individuated couplets into richly integrated systems. There is, for instance, the continuity of allusion such as that in the Midas passage of the *Epistle to Dr. Arbuthnot* (ll. 69–82). More common than this is the dramatic vignette: *Moral Essay I* closes on a series of these. There is, for instance, the three-couplet drama between the miserly Euclio and his attorney:

> 'I give and I devise, (old Euclio said,
> And sigh'd) My lands and tenements to Ned.'
> Your money, Sir? 'My money, Sir, what all?
> Why, — if I must — (then wept) I give it Paul.'
> The Manor, Sir? — 'The Manor! hold,' he cry'd,
> 'Not that, — I cannot part with that' — and dy'd.

The varieties of couplet punctuation define every step of the action. Each of Euclio's three statements is focussed in its own couplet, and each couplet makes use of its first-line break and its caesuras to punctuate the statement it defines. Th midpoint of the third line, for instance, separates the lawyer's prompting from Euclio's response, and the pause at the end of this line separates Euclio's first response, a question, from his second, the statement of bequest. At the same time the little drama develops — from sighs, to tears, to mortal agony and death. This development obviously unifies the three couplets into one single poetic statement, a statement, however, whose elements are brilliantly defined and illuminated.

This passage from the *Epistle to Dr. Arbuthnot* presents us with a more complex composition of the same kind:

Bless me! a Packet. — ' 'Tis a stranger sues,   55
A Virgin Tragedy, an Orphan Muse.'
If I dislike it, 'Furies, death and rage!'
If I approve, 'Commend it to the Stage.'
There (thank my Stars) my whole Commission ends,
The Play'rs and I are, luckily, no friends.   60
Fir'd that the House reject him, ' 'Sdeath I'll print it
And shame the Fools — your Int'rest, Sir, with *Lintot*.'
Lintot, dull rogue! will think your price too much.
'Not Sir, if you revise it, and retouch.'
All my demurrs but double his attacks,   65
At last he whispers 'Do, and we go snacks.'
Glad of a quarrel, strait I clap the door,
Sir, let me see your works and you no more.

What we have here is a remarkably compact two-act comedy. Its first act
(ll. 55–60) shows Pope coming to agree to recommend the young
poet's "Virgin Tragedy" to the players; its second presents the return of
the young poet after his tragedy has been hooted off the stage. The open-
ing of the second act, with the young poet's return, gives a nice comic
shock, since Pope had concluded the first act by remarking with a sigh of
relief that he would never have to help that fellow again.[2] The dramatic
continuity in such passages as this, once again, binds their separate cou-
plets into larger discursive systems, not, however, at the sacrifice of cou-
plet correctness. The varieties of closed-couplet punctuation, indeed,
allow Pope to compose dramatic confrontations like this one in the
extremely narrow confines his broader discursive purposes required and
to present them with the sharpness, the emphasis, and the detachment
on which their comic effects depend.

   Such dramatic vignettes as the two we have discussed are quite com-
mon in Pope's later poems. But still more common as an element of
larger poetic unity and, indeed, quite central to Pope's maturing art is
the persistent conversational movement one finds in all of the late essays
and epistles — a movement in which the dramatic vignettes, the allusive
systems, and the great satiric portraits are, of course, embedded. From
the *Moral Essays* on, the impression of conversation is strong enough to

---

[2] Actually my description oversimplifies this passage: notice, for example, that
lines 57–58 must be understood as representing not Pope's speech but the internal
workings of his mind, as must the expression "dull rogue" in line 63, and that
line 65 *implies* a series of dramatic exchanges, a series whose particulars we can
easily imagine, rather than *rendering* it.

explain the course and the shape of Pope's poems and to establish for each a pervasive, unifying tone. Dr. Arbuthnot's interruptions of Pope's discourse with him cut off some topics with a scandalized exclamation and modify the progress and the force of others. And the two dialogues of the *Epilogue to the Satires* are almost completely determined by the dismayed or disapproving interruptions of his friends and by Pope's effort to preserve their comfort and approval. Even the earlier *Moral Essay II*, whose addressee, Mrs. Blount, only once actually interrupts its flow, derives its special tone and a number of its transitions from the speaker's awareness of her presence as his conversational correspondent. The impression of conversation is, however, so persistent and so important an aspect of Pope's poetry that its development, which is as great as the development of Pope's metrical correctness, and its expressive value must be treated separately.

Before turning to this, the second major element in our study of Pope's couplet, perhaps I can suggest the expressive force of the first, that is, Pope's correctness of metrical practice. The mere regularity and polish of the couplet, as Pope achieved it from the beginning, carries a philosophical, a didactic, implication: that it is necessary for limits to be put on human intellectual ambitions and, contrariwise, that the human mind, working within its proper limits, has tremendous powers: "Each might his several Province well command, / Would all but stoop to what they understand." The explicit teaching of this couplet, variations of which crop up again and again in Pope, dwells implicitly in all his couplet practice. If a man will confine himself to the limited area of his understanding, he can make extremely precise distinctions between the elements of his thought; he can balance them as they oppose one another, and line them up as they agree; he can modify old general principles by redefining them or by squaring them with new evidence; and he can formulate new principles as his experience warrants them. In short, he can organize and judge the totality of his knowledge and derive from it a lucid and sufficient understanding of his condition, his duties, and his destiny. Pope's metrical practice, even when he exercises it on Eloisa's lost love or on Belinda's coquetry, indicates the view that the mysterious ways of God can be vindicated and the proper ways of man discovered.

2. Pope's Politeness

Pope focussed this teaching, implicit in his metrical practice, on society, on an audience of ladies and gentlemen in the aspect of polite intercourse. The impression of this social milieu in which his individual speakers perform is created primarily by the conversational style and movement of their discourse and, in his later poetry, by an explicit conversational give-and-take between each speaker and a gentleman or lady of the speaker's acquaintance. This conversational style, which was cultivated by virtually all the Augustan writers under the general heading of "politeness," is, of course, most striking in Pope's many essays and epistles, but its presence illuminates, although to a less extent, *The Rape of the Lock* and *The Dunciad*.

Conversation, which was the necessary condition of Martial's epigrams and, only a little less so, of Ovid's elegies, was imposed on the English decasyllabic couplet, as we have seen, in the same operation that brought to the native form the metrical practices of these Latin poets. It remained a natural and persistent element of the form throughout its development — sounding clear in such great couplet poets as Donne, Jonson, and Dryden, fading away in the preconceived pleasantries of Waller and Walsh, but always accessible to a couplet poet and, as things were to turn out, always necessary to the utterance of great couplet poetry. Thus Pope inherited it as he inherited his meter but, since his primary models were Waller and Walsh, in an attenuated form. To develop this aspect of his form and to derive its expressive benefits were, like his development and expressive application of his meter, the work of a lifetime.

Pope's speech tone was, from the first, conversational, polite, and not, like Dryden's, oratorical. It was the medium of graceful retirement, of easy and elegant society. This impression is constant from the time of *Windsor Forest*, in which Pope congratulates Trumbull on his retirement, through the *Essay on Man*, which opens with Pope's advising Bolingbroke on the pleasures and uses of his retirement, and on through his complaint in his *Epistle to Dr. Arbuthnot*, on the interruptions of his own retirement.

Lord Lansdowne, whom Pope was to call "Granville the polite," had celebrated retirement — his own, Cato's, and that of other great men — in "An Address to Mrs. Elizabeth Higgons, Occasioned by her Verses to the Poet, intreating him to Return to Public Life, written in the year 1690."[3] The Glorious Revolution and the eventual Whig ascendency no doubt had much to do with giving this attitude, this choice of political aloofness, a broad currency among English aristocrats and English

---

[3] Pp. 355–57 in this book.

gentlemen of a Tory leaning, but it is rooted in English and Latin literary tradition. One can find it stated, for example, in a couple of Martial's epigrams that the retiring Abraham Cowley translated soon after the Restoration.[4] This attitude in general is one of withdrawal from public life, that is, from the turbulent political world of Dryden, or, more positively, one of removal to what we still understand as private life, that is, to the quiet and courtesy of the social world. Pope's essays and epistles provide us with the most brilliant literary expression of it and of the world of social intercourse to which it leads.

His mature essays and epistles project two rings of social intercourse, two rings of social life: the first an intimate one comprised of Pope and St. John Bolingbroke, say, or of Pope and Dr. Arbuthnot; the second a broad one including the whole polite world. In this passage from the *Epistle to Dr. Arbuthnot*, for instance, Pope uses the friend's interruption to insist on the second and broader, as well as the first, circle of social address:

> Does not one Table *Bavius* still admit?
> Still to one Bishop *Philips* seem a Wit?
> Still *Sapho* — 'Hold! for God's-sake you'll offend.
> No names — be calm — learn Prudence of a Friend:
> I too could write, and I am twice as tall,
> But Foes like these!' — One Flatt'rer's worse than all.

Dr. Arbuthnot's fear that the speaker will offend asserts the wider audience of the speaker's words so that we catch his response, "One Flatt'rer's worse than all," as a statement of widely public defiance. This double ring of social attention, which the poets contemporary with Pope also achieved to varying degrees, stood out more and more clearly as he developed and matured.

Closure, which is more decisively marked by Pope than by Dryden, has several values as an element of such social poetry. First, it promotes clarity, making the discourse widely and easily understandable — as virtually every one of Pope's couplets shows. Second, it punctuates the speaker's smart epigrammatic turn, his tendency to the bon mot, which is, as Boswell's *Life of Johnson* exemplifies over and over again, the climax of social conversation. Third, closure suggests the speaker's courteous brevity, his willingness to stop or to change course in response to his company. As we consider the first and third of these points, we can

---

[4] Pp. 299–300 in this book.

see how correctness and politeness might seem almost synonymous terms to an Augustan poet.

Every close and, indeed, every pause in Pope's late couplets, to expand on the third point, become susceptible to a courteous shifting of statement and, indeed, to an actual interruption by the speaker's correspondent. In the passage quoted just above, for instance, the caesura of the line in which the friend interrupts, "Still *Sapho* — 'Hold! for God's-sake you'll offend," comes after the friend's first word; the first half-line thus unites and heightens the disagreement between the two speakers, and the caesura separates the friend's cry of alarm — thus intensifying it — from its explanation. Or take the third line of the following passage from the *Epilogue to the Satires*:

Who starv'd a Sister, who forswore a Debt,
I never nam'd — the Town's enquiring yet.
The pois'ning Dame — *Fr.* You mean — *P.* I don't. — *Fr.* You do.
P. See! now I keep the Secret, and not you.

Pope makes all the formal segments of his measure — right down to its iambic feet — help him indicate the intensity with which this speaker observes his social immersion.

The tremendously discursive organization of Pope's essays and epistles reinforces this use of the closed couplet to indicate the poet's social responsiveness. We might remember the elaborate "Arguments" Pope affixed as guides to the separate epistles of *An Essay on Man* or his three-part outline to *An Essay on Criticism*. Here, for example, is his outline of Part III of the earlier work:

> *Rules for the* Conduct *of* Manners *in a Critic,* I. Candour, v 563. Modesty, v 566. Good-breeding, v 572. Sincerity, *and* Freedom *of Advice,* v 578. 2. *When one's Counsel is to be restrained,* v 584. *Character of an* incorrigible Poet, v 600. *And of an* impertinent Critic, v 610, *&c. Character of a* good Critic, v 629. *The* History *of* Criticism, *and Characters of the best Critics,* Aristotle, v 645. Horace, v 653. Dionysius, v 665. Petronius, v 667. Quintilian, v 670. Longinus, v 675. *Of the Decay of Criticism, and its Revival.* Erasmus, v 693. Vida, v 705. Boileau, v 714. *Lord* Roscommon, *&c* v 725. *Conclusion.*

As this outline indicates, Part III modulates from a set of rules, which are not perfectly parallel in articulation or equivalent in development, to a set of variously opposed characters, to an eclectic history. Part II of this *Essay* is equally discursive but in a totally different way: until rather near its end, it is a long catalogue of hindrances to true judgment, ten of them in all, the third of which, "Judging by parts," is subdivided and developed over fifty lines, and the seventh of which, "Singularity," gets only six. The movements of the later essays and epistles, as one will discover who consults the outlines Pope provided to his *Moral Essays* or who makes his own outline to *An Epistle to Dr. Arbuthnot,* are even less susceptible to pyramidal or numerical explanations.

This discursiveness, which is the rule in all of Pope's essays and epistles, this lack of an ironbound structure, suggests the ease, the graceful associative quality of polite talk. Such an unforced, such a flexible, notion of topics and arguments and evidence is naturally capable of being interrupted or amended, extended or cut off short without loss of order and coherence. It is, of course, the couplet, with its persistent impression of intelligence and control, that allows the poet to organize in so easy and polite a way without giving the impression of mental weakness or confusion. Thus the closed couplet, with its close-grained system of pauses, allows the poet to suggest a persistent responsiveness to his society, a persistent readiness to change course in order to accommodate his interlocutors' questions and doubts. And, with its impression of continuous order and control, it allows him a freedom in the larger ranges of his utterance by which this impression of his social responsiveness is augmented.

This impression, once again, although it is an essential aspect of Pope's style, becomes more richly developed and forcefully articulated in the late essays and epistles, most richly and forcefully of all in the *Epilogue to the Satires* of 1738. The address of Pope's early poems is generalized and imprecise. *Windsor Forest* opens, indeed, with an address to the forest and its "Sylvan Maids." Lord Lansdowne, to whom the poem is dedicated, is referred to only obliquely, in the third person, as the instigator of the piece. Compliments to Sir William Trumbull and Queen Anne are also referentially phrased in the third person. The *Essay on Criticism,* although it lacks a clear interlocutor, that is to say, an intimate conversational circle, makes a more pointed social address. The repeated use of "our," especially in the opening lines, the elegant watch simile (ll. 9–10), and the mention of fools exposing themselves to public scorn (ll. 7–8) all help project the broad circle of social solicitation.

The speaker of *An Essay on Criticism* may, nevertheless, strike us the way he struck Pope's older contemporary, John Dennis,[5] as an extremely

---

[5] "Reflections on *An Essay upon Criticism,*" in *The Critical Works,* ed. E. N. Hooker (Baltimore, 1939), I, esp. 413–15.

arrogant young man. This is because Pope persistently used the couplet here, as in his youthful poetry generally, as an epigrammatic device and failed to capitalize on its chances for social courtesy. No one interrupts the speaker of this poem, we may remember. No matter how complex or controversial the topic, its style suggests, this young man can snap it shut. The actual difficulty, the imprecision, of some of his formulations, such as that on the limitedness of human intelligence, augments this impression of the speaker's youthful arrogance; the positiveness, the sharpness of the utterance, coupled with this imperfect clarity, presents him to us as a young man who understands things somehow better than we can or, possibly, as one whose own understanding is less great than his confidence.

In his later poetry, as the examples of it which we have examined make clear, Pope greatly increased the politeness of his utterance, doing so, however, without sacrificing its epigrammatic uses. The greater economy of actually crystallized epigrams in the later poetry and the increased contextual support with which Pope came to enunciate them give this aspect of his poetry a new emphasis, a new force. And so does the politeness, the regard for others' feelings and opinions with which these strokes are delivered. "I fain wou'd please you, if I knew with what," says the speaker of Pope's last poem of social address, the *Epilogue to the Satires*. It is his effort to find ways of pleasing society which are consonant with the truth and his conscience — an effort which finally becomes hopeless in the *Epilogue* — that makes the strokes he lays on it so comprehensive and stinging. Pope's later poetry, which became more and more focussed on the inhabitants of society and on society itself, thus became at once more polite in its social solicitations and more incisive in its social commentary — more incisive because more polite.

The expressive force of Pope's conversational politeness, that is, of his social solicitation, can be generally described. It suggests both the best mode of man's efforts to command his limited knowledge and the nature of this knowledge as well. The knowledge proper and relevant to man is that which he can share with others, which he can discuss and refine in social intercourse. Virtually all of Pope's own arguments are, as they must be, *ad hominem* arguments, and his conclusions are, likewise, socially viable, socially acceptable statements. He attempts, for instance, to cajole Mrs. Fermor into recognizing the difference between hearts and necklaces and the greater social utility of virtue to beauty; he clears his own understanding on the divine plan and the divine benevolence by expatiating on man and the universe with St. John Bolingbroke, his guide, philosopher, and friend; he works toward an agreement with Lord Bathurst on the use of riches, with Mrs. Blount on the characters of women, and with Dr. Arbuthnot on the nature of his own career. His effort throughout is to reach an agreement with each of his correspondents, a common sense of their common interest, and, in doing so, to articulate opinions to which the world in general will agree. To particularize this further: if he and Lord Bathurst can come to an agreement on the uses of wealth, if he and Mrs. Blount can come to an agreement on the characters of women, if he and Dr. Arbuthnot can come to an agreement on the nature of his career, then ladies and gentlemen all over England may be expected to be agreeable too.

Pope's design of a socially derived common sense is most neatly indicated in the opening of *Moral Essay II*, to Mrs. Blount: "Nothing so true as what you once let fall, / 'Most Women have no Characters at all.' " This flattering dependence on a casual remark of Mrs. Blount naturally implicates her in all the sharp remarks Pope is about to let fall on other members of her sex and on her sex in general. There are similarly apposite conversational openings to *Moral Essay III*, in which Pope addresses his remarks on riches to a rich friend, and to "The First Satire of the Second Book of Horace Imitated," in which he turns to a friend in the legal profession for advice on the charges of libel that seem to threaten his satiric writings. The end of a poem usually reveals most clearly Pope's confidence that he has achieved an agreement with his correspondent and extended it to society at large. "One truth is clear," he says at the close of the first epistle of the *Essay on Man*. Again, he and Arbuthnot agree at the close of their conversation — it hardly matters which one says it — "Thus far was right." He has little agreement to disclose at the end of the *Epilogue to the Satires* — little common sense to define. But there, as in earlier poems, Pope indicates what common sense he has been able to work out: none at the end of this poem's "Dialogue I," and none, except at the cost of his making an impossible retreat, at the end of its "Dialogue II." It is by recognizing the failure of common sense in these poems of social address, the last such poems Pope ever wrote, that we can understand their essentially anguished brilliance and the painful propriety of their being described as an *Epilogue to the Satires*.

The projection of a social milieu with its implications of common evidence and common sense is, of course, a persistent literary property of the Augustan Age. Fielding made it the constant ground of *Tom Jones* and Sterne, of *Tristram Shandy*; [6] Boswell conjured it only less potently than these great novelists as the atmosphere of his *Life of Johnson*. Swift, similarly, resorted to a conversation as the ground for the commonsensical King of Brobdingnag's judgment of mankind — a judgment which Gulliver, who had presented all the evidence for it, could not withstand. Bishop Berkeley, again, posed his late work *Alciphron* and his early *Three Dialogues between Hylas and Philonous* in this polite, conversational form. Early in the *Dialogues*, Hylas says, "My thoughts always flow more easily in conversation with a friend, than when I am alone." And Philonous, who perfectly agrees, goes on to praise "the plain dictates of nature and common sense." Both Hylas and Philonous, moreover, respect the needs and the notions of "the vulgar" — that is, of society in general as opposed to the philosophers, and they square each step in their discourse with vulgar opinion. Thus Berkeley recognizes and responds to the two circles of society we have described in Pope. For all these great Augustan writers, common conversation — the common conversation of polite, well-read ladies and gentlemen — was the proper testing ground for sense and reason. Truth, that truth which is necessary and proper for mankind, is not found in the dark solitude of the library or in the singular involutions of the secret soul, or in those vaporous intuitions that lie too deep for expression; truth is the product of spirited but lucid talk between plain, sensible men — plain, sensible men like Berkeley, Fielding, Johnson, and, of course, Pope. Pope's later essays and epistles, which give us the most brilliant and pointed representations of the processes of common sense, thus epitomize the Augustan Age.

Let us pause to make a general comparison between the two great closed-couplet styles in our literature. Dryden's articulation of this form projected the impression that all sides of the most urgent, the most divisive, political argument could be comprehended by sensible men of all factions; that all the arguments could be represented; that, with the proper spirit of national solidarity and the proper feeling for compromise and moderation, a political consensus could be achieved; and that the ground of a bloodless national adjustment could be found. Pope's couplets project a confidence that a conversational sharing of intelligence, that a courteous responsiveness to the polite attention of ladies and gentlemen will allow one of their number to refine upon their various opin-

---

[6] See my book, *Laurence Sterne* (New York, 1965), esp. pp. 21–87, for a discussion of the conversational address and the conversational implications of *Tristram Shandy*.

ions and by doing so achieve a harmonious statement, a general agreement on all of life's great problems — even to the point of vindicating God's ways to man. The difference between the public ear and the private ear, as F. R. Leavis describes it,[7] is of the essence to Pope, but not to Dryden. The political poet derives most of his special force as a poet from the sense he gives of urgent public disagreements. His great sweep of verse suggests the national danger that prompts every political compromise and the tremendous complexity involved in reaching a compromise. What he himself thinks, which is a crucial element in the social poetry of Pope, is, obviously, irrelevant, improper. He must not write as severely as he can, as severely as the secret truths in his heart might prompt him to do; rather, he must confine himself to those issues he and his party share, those issues of public conflict between themselves and the members of other parties, and he must define or suggest the grounds on which those issues can be resolved. Pope, on the other hand, must represent as deeply as possible those elements in his own thoughts, those annoyances and reservations and doubts — along with the experiences and observations underlying them — which separate or might separate him from society at large. These he must publicize as precisely, but also as tentatively and courteously, as possible, submitting them for scrutiny to the friends and, as he understood, the foes who might question them. Dryden conveys a sense of major national urgency and danger as the background of his oratorical efforts; Pope conveys, as the background of his conversational efforts, first, a fear of insults or slander or public anger, in short, of social rejection and, second, a fear that society may not think right on the great issues of its concern.

3. The Expressive Value of Pope's Couplet Practice

We have discussed Pope's couplet practice under two aspects, its metrical correctness and its conversational politeness, describing the development and the expressive force of each. Actually, of course, Pope's practice presents us with one great style and one great vision. We can describe this vision in general as that of unity in diversity, of order in variety, of actual pattern in apparent chaos, or, to use an ancient and venerable expression, of a *concors discordia rerum*.[8] Each aspect of Pope's

---

[7] *Revaluation* (London, 1949), pp. 31–33.

[8] I have been partially anticipated in thus affixing this ancient notion to Pope's heroic couplet style by two or three scholars: by Earl Wasserman, *The Subtler Language* (Baltimore, 1959), esp. pp. 53–82 and 103–13, who was chiefly concerned, however, to describe it in the couplets of Denham; by Maynard Mack, in his edition of *An Essay on Man* (London, 1950), p. xxxiv; and by Reuben Brower, *The Fields of Light* (New York, 1951), pp. 138–63.

style represents an aspect of this vision. Pope's metrical practice projects his faith in a metaphysical harmony, that is, in a harmony in nature: each of his poems is thus an attempt to comprehend one element of natural diversity and complexity and to articulate the principles that govern it, the pattern that dwells in it. Pope's conversational practice projects his confidence in a social harmony, in a harmony abiding in the conversation and in the minds of men; common sense was the Augustan expression for this harmony. Pope's correctness, then, is his reflection of the harmony in nature, and his politeness, the means by which he can promote a harmony among men.

Each of his poems is thus an attempt to comprehend one element of observable natural diversity and complexity — that diversity, say, in the groves of Windsor, the types of literary criticism, or the characters of men — and to reach a sense of its general harmony, a sense which all ladies and gentlemen can hold in common. The concern with the harmonies in nature, that is, with the harmonies in the subject matter he takes up, is Pope's chief interest in his early poems; the concern with social harmony, which Pope seems almost to have taken for granted until *An Essay on Man*, that is, with the harmony between himself and his friends and between himself and society at large, becomes increasingly at issue in the later ones. Both, however, dwell together as the twin halves of one faith and of one persistent literary ambition in virtually all of Pope's major poems.

In *Windsor Forest* the youthful Pope, following Sir John Denham, enunciated his vision of a *concors discordia rerum* as he found it in nature:

> Here Hills and Vales, the Woodland and the Plain,
> Here Earth and Water seem to strive again,
> Not *Chaos*-like together crush'd and bruis'd,
> But as the World, harmoniously confus'd:
> Where Order in Variety we see,
> And where, tho' all things differ, all agree.
> Here waving Groves a checquer'd Scene display,
> And part admit and part exclude the Day;
> As some coy Nymph her Lover's warm Address
> Nor quite indulges, nor can quite repress.
> There, interspers'd in Lawns and opening Glades,
> Thin Trees arise that shun each others Shades.
> Here in full Light the russet Plains extend;
> There wrapt in Clouds the blueish Hills ascend:

> Ev'n the wild Heath displays her Purple Dies,
> And 'midst the Desart fruitful Fields arise,
> That crown'd with tufted Trees and springing Corn,
> Like verdant Isles the sable Waste adorn.

The timid observation of the couplet's mechanical closes and balances in these lines reduces the expressive reinforcement the form has obviously been asked to give to the poet's vision. Pope may have seen harmony between lawns and glades, between light and shade, between earth and water simply because he did not see them very precisely. We know, at any rate, that the range of nature is much greater than the range of the poet's descriptive medium; that its variety, its apparent confusion, is much greater than such a form of description can indicate. Thus we doubt the poet's assertion of this natural harmony.

But as Pope's couplets encompass a richer array of evidence — as he makes them more individually various, making them, that is, more responsive to nature's varieties, and weaves them into more and more complex webs of discourse, making them, that is, more reflective of nature's complexity — they come more and more adequately to express the varieties and the complex connections of things. The verse's assertion of an abiding harmony in each subject it takes up thus becomes more convincing, more profound. Compare, for instance, this description of a harmony between reason and self-love, which comes from *An Essay on Man*, with the *Windsor Forest* passage just above:

> Two Principles in human nature reign;
> Self-love, to urge, and Reason, to restrain;
> Nor this a good, nor that a bad we call,
> Each works its end, to move or govern all:
> And to their proper operation still,
> Ascribe all Good; to their improper, Ill.
>   Self-love, the spring of motion, acts the soul;
> Reason's comparing balance rules the whole.
> Man, but for that, no action could attend,
> And, but for this, were active to no end;
> Fix'd like a plant on his peculiar spot,
> To draw nutrition, propagate, and rot;
> Or, meteor-like, flame lawless thro' the void,
> Destroying others, by himself destroy'd.

An Essay on Man is dedicated throughout to convincing society that "All Discord [is] Harmony, not understood," or, more precisely, to bringing into the focus of common sense the certainty that creation entire, despite the many observable imperfections of the human condition, is perfect and good. And with the helpful concurrence of his guide, philosopher, and friend, Pope found it possible to do this. One human imperfection after another could be resolved, and, in the process, sufficient principles of human life and action could be established. Only pride, the one aspect of society at large to which Pope seriously attended in this poem, blocked the achievement of the common sense Pope was enunciating.

The later poems, however, show Pope's increasing awareness of the difficulties in reaching the perfectly harmonious resolution of this double ground of discord, first, that in the nature of things and, second, that in the minds of ladies and gentlemen.

We may recall the remarkable variety of modifications with which Pope articulates the common principle of the ruling passion in the first *Moral Essay*. His sensitivity to the diversity of human character, a sensitivity recognizable in the tremendous variety of the couplets and couplet systems with which Pope expressed it, forces him to give the narrowest imaginable range to this one principle by which all human differences can be brought to bear — reducing its practical application, finally, to each person only at the point of his death. The scope of this one harmonious principle, once Pope has reconciled it to the discordancies of individual human life, is so narrow as to make it virtually useless as a piece of common human knowledge. We may also think of the second *Moral Essay*, that on the characters of women, in which Pope begins, at least, by attempting to form his abiding principle from the fact that no principle will serve, that the discordancies in feminine character are irreducible.

On the other hand, all the separate portraits and, indeed, all the separate couplets show how in every individual case, how at every single moment, a pattern, a harmony, can be described:

> Rufa, whose eye quick-glancing o'er the Park,
> Attracts each light gay meteor of a Spark,
> Agrees as ill with Rufa studying Locke,
> As Sappho's diamonds with her dirty smock,
> Or Sappho at her toilet's greasy task,
> With Sappho fragrant at an ev'ning Mask:
> So morning Insects that in muck begun,
> Shine, buzz, and fly-blow in the setting sun.

Rufa's shift from flirtation to philosophy can be seen, first of all, as a pattern of antithesis. In her absurd shiftiness of mind, moreover, she harmonizes with Sappho's absurd shiftiness in physical appearance. And both are in some kind of harmony, Rufa by way of Sappho, with the shifting appearances of sparkling bugs.

There is, of course, a further harmony in this passage and, indeed, in all the *Moral Essays*, and that is the social harmony with which it is enunciated, the agreement between the speaker and his interlocutors on the justness of his discourse. Pope has frozen the absurd diversity of Rufa and Sappho into a single satiric definition which he and Mrs. Blount and which, by natural extension, all ladies and gentlemen may share. The diversities of Atticus in the *Epistle to Dr. Arbuthnot*, likewise, the poet will resolve into the harmony of social agreement: "Who would not laugh if such a man there be? / Who would not weep if Atticus were he?" And even the horrid ambivalencies of Sporus, which Dr. Arbuthnot advised Pope to avoid, the poet may be able to satirize with social approval. He can hope to define the elements of this gilded bug so as to demonstrate that it is made throughout of "parts that none will trust."

However, all his later essays and epistles, those poems in which the poet attempts to maintain a harmony between social politeness and social satire, reveal Pope's poetic practice and his poetic vision under virtually explosive pressure. In the latest of these, the *Epilogue to the Satires*, Pope defines in his most richly composed social utterance a final disharmony between himself and society, a disharmony between his insistence on the truth and society's incurable hypocrisy. In its second and last dialogue he confronts an interlocutor who is both a normally uncritical gentleman of the poet's acquaintance and the epitome of complacent social hypocrisy and who, thus, embodies both rings of Pope's social solicitation. This dialogue is devoted throughout to the attempt of Pope and this representative of society to reach a common sense of Pope's social satire and of society itself — a hopeless attempt, as every word of the dialogue makes clear. This dialogue and thus the *Epilogue* ends with Pope's correspondent advising him to return to less incendiary topics, in particular to "more *Essays on Man*" — as if those who could not agree about the nature of man's social life could agree about the whole nature of man.

Thus at the end of his career, Pope reached beyond the implicit bounds of his form, devoting its harmonies to a demonstration, first, of the disharmony in his world between its words and its deeds, between its professions and its principles, and, second, of the consequent disharmony between his world and himself. This does not mean, of course, that he destroyed his form but, rather, that he tested it to and beyond the limits of its efficacy. In the process, he left behind him many great assertions of various harmonies in nature and many living achievements of great harmonies among men.

X

✦✦✦✦✦✦✦✦✦✦✦✦✦✦✦

THE COUPLET AFTER POPE

With Pope we have touched the highest point of all our greatness. He comprehended the total expressive power of the closed couplet, using its definitive correctness to cut into his age's most vital issues and using its social politeness to cut into his age's most vital condition. Indeed, he forced this form, as we have seen, beyond the limits of its efficacy, attempting to bring into harmonious definition a system of social practices and into harmonious agreement a set of social attitudes that could not be resolved. I wonder if it was not Pope's comprehension of the closed couplet, his virtual exhaustion of its potential, that Dr. Johnson recognized when, in contemplating Pope's achievement, he asserted that it would be "dangerous . . . to attempt any further improvement in versification." [1] Johnson, like Pope, believed in the closed couplet as the best medium for portraying polite conversation and in polite conversation as the best ground for pursuing the intellectual life, for considering mankind's most basic and persistent problems. Thus Johnson, if not Wordsworth, may well have thought of Pope as reaching and exploring the crest of Parnassus. After Pope, at all events, the expressive power of the couplet diminished.[2]

---

[1] "Alexander Pope," in *Lives of the Poets*, in *Works* (Troy, N. Y., 1903), x, 334.

[2] This diminution in the responsiveness and the range of the closed couplet is, of course, evident in the late poetry of Pope, especially in *Dunciad* IV. The celebrated Miltonic quality of that work is actually a kind of controlled perversion of the couplet, a painful insistence by Pope of the failure of common sense, of the failure of that climate in which men could refine their minds and their lives by conversation. "Fit audience . . . though few" suggests the proper attitude of the Miltonic style — even if Milton struck it in disappointment and defiance, but it signifies a tragic defeat for Pope, a dreadful abnegation of the faith on which his style had been built. The monolithic declamations of the pedagogues and scientists in *Dunciad* IV, each of them totally absorbed in his own work and in his own wisdom, and the tone of incontrovertible declaration in Pope's own descriptions of the encroaching darkness bespeak not an advance in his style but the collapse of its basic assumptions. It is in this poem, naturally, that we chiefly find those

The great couplet poets who followed him, Johnson, Goldsmith, Churchill, and Crabbe, all made interesting and valuable adaptations of the meter of the closed couplet — each one of them a unique and uniquely expressive adaptation, but they all sacrificed Pope's effort to include society as a living and dynamic aspect of their poetry, to articulate their perceptions in the form of common sense. To put this another way, each of them maintained and augmented the correctness of the closed couplet in his own fashion, but they all abandoned its politeness: Johnson lectured, Goldsmith and Crabbe ignored, and Churchill defied, the world. We may no doubt see this narrowing of their ambitions as the logical and proper consequence to Pope's last poems — those poems whose implicit but overwhelming theme is the impossibility of communication between truthful poetic intelligence and an incurably foolish and hypocritical society. Only in the novel, chiefly in *Tom Jones* and *Tristram Shandy*, was Pope's more ambitious literary endeavor carried on. It is the later poets' failure to make total use of the closed couplet, a use which remained centrally relevant to the English sensibility and to cultivated English life until the beginning of the nineteenth century, which makes their extremely interesting poetry seem like minor literary utterance — while the novel is clearly blossoming into a major form.

Every one of these poets whose names I have mentioned has, nevertheless, made unique contributions to our literature, each of them articulating the closed couplet to fit his own designs. Because of their individuality and because each one marks a dead end in our history, the work of none having been significantly followed by other poets, each of them can best be treated separately, as I have done in my separate essays on their work.

The degradation and the abandonment of the couplet, which had been accomplished before Crabbe died, can also be treated best — insofar as it must be treated at all — in a few essays. I have already said enough about the romance couplet, that perversion of the closed form which had such a vast fascination for Leigh Hunt, Thomas Moore, and the young Keats. Keats's refinement of the romance couplet in *Endymion,* his unsuccessful effort to return to the closed couplet in *Lamia,* and Byron's rather crude employment of the form in several of its aspects I acknowl-

---

indications of the various styles of the later couplet masters which Yvor Winters has mentioned in "The Heroic Couplet and Its Recent Rivals," in *In Defense of Reason* (Denver, 1943), pp. 134–50. However, one also detects signs of the new diminution in couplet style in *Epilogue to the Satires,* that work which precisely marks the failure of conversation and the impossibility of an acceptable common sense; see esp. I, 141–70 and II, 211–53.

edge in detail in my separate essays on their work. Otherwise, the rejection of our greatest form of public poetry has been sufficiently celebrated.[3]

Let me summarize. The closed couplet provided a remarkable medium for public poetry, for the definition of public concerns and the address to a publicly situated audience. Two great poets realized its full expressive range, the first in articulating a poetry of political discourse, the second in achieving a poetry of social conversation. After its second great employment it served several minor but excellent poets, allowing each of them to attain a rather special mode of poetic expression. Then, after almost two centuries as the central medium of English poetry, at the time when its public implications and its powers of definition seemed to have lost their relevance for English-speaking people, it was discarded. Recent efforts to revive it by poets who naturally lack the tradition of poetry as a public discourse, although very interesting in some cases, have been unsuccessful or, more properly perhaps, successful only in limited ways. They may indicate, however, our growing need of an utterance which can be both public and profound, our need, that is, for social conversation and political discussion that can make sense out of issues whose vital importance we all recognize and whose vital ramifications we all share. We can recapture the feeling for such an utterance and possibly a clue by which we might achieve it in our own way, so far as I know, only by submitting ourselves to our one great tradition of public poetry, the tradition of the closed heroic couplet.

[3] For an illuminating description of the decay of closed-couplet composition see Earl Wasserman, "The Return of the Enjambed Couplet," *ELH*, VII (1940), 239–52.

ESSAYS AND ILLUSTRATIONS

I

✦✦✦✦✦✦✦✦✦✦✦✦✦✦

GEOFFREY CHAUCER
(1340-1400)

Chaucer made no effort to form his rhyming decasyllabic couplets in the mold of Ovid's elegiac distichs even in the passage from his "Legend of Ariadne" in which he was virtually translating from the Latin poet. Chaucer, for instance, completely avoided such witty word play as that in Ovid's "*nullus erat . . . / nullus erat*" (ll. 11–12) and "*locus ipse . . . / ipse locus*" (ll. 23–24) distichs and in his "*verbera cum verbis*" pentameter line (l. 38). He reduced the elaborate balance of the "*Luna fuit*" distich (ll. 17–18) to the direct "No man she sawe / and yet shone the mone" (l. 2194), and the fancy "*ut vidi haut*" distich (ll. 31–32) to "Colde waxe her hert" (l. 2197). Ovid's two gracefully parallel distichs, which end with the pointed "*lapis . . . tam lapis*" pentameter (ll. 47–50), again, became in Chaucer quite simply "And doune she felle a-swoune / on a stoon" (l. 2207). Ovid's detachment and the theatricality of his heroine, which his pointed and witty verses bespeak, Chaucer has rejected. It was the pitiful plight of the lady ("Hathe he not synne / that he hir thus begylde") that stirred the medieval poet. The single trick of Ovidian style which Chaucer did keep (ll. 55–58) he kept because it defined Ariadne's desolation and heightened her sense of loss, and even this he revised. Ovid had distinguished between Ariadne's past and present not once in one witty line, but twice in two: " '*pressimus,*' *exclamo, 'te duo — redde duos!*' " and " '*venimus huc ambo; cur non discedimus ambo?*' " Chaucer has rendered it once in a two-line noncouplet: "Thow bedde quod she / that haste receyved twoo // Thow shalt answere of twoo / and nat of oon." Ovid's Ariadne is shrill and sophisticated, almost the object of comedy, in her command and then in her plea for absolute equivalencies; Chaucer's Ariadne is pitiful in her despairing recognition of an irrevocable change.

Chaucer's meanings do not reveal themselves, in either the *Legend of Good Women* or the *Tales*, a couplet at a time, nor do they commonly depend on specifically couplet emphasis. Couplets do not usually punctuate even those passages in which Chaucer enforces his rhetoric with verse as, for instance, in Ariadne's address to her bed, above, or in the parallel description he gives of the Canon's and of the Canon's Yeoman's horses:

> His hakeney / that was al pomely grys
> So swatte / that it wonder was to see
> It semed / he hadde priked myles three
> The hors eek / that his yeman rood up on
> So swatte / that unnethe myghte he gon
> Aboute the peitrel / stood the foom ful hye
> He was of foom / al flekked as a pye.

This rhetorical parallel is diffused, first, by one member's filling a non-couplet and the other a couplet; second, by their being separated with a line of totally different matter, a narrative surmise; and, third, by the fact that the second member, the description of the Yeoman's horse, does not stop in two lines but continues on for two more. The catalogue of the poor widow's eating habits ("Nun's Priest," ll. 4024–36) [1] does not fall into defining couplets either — not at least until it falls into the hands of John Dryden. The lines of it that tend to pair off, due to similarities of substance (ll. 4030–31) or syntactical connections (ll. 4028–29), form noncouplet units. The passage unfolds in units of one, one, one, one, two, two, one, three, and one lines. Virtually no two of these nine units are parallel in form or substance, and none of them is subordinated to any other or to an explicit theme.

Chaucer's usual practice as a verse writer can best be described, perhaps, by saying that he composed in linear segments of utterance, variously one, two, three, and four lines long. Although he made some definitive use of the midpoints of his lines, his major breaks in sense usually come at line ends, not at couplet ends. Major breaks came as naturally for Chaucer at the ends of first lines as at the ends of second lines. Virtually every line end serves some definitive purpose and, almost always, a more forceful one than any midpoint pause. Recognizing that enjambment is relative, we may suggest that Chaucer wrote in enjambed couplets but not in enjambed lines.

Chaucer used his lines not only to define materials, but often to define shifts in attitude and tone as well. One might notice the shifts in the

---

[1] My line references correspond to the line notations in *The Text of the Canterbury Tales*, ed. John M. Manly and Edith Rickert (Chicago, 1940), III and IV; and, substantially, to those in *The Poetical Works of Chaucer*, ed. F. N. Robinson (Boston, 1933).

"Canon's Yeoman's Prologue" between straight description, expressions of surprise, curiosity, joyful sympathy, and suspicion — each of these attitudes defined by a line or a set of lines and each shift line-punctuated. Take, for instance, the opening lines on the Canon's array ("Canon," ll. 567 ff.): the first line is virtually pure observation; the second is a reflection on the odd disparity between the Canon's "worthiness" and his skimpy dress; in the next three lines Chaucer drops this puzzling disparity and tries to guess the Canon's profession; the next two lines present his decision on it; and the next two give more pure observation. The puzzling problem of so worthy a man's riding in light summer attire during April is left until later as Chaucer's sharp eye and his attentive mind focus on things as they present themselves.

Chaucer occasionally imposed parallels, antitheses, distinctions, and the like on his lines and couplets which remind us of neoclassical effects. There is, for instance, "A likerous mouth / moste han a likerous tayl" from the "Wife's Prologue" (l. 466), whose pointedness Pope did his best, when translating this prologue, to retain. And the metaphorical couplet in which the Wife surveys her life (ll. 477–78), with its 'flour–bren' opposition and its periodic last line, also seems to look ahead. Oddly enough, Pope destroyed its trenchancy when he tried to do something about the expletive which makes up the last half of its first line. Here and there throughout the satiric attack on women in the "Merchant's Tale" one also hits a fairly sharp couplet formulation (ll. 1345–46, 1347–48, 1375–76), but not nearly so often as might be expected. Even in so discursive and so satiric a passage as this we can see that Chaucer's literary ideals and practices were never those of Pope.

Chaucer never wanted to confine himself to the continuous attitude of detachment and judgment which the closed couplet, with its short-term complexities and resolutions, pervasively suggests. Neither could he have wished to retard his utterance, which was prevailingly narrative, with the closed couplet's recurrent click. By variously defining his stories and observations with the sturdy lines his paired rhymes allowed him, Chaucer achieved a swift and economical discourse, each of whose shifts in mood or attention is sharply but unobtrusively delineated and each of whose substantial elements is articulated with special force and clarity. These elements, like the many particularized figures in a medieval painting or, better perhaps, like the individual pieces in a stained glass window, are separately realized and left to compose with others in the reader's mind as patterns and affinities occur to him.

Chaucer's line segments and line-end punctuations are more necessary to the clarity and impetus of the *Tales*, with its remarkable range of elements and attitudes, than to the *Legend*, but his verse production is much the same in both — and throughout the great variety of the *Tales*. "The Squire's Tale," which Robinson calls a typical romance,[2] unfolds, for all the strangeness and diffuseness of its material, with the same clarity and economy as "The Nun's Priest's Tale" and "The Merchant's Tale." The chief quality of "The Squire's Tale," indeed, arises from a tension between the diffuse and mysterious story and its terse, straightforward presentation. This is a tension, by the way, that Chaucer has insisted on explicitly (ll. 283–90, 298–301). In coping with this romantic matter, as throughout his couplet practice, Chaucer employed a flexible, unobtrusive metrical instrument which perfectly suited the comprehensiveness and particularity of his sensibility and the prevailingly narrative mode of his art.

THE LEGEND OF GOOD WOMEN, VI, THE LEGEND OF ARIADNE

Ryght in the dawenynge / a-waketh she	2185
And gropeth in the bed / and fonde ryght nought	
Allas quod she / that ever I was wrought	
I am betrayed / and hir heer to-rent	
And to the stronde / barefote faste she went	
And cryed / Theseus myn / hert swete	2190
Where be ye that I may not / with yow mete	
And myght thus with bestes / ben y-slayne	
The holowe rokkes answerde her agayne	
No man she sawe / and yet shone the mone	
And hye upon rokke / she went sone	2195
And saw his barge / saylynge in the see	
Colde waxe her hert / and ryght thus sayde she	
Meker than ye / fynde I the bestes wilde	
Hathe he not synne / that he hir thus begylde	
She cried O turne agayne / for routhe and synne	2200
Thy barge hath not / al thy meyne inne	
Hir kerchefe on a pole / up styked shee	
Aschaunce he shulde / hyt wel y-see	
And hym Remembre / that she was behynde	
And turne agayne / and on the stronde hir fynde	2205

---

[2] *The Poetical Works of Chaucer*, p. 821.

But al for noght / his wey he is goon
And doune she felle a-swoune / on a stoon
And up she riste / and kyssed in al hir care
The steppes of his fete / there he hath fare
And to hir bedde ryght thus / she speketh thoo   2210
Thow bedde quod she / that haste receyved twoo
Thow shalt answere of twoo / and not of oon
Where is thy gretter parte / away goon

.   .   .   .

OVID, HEROIDES, X,
ARIADNE TO THESEUS

Incertum vigilans a somno languida movi
   Thesea prensuras semisupina manus —   *10*
nullus erat! referoque manus iterumque retempto,
   perque torum moveo bracchia — nullus erat!
excussere metus somnum; conterrita curgo,
   membraque sunt viduo praecipitata poro.
protinus adductis sonuerunt pectora palmis,   *15*
   utque erat e somno turbida, rapta coma est.
Luna fuit; specto, siquid nisi litora cernam.
   quod videant oculi, nil nisi litus habent.
nunc huc, nunc illuc, et utroque sine ordine, curro;
   alta puellares tardat harena pedes.   *20*
interea toto clamanti litore "Theseu!"
   reddebant nomen concava saxa tuum,
et quotiens ego te, totiens locus ipse vocabat.
   ipse locus miserae ferre volebat opem.
Mons fuit — apparent frutices in vertice rari;   *25*
   hinc scopulus raucis pendet adesus aquis.
adscendo — vires animus dabat — atque ita late
   aequora prospectu metior alta meo.
inde ego — nam ventis quoque sum crudelibus usa —
   vidi praecipiti carbasa tenta Noto.   *30*
ut vidi haut dignam quae me vidisse putarem,
   frigidior glacie semianimisque fui.
nec languere diu patitur dolor; excitor illo,
   excitor et summa Thesea voce voco.

"quo fugis?" exclamo; "scelerate revertere Theseu!   35
   flecte ratem! numerum non habet illa suum!"
Hæc ego; quod voci deerat, plangore replebam;
   verbera cum verbis mixta fuere meis.
si non audires, ut saltem cernere posses,
   iactatae late signa dedere manus;   40
candidaque inposui longae velamina virgae —
   scilicet oblitos admonitura mei!
iamque oculis ereptus eras. tum denique flevi;
   torpuerant molles ante dolore genae.
quid potius facerent, quam me mea lumina flerent,   45
   postquam disieram vela videre tua?
aut ego diffusis erravi sola capillis,
   qualis ab Ogygio concita Baccha deo,
aut mare prospiciens in saxo frigida sedi,
   quamque lapis sedes, tam lapis ipsa fui.   50
saepe torum repeto, qui nos acceperat ambos,
   sed non acceptos exhibiturus erat,
et tua, quae possum pro te, vestigia tango
   strataque quae membris intepuere tuis.
incumbo, lacrimisque toro manante profusis,   55
   "pressimus," exclamo, "te duo — redde duos!
venimus huc ambo; cur non discedimus ambo?
   perfide, pars nostri, lectule, maior ubi est?"

.   .   .   .

II

✦✦✦✦✦✦✦✦✦✦✦✦✦✦✦

WILLIAM BALDWIN
(fl. 1532-1563)

The very first lines of Baldwin's "Funeral of King Edward VI," which echo the opening of *The Canterbury Tales*, suggest how strongly Baldwin felt the influence of his great predecessor. In these lines and throughout his poem, Baldwin has followed Chaucer in organizing his utterance in units of varying numbers of lines. Baldwin's first eighteen lines, for instance, fall into segments of four, two, three, one, four, and four lines, and lines 163–78, again, are composed of two-, four-, four-, five-, and one-line units. Baldwin also follows Chaucer in commonly soft-pedalling the mid-line pause and in rounding lines with expletives (ll. 59, 62, 136, 185). There are smudgy spots in Baldwin's verse: in lines 1–6, for instance, where metrical exigencies have forced a confused disposition of the compound object of "forced had"; and in lines 81–86, where apparently parallel "what" clauses are finally neither parallel rhetorically (what kind of man being set beside what kind of land) nor, owing to an enjambed couplet, parallel in position. Despite these incidental smudges, however, Baldwin's verse has much of the movement and the flavor of Chaucer's.

The differences there are between Baldwin's couplet production and that of his great model bespeak, at least in part, Baldwin's different intention. Unlike Chaucer, Baldwin was possessed by one overriding theme, namely, that the English must repent and reform. In keeping with this singularity of theme, he has infused his poem with a logical and rhetorical thrust: in lines 19–28, for instance, where an eight-line passage on God's view of England reaches a climax in a two-line utterance of God's dismay, or, again, in lines 163–78, which contain God's carefully calculated complex of instructions to his servant Crasy Cold. Baldwin's purpose was, moreover, partially satiric, especially in enunciating the evils of England, and that prompted him to close off some of his couplets (ll. 59–88). The individual couplets here are not worked out as a series of rhetorically parallel items — in this they are Chaucerian; but each of them does define and heighten one element of God's angry vision. The stiffness of their closure; their usual neglect of the mid-line pause as a rhetorically definitive point; their occasional settling into essentially single-line utterance (ll. 61, 62, 73, 75, 87) and, on the other hand, their incidental enjambment (l. 82): all these suit the application of the medieval couplet to what the age called "complaint." [1]

Baldwin's observance of the couplet unit actually extends beyond the satiric passages. It is apparent, indeed, throughout the poem: in the opening, for instance, which runs along largely in doubled couplet units, and even in those passages, mentioned above, in which the thought thrusts through eight or ten lines (ll. 19–28). One might also observe the couplet-phased description of Crasy Cold (ll. 179–88) and compare it to Chaucer's description of the Canon. In these cases Baldwin seems, quite simply, to be submitting to the natural promptings of his rhyme scheme, somewhat as Spenser will do soon afterwards in his *Mother Hubberd's Tale*. Reading these followers of Chaucer makes one wonder afresh at the power with which he resisted this recalcitrant form of verse and the skill with which he worked it into a sufficiently flexible vehicle for the expression of his comprehensive medieval curiosity and his vast human sympathy.

THE FUNERAL OF KING EDWARD VI

When bytter Wynter forced had the Sun
Fro the horned Goat to Pisces ward to run,
And lively sap, that greneth gardins soote,
To flye the stocke to save her nurse, the roote,
And sleety Cech that blowth by North fro East   5
Decayd the health and welth of man and beast,
The almighty minde that rayneth thre in one,
Disposing all thinges from his stable throne,
Beheld the earth, and man among the rest:
Movde by the crye of such as wer opprest.   10
And when he had the maynland throughly vewed,
With Mahometrie and Idol blud embrewed,

---

[1] For a discussion of this term and the literature to which it refers, see John Peter, *Complaint and Satire in Early English Literature* (Oxford, 1956).

Wherthrow his Law and Gospel were defylde,
His love, his awe, his worship quite exilde,
He turnd his iyes from that so fowle a sight,   15
And toward the Iles he cast his looke a right:
In hope that where true knowledge did abound,
He should sum lovelyer sight have quickely found.
But when he sawe all vice most vile and naught
Most rifely swarme, where truth had most be taught,   20
In England chefe, which he of speciall grace
Had made his wurd and chosens resting place,
And had for that cause powrd on it such store
Of welthy giftes as none could wishe for more,
Joynt with a King, of such a godly minde,   25
As seldome erst he elsewhere had assinde,
All wo and wroth he flang away his face,
And to him selfe he thus bewayld the case.

. . . .

Beholde the heades, what els do they devise,
Save in our name to cloke their covetise? [2]   60
Thine herytage they have thee whole bereft,
Except thy shurt, let see, what have they left?
Thy golde, thy plate, thy lodgyng, yea thy landes
That are the poores, are in the richest handes:
They waste, they spoyle, they spill upon their pride   65
That which was geven the nedy corse to hide:
And thou lyest naked starving at their gates
While they consume thy substaunce with theyr mates.
As for theyr lawe wherby men should have right
Is ruled hole by money and by might.   70
And where the riche the nedy should relive
They do their best to beggry all to drive.
What titles forge they falsely to their landes,
Untill they wrongly wring them from their handes?
How joyne they house to house, how farme to farme?   75
How lease to lease, the selly sort to harme?
How rayse they rents, what income, yea what fines
Exact they still though all the world repines?
How suffer they theyr grayne to rot and hore

---

[2] God is here addressing Christ.

To make a dearth when I geve plenty store? 80
And where they brag they do thy word avaunce,
Have they not spoyld or fliste all mayntenaunce,
That therto servde? what kinde of Clergy lande
Or fee, is free now from the Lay mans hande?
What gentleman, what marchant, yea what swayne, 85
But hath or may have a parsonage or twayne?
I loth to name the vilenes of the rest,
So sore my hart theyr robbry doth detest.

.   .   .   .

This sayd, he called to his servaunt Crasy Cold,
Whom the Isy king kept prisoner in his hold
Beneath the Poales, where under he doth dwell
In grysly darke like to the diepe of hell,
In rockes and caves of snow and clottred yse 135
That never thaw, and sayd him in this wise.

.   .   .   .

And when thou hast his place and person found,
I will thou shalt his helthy body unsound:
But see thou hurt him not unto the death, 165
Thou shalt but stop his Loungpipes, that his breth
Constraynd, may cause the cough brede in his brest:
Els what shall cure or quel up all the rest.
But in this feat I charge the see thou looke
Thou harme him not while he is at his booke, 170
Or other kinde of vertuous exercise:
Neyther yet at game so it be voyd of vice.
But if this Winter time thou mayst him marke
To ride all day all armde about the parke,
Or els at dice, or tenis out of time 175
To overwatch or toyle him selfe, for such a crime
Strike hardily, but not to hard, I say:
This is thy charge, about it, go thy way.
    Scarce was this errand throwly to him tolde,
But forth he came this shivering Crasy Cold, 180
With Ysikles bebristled like a Bore,
About his head behind and eke before.
His skin was hard al made of glassy yse,
Overheard with hore frost, like gray Irishe Frise,
His armes and legges, to kepe him warm I trow, 185

Wer skaled through with flakes of frosen snowe,
And from his mouth there reekt a breth so hot,
As touched nothing that congeled not.
   And when he had arowsd him selfe a while,
And stretcht his joyntes as stiffe as any stile: 190
Because he would his charge no longer slacke.
He got him up on blustring Boreas backe,
And forth he went: but his horse so heavy trode,
That al the world might knowe which way he rode.
For in his way there grew no maner grene,   195
That could in thre dayes after wel be sene.
His breth and braying was so sharpe and shryl,
That fluds for feare hard cluddered stoode full stil.
The seas did quake and tremble in such sort,
That never a ship durst venter out of port.   200
The holtes, the heathes, the hilles became al hore,
The trees did shrinke, al thinges were troubled sore.

.   .   .   .

III

✶✶✶✶✶✶✶✶✶✶✶✶✶✶✶

NICHOLAS GRIMALD
(1519-1562)

Nicholas Grimald was the earliest of the English poets to derive English heroic couplets from Latin elegiac distichs.[1] His "Praise of Measure Keeping," for instance, is a couplet-for-distich rendering of Theodore de Beza's "Elegia II," thirteen distichs of Beza coming over into thirteen exactly correspondent couplets of Grimald. "The Lover Asks Pardon," is, likewise, except for its sixth couplet, a couplet-for-distich transcription of Beza's "Elegia V." Finding a difference between Grimald and his source which is not attributable to the inescapable differences between Latin and English requires some study. One does find, for instance, that in his translation of "Elegia II" Grimald lost its *'truculente–truculentus'* echo (ll. 11–14) but that he added a 'mid–middle' echo, for which he found no sanction in Beza (ll. 5–6). The couplet which Grimald contrived to improve this latter distich is not very good, but Beza's equivocating of his main theme, that is, the middle way, by introducing the distracting idea of filial obedience had left Grimald a hopeless problem. He might have done better with it if he had had the independence to cut out Icarus's father.

It was, however, by following Beza closely that Grimald captured in English couplets the patterning which was to become an essential element in closed-couplet composition. He achieved the metrical reinforcement of rhetorical antithesis: for instance, between the two lines of one closed couplet ("Lover," ll. 3–4; "Praise," ll. 11–12) and between the two halves of a closed line ("Praise," ll. 21, 22). He also gave couplet definition to rhetorical parallels: between the two halves of a line ("Praise," ll. 9, 14, 17), between the two lines of a couplet ("Lover," ll. 13–14, 17–18), and between two or more couplets ("Lover," ll. 7–12).

---

[1] George P. Shannon, "Nicholas Grimald's Heroic Couplet and the Latin Elegiac Distich," *PMLA*, XLV (1930), 532–42.

[168]

He achieved a pattern of three consecutive if-then couplets ("Lover," ll. 7–12) by copying two distichs from Beza and by condensing three others ("Elegia V," 7–16). In all this Grimald was a portent of the transmission into English couplets of better and livelier Latin elegiac distichs, especially those of Ovid and Martial.

His verse, however, in addition to its academic staleness, lacks the dynamics essential to good couplet writing. There are rather few couplets in which the two lines flow together ("Lover," ll. 1–2, 9–10; "Praise," ll. 5–6, 15–16) and almost no well-tied groups, or even pairs, of couplets. Except for such an original effort as "Of Nicholas Chambers," which does have some rude pace and flow, Grimald's couplets lie still in their banks. Of course, in this he was following his model, who had apparently not been gripped by a subject whose force or complexity put any strain on the elegiac measure. Grimald's verse, then, is subliterary, but it shows the sense of affinity between Latin elegiac distichs and English pentameter couplets which was to possess English poets thirty years after his death and drive them to revolutionize English poetry.

THE LOVER ASKS PARDON OF HIS DEAR FOR FLEEING FROM HER

Lovers men warn the corps beloved to flee,
From the blinde fire in case they wold live free.
Ay mee, how oft have I fled thee, my Day?
I flee, but love bides in my brest alway.
Lo yet agayn, I graunt, I gan remove: 5
But both I could, and can say still, I love.
If woods I seek, cooms to my thought Adone:
And well the woods do know my heavy mone.
In gardens if I walk: Narcissus there
I spy, and Hyacints with weepyng chere: 10
If meads I tred, O what a fyre I feel?
In flames of love I burn from hed to heel.
Here I behold dame Ceres ymp in flight:
Here bee, methynk, black Plutoes steeds in sight.
Stronds if I look upon, the Nymphs I mynde: 15
And, in mid sea, oft fervent powrs I fynde.
The hyer that I clyme, in mountanes wylde,
The nearer mee approcheth Venus chylde.

Towns yf I haunt: in short, shall I all say?
There soondry fourms I view, none to my pay.   20
Her favour now I note, and now her yies:
Her hed, amisse: her foot, her cheeks, her guyse.
In fyne, where mater wants, defautes I fayn:
Whom other, fayr: I deem, she hath soom stayn.
What boots it then to flee, sythe in nightyde,   25
And daytyme to, my Day is at my side?

.   .   .   .

BEZA, ELEGIA V

Quisquis amas (aiunt cuncti) fuge corpus amatum,
    Vivere si caeco liber ab igne cupis.
Hei mihi, te quoties fugi, mea Candida fugi:
    Semper at in nostro pectore regnat amor.
Ecce iterum fateor, fugi te, Candida: verum   5
    Et potui et possum dicere semper, amo.
Sive abeo in sylvas, nobis succurrit Adonis,
    Et fit tristitiae conscia sylva meae:
Sive placent horti, quot florum hic millia cerno,
    Tot stimulis captum me premit asper amor: 10
Narcissum hinc croceum video, hinc flentes Hiacynthos,
    Hinc miser ante oculos pulcher Adonis adest:
Magna quidem nostrae fateor midicamina flammae,
    Sed me qui vincit, vincit et ille Deos.
At si prata juvant, o quantas sentio flammas!   15
    Ardeo tunc flammis totus amoris ego.
Hic videor Cereris fugientem cernere natam,
    Hic videor furvi cernere Ditis equos,
Littora si specto, vitreas tunc cogito Nymphas,
    Fervidaque in medio numina saepe mari.   20
Quo magis evado montes sublimis in altos,
    Hoc proprior Veneris fit puer ille mihi,
Si placeant urbes: vis semel omnia dicam?
    Illic quum videam plurima, nulla placent.
Illius nunc carpo oculos, nunc illius ora,   25
    Haec capite, haec pedibus displicet, illa genis
Denique materies si desit, crimina fingo:
    Et quaecunque aliis candida, nigra mihi est.

Quid prodest fugisse igitur, cum Candida praesens,
   Atque adeo lateri sit comes usque meo?   30

.   .   .   .

PRAISE OF MEASURE KEEPING

The auncient time commended, not for nought,
The mean: what better thing can ther be sought?
In mean, is vertue placed: on either side,
Bothe right, and left, amisse a man shall slide.
Icar, with sire hadst thou the mid way flown,   5
Icarian beck by name had no man known.
If middle path kept had proud Phaeton,
No burning brand this erth had falln upon.
Ne cruell powr, ne none to soft can raign:
That keeps a mean, the same shall styll remain.   10
Thee, Julie, once did too much mercy spill:
Thee, Nero stern, rigor extreem did kill.
How could August so many yeres well passe?
Nor overmeek, nor overferse he was.
Worship not Jove with curious fansies vain,   15
Nor him despise: hold right atween these twayn.
No wastefull wight, no greedy goom is prayzd.
Stands largesse just, in egall balance payzd.
So Catoes meal surmountes Antonius chere,
And better fame his sober fare hath here,   20
To slender buildyng, bad: as bad, to grosse:
One, an eyesore, the tother falls to losse.
As medcines help, in measure: so (God wot)
By overmuch, the sick their bane have got.
Unmeet mee seems to utter this, mo wayes: 25
Measure forbids unmeasurable prayse.

BEZA, ELEGIA II,
IN MEDIOCRITATIS LAUDEM

Non frustra solita est medium laudari vetustas,
   Nam nil laudari dignius orbis habet.
In medio posita est virtus hinc indeque fallax:

Tota sinistra via est, totaque dextra via est.
Icare, si patrem esses inter utrumque secutus,   5
    Icarias nullus nomine nosset aquas.
Si medio Phaeton mansisset calle superbus,
    Non esset saeva terra perusta face.
Nec lenis nimium, nec durat saeva potestas,
    Quae medium servat, sola perennis erit: 10
Te nimia, O Juli, clementia perdidit olim:
    Occidit feritas te truculente Nero.
Augustus felix cur multos mansit in annos?
    Nec facilis nimium, nec truculentus erat.
Nec nimis ipse coli, nec sperni Juppiter optat,   15
    Sed magis una iuvat mens moderata deos.
Largus opum nullus, nullus laudatur avarus:
    Magnus, in his potuit qui tenuisse modum.
Antonii mensas sic vicit coena Catonis,
    Et tenuem melior fama secuta larem.   20
Nec gracilis structura nimis, nec crassa probatur:
    Haec spectatori displicet, illa ruit.
Ut moderata juvant, sic aegris pharmaca multis,
    Heu nimium multis, saepe petita nocent.
Dicere plura nefas credo, nam laude nequaquam   25
    Efferri immodica sustinet ipse modus.

IV

＊＊＊＊＊＊＊＊＊＊＊＊＊＊＊＊

EDMUND SPENSER

(1552-1599)

Mother Hubberd's Tale, for the most part, flows along in a somewhat stiffer version of the Chaucerian couplet style. But Spenser lacked Chaucer's medieval breadth of human interest and, correspondingly, did not define the separate items of his poetic material as vividly as Chaucer had done or move between them with Chaucer's diffidence and grace. Spenser had an overriding satiric intention; this naturally prompted him to be more observant of the couplet stop — with its chances for definition, its narrowing of focus, and its implications of judgment — than Chaucer was. The opening of *Mother Hubberd's Tale*, although reminiscent of the opening of Chaucer's "Nun's Priest's Tale," proceeds quite a way (ll. 1–24)[1] in fairly strict four-line, double-couplet units; the famous passage on the suitor's state (ll. 897–906) has a kind of closed-couplet movement; and so does the description of the hypocritical ape's military dress (ll. 209–22), as a comparison with Chaucer's description of the Canon would make clear. Nevertheless, Spenser did follow Chaucer significantly in his couplet production: he usually subordinated mid-line pause to line-end pause; he seldom used mid-line pause to gain balance or definition; and he commonly composed in noncouplet systems of verse whose variety and lengths approach the Chaucerian (ll. 25–44, 727–52). As the opening of *Mother Hubberd's Tale* and its description of the ape show, Spenser's verse is a compromise between his satiric intention and his Chaucerian discipleship.

The passage on the suitor's state, which is clearly not Chaucerian, approximates a closed-couplet effect in a remarkable way. Every one of the *lines* in the heart of this passage (ll. 897–906), each of which defines a separate infinitive phrase (or phrases), is strongly end-stopped; in this it

---

[1] My line references correspond to line notations in *The Complete Poetical Works of Spenser*, ed. R. E. Dodge (Cambridge, Mass., 1936).

resembles the medieval practice of Baldwin and Breton, as it does also in the generality of its address. But since each member of every rhyming pair of lines shares rhetorical and musical qualities with its mate and with no other line, every pair, every couplet, achieves its own special chime. For instance, the opening verbs in the two lines of the second couplet rhyme ('speed–feed'), and the second half of each one contains a second infinitive phrase ('to be–to pine'); the opening verbs of the next couplet's two lines, again, are identical ('have–have'), and the second half of each line begins "yet w . . ."; even the climactic couplet is a pair of mirroring lines — each one being a series of infinitives whose first three members take up just six syllables, whose third member begins with a *w* ('waite–want'), and whose mid-line pause comes after this alliterating member. To call this brief achievement of a closed-couplet organization freakish does not deny its brilliance, but it does set it outside that tradition which commenced at the turn of the sixteenth century. The central aesthetic of that new tradition is the dynamic interplay between metrical confinement and conversational ease, between artificial division and the natural flow of speech. But in this passage on the suitor's state, Spenser has modified the artifice of verse closure, of line closure in fact, with the artifice of verbal music. The effect is striking, but not even Spenser could keep it up for long. And it is, of course, further from the pointed, colloquial tone of address which will characterize the new couplet than Chaucer or even Baldwin.

V

ᛉᛉᛉᛉᛉᛉᛉᛉᛉᛉᛉᛉᛉᛉᛉ

SIR JOHN HARINGTON
(1561-1612)

Harington turned more than twenty of Martial's elegiac distich epigrams into heroic couplet epigrams of his own. These exercises in transference do not make quite the couplet-for-distich reflection Marlowe achieved in translating Ovid's *Amores*: Harington sometimes embellished and sometimes expanded his model. But the impress of Martial on these poems is tremendous, nevertheless. His sharply closed distichs with their witty turns drove Harington to similarly closed and witty couplets.

Consider, for instance, Harington's "Epigram on Paulus." Every one of its five separate law cases has been screwed into its own separate couplet (ll. 5–14); moreover, each first line gives a case and each second line, Paulus's response to it. Harington found this exact pattern in Martial's *Epigrammaton*, II, xxxii; the difference is that he has repeated five times — beyond the point of good effect — the pattern Martial used only twice. The same stiffness of couplet closure and the same repetitiveness of couplet employment shows up in Harington's original poems. Each couplet beyond the first one in Harington's poem "At the Birth of his Son," for example, asserts one perfectly isolated analogy between the diamond, which the poet has given his wife on this occasion, and his wife. In every couplet, moreover, the first line describes an aspect of the diamond and the second line, a like (or, in the last couplet, a different) aspect of the wife.

In this poetry we catch the couplet, as it were, half changed from its medieval into its classical attire.[1] Since Harington was applying it to pithy classical epigrams, and not to discursive medieval complaints, the

---

[1] On the transitional nature of Harington's style see John Peter, *Complaint and Satire in Early English Literature* (Oxford, 1956), pp. 162–63; and Wesley Trimpi, *Ben Jonson's Poems* (Stanford, 1962), pp. 170–73.

medieval stylistic remnants appear as flaws. We have already noticed the repetitiveness of Harington's couplet practice. The last couplet of Harington's original "Epigram to Bastard," to exemplify it further, repeats and squanders the well-turned point of the next-to-last couplet; and the last twelve lines of the "Epigram to his Wife, on Praying" rehash, in the medieval way of good counsel, adjuration and reasoning already sufficiently expounded. We have also noticed the stiffness of Harington's couplet practice. We might lay this to Martial's neatly clipped distichs as well as to the medieval couplet of complaint, but Martial would never approve a way Harington often used of closing and stiffening his couplets, that is, the way of expletives, whereas, of course, Chaucer and Baldwin might. One notices the empty expressions, "as I heard it said" ("Pedro," l. 6) and "I dare lay my life" ("Cuckold," l. 12) — the latter of these coming unluckily at the very end of a poem. Worse than this, there are whole expletival couplets, whole couplets, that is, which bear no necessary meaning or which repeat points that were already established. The first two couplets of the "Epigram on Paulus," for example, couplets for which Martial's epigram gave no sanction, are largely irrelevant to its central point — a point which, as has already been suggested, Harington labored more than twice as long as his model. Despite such failings, Harington has realized in English couplets some of the epigrammatic wit and pointedness and some of the conversational tone of his Latin predecessor. He caught Martial's 'res–res' word play (*Epigrammaton*, V, lxi, 14) quite felicitously with his 'business–business' turn of wit ("Cuckold," ll. 11–12), for instance — although he has lost the emphasis Martial got by defining this repetition in a single line. And he achieved a pointed personal address not only in translations from his model but in his original epigrams as well. We have already mentioned, for instance, poems directed at his wife and at his fellow epigrammatist, Thomas Bastard.

What Harington's closed couplets entirely lack that the mature form will come characteristically to have — namely, a supracouplet dynamics between stability and movement, between lucidity and complexity — Martial's epigrams lack too. So too, of course, do Ovid's and Marlowe's elegies. The English satirists and the tribe of Ben, both of which followed Harington in paying close attention to Martial, attempted, each group in its own way, to achieve this dynamics: the satirists by qualifying their allegiance to the neat distichs of Martial with a counterallegiance to the rough, enjambed hexameters of Juvenal and Persius; Jonson and his disciples by modifying the epigrammatic effect with a broad selection of classical effects, especially those of the informal epistle.

EPIGRAM ON A DIAMOND GIVEN TO HIS WIFE AT THE BIRTH OF HIS ELDEST SON

Deare, I to thee this Diamond commend,
In which, a modell of thy selfe I send,
How just unto thy joynts this circlet sitteth,
So just thy face and shape my fancy fitteth.
The touch will try this Ring of purest gold,   5
My touch tries thee as pure, though softer mold.
That metall precious is, the stone is true,
As true, as then how much more precious you?
The Gem is cleare, and hath nor needes no foyle,
Thy face, nay more, thy fame is free from soile.   10
Youle deem this deere, because from me you have it,
I deem your faith more deer, because you gave it.
This pointed Diamond cuts glasse and steele,
Your loves like force in my firme heart I feele.
    But this, as all things else, time wasts with wearing,   15
    Where you, my Jewels multiply with bearing.

EPIGRAM ON PAULUS, A GREAT MAN WHO EXPECTED TO BE FOLLOWED

Proud *Paulus* late advanc't to high degree,
Expects that I should now his follower be.
Glad I would be to follow ones direction,
By whom my honest suits might have protection.
But I sue *Don Fernandos* heyre for land,   5
Against so great a Peere he dare not stand.
A Bishop sues me for my tithes, that's worse,
He dares not venter on a Bishops curse.
Sergeant Erifilus beares me old grudges,
Yea but, saith *Paulus, Sergeants* may be Judges.   10
Pure *Cinna* o're my head would begge my Lease,
Who? My Lord — ? Man, O hold your peace.
Rich widdow *Lesbia* for a slander sues me.
Tush for a womans cause, he must refuse me.
Then farewell frost: *Paulus,* henceforth excuse me,   15
    For you that are your selfe thrall'd to so many,
    Shall never be my good Lord, if I have any.

MARTIAL, EPIGRAMMATON, II, xxxii

Lis mihi cum Balbo est, tu Balbum offendere non vis,
    Pontice: cum Licino est, hic quoque magnus homo est.
vexat saepe meum Patrobas confinis agellum;
    contra libertum Caesaris ire times.
abnegat et retinet nostrum Laronia servum;   5
    respondes "Orba est, dives, anus, vidua."
non bene, crede mihi, servo servitur amico:
    sit liber, dominus qui volet esse meus.

EPIGRAM ON DON PEDRO
AND HIS POETRY[2]

Sir, I shall tell you newes, except you know it,
Our noble friend *Don Pedro*, is a Poet.
His verses all abroad are read and showne,
And he himselfe doth sweare they are his owne.
His owne? tis true, for he for them hath paid   5
Two crownes a Sonnet, as I heard it said.
So *Ellen* hath faire teeth, that in her purse
She keepes all night, and yet sleepes ne're the worse.
So widdow *Lesbia*, with her painted hide,
Seem'd, for the time, to make a handsome bride.   10
    If *Pedro* be for this a Poet cald,
    So you may call one hairie that is bald.

EPIGRAM TO MASTER THOMAS BASTARD,
TAXING HIM FOR FLATTERY

It was a saying us'd a great while since,
The subjects ever imitate the Prince,
A vertuous Master, makes a good Disciple,
Religious Prelates breede a godly people.
And evermore the Rulers inclination,   5
Workes in the time the chawnge and alteration.

---

[2] See p. 57 in this book for the epigram of Martial from which this derives
and for Marston's adaptation of it.

Then what's the reason, *Bastard*, why thy Rimes
Magnifie Magistrates, yet taunt the times?
   I thinke that he to taunt the time that spares not,
   Would touch the Magistrate, save that he dares not.   10

EPIGRAM TO A CUCKOLD

What curld-pate youth is he that sitteth there
So neere thy wife, and whispers in her eare,
And takes her hand in his, and soft doth wring her,
Sliding her ring still up and downe her finger?
Sir, tis a Proctor, seene in both the Lawes,   5
Retain'd by her, in some important cause;
Prompt and discreet both in his speech and action,
And doth her busines with great satisfaction.
And thinkest thou so? a horne-plague on thy head:
Art thou so like a foole, and wittoll led,   10
   To thinke he doth the businesse of thy wife?
   He doth thy business, I dare lay my life.

MARTIAL, EPIGRAMMATON, V, lxi

Crispulus iste quis est, uxori semper adhaeret
   qui, Mariane, tuae? crispulus iste quis est?
nescio quid dominae teneram qui garrit in aurem
   et sellam cubito dexteriore premit?
per cuius digitos currit levis anulus omnis,   5
   crura gerit nullo qui violata pilo?
nil mihi respondes? "Uxoris res agit" inquis
   "iste meae." sane certus et asper homo est,
procuratorem voltu qui praeferat ipso:
   acrior hoc Chius non erit Aufidius.   10
o quam dignus eras alapis, Mariane, Latini:
   te successurum credo ego Panniculo.
res uxoris agit? res ullas crispulus iste?
   res non uxoris, res agit iste tuas.

VI

✼✼✼✼✼✼✼✼✼✼✼✼✼✼✼✼

JOSHUA SYLVESTER
(1563-1618)

Sylvester's decasyllabic couplets conform rather closely to the early English practice, being by turns stiff and irregular. His own early interpolation into his translation of DuBartas (I, 13–26), for instance, reveals a series of six rigidly parallel lines, the odd and even ones being equally closed, none of which makes a significant use of mid-line caesura; and then a six-line thrust, an expansive, imperative system which is articulated with interruptive interpolations and emphatic repetitions — variously defined by couplet, line, and caesural pauses. Generally speaking, however, Sylvester's translation clicks along in stiffly closed pentameter couplets which correspond to the stiffly closed hexameter couplets of DuBartas. Like both his French model and his early English predecessors in couplet writing, Sylvester made only occasional, only incidental rhetorical use of the caesura (I, 11, 17, 178; II, 8); many of his lines have, of course, no mid-line pause at all (I, 1, 4, 6, 10, etc.). On the other hand, we sometimes find a heavy pause within a line (I, 39, 196), and as often a pause toward the extremity of a line (I, 35, 163, 173) as one toward the center. The usually stiff couplet close, similarly, is occasionally compromised by a strong enjambment (I, 170, 190; II, 30). Sylvester's employment of such a metrical practice for his long, didactic, and at least partially narrative poem makes him fit very nicely in the tradition of the early English couplet.

Sylvester's practice is somewhat more regular in its movement than that of Baldwin and Spenser, no doubt owing to the rather stodgy and diffuse regularity of his model. His very first six couplets, for example, are all strongly stopped in precise reflection of the first six of DuBartas. He has duplicated one of his model's rhymes in this passage ('verse–*Universe*'), and its balanced twelfth line mirrors that of DuBartas even down to the slant of its syntax. In the passage likening the world to a school, a stairway, a hall, and a half-dozen other things (I, 157–200), again, Sylvester has transferred twenty-two couplets of his model (I, 135–78) into twenty-two closely similar couplets of his own. There are, however, cases in this passage and in Sylvester's translation at large of metrical displacement and slosh. Sometimes the English poet made oblique, flowing matter in the French poem (I, 137–42) conform to the stiffness of early English couplet practice (I, 159–64); sometimes, on the other hand, he made a stiff metrical articulation in his model (I, 19–20; II, 5–6) conform to early English looseness of organization (I, 35–36; II, 9–10). Every now and then he expanded on his model, usually however in a ratio of lines and couplets: turning one French line (I, 15) into one English couplet (I, 29–30), for example, or one French couplet (II, 1–2) into three English ones (II, 1–6), or two (II, 15–18) into three (II, 19–24). On the whole, Sylvester was able to bring the stiff, diffuse hexameter couplets of DuBartas into English pentameter couplets of the old-fashioned kind his interpolations reveal to have been natural to him without much trouble or, more significantly, without the kind of artistic transformation of the English couplet which translations and imitations of the Latin elegiac distich were requiring of Sylvester's contemporaries.

The abstract, generally didactic tone of DuBartas's poem was even more congenial with early English poetic practice than his meter. Once again, then, nothing like the revolution in Sylvester's poetry that Ovid and Martial and Horace were inspiring in that of Marlowe and Donne and Jonson. DuBartas was not pointed or particular either in his poetic reference or in his poetic address, and neither, of course, is Sylvester. The list of figures for the world (I, 157–200) reminds us in its abstract articulation and its stiffly seriatim organization — and in its universal didacticism as well — of much early English practice in couplets and in other poetic forms. To illuminate the medieval quality of this catalogue one might compare it with the particularized, colloquial catalogue of poetic vices which opens John Donne's "Satire II." A still more precise comparison may be drawn between the stiffly assertive poetic morality opening "The Second Day" of Sylvester (and, of course, DuBartas) and the flexibly articulated argument on poetic morality Lord Falkland addressed to George Sandys on the occasion of the latter's *Paraphrase Upon the Psalms*.[1]

As these comparisons should suggest, Sylvester's poetic practice, which Dryden came to describe as "abominable fustian," [2] was close in

---

[1] Pp. 279–81 in this book.
[2] *Essays*, ed. W. P. Ker (Oxford, 1900), I, 247.

both meter and tone to English medieval couplet poetry, not to that which contemporary poets were establishing under the inspiration of Latin poetry. The windy grandeur and high seriousness of DuBartas, which could not have endured the sharp definitions of the elegiac couplet or the sharp scrutiny of public conversation, Sylvester was able to acclimatize easily to the more assertive and the less self-conscious measures of the early English couplet. His influence, correspondingly, was negligible in the establishment of the closed couplet; its chief beneficiaries were the composers of vast, exalted, and improving poems, the Fletchers, John Milton, and Sir Richard Blackmore.

THE FIRST DAY OF THE FIRST WEEK

Thou glorious Guide of Heavns star-glistring motion,
Thou, thou (true *Neptune*) Tamer of the *Ocean*,
Thou Earths dread Shaker, at whose only word,
Th' *Eolian* Scoutes are quickly still'd and stirr'd:
Lift up my soule, my drossie spirits refine,   5
With learned Arte enrich this Worke of mine:
O Father, graunt I sweetly warble forth
Unto our seed the *Worlds* renowned *Birth*:
Graunt (gracious God) that I record in verse
The rarest Beauties of this *Universe*,   10
And graunt therein, thy power I may discerne,
That teaching others, I my selfe may learne.
    And also graunt (great Architect of Wonders,
Whose mighty Voice Speakes in the midst of Thunders,
Causing the Rockes to rocke, and Hills to teare;   15
Calling the things that are not, as they Were;
Confounding mighty things by meanes of weake;
Teaching dumbe Infants thy dread Praise to speake;
Inspiring Wisedome into those that want,
And giving knowledge to the ignorant)   20
Graunt me good Lord (as thou hast giv'n me hart
To undertake so excellent a Part)
Graunt me such Judgement, Grace, and Eloquence,
So correspondent to that Excellence,
That in some measure, I may seeme t'inherit   25
(Elisha-*like*) *my dear* Elias *Spirit.*

CLEARE FIRE for ever hath not Ayre imbrast,
Nor aye the Ayre inviron'd Waters vaste,
Nor Waters alwayes wrapt the Earth therein
But all this *All* did once (of nought) begin.   30
Once All was made; not by the hand of *Fortune*
(As fond *Democritus* did yerst importune)
With jarring Concords making Motes to meete,
Invisible, immortall, infinite.
    Th' immutable devine decree, which shall   35
Cause the Worlds End, caus'd his originall:
Neither in Time, nor yet before the same,
But in the instant when Time first became,
I meane a Time confused; for the course
Of yeares, of monthes, of weekes, of dayes, of howers,   40
Of Ages, Times, and Seasons is confin'd
By th' ordred Daunce unto the Starres assign'd.

.   .   .   .

The World's a Schoole, where (in a generall Storie)
God alwayes reades dumbe Lectures of his Glorie:
A paire of Staires, whereon by certaine steps,
Our mounting Soule above Heav'ns arches leapes: 160
A sumptuous Hall, where God on every side,
His wealthy Shop of wonders opens wide:
A bridge, whereby we may passe o're at ease
Of sacred Secrets the broad bound-lesse Seas.
    The World's a Cloud, through which there shineth cleere   165
Not faire *Latona's* quiv'red Darling deere,
But the true *Phoebus*, whose bright countenance
Through thickest vaile of darkest night doth glance.
    The World's a Stage, where Gods Omnipotence,
His Justice, Knowledge, Love, and Providence,   170
Doo act their parts; contending in their kindes,
Above the Heav'ns to ravish dullest mindes.
    The World's a Booke in *Folio*, printed all
With God's great Workes in Letters Capitall:
Each Creature, is a Page, and each effect,   175
A faire Caracter, void of all defect.
    But, as young Trewants, toying in the Schooles,
Instead of Learning, learne to play the fooles:
We gaze but on the Babies and the Cover,

The gawdie Flowers, and Edges guilded over;   180
And never farther for our *Lesson* looke
Within the Volume of this various Booke:
Where learned Nature rudest ones instructs,
That by his wisedome God the World conducts.
    To read this Booke, we neede not understand   185
Each Strangers gibbrish; neither take in hand
Turkes Caracters, nor *Hebrue* Points to seeke,
Nyle's Hieroglyphikes, nor the Notes of *Greeke.*
The wandring *Tartars,* and th' *Antartikes* wilde,
Th' *Alarbies* fierce, the *Scithians* fell, the Childe   190
Scarce seav'n yeare old, the bleared aged eye,
Though void of Arte, read heere indifferently.
But he that weares the spectacles of *Faith,*
Sees through the Spheares above their highest heigth:
He comprehends th' Arch-moover of all Motions,   195
And reades (though running) all these needfull Notions.
Therefore, by *Faith's* pure rayes illumined,
These sacred *Pandects* I desire to read;
And, God the better to behold, behold
Th' Orbe from his Birth, in's Ages manifold.   200

.   .   .   .

DuBARTAS, LA CREATION DU MONDE, LE PREMIER JOUR

Toy qui guides le cours du ciel porte-flambeaux,
Qui, vray Neptune, tiens le moite frein des eaux,
Qui fais trembler la terre, et de qui la parole
Serre et lasche la bride aux postillons d'AEole,
Esleve à toy mon ame, espure mes esprits,   *5*
Et d'un docte artifice enrichy mes escrits.
O Pere, donne-moy que d'une voix faconde
Je chante à nos neveux la naissance du monde.
O grand Dieu, donne-moy que j'estale en mes vers
Les plus rares beautez de ce grand univers;   *10*
Donne-moy qu'en son front ta puissance je lisse,
Et qu'enseignant autruy, moy-mesme je m'instruise.
    De tousjours le clair feu n'environne les airs,
Les airs d'eternité n'environnent les mers;

La terre de tout temps n'est ceinte de Neptune;   15
Tout ce Tout fut basti, non des mains de fortune,
Faissant entrechoquer par discordans accords
Du resveur Democrit les invisibles corps:
   L'immuable decret de la bouche divine,
Qui causera sa fin, causa son origine.   20
Non en temps, avant temps, ains mesme avec le temps,
J'entens un temps confus, car les courses des ans,
Des siecles, des saisons, des moys, et des journees,
Par le bal mesuré des astres sont bornees.

.   .   .   .

Vrayment, cest univers est une docte eschole,   135
Où Dieu son propre honneur enseigne sans parole,
Une vis à repos, qui, par certains degrez,
Fait monter nos esprits sur les planchers sacrez
Du Ciel porte-brandons, une superbe sale
Où Dieu publiquement ses richesses estale;   140
Un pont sur qui l'on peut sans crainte d'abysmer,
Des mysteres divins passer la large mer.
   Le monde est un nuage, à travers qui rayone,
Non le fils tire-traits de la belle Latone,
Ains ce divin Phoebus, dont le visage luit   145
A travers l'espesseur de la plus noire nuict.
   Le monde est un theatre, où de Dieu la puissance,
La justice, l'amour, le sçavoir, la prudence,
Jouent leur personnage, et comme à qui mieux mieux,
Les esprits plus pesans ravissent sur les cieux.   150
Le monde est un grand livre, où du souverain maistre
L'admirable artifice on list en grosse lettre.
Chasque oeuvre est une page, et chasque sien effect
Est un beau charactere en tous ses traits parfaict.
Mais tous tels que l'enfant qui se paist dans l'eschole,   155
Pour l'estude des arts, d'un estude frivole,
Nostre oeil admire tant ses marges peinturez,
Son cuir fleurdelizé, et ses bords sur-dorez,
Que rien il ne nous chaud d'apprendre la lecture
De ce texte disert, où la docte nature   160
Enseigne aux plus grossiers qu'une Divinité
Police de ses loix ceste ronde Cité.
Pour lire là dedans il ne nous faut entendre
Cent sortes de jargons, il ne nous faut apprendre

Les characteres turcs, de Memphe les pourtraits,   165
Ny les points des Hebrieux, ny les notes des Grecs.
L'Antarctique brutal, le vagabond Tartare,
L'Alarbe plus cruel, le Scythe plus barbare,
L'enfant qui n'a sept ans, le chassieux vieillard,
Y lit passablement, bien que despourveu d'art.   170
Mais celuy qui la Foy reçoit pour ses lunettes,
Passe de part en part les cercles des planettes,
Comprend le grand Moteur de tous ces mouvemens,
Et lit bien plus courant dans ces vieux documens.
    Ainsi donc, esclairé par la Foy, je desire   175
Les textes plus sacrez de ces panchartes lire.
Et depuis son enfance, en ses aages divers,
Pour mieux contempler Dieu, contempler l'univers.

.   .   .   .

THE SECOND DAY OF THE FIRST WEEK

Those learned Spirits, whose wits applied wrong,
With wanton Charmes of their inchanting song,
Make of an old, foule, frantike *Hecuba*,
A wondrous fresh, faire, wittie *Helena*:
Of lewd *Faustine*, that loose Emperesse,   5
A chaste *Lucretia*, loathing wantonnesse:
Of a blind Bowe-Boy, of a Dwarfe, a Bastard,
No pettie Godling, but the Gods great Maister.
On thank-lesse furrowes of a fruit-lesse sand
Their seed and labour lose, with heed-lesse hand: 10
And pitching of a Net to catch the winde
Of a fond Fame that doth bewitch their minde.
Resemble Spiders, that with curious paine
Weave idle Webs, and labour still in vaine.
    But (though then time we have no deerer treasure,)   15
Lesse should I waile their mis-expence of leasure,
If their sweet *Muse* with too-well-spoken Spell,
Drew not their Readers with themselves to Hell.
    Under the honey of their learned Workes
A hatefull draught of deadly poyson lurkes,   20
Whereof (alas) young Spirits quaffe so deepe,

That drunke with Love, their Reason falls a sleepe;
And such a habite their fond Fancie gets,
That their ill stomack still loves evill meates.
    Th' inchanting force of their sweet Eloquence   25
Tumbles downe headlong their soft audience,
Who from the steepe Mount of this Icie life
Slide for the first fall, with a foolish strife.
    The Songs their *Phoebus* doth so sweet inspier,
Are even the Bellowes whence they blow the fier   30
Of raging Lust (before) whose wanton flashes
A tender brest rakt-up in Shame-fac'd ashes.
    Therefore, for my part I have vow'd to Heav'n
Such wit and learning as my God hath giv'n,
To write to th' honour of my Maker dread,   35
Verse that a Virgine without blush may read.

.   .   .   .

DuBARTAS, LA CREATION DU MONDE, LE SECOND JOUR

Tous ces doctes esprits, dont la voix flateresse
Change Hecube en Helene et Faustine en Lucresse,
Qui d'un nain, d'un bastard, d'un archerot sans yeux,
Font, non un dieutelet, ains le maistre des dieux,
Sur les ingrats seillons d'une infertile arene,   5
Perdent, mal-avisez, leur travail et leur graine,
Et tendans un filé pour y prendre le vent
D'un los, je ne sçay quel, qui les va decevant,
Se font imitateurs de l'araigne qui file
D'un art laborieux une toile inutile.   10
Mais bien que nous n'ayons rien plus cher que le temps,
Peu je regretteroy la perte de leurs ans,
Si par ces vers pipeurs leur muse trop diserte,
Se perdant, ne trainoit des auditeurs la perte.
Sous le meilleux apast de leurs doctes escrits   15
Ils cachent le venin que les jeunes esprits
Avalent à longs traicts, et du vin d'amour yvres,
Leur mauvais estomach aime les mauvais vivres.
D'un rude eslancement leurs carmes enchanteurs

Precipitent en bas les novices lecteurs,   20
Qui font à mieux glisser d'une folastre envie
Par le pendant glacé du mont de ceste vie.
Les vers que leur Phoebus chante si doucement,
Sont les soufflets venteux dont il vont r'alumant
L'impudique chaleur, qu'une poitrine tendre   25
Couvoit sous l'espaisseur d'une honteuse cendre.
   Or tout tel que je suis, du tout j'ay destiné
Ce peu d'art et d'esprit que le ciel m'a donné
A l'honneur du grand Dieu, pour nuit et jour escrire
Des vers que sans rougir la vierge puisse lire.   30

.   .   .   .

VII

✠✠✠✠✠✠✠✠✠✠✠✠✠✠✠

MICHAEL DRAYTON
(1563-1631)

In the elegies, which he wrote toward the end of his career, Drayton achieved a flexible couplet production that no doubt owed much to Ben Jonson. The first lines of his "Elegy to Henry Reynolds," with their mingled ease and trenchancy, especially suggest this debt. But Drayton has also caught something of Jonson's style in the witty, Ovidian "Elegy on his Lady's not Coming to London." There are several neatly closed couplets in this poem (ll. 35–36, 39–40),[1] but usually Drayton has worked out a lively interplay between couplet definition and the flow of the thought: the meter sharpens relationships (ll. 49–50) and emphasizes major elements (ll. 43–44) without retarding the poem's movement. The English of this poem, although not perfect (notice the unlucky repetition of "you" in lines 35–36 and the dangling "by" phrase), is cleaner and more natural than that for which Drayton often settled.

England's Heroical Epistles, that adaptation of Ovid's *Heroides* which the patriotic Drayton made near the beginning of his career, although popular among his countrymen, was not very successful. Drayton composed this long work, like Marlowe in his translation of *Amores*, in pervasively closed elegiac couplets: in "Rosamond to King Henry the Second," for example, he achieved variously balanced half-lines (ll. 3, 6, 7, 8, 63, 129), lines (ll. 13–14, 14–15, 65–66, 71–72, 129–30), and couplets (ll. 67–70), and often used periodic inversion to emphasize the integrity of lines (ll. 5, 14, 63, 66, 70) and couplets (ll. 11–12, 120–21). One occasionally finds an Ovidian density in the ordering, in the second line of this couplet, for instance — "Once did I sinne, which Memorie doth cherish, / Once I offended but I ever perish" — which defines half of a 'Once–Once' parallel and all of a 'Once–ever' antithesis. The effect

---

[1] My line references correspond to the line notations in *The Works of Michael Drayton*, ed. J. William Hebel (Oxford, 1965), 5 vols.

is, of course, weakened by the two-syllable rhyme and much more by the fact that the half-line "Once I offended," is a mere rewording of the half-line "Once did I sinne." Such diffuseness as this is the besetting sin of *England's Heroical Epistles*. The three couplets on Rosamond's rejection by her own family (ll. 133–38), to further exemplify it, could easily have been condensed into one, "The Clifford's take from me their famous name, / And call me bastard since I whore became," a couplet whose English, by the way, should not have offended Drayton. Even so seemingly neat and pithy a couplet as "This scribbled Paper which I send to thee, / If rightly noted, doth resemble me" is really only the one line, "This scribbled Paper doth resemble me," interrupted and blown up. The formal emphasis of the couplet, the integrity and weight it gives each of its elements, naturally exaggerates this diffuseness, this dependence on expletives to fill up the measures. The stiffness of these couplets, a stiffness whose chief characteristic is an extremely heavy first-line stop (ll. 5, 7, 63, 65, 73, 121, 129, 137), obviously makes matters worse. In this poem, then, Drayton has used the emphatic and definitive powers of the couplet to bring out the meagerness of his imagination.

If *England's Heroical Epistles* looks to *Heroides* for its source and its sanction, *Endymion and Phoebe* looks to *Hero and Leander*. Each item of action and description in Drayton's poem, as in that of Marlowe, receives some kind of couplet definition — but so transient and so oblique a definition that its flow into the next item is easy and smooth. In the description of Phoebe, for instance, Phoebe's mantle takes up three full couplets (ll. 111–16) — not just one, however, be it noticed — and her smock three more (ll. 121–26). The descriptive force of each of the first two couplets on the mantle is strengthened by ending on a brief simile. The whole description of Phoebe, again, is concluded with a brief general observation and closed with the close of a couplet (ll. 130–32) — a Marlovian practice, we may remember.

Drayton recast this description of Phoebe some years later in writing *The Man in the Moon*, running it to a hundred and twenty lines. Phoebe's mantle in this new description is introduced so obliquely, coming as the object in a subordinate clause well along in a long sentence (ll. 139–46), described at such length (ll. 146–220), and dismissed with so complete a lack of notification that a reader is aware only faintly and only here and there that he is being presented all the while with Phoebe's mantle. This description, some notice of which we took in the "History," is hazy throughout. In lines 163–78, for instance, one is unable, without the kind of close study that runs counter to the promptings of the verse, to determine simple syntactic relationships: who do the "Waters . . . scold" (ll. 163–72)? does the same actor/actors engage in the thrusting (l. 168) as in the looking (l. 169)? and who is/ are he/they? The relevance, the grammatical connection, and even the extent of the "Rich men" figure (ll. 170 ff.) are, likewise, unclear. And there is nothing here, even if we decide on the elements of this description, to remind us that it is all a part of the decoration of Phoebe's mantle. In this recasting of materials, Drayton has gone in one step from the controlled enjambment of Marlowe's romance to the romantic abandonment, the romantic perversity, of William Chamberlayne's *Pharonnida*.

Drayton picked up the couplet style for his *Moon Calf* from still another great source, from the medieval practice of Chaucer and Spenser. Drayton's introduction of his four storytellers (ll. 575–626) proclaims this ancestry, most closely echoing Spenser's opening of his *Mother Hubberd's Tale*. Drayton's complaint of the universal prevalence and triumph of vice (ll. 243–54, 263–72) and his catalogue of monsters (ll. 684–774), a part of which I here quote, have more general roots in the Middle Ages:

> Another foole, to fit him for the weather,
> Had arm'd his heeles with Cork, his head with feather;
> And in more strange and sundry colours clad,
> Then in the Raine-bowe ever can be had:
> Stalk'd through the Streets, preparing him to flie,
> Up to the Moone upon an Embassie.
> Another seeing his drunken Wife disgorge
> Her pamperd stomack, got her to a Forge,
> And in her throat the Feverous heat to quench
> With the Smiths horne, was giving her a Drench:
> One his next Neighbour haltred had by force,
> So frantique, that he tooke him for a Horse,
> And to a Pond was leading him to drinke;
> It went beyond the wit of man to thinke,
> The sundry frenzies that he there might see,
> One man would to another married be:
> And for a Curate taking the Towne Bull,
> Would have him knit the knot.

Drayton's horrified surrender to the panorama of vice and folly in this passage, a surrender signalled by the widely diverse degrees to which the different items are developed and by the confusedly enjambed and broken verses in which they realize themselves, resembles a satiric painting of Bosch or, closer still, one of Breughel at his most miscellaneous and incidental. Each item in Drayton's catalogue is forceful and frightful enough in itself, but there is nothing, except the wedged-in exclamations of Drayton's passive observer, to bring them to bear — to assert a pattern among them or to suggest an ideal against which they can be judged. The necessary ethical understanding had been built into the Middle Ages, but, as John Donne painfully recognized, that understanding was crumbling terribly during the time that he and Drayton were living. *The Moon Calf* was thus an anachronism in its very conception. So stiff, so irregular, and so unresponsive an utterance could not represent the new age or cope with its problems.

The variety of Drayton's couplet poems, none of which is perfectly valuable in itself, suggests the tremendous ferment the heroic couplet was making in English poetry between 1590 and 1630. These poems reveal, first, the range of poetic opportunities the form offered to the poets of this time and, second, the dangers with which it confronted them — the problem they faced in working it into a coherent poetic medium.

VIII

𐀭𐀭𐀭𐀭𐀭𐀭𐀭𐀭𐀭𐀭𐀭𐀭𐀭

CHRISTOPHER MARLOWE
(1564-1593)

Marlowe translated the closed elegiac distichs of Ovid's *Amores*, in his *Ovid's Elegies*, into almost exactly corresponding closed heroic couplets. And he was able, by doing so, to duplicate in English much of his Latin model's balance and precision. Marlowe brought over, for instance, the *'oscula–oscula'* (I, iv, 64), *'ante–ante'* (I, iv, 13–14), and *'tangere–tange'* (I, iv, 57–58) verbal patterns from Ovid, and others, such as the *'canit–cantanti'* echo (II, iv, 25–26), he approximated. Marlowe may even be argued to have overgone his master in a few cases — such as the *'molliter–mollior'* echo (and off-pun?) (II, iv, 23–24), for which he substituted the 'nimbler–lying' paradox. Admittedly, Marlowe lost many of Ovid's verbal patterns — the *'surges–surgemus'* (I, iv, 55) and *'Placeo–placet'* (II, iv, 20) echoes, for instance — and thus has given only a weakened impression of his model's pervasive polish and grace. Still, he achieved a remarkable equivalency of Ovid in his translation.

In doing so Marlowe was forced to leave here and there whole couplets, whole units of this most lucid form of verse, in poor and even nonsensical English (I, iv, 59–60; II, ix, 9–10; II, xix, 11–12). He also closed off many first lines that he found enjambed in his model (I, iv, 11; II, iv, 19; II, xix, 13; II, xix, 17), thus reducing the flexibility of verse that was already, as Ovid had practiced it, dangerously mannered and static. Sometimes, however, Marlowe duplicated Ovid's intradistich enjambment (I, iv, 15; I, xv, 19) or even practiced it where Ovid had not (II, iv, 25–26). More striking than these incidental improvements is Marlowe's success in capturing the periodic inversions by which Ovid defined first lines of his distichs. One such Ovidian distich comes out in Marlowe: "Why me that always was thy souldiour found, / Doest harme, and in thy tents why doest me wound?" (II, ix, 3–4). Another reads in Marlowe: "Thou also that late tookest mine eyes away, / Oft

[193]

couzen me, oft being wooed say nay" (II, xix, 19–20). The parallel predicates in this second line, by the way, also reflect the Ovidian original. It will be noticed that the periodic definition of these two first lines encounters, in both cases, syntactic thrust. This practice, by which a first line is both defined and enjambed at once, marks a step toward closed-couplet dynamics of great formal importance.

Some of Marlowe's English adaptations of essentially Latin effects are also formally portentous. The impression of poise Ovid gets in such a line as *"non est certa meos quae forma invitet amores"* by placing terms syntactically in agreement, *"certa . . . forma"* and *"meos . . . amores,"* on either half of his line Marlowe could only achieve by an explicit balance: "No one face likes me best, all faces move." The witty distinction Ovid could focus in the second half of the pentameter line of this distich — *"Battiades semper toto cantabitur orbe; / quamvis ingenio non valet, arte valet"* — drove Marlowe, again, to a fully balanced second line: "The world shall of *Callimachus* ever speake, / His Arte excelld, although his witte was weake." Thus Marlowe led the way toward the even-flowing, bipartite couplet line. Jonson, by the way, translated the above distich *"Callimachus*, though in invention lowe, / Shall still be sung: since he in art doth flowe," sacrificing Marlowe's line-defined antithesis to achieve intracouplet movement. Pope and Dryden would find ways to realize Marlowe's emphasis and Jonson's movement at once.

As a comparison of *Ovid's Elegies* and *Hero and Leander* shows, Marlowe was at different times a writer of closed and a writer of enjambed couplets. In this he would be followed by Drayton, Shakespeare, Donne, and many others.

Hero and Leander, which stands at the head of a long list of Renaissance romances in enjambed couplets, resembles both Ovidian and Chaucerian couplet practice in incidental ways. There are in this poem several cases of line-strengthening inversions like those Marlowe had copied out of *Amores* (ll. 10, 20, 261)[1] and a number of fairly well-defined couplets — especially in the handling of such material as reasoning (ll. 167–76) and descriptive cataloguing (ll. 145–52), which were susceptible to couplet promptings. On the other hand, one finds heavy first-line pauses (ll. 135, 141) and enjambed couplets (l. 132) which characterize the verse of Chaucer. Marlowe occasionally practices epigrammatic lines (ll. 166, 176) which might remind us either of Ovid's pointed wit or Chaucer's pithy generalizations. But for all this, *Hero and Leander* is neither an Ovidian nor a Chaucerian poem.

---

[1] My line references correspond to the line notations in *The Works of Christopher Marlowe*, ed. C. F. Tucker Brooke (Oxford, 1925).

Marlowe almost never engages in precise rhetorical paralleling in this poem even when his material, a series of mythical lovers (ll. 145–56), say, indicates that form of display. He does not even maintain Chaucer's strong line, but often uses mid-line pause as a main divider of this poem's sense (ll. 15, 53, 65, 71). *Hero and Leander* thus flows along in variously measured waves with no normal place for the reader to pause and, consequently, neither a prompting toward the judgment of statements and their relationships nor a sense of discursive dynamics.

Marlowe does not make any pointed address to his readers or any attempt to define them. His poem glides from one incidental pause and from one incidental item of expression to the next as though its author — one can hardly say speaker — were totally neglectful of his audience and responsive only to the wayward impulses of his fancy. The poem, thus, merely allows those readers who desire it to drift into an escapist reverie, using the poet's rich and highly educated imagination instead of their own. The impressionistic responsiveness and seductive fluency of its verse, which especially pervade the description of Leander (ll. 51–76), wonderfully suited Marlowe's romantic, luxurious intentions. But his example prompted less imaginative and less artful poets to cultivate a metrical perversity which made their poems confusing and tedious.

OVID'S ELEGIES, I, iv

Thy husband to a banquet goes with me,
Pray God it may his latest supper be.
Shall I sit gazing as a bashfull guest,
While others touch the damsell I love best?
Wilt lying under him his bosome clippe?   5
About thy neck shall he at pleasure skippe?
Marveile not, though the faire Bride did incite
The drunken *Centaures* to a sodaine fight.
I am no halfe horse, nor in woods I dwell,
Yet scarse my hands from thee containe I well.   10
But how thou shouldst behave thy selfe now know:
Nor let the windes away my warnings blowe.
Before thy husband come, though I not see
What may be done, yet there before him bee.
Lie with him gently, when his limbes he spread   15
Upon the bed, but on my foote first tread.

.   .   .   .

Entreat thy husband drinke, but do not kisse,
And while he drinkes, to adde more do not misse,
If hee lyes down with Wine and sleepe opprest,
The thing and place shall counsell us the rest.
When to go homewards we rise all along,   55
Have care to walke in middle of the throng.
There will I finde thee, or be found by thee,
There touch what ever thou canst touch of mee.
Aye me, I warne what profits some few howers,
But we must part, when heav'n with black night lowers.   60
At night thy husband clippes thee, I will weepe
And to the dores sight of thy selfe keepe:
Then will he kisse thee, and not onely kisse
But force thee give him my stolne honey blisse.
Constrain'd against thy will give it the pezant,   65
Forbeare sweet wordes, and be your sport unpleasant.
To him I pray it no delight may bring,
Or if it do, to thee no joy thence spring:
But though this night thy fortune be to trie it,
To me to morrow constantly deny it.   70

OVID, AMORES, I, iv

Vir tuus est epulas nobis aditurus easdem —
  ultima coena tue sit, precor, illa viro!
ergo ego dilectam tantum conviva puellam
  adspiciam? tangi quem iuvet, alter erit,
alteriusque sinus apte subiecta fovebis?   5
  iniciet collo, cum volet, ille manum?
desine mirari, posito quod candida vino
  Atracis ambiguos traxit in arma viros!
nec mihi silva domus, nec equo mea membra cohaerent —
  vix a te videor posse tenere manus!   10
Quae tibi sint facienda tamen cognosce, nec Euris
  da mea nec tepidis verba ferenda Notis!
ante veni, quam vir — nec quid, si veneris ante,
  possit agi video; sed tamen ante veni.
cum premet ille torum, vultu comes ipsa modesto   15
  ibis, ut accumbas — clam mihi tange pedem!

.   .   .   .

vir bibat usque roga — precibus tamen oscula desint! —
  dumque bibit, furtim si potes, adde merum.
se bene conpositus somno vinoque iacebit,
  consilium nobis resque locusque dabunt.
cum surges abitura domum, surgemus et omnes,   55
  in medium turbae fac memor agmen eas.
agmine me invenies aut invenieris in illo:
  quidquid ibi poteris tangere, tange mei.
Me miserum! monui, paucas quod prosit in horas;
  separor a domina nocte iubente mea.   60
nocte vir includet, lacrimis ego maestus obortis,
  qua licet, ad saevas prosequar usque fores.
oscula iam sumet, iam non tantum oscula sumet:
  quod mihi das furtim, iure coacta dabis.
verum invita dato — potes hoc — similisque coactae;   65
  blanditiae taceant, sitque maligna Venus.
si mea vota valent, illum quoque ne iuvet, opto;
  si minus, at certe te iuvet inde nihil.
sed quaecumque tamen noctem fortuna sequetur,
  cras mihi constanti voce dedisse nega!   70

OVID'S ELEGIES, I, xv

Homer shall live while *Tenedos* stands and *Ide*,
Or into Sea swift *Simois* doth slide.   10
Ascraeus lives, while grapes with new wine swell,
Or men with crooked Sickles corne downe fell.
The world shall of *Callimachus* ever speake,
His Arte excelld, although his witte was weake.
For ever lasts high *Sophocles* proud vaine,   15
With Sunne and Moone *Aratus* shall remaine.
While bond-men cheate, fathers hard, bawds whorish,
And strumpets flatter, shall *Menander* flourish.
Rude *Ennius*, and *Plautus* full of witt,
Are both in fames eternall legend writt.   20

.   .   .   .

Therefore when Flint and Iron weare away,
Verse is immortall, and shall nere decay.
To verse let Kings give place, and Kingly showes,
And bankes ore which gold-bearing *Tagus* flowes.

Let base conceipted witts admire vilde things,   35
Faire *Phoebus* lead me to the Muses springs.
About my head be quivering mirtle wound,
And in sad lovers heads let me be found.

. . . .

OVID, AMORES, I, xv

Vivet Maeonides, Tenedos dum stabit et Ide,
   dum rapidas Simois in mare volvet aquas;   10
vivet et Ascraeus, dum mustis uva tumebit,
   dum cadet incurva falce resecta Ceres.
Battiades semper toto cantabitur orbe;
   quamvis ingenio non valet, arte valet.
nulla Sophocleo veniet iactura cothurno;   15
   cum sole et luna semper Aratus erit;
dum fallax servus, durus pater, inproba lena
   vivent et meretrix blanda, Menandros erit;
Ennius arte carens animosique Accius oris
   casurum nullo tempore nomen habent.

. . . .

Ergo, cum silices, cum dens patientis aratri
   depereant aevo, carmina morte carent.
cedant carminibus reges regumque triumphi,
   cedat et auriferi ripa benigna Tagi!
vilia miretur vulgus; mihi flavus Apollo   35
   pocula Castalia plena ministret aqua,
sustineamque coma metuentem frigora myrtum,
   atque ita sollicito multus amante legar!

. . . .

OVID'S ELEGIES, II, iv[2]

No one face likes me best, all faces move,
A hundred reasons make me ever love.   10
If any eye me with a modest looke,

---

[2] See pp. 334–35 in this book for John Oldham's translation of this Ovidian material.

I burn, and by that blushfull glance am tooke.
And she thats coy I like for being no clowne,
Me thinkes she would be nimble when shees downe.
Though her sowre lookes a *Sabines* browe resemble,   15
I thinke sheele do, but deepely can dissemble.
If she be learn'd, then for her skill I crave her,
If not, because shees simple I would have her.
Before *Callimachus* one preferres me farre,
Seeing she likes my bookes why should we jarre?   20
An other railes at me and that I write
Yet would I lie with her if that I might.
Trips she, it likes me well, plods she, what then?
Shee would be nimbler, lying with a man.
And when one sweetely sings, then straight I long   25
To quaver on her lips even in her song.
Or if one touch the Lute with arts and cunning
Who wold not love those hands for their swift running?

.   .   .   .

OVID, AMORES, II, iv

Non est certa meos quae forma invitet amores —
    centum sunt causae, cur ego semper amem.   *10*
sive aliqua est oculos in se deiecta modestos,
    uror, et insidiae sunt pudor ille meae;
sive procax aliqua est, capior, quia rustica non est,
    spemque dat in molli mobilis esse toro.
aspera si visa est rigidasque imitata Sabinas,   *15*
    velle, sed ex alto dissimulare puto.
sive es docta, places raras dotata per artes;
    sive rudis, placita es simplicitate tua.
est, quae Callimachi prae nostris rustica dicat
    carmina — cui placeo, protinus ipsa placet.   *20*
est etiam, quae me vatem et mea carmina culpet —
    culpantis cupiam sustinuisse femur.
molliter incedit — motu capit; altera dur est —
    at poterit tacto mollior esse viro.
haec quia dulce canit flectitque facillima vocem,   *25*
    oscula cantanti rapta dedisse velim;

haec querulas habili percurrit pollice chordas —
  tam doctas quis non possit amare manus?

.   .   .   .

OVID'S ELEGIES, II, ix[3]

O *Cupid* that doest never cease my smart,
O boy that lyest so slothfull in my heart.
Why me that alwayes was thy souldiour found,
Doest harme, and in thy tents why doest me wound?
Why burnes thy brand, why strikes thy bow thy friends?   5
More glory by thy vanquisht foes assends.
Did not *Pelides* whom his Speare did grieve,
Being requirde, with speedy helpe relieve?
Hunters leave taken beasts, pursue the chase,
And then things found do ever further pace.   10
We people wholy given thee feele thine armes,
Thy dull hand stayes thy striving enemies harmes.
Doest joy to have thy hooked Arrowes shaked
In naked bones? love hath my bones left naked.
So many men and maidens without love,   15
Hence with great laude thou maiest a triumph move.
Rome if her strength the huge world had not fild,
With strawie cabins now her courts should build.
The weary souldiour hath the conquerd fields,
His sword layed by, safe, though rude places yeelds.   20
The Docke inharbours ships drawne from the flouds,
Horse freed from service range abroad the woods,
And time it was for me to live in quiet,
That have so oft serv'd pretty wenches dyet.

.   .   .   .

OVID, AMORES, II, ix

O numquam pro me satis indignate Cupido,
  o in corde meo desidiose puer —
quid me, qui miles numquam tua signa reliqui,
  laedis, et in castris vulneror ipse meis?

---

[3] The Earl of Rochester also translated this elegy.

cur tua fax urit, figit tuus arcus amicos?   5
  gloria pugnantes vincere maior erat.
Quid? non Haemonius, quem cuspide perculit, heros
  confossum medica postmodo iuvit ope?
venator sequitur fugientia; capta relinquit
  semper et inventis ulteriora petit.   10
nos tua sentimus, populus tibi deditus, arma;
  pigra reluctanti cessat in hoste manus.
quid iuvat in nudis hamata retundere tela
  ossibus? ossa mihi nuda relinquit amor.
tot sine amore viri, tot sunt sine amore puellae! —   15
  hinc tibi cum magna laude triumphus eat.
Roma, nisi inmensum vires movisset in orbem,
  stramineis esset nunc quoque tecta casis.
Fessus in acceptos miles deducitur agros;
  mittitur in saltus carcere liber equus;   20
longaque subductam celant navalia pinum,
  tutaque deposito poscitur ense rudis.
me quoque, qui totiens merui sub amore puellae,
  defunctum placide vivere tempus erat.

.   .   .   .

OVID'S ELEGIES, II, xix[4]

What should I do with fortune that nere failes me?
Nothing I love, that at all times availes me.
Wily *Corinna* sawe this blemish in me,
And craftily knowes by what meanes to winne me.   10
Ah often, that her haole head aked, she lying,
Wild me, whose slowe feete sought delay by flying.
Ah oft how much she might she feignd offence;
And doing wrong made shew of innocence.
So having vext she nourisht my warme fire,   15
And was againe most apt to my desire.
To please me, what faire termes and sweet words ha's shee?
Great gods what kisses, and how many gave she?
Thou also that late tookest mine eyes away,
Oft couzen me, oft being wooed say nay.   20
And on thy threshold let me lie dispred,

---

[4] Dryden also made a translation of this elegy.

Suffring much cold by hoary nights frost bred.
So shall my love continue many yeares,
This doth delight me, this my courage cheares.
Fat love, and too much fulsome me annoyes,   25
Even as sweete meate a glutted stomacke cloyes.

.   .   .   .

OVID, AMORES, II, xix

Quo mihi fortunam, quae numquam fallere curet?
   nil ego, quod nullo tempore laedat, amo!
Viderat hoc in me vitium versuta Corinna,
   quaque capi possem, callida norat opem.   10
a, quotiens sani capitis mentita dolores
   cunctantem tardo iussit abire pede!
a, quotiens finxit culpam, quantumque licebat
   insonti, speciem praebuit esse nocens!
sic ubi vexarat tepidosque refoverat ignis,   15
   rursus erat votis comis et apta meis.
quas mihi blanditias, quam dulcia verba parabat
   oscula, di magni, qualia quotque dabat!
Tu quoque, quae nostros rapuisti nuper ocellos,
   saepe time insidias, saepe rogata nega;   20
et sine me ante tuos proiectum in limine postis
   longa pruinosa frigora nocte pati.
sic mihi durat amor longosque adolescit in annos;
   hoc iuvat; haec animi sunt alimenta mei.
pinguis amor nimiumque patens in taedia nobis   25
   vertitur et, stomacho dulcis ut esca, nocet.

.   .   .   .

IX

‡‡‡‡‡‡‡‡‡‡‡‡‡‡‡‡

WILLIAM SHAKESPEARE
(1564-1616)

Shakespeare fit passages of heroic couplets into his plays throughout his career. Examples are: *Two Gentlemen of Verona*, III, i, 89–105; *A Midsummer Night's Dream*, II, i, 32–59; *Richard II*, I, i, 152–205; *Romeo and Juliet*, II, iii, 1–30; *Hamlet*, III, ii, 192–231; *Othello*, II, i, 149–61; and *The Winter's Tale*, IV, i, 1–32.[1] The examples from *Two Gentlemen*, *Romeo and Juliet*, *Hamlet*, and *Othello* are in predominately closed couplets, that from *Two Gentlemen*, indeed, with its witty and balanced love advice, being distinctly Ovidian. The couplet passage from *The Winter's Tale*, which is the prologue to the second part of this dramatic romance, has close stylistic affinities with the enjambed romance couplet and, on the other hand, with the couplet of Ben Jonson, especially with the practice one finds in Jonson's prologues.

In the couplet passage from *Richard II*, for virtually the only time in his career, Shakespeare worked out a kind of couplet dynamics. It is really a dramatic dynamics, however, which the oscillation of the couplets between a closed and an enjambed movement underscores. We find assembled here the ingredients for an elegant interlude in closed couplets, that is, for an elegant dramatic tableau: two antagonists and two peacemakers with balanced pleadings and professions. But the ceremonial pattern of utterance, inaugurated by Richard, gives way, with wonderfully expressive effect, before the energy and passion of Bolingbroke. Richard loves kingly show but not kingly exertion, the forms but not the stresses of royalty. The closed couplets with which the passage opens and the closed-couplet situation Richard attempts to prescribe declare his plans: he will calm Mowbray, and Gaunt will calm Bolingbroke in

---

[1] My act, scene, and line references correspond to the notations in *The Complete Plays and Poems of William Shakespeare*, ed. W. A. Neilson and C. J. Hill (Cambridge, Mass., 1942).

beautifully mirroring attitudes of command and obedience. But the very first application of this inappropriately aesthetic impulse, his and Gaunt's antiphonal commands of peace (ll. 160–65), fails when the two foes, whose motives are deep and complex, resist. Their resistance is, of course, reflected in the breakdown of couplet closure and balance. Mowbray comes, finally, to submit to the king's mode of utterance, that is, to the king's wishes (ll. 178–85), but not Bolingbroke. His powerfully enjambed speech (ll. 187–95) underscores his recalcitrance. Richard's apparent recapturing of this situation, signalized by his reassertion of closed-couplet utterance after a brief lapse into blank verse (ll. 196–205), is hollow; the antagonists, or at least one of them, have not submitted and will not submit to play parts in Richard's royal puppet show. Shakespeare's handling of the couplet throughout this passage, then, underscores the inadequacy of Richard as a king and the fragility of his rule.

The couplet passage from *A Midsummer Night's Dream*, a passage of enjambed couplets, presents a two-part account of Puck's mischievousness. A fairy gives a series of Puck's tricks (ll. 34–39), which receive line, but not couplet, definition, and a general statement on Puck's favor, which fills a couplet. Then Puck describes three of his tricks in some detail. The first of these descriptions overruns a couplet and ends with the next line (ll. 44–46). The second covers four lines (ll. 47–50), rhyming a, b, b, c, and suffers its chief break in thought at the end of its second line. The third, which covers seven lines (ll. 51–57), breaks into two main segments: the first of which, describing Puck's victim, runs four lines but, once again, not two couplets; the second of which, describing the bystanders, runs three lines, ending finally at a couplet break. The whole passage thus moves, as with Chaucer, not in couplets, but in odd sets of lines. But it is more tightly woven than Chaucer's verse, in accordance with its narrower focus, and makes up a system of series and balances. Shakespeare's occasional line-defined parallels (ll. 54, 55, 56) and periods (ll. 45, 51–52) — especially the periods with their dramatic emphases — further remove this verse from the practice of Chaucer.

The couplet passages from *Romeo and Juliet*, *Hamlet*, and *Othello*, are, in the first place, extremely stiff and mannered in their production and, in the second place, mere interludes in the dramatic action. The passage from *Romeo and Juliet*, although it gives us the necessary information of Friar Laurence's herbal expertise, stands here as a didactic interlude. The closed, tediously measured couplets of the Player King, again, seem expressly designed to make it clear that this stuff, unlike the tragedy of Hamlet, is merely a play, an artifice. Iago's speech, with its courteous address to Desdemona and its mannered misogyny, is the stuff of Pope's *Moral Essay II*—although Pope will achieve a much more fluent and pointed medium for it. But it is merely a diversion in Shakespeare's tragic world; Othello's danger at sea and his imminent deliverance are our chief concern, as they are Desdemona's, all the while Iago is addressing this speech to her. As time transforms the English sensibility, centering it on the social rather than the dramatic modes of life, it will also transform this stiff and consequently meager mode of poetic organization, turning it into a flexible and subtle instrument which can comprehend and punctuate concerns of central importance.

X

JOHN DONNE
(1572-1631)

Even the freest, the roughest, the most enjambed of Donne's couplet productions show some signs of his Ovidian apprenticeship. "The First Anniversary," for instance, quite often steps forward a couplet at a time (ll. 19–24, 121–30).[1] Some of its individual couplets, moreover, show something of the inner patterning which is common in this author's elegies and in his heroic epistle, "Sapho to Philaenis": there is, for instance, one couplet (ll. 23–24) whose second line is balanced between health and lethargy and another (ll. 129–30) which concludes on a tightly wedged right-wrong opposition. The elegies, of course, especially I and IX, and "Sapho to Philaenis" are strikingly Ovidian. In one couplet of "Elegy I" (ll. 15–16), for instance, whose first line makes a general assertion (that the husband is courteous) and whose second validates the assertion with a witty refinement (that his suspicion is a kind of warning), Donne has given an Ovidian sentiment an Ovidian utterance. Several couplets in "Elegy IX" (ll. 3–4, 21–22, 23–24) also achieve an Ovidian closure and rhythm. That poem and "Sapho to Philaenis," moreover, move from couplet to couplet, at least for a long way, in the pointed, fairly static Ovidian manner.

The Ovidian is not, however, Donne's only mode of couplet production. His satires, which were discussed in the preceding "Brief History," reveal that mixture of Juvenalian scope (or roughness) and the epigrammatic point of Martial which characterizes virtually all couplet satire at this time. His anniversary poems, on the other hand, look back to the medieval complaint; one might compare the drawn-out personification of the world in "The First Anniversary" (ll. 1–24), by the way, with an

---

[1] My line references correspond to the line notations in *The Poems of John Donne*, ed. H. J. C. Grierson (Oxford, 1953), 2 vols.

equally drawn-out personification of it at the beginning of Drayton's strongly medieval poem, *The Moon Calf.*

Donne, who often uses caesuras to define the major pivots of his thought (ll. 179, 183, 217, 229), has composed "The First Anniversary" much less in lines and multiline units than such predecessors as Baldwin and Chaucer. He formulates neat Ovidian couplets now and then, as we have already noticed, and he sometimes swirls his verse along with sweeping periods — especially in the "She" passages (ll. 175–84). In these latter cases his verse production approximates blank verse. Nevertheless, Donne has organized this poem basically in the old Chaucerian way, defining his material in segments of varying numbers of lines and, correspondingly, making indiscriminate use of his line and couplet closures.[2] Lines 205–18, for instance, advance, roughly speaking, in one, one, two, two and one-half, one and one-half, two, two and one-half, and one and one-half lines; two of its seven couplets are enjambed, and three of its first lines suffer a major stop. In terms of verse movement, then, it is a medieval poem modified by several Renaissance innovations.

The Renaissance influence is much more evident in the last half of Donne's "Good Friday" (ll. 23–42), a poem which opens in rather a medieval vein, and in virtually all of Donne's verse letters. Their mode of organization and movement, more specifically, is that which in the "Brief History" we called Jonsonian. The couplet in these poems is only one element of a broadly based classical plainness, one aspect of a flexible and diffused design of lucidity and emphasis. One notices, for instance, the paralleling of "that blood" and "that flesh" in corresponding places of succeeding couplets of "Good Friday" (ll. 25–28), but not in the most emphatic places. The grace and control of these poems, their noble reasonableness, explains why Donne's and Jonson's work might occasionally have been confused.

There is, however, in all Donne's poems evidence of his own witty and active spirit. The intellectual acrobatics by which Donne explains his fear of looking on God in "Good Friday" (ll. 15–18), for instance, makes less of an appeal to reason, as Jonson would have done, than a challenge to reason. Or take "Elegy XVI": the twelve-line periodic thrust with which it opens, its enjambed presentation of the series of seducers (ll. 33–43), its parenthetical qualifications and plays of wit (ll. 15,

---

[2] Louis Martz, *The Poetry of Meditation* (New Haven, 1965), p. 233, remarks that "'The First Anniversary' . . . is rigidly divided into sections and subsections . . . [which are] marked by strong pauses and clumsy transitions."

19), its obvious preference of terseness to polish, and its argumentative texture — all these bespeak the poetic genius of Donne. Donne's own witty and contentious qualities of mind and imagination break forth even in an imitative poem like "Sapho to Philaenis" (ll. 37–50) and in a quietly meditative one like "Elegy IX" (ll. 37–44). In both these poems, smooth couplets and neatly lucid thought give way to more trenchant and crabbed utterance — in the first case when Donne argues the relative merits of heterosexual and homosexual love-making, in the second case when his mind snags on the vision of extreme age. "The First Anniversary," likewise, has a trenchancy and refinement of thought and bright shoots of intellectual light that no medieval poet would have recognized. Take, for instance, the parenthesis in this line, "And that except thou feed (not banquet) on," the universal agony of " 'Tis all in pieces, all cohaerence gone," or, finally, the witty analogy between the diminution of the seasons and the procreative diminution of aging women.

The satires reveal Donne's remarkable wit and vigor, probably, better than any other of his couplet poems. Consider, for instance, the first forty lines of "Satire II." [3] They make one great period, a period some of whose subordinate elements are themselves periodic (ll. 11–14, 28–30), and whose conclusion is reached, moreover, only by degrees at lines 44, 48, and 60. The four-line period on the dramatic poet, which is included in this longer measure, is fairly typical of Donne's satiric practice:

> One, (like a wretch, which at Barre judg'd as dead,
> Yet prompts him which stands next, and cannot reade,
> And saves his life) gives ideot actors meanes
> (Starving himselfe) to live by his labor'd sceanes.

The suspensive material which introduces the elements of a double analogy (poet–wretch; actor–illiterate) runs two and one-half lines. The couplet break, which separates the prompting of the illiterate from his salvation, gives this as yet unrelated material a dramatic emphasis — if one can catch and enjoy it. The application of this analogy, which is squeezed into the last line and one-half of the passage, is also dramatically suspended by the splintering of the predicate, "gives . . . meanes . . . to live," and, especially, by line-end emphasis on the quite empty term "meanes": it thus bursts forth only in the last half-line of the passage. Of course, the compression of this complicated figure and its dramatic mode of discovery forced Donne into obscurity:

---

[3] See pp. 58–59 of this book, in which this passage is quoted and discussed.

the pronoun "his" is unclear in reference, and the "Starving himselfe" phrase dangles dangerously. This phrase, moreover, opposes "to live" (whose actual connection to "actors" is also dangerously distant) only obliquely; so the point of this passage, the irony of a poet's starving to death while giving actors the means of life, is hard to grasp. Pope's untangling of this passage wonderfully highlights Donne's and his own aesthetic difference — the one choosing wit and drama, the other politeness and lucidity. Nevertheless, Donne has crammed this matter into two couplets and achieved an epigrammatic balance, if a syntactically slanted one, in his closing line. One can find a similarly eclectic use of closed-couplet effects a few lines later in the plagiarist passage (ll. 25–30), a three-couplet system with a sharply defined last couplet and a brilliantly balanced last line.

Donne, then, responded to virtually every aspect of the heroic couplet which his age had discovered, using the form eclectically to embellish and enrich his own special creative intentions.

XI

✰✰✰✰✰✰✰✰✰✰✰✰✰✰

BEN JONSON
(1572-1637)

The first three couplets of "To Penshurst" —

> Thou art not, PENSHURST, built to envious show,
>   Of touch, or marble; nor canst boast a row
> Of polish'd pillars, or a roofe of gold:
>   Thou hast no lantherne, whereof tales are told;
> Or stayre, or courts; but stand'st an ancient pile,
>   And these grudg'd at, art reverenc'd the while —

fall into two three-line units, not three two-line units, which parallel one another fairly closely: "Thou art not . . . Thou hast no." This passage's second line partially parallels its third line, "Of . . . or . . . / Of . . . or," and not its first or fourth. Lines one through half-two, again, run in series with the next line and one-half; and lines four through half-five balance the second half of five. Only the sixth line, with its 'grudg'd–reverenc'd' opposition, achieves the metrical-rhetorical reinforcement which will be common in closed-couplet poetry after Waller. Still, of course, the passage gives lucid and trenchant, if not perfectly explicit, utterance to the distinction between Penshurst and more flashy dwellings.

The whole first half of "To Penshurst," to further exemplify Ben Jonson's flexible couplet production, is a series of Penshurst's possessions rendered in nonequivalent, imperfectly parallel units. The series's general introduction (ll. 7–8) [1] takes up one single, unbalanced couplet. Its first particular item, walks, covers one line; its second item, mount, fills out this couplet and then covers four more couplets; the coppice covers

---

[1] My line references correspond to the line notations in *Ben Jonson*, ed. C. H. Herford and Percy and Evelyn Simpson (Oxford, 1947), VIII.

[210]

three lines; the lower lands, two (although not a couplet); and so it goes. The general introduction, moreover, is signified differently ("Thou joy'st") from the particular items ("Thou hast"). And this formal sign, yet again, holds its normal position at a couplet's beginning only once after its first use (l. 32); and in several cases (ll. 22, 39) it has vanished altogether. The catalogue of game further shows this orderly and yet flexible style: "coneyes" takes up a long half-line, "pheasant," three and one-half, and "partrich," a full couplet; "carps," again, after a couplet on fish in general, takes up a line, "pikes," three lines, and "eeles" another full couplet. The two sections of this catalogue thus advance in accordance with the particular expository requirements of the individual members, but not in perfect accordance with the poetic form.

The syntax of this and, indeed, of the whole catalogue of Penshurst's possessions is also flexible — with a wonderfully expressive effect. The inanimate possessions shift back and forth between their normal accusative condition ("Thou hast . . . walkes . . . copp's . . . ponds") and the grammatically more eminent nominative condition ("The middle grounds . . . breed"; "Each banke doth yeeld"). Further still, the animate provisions of these inanimate parts of the estate also leap on two occasions into the nominative case ("partrich . . . is willing"; "pikes . . . themselves betray"). This exaltation of subordinate items may seem, at first, to give them a kind of Chaucerian dignity, each one taking the center of the poem for its moment, but since Jonson has conferred this dignity eclectically — the purple pheasant being provided willy-nilly by the coppice whereas the metrically and substantially equivalent painted partridge is himself willing to be killed — we must recognize a more sophisticated effect. The theme of this section of "To Penshurst" is Penshurst's hospitality. Jonson's endowing of some of its places and some of its game with nominative dignity, with wills of their own as it were, deepens this theme: Penshurst's middle grounds are not merely possessed by it, but they breed its horses, and its banks actively yield up rabbits; the partridges, joining in the prevailing hospitality of the place, are willing to be killed for food, and the pikes generously betray themselves in the same convivial cause.

As the versification of "To Penshurst" should suggest, Jonson responded to the formal promptings of the couplet eclectically, employing its divisions and emphases only as part of a more broadly based poetic order. His various and flexible control of his material is also clearly evident in the man-muse opposition in the "Epistle to my Lady Covell" (ll. 6–27) and in the nature-art opposition in the poem on Shakespeare (ll. 47–64) —

both of which would have fitted nicely in strictly closed couplets had Jonson been inclined so to confine them. We can also study this flexible control of Jonson in the passage in "To Penshurst" on the peasants (ll. 45–56), where, in order to accommodate the complexity of the peasants' motives, Jonson's couplets approximate a blank-verse movement.

Despite the willingness to practice couplet enjambment evident in this passage, however, Jonson's couplets are never like Chaucer's. His couplets always suggest his own intellectual presence, his persistent attitude of judicial detachment. For one thing, he seldom allowed a major pause at a first line, so that his utterance, however broadly it may flow, resolves at last within the bounds of a couplet, that is, within the bounds of formal control and conscious judgment. For another thing, Jonson habitually practiced distinctions, parallels, and antitheses — all proofs of an abstract, external intelligence, and he often used not only line and couplet breaks, but the mid-line pause as well, to define these palpable exercises of mind. But Jonson's couplets, if not like Chaucer's, are not like Waller's or Pope's, either. The use Jonson made of mid-line pause to define material which stretched beyond line and couplet bounds ("Penshurst," l. 52; "To Heaven," l. 7; "Covell," l. 26; "Shakespeare," ll. 17, 37, 58), as well as his generally more flexible practice, separates him from all the writers of insistently closed couplets.

Jonson is in some sense less in line with the closed-couplet tradition than was Marlowe in his *Ovid's Elegies*, less in line with it, indeed, than was Ovid in his *Amores*. It has been pointed out how Jonson loosened Ovid's witty judgment of Callimachus, running it over the whole couplet, "*Callimachus*, though in invention lowe, / Shall still be sung: since he in art doth flowe" (*Poetaster*, I, ll. 55–56), thus sacrificing Marlowe's neat formulation, "His Arte excelld, although his witte was weake," and how Jonson reduced the clipped and pointed quality of Martial's *Epigrammaton*, XII, xciv, in composing his own "Epigram to a weak Gamester in Poetry." In both these cases, it may be worth noticing, Jonson sacrificed word play that he found in his models — the '*valet–valet*' repetition in Ovid, for instance, and a '*ludo–ludis*' play in Martial. In general, Jonson practiced a more serene, a less intense form of discursive poetry than that which the next two centuries would demand.

He does, however, have important affinities with writers of the closed couplet. His continuous intellectual control over his material, his strong suggestion of a speaking voice, his appeal to common sense in a common style: all these qualities dwell in the best neoclassical couplet writing.

XII

✠✠✠✠✠✠✠✠✠✠✠✠✠✠

THOMAS HEYWOOD
(1573-1641)

Our two original poems by Heywood beautifully illustrate the problem early couplet writers had in resolving the conflicting demands between fluency and precision. In the "Prologue at Hampton Court" Heywood accommodated the form to the flowing motion of public address but sacrificed, especially in the crucial lines at the poem's center (ll. 11–16), its precision, indeed, its lucidity. In the pretty epitaph on Mary Littleboyes, he opened with extremely pointed formulations (ll. 1–4), then slid into a patch of quite shapeless and irregular verse (ll. 5–10), and closed on a pretty parallel couplet — but one more musical and ceremonial than discursive and descriptive. This poem is thus formally a mixture, a hodgepodge of styles.

Heywood more nearly approached an extensively coherent closed-couplet practice, that is, a system of couplets both fluent and lucid, in his translations of Ovid's Helen-Paris epistles. He did so, however, by expanding on his model — thus gaining a measure of movement by sacrificing a measure of precision. There are, for instance, several four-line units of utterance that give the epistle a sense of increased movement, which Heywood got by simply doubling Ovidian distichs (ll. 3–6, 7–10, 11–14, 416–20). One could cut out the middle two lines of several of these bundles (ll. 7–10, 416–20) without losing any of Ovid's meaning — or much thought of any kind. The condensation of a line and one-half into one line — one such as "I'll urge more fitting battles, every night" — would, at another point (l. 426), have allowed as a bonus a neat couplet closure. Obviously, Heywood did not, any more than Drayton, think of the couplet as a prompting to trenchancy.

Heywood did, however, transfer into English some of Ovid's rhetorical elegance and wit — although in an expanded form. His courtship-

[213]

war antithesis, although it took him a line to set it up (ll. 421–22), duplicates Ovid's balancing of Venus and Mars (l. 253); his soldiers-Paris antithesis (ll. 423–24) spreads a one-line pattern in Ovid (l. 254) over a couplet; his friend-enemy opposition (l. 18) inflates to a whole line Ovid's half pentameter "*hospes an hostis eras.*" Heywood's one-line wrong-right antithesis (l. 15), however, actually sharpens a one-line Ovidian utterance (l. 9).

Heywood had a diffuse poetic soul, but, in following Ovid, even imperfectly, he achieved patterns and approached modes of verse that would allow couplets, in time, to be both fluent and trenchant.

TROIA BRITANNICA, X,
HELEN TO PARIS[1]

No sooner came mine eye unto the sight
Of thy rude Lynes, but I must needes re-wright:
Dar'st thou (Oh shamlesse) in such heynous wise,
The Lawes of Hospitality despise?
And being a straunger, from thy countries reach,   5
Solicite a chast wife to Wedlocks breach?
Was it for this, our free *Tenarian* Port,
Receiv'd thee and thy traine, in friendly sort?
And when great Neptune nothing could appease,
Gave thee safe harbour from the stormy Seas?   10
Was it for this, our Kingdomes armes spread wide,
To entertaine thee from the waters side?
Yet thou of forren soyle remote from hence,
A stranger, comming we scarce know from whence,
Is perjur'd wrong the recompence of right?   15
Is all our friendship guerdoned with despight?
I doubt me then, whither in our Court doth tarry,
A friendly guest, or a fierce adversary.

.   .   .   .

So where your valour and rare deedes you boast,
And warlike spirits in which you tryumph most,
By which you have attained mongst Souldiers grace,
None will beleeve you that but sees your face,   420

---

1 Dryden also translated this Ovidian epistle.

Your feature and fayre shape, is fitter farre
For amorous Courtships, then remorselesse warre:
Let rough-hew'd Soldiers warlike dangers prove,
Tis pitty *Paris* should do ought save love.
Hector (whom you so praise) for you may fight,   425
Ile finde you warre, to skirmish every night,
Which shall become you better: Were I wise
And bold withall, I might obtaine the prize,
In such sweete single Combats, hand to hand,
Gainst which no woman that is wise will stand: 430
My champion Ile encounter breast to breast,
Though I were sure to fall, and be o'repreast.

.   .   .   .

OVID, HEROIDES, XVIII, HELEN TO PARIS

Nunc oculos tua cum violarit epistula nostros
    non rescribendi gloria visa levis.
ausus es hospitii temeratis, advena, sacris
    legitimam nuptae sollicitare fidem!
scilicet idcirco ventosa per aequora vectum   5
    excepit portu Taenaris ora suo,
nec tibi, diversa quamvis e gente venires,
    oppositas habuit regia nostra fores,
esset ut officii merces iniuria tanti!
    qui sic intrabas, hospes an hostis eras?   10

.   .   .   .

Quod bene te iactes et fortia facta loquaris,
    a verbis facies dissidet ista tuis.
apta magis Veneri, quam sunt tua corpora Marti.
    bella gerant fortes, tu, Pari, semper ama!
Hectora, quem laudas, prote pugnare iubeto;   255
    militia est operis altera digna tuis.
his ego, si saperem pauloque audacior essem,
    uterer; utetur, siqua puella sapit —
aut ego deposito sapiam fortasse pudore
    et dabo cunctatas tempore victa manus.   260

.   .   .   .

A PROLOGUE SPOKEN TO THEIR SACRED MAJESTIES AT HAMPTON COURT

If *Caesar*, greatest in great *Pompeis* fall,
As being made the soveraigne over all
The (then knowne) world; or if *Augustus*; Hee
Who left his ample name Hereditarie
To all succeeding Emperours; If to th' last   5
Of the twelve *Caesars*, Theaters were grac't,
And when the Julian family expir'd
In many ages after were admir'd?
And the more fame from forraigne parts to win,
Adornd without, and beautified within.   10
If by succession we can draw them downe
Through nations, realmes and tongues, even to our own,
Proving these flourishing Kingdomes prosperd well,
And never faild before these structures fell:
Or were supprest; for 'tis a bad presage,   15
(All mirth exil'd) still followes wrack and strage.
If then a factious peevish male-content,
Envying a blest state; shall his malice vent
In bald unlicenc't papers? so much daring
As neither Soveraigne, nor the subject sparing: 20
Assuming in a strange libellious straine,
To thinke all wisedome treasur'd in his braine?
Be all such frustrate in their vaine indeavour,
Whilst you oh Royall *Caesar* live for ever.

AN INSCRIPTION FOR MISTRESS MARY LITTLEBOYES'S TOMBSTONE

Hereunder lyes a Casket, that containd
A life unspotted, and a soule unstaind,
A virgin chaste, beyond example faire,
For outward gifts remark't, for inward, rare,
Of natures pieces, one the prime and choice,   5
So naturd, that for needle, booke and voice
She was unpeer'd: matchles in mind and face,
And all the vertues that her sex most grace.

Who after twenty yeares scarce fully expird,
Arriv'd at that safe port she most desird: 10
In life, to friends and parents fresh joyes bringing:
In death; to God sweet *Halelujaes* singing.

OF LUCRECE

If to thy bed the adulterer welcome came,
O *Lucrece*, then thy death deserves no fame.
If force were offred, give true reason why,
Being cleare thy selfe thou for his fault wouldst dye?
Therefore in vaine thou seekst thy fame to cherish,   5
Since mad thou fal'st, or for thy sinne dost perish.

BEZA, LUCRETIA

Si fuit ille tibi, Lucretia, gratus adulter,
  Immerito ex merita praemia morte petis.
Sin potius casto vis est allata pudori,
  Quis furor est, hostis crimine velle mori?
Frustra igitur laudem captas, Lucretia: namque   5
  Vel furiosa ruis, vel scelerata cadis.

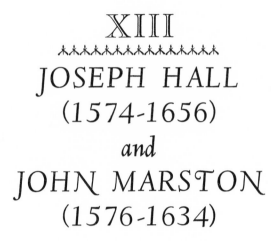

XIII

JOSEPH HALL
(1574-1656)
and
JOHN MARSTON
(1576-1634)

Hall and Marston drew significantly for their satiric inspiration on two of the same Latin poets: on Martial, whose epigrams encouraged neatness, clarity, and detachment, and on Juvenal, whose satires encouraged largeness and cloudiness of utterance and raging indignation. Martial often composed in elegiac distichs, Juvenal in largely enjambed hexameters.

Hall, the more learned and the less adventurous of the two English poets, attempted to resolve these conflicting Latin impulses arithmetically by writing the first three books of his *Virgidemiarum* in the neat, lucid vein of Martial and the last three in the harsh, mysterious vein of Juvenal. He announces this poetic compromise at the end of his third book:

> Thus have I writ in smother Cedar tree,
> So gentle Satyrs, pend so easily,
> Henceforth I write in crabbed oke-tree rinde:
> Search they that meane the secret meaning finde.

Actually, Hall is closer to Martial than to Juvenal throughout his satires although he never quite caught the tone of personal address, which he could have imbibed from Ovid's elegiac poems as well as from Martial's epigrams, that gives the tightly constructed verse form its necessary flexibility and affective point. Marston, on the other hand, is Juvenalian; one only finds the epigrammatic note of Martial in his work, indeed, imbedded in the flow of larger and cloudier utterance (*Certain Satires*, II, 41–54).[1] It may be well to mention that Hall seems to have been impelled toward his style of clear but generalized address by examples of medieval satiric writing, especially by Chaucer and Spenser, and that Marston may have been made as furious and as heedless of his audience as he was in part by the example of Thomas Nashe's furiously ebullient satiric prose.

Both of these poets, broadly speaking, attempted to reap the satiric benefits, on the one hand, of closed couplets with their regularly pointed definitions and segmented emphases and, on the other hand, of enjambed couplets with their chances for comprehensive utterance. Closed couplets are quite common in Hall: he composed many parallel couplets (*Virg*, II, vi, 5–8) and couplet-defined parallel lines (*Virg*, III, ii, 21–22; *Virg*, IV, iv, 115–16; *Virg*, VI, i, 26–30); many intraline (*Virg*, IV, iv, 123; *Virg*, III, ii, 11, 12), intracouplet (*Virg*, II, vi, 5–6), and intercouplet (*Virg*, III, ii, 5–8) antitheses; and many passages in which sets of parallel or opposing items receive persistent couplet definition (*Virg*, VI, i, 35–74; *Virg*, IV, iv, 37–65). Such practices are less common in Marston, but they illuminate much that is best in his satire. One finds his mysterious anger sometimes miraculously focussed in such a line as "Smooth seeme-Saints, yet damn'd incarnate devils," which suddenly declares the maddening hypocrisy of lawyers and brings a whole passage of vituperation to bear. Again, the five major crimes that Marston says he should concern himself with (*Scourge*, III, 181–90) are defined in five separate couplets, each containing a "Shall" question. The five are imperfectly parallel, no doubt, but much clearer and stronger for what paralleling there is.

Both poets, Hall especially in the last three books of *Virgidemiarum* and Marston always, have striven for extracouplet systems of satiric utterance, for grandly enjambed bursts of harsh and purposefully difficult exclamation. The conclusion of Hall's *Virgidemiarum*, IV, iv (98–132) is completely governed and yoked together by the theme that young Gallio should marry. Its unity is rhetorically driven home, at least through part of its course, by Hall's repeated "Hy thee" command to Gallio. Hall achieved a larger and more coherent unity in *Virgidemiarum*, VI,

---

[1] My line references to the poems of these two poets correspond to the line notations in *The Collected Poems of Joseph Hall*, ed. Arnold Davenport (Liverpool, 1949); and *The Poems of John Marston*, ed. Arnold Davenport (Liverpool, 1961).

throughout which the speaker asserts the mock resolve to repent of his satires and explains the basis for this resolve — his ironical description of the world's recent, miraculous improvement. The natural rhetorical device of contrasting the vicious past with the virtuous present (ll. 25–128) helps Hall maintain the singleness of his satiric impulse. Marston achieved a similarly large-scale unity in *Scourge of Villany*, VII, in which he developed the theme that there are no true men in the world by considering and rejecting a series of candidates, among them usurers and lawyers. His use of two arguing masks throughout the satire, the naive Linceus and the cynical Diogenes, and his exclamatory repetition of "A man, a man" underscore the poem's unity. A shorter and tighter satiric system is that at the end of *Scourge*, III (157–96) in which Marston describes the minor vices he should ignore and the major ones he should attack.

Neither Marston nor Hall achieved a perfect resolution of the two poetic impulses both responded to. Marston's most obvious failure is fuzziness, such as that which diminishes, for instance, his whole portrait of the usurer (*Scourge*, VII, 46–74). He is, of course, a very sloppy writer. In *Scourge*, VII, 74–77, for instance, he has botched his transition from usurers to lawyers: he overruns the couplet that should have defined the break and must resort to the Linceus-Diogenes conversation to force a break — not, however, before he has made a metaphorical distinction between the two which, since the lawyers have not been introduced, makes no sense. Marston's draping of three straight statements across line breaks in managing this transition makes line and couplet emphasis work against him and adds to the confusion. Hall suffered from the opposite problem, a medieval stiffness of utterance and lack of movement. In *Virgidemiarum*, IV, i, for instance, Hall's governing theme, that his victims suffer only when they are named, vanishes as case after sharply defined case usurps our whole attention. Like other of his contemporaries, Hall sometimes suffered from an oscillation between metrical stiffness and metrical shiftlessness, between strongly defined couplets and shapeless ones. One might notice, for instance, the change in *Virgidemiarum*, III, ii, from the tightly closed verse of lines 9–14 to the irregularity and imprecision of lines 17–22.

Hall, although the more readable poet today, had no followers. His style had no really distinctive features for later poets to ape or to develop. But Marston's wild way crops up again and again in the couplet tradition — in John Oldham during the Restoration, for instance, and in Charles Churchill during the eighteenth century. Both of these later poets composed in long-winded blasts of invective, like Marston, and both absorbed his way of punctuating and unifying such utterances with repeated exclamatory tags. Only Churchill, however, who also enjoyed the beneficial examples of Dryden and Pope, was able to articulate such practices in effective public address, to turn the style of Marston, that is to say, into enduring closed-couplet poetry.

XIV

ㅅㅅㅅㅅㅅㅅㅅㅅㅅㅅㅅㅅㅅㅅ

GEORGE SANDYS
(1578-1644)

In his translation from Ovid of Galatea's good and bad points (*Metamorphosis*, XIII, 989–1005), Sandys confined himself to three or four forms of line organization. He repeated the comparative-substantive-substantive-comparative pattern four times (ll. 990, 991, 994, 1002), for instance, and the comparative-substantive-comparative-substantive pattern thrice (ll. 995, 1003, 1005). Thus, although each of the sharply closed lines in this series is pretty and graceful, the series is tedious; the metrical repetition weakens the individuality, the pungency of the different comparisons, and the persistent click of the line ends makes the passage's movement mechanical. Much of the trouble here may be due to Sandys's model: the corresponding passage in Ovid (*Metamorphoses*, XIII, 789–804) is made up of closed hexameter lines many of which are formally repetitious. But Sandys sometimes overused his limited stock of line and couplet patterns in his own creations; four of the first six lines "To the King," and nine of its twenty are defined by inverted verbs, and the four seriatim "To" couplets in "Deo Optimo Maximo" (ll. 53–60) have an almost mechanical similarity.

Opposed to these monotonously patterned patches of strongly closed lines and couplets are others in which the verse elements completely fail to define or illuminate the material. This formal breakdown is especially common at points of transition: between Galatea's good and bad points (*Metamorphosis*, XIII, 997–1000), which Ovid had achieved neatly and which Dryden would turn into a triumph; between the number and the quality of Polyphemus's flocks (*Metamorphosis*, XIII, 1023–26); between Polyphemus's size and his hairiness (ll. 1043–46). Sandys resorted to nonsense to maintain the first couplet in this last example and then abnegated his couplet responsibility in the second. Sometimes his couplets fail to handle material that should have suited them perfectly:

in defining a series of five antitheses (*Ecclesiastes*, IX, 14–18), for instance, and a series of God's mercies ("Deo Optimo Maximo," ll. 70–76). Or take, as an example, the following couplet: "Nor will we gifts for thy delight prepare / Of easie purchase, or what are not rare." Here Sandys has patterned his first line and subverted its meaning at one stroke; his shifting of "prepare" to the line end strengthens the integrity of the line and thus allows exactly the wrong impression, that is, that Polyphemus will *not* prepare gifts for his beloved's delight. In such passages as these, couplet divisions and emphases obfuscate material instead of clarifying it.

Other of Sandys's lines and couplets, however, suggest the lucidity and grace of which the form was capable — a lucidity and grace which Waller and still later poets would cultivate. Such a couplet as this, "Yet those have hope, who with the living dwell: / For living Dogs dead Lyons farre excell," in whose second line a crisscross antithesis receives periodic heightening, strongly anticipates mature closed-couplet composition.

OVID'S METAMORPHOSIS, XIII, POLYPHEMUS'S LAMENT[1]

O *Galatea*, more then lilly-white,
More fresh then flowrie meads, then glasse more bright,   990
Higher then Alder trees, then kids more blithe,
Smoother then shels whereon the surges drive,
More wisht then winters Sun, or Summers aire,
More sweet then grapes, then apples farre more rare,
Clearer then Ice, more seemely then tall Planes   995
Softer then tender curds, or downe of Swans,
More faire, if fixt, then gardens by the fall
Of springs inchac't. Though thus, thou art withall
More fierce then salvage bulls, who knowe no yoke,
Then waves more giddy, harder than the oke,   1000
Then vines or willow twigs more eas-lie bent,
More stiffe then rocks, then streames more violent,
Prowder then peacocks prais'd, more rash then fire,
Then Beares more cruell, sharper then the brier,

---

[1] This passage of *Metamorphoses* has also been translated into couplets by Dryden and by Pope.

Deeper then Seas, more fell then trod-on snake;   1005
And, if I could, what I would from thee take,
More speedie then the hound-pursued Hind,
Or chaced clouds, or then the flying wind.
If knowne to thee, thou wouldst thy flight repent;
Curse thy delay, and labour my content.   1010
For I have caves within the living stone;
To Summers heat, and Winters cold unknowne;
Trees charg'd with apples; spreading vines that hold
A purple grape, and grapes resembling gold.
For thee I these preserve, affected Maid.   1015
Thou strawberries shalt gather in the shade,
Autumnal cornels, plummes with azure rind,
And wax-like yellow of a generous kind;
Nor shalt thou ches-nuts want, if mine thou be,
Nor scalded wildings: serv'd by every tree.   1020
These flocks are ours: in vallies many stray,
Woods many shade, at home as many stay.
Nor can I, should you aske, their number tell:
Who number theirs, are poore. How these excell,
Believe not me, but credit your owne eyes: 1025
See how their udders part their straddling thighes.
I in my sheepe-coats have new-weaned lambs;
And frisking kids late taken from their dams.
New milke, fresh curds and creame, with cheese well prest,
Are never wanting for thy pallats feast.   1030
Nor will we gifts for thy delight prepare
Of easie purchase, or what are not rare:
Deere, red and fallow, Roes, light-footed Hares,
Nests scal'd from cliffes, and Doves produc't by paires.
A rugged Beares rough twins I found upon   1035
The mountaine late, scarce from each other knowne,
For thee to play with: finding these, I said,
My Mistris you shall serve. Come lovely Maid,
Come *Galatea*, from the surges rise,
Bright as the Morning; nor our gifts despise.   1040
I knowe my selfe; my image in the brooke
I lately saw, and therein pleasure tooke.
Behold, how great! Not *Jupiter* above
(For much you talke I knowe not of what *Jove*)

Is larger siz'd: curles, on my browes displaid, 1045
Affright; and like a grove my shoulders shade.
Nor let it your esteeme of me impaire,
That all my bodie bristles with thick haire.
Trees without leaves, and horses without maines,
Are sights unseemely: grasse adornes the plaines, 1050
Wooll sheepe, and feathers fowle. A manly face
A beard becomes: the skin rough bristles grace.
Amid my fore-head shines one onely light;
Round, like a mighty shield, and cleere of sight.
The Sunne all objects sees beneath the skie: 1055
And yet behold, the Sunne hath but one eye.
Besides, your Seas obey my fathers throne:
I give you him for yours. Doe you alone
Vouchsafe me pitty, and your suppliant heare:
To you I onely bow; you onely feare. 1060
Heaven, *Jupiter*, his lightning I despise:
More dread the lightning of thy angry eyes.
And yet your scorne my patience lesse would move,
Were all contemn'd. Why should you *Acis* love,
And slight the *Cyclop*. why to him more free? 1065
Although himselfe he please; and pleaseth thee,
(Which frets me most) could I your darling get,
He then should finde my strength and me like great.
His guts I would extract, squeaze out his braines,
Throw his dissevered lims about the plaines: 1070
And if with thee he mingle, mix thy wave
With his hot blood; and make thy deepe his grave.
For O, I frye! despisd affection burnes
With greater rage: my bulke to Aetna turnes,
And all her flames are in my bosome pent: 1075
Yet *Galatea*, wilt not thou relent.

.   .   .   .

OVID, METAMORPHOSES, XIII

Candidior folio nivei Galatea ligustri,
floridior pratis, longa procerior alno, 790
splendidior vitro, tenero lascivior haedo,

levior adsiduo detritis aequore conchis,
solibus hibernis, aestiva gratior umbra,
nobilior pomis, platano conspectior alta,
lucidior glacie, matura dulcior uva,   795
mollior et cygni plumis et lacte coacto,
et si non fugias, riguo formosior horto;
    Saevior indomitis eadem Galatea iuvencis,
durior annosa quercu, fallacior undis,
lentior et salicis virgis et vitibus albis,   800
his immobilior scopulis, violentior amne,
laudato pavone superbior, acrior igni,
asperior tribulis, feta truculentior ursa,
surdior aequoribus, calcato inmitior hydro,
et, quod praecipue vellem tibi demere possem,   805
non tantum cervo claris latratibus acto,
verum etiam ventis volucrique fugacior aura,
(at bene si noris, pigeat fugisse, morasque
ipsa tuas damnes et me retinere labores).
sunt mihi, pars montis, vivo pendentia saxo   810
antra, quibus nec sol medio sentitur in aestu,
nec sentitur hiems; sunt poma gravantia ramos,
sunt auro similes longis in vitibus uvae
sunt et purpureae: tibi et has servamus et illas.
ipsa tuis manibus silvestri nata sub umbra   815
mollia fraga leges, ipsa autumnalia corna
prunaque non solum nigro liventia suco,
verum etiam generosa novasque imitantia ceras.
nec tibi castaneae me coniuge, nec tibi deerunt
arbutei fetus: omnis tibi serviet arbor.   820
    Hoc pecus omne meum est, multae quoque vallibus errant,
multas silva tegit, multae stabulantur in antris,
nec, si forte roges, possim tibi dicere, quot sint:
pauperis est numerare pecus; de laudibus harum
nil mihi credideris, praesens potes ipsa videre,   825
ut vix circumeant distentum cruribus uber.
sunt, fetura minor, tepidis in ovilibus agni.
sunt quoque, par aetas, aliis in ovilibus haedi.
lac mihi semper adest niveum: pars inde bibenda
servatur, partem liquefacta coagula durant.   830
    Nec tibi deliciae faciles vulgataque tantum

munera contingent, dammae leporesque caperque,
parve columbarum demptusve cacumine nidus:
inveni geminos, qui tecum ludere possint,
inter se similes, vix ut dignoscere possis, 835
villosae catulos in summit montibus ursae:
inveni et dixi "dominae servabimus istos."
   Iam modo caeruleo nitidum caput exere ponto,
iam, Galatea, veni, nec munera despice nostra!
certe ego me novi liquidaeque in imagine vidi 840
nuper aquae, placuitque mihi mea forma videnti.
adspice, sim quantus: non est hoc corpore maior
Iuppiter in caelo, nam vos narrare soletis
nescio quem regnare Iovem; coma plurima torvos
prominet in vultus, umerosque, et lucus, obumbrat; 845
nec mea quod rigidis horrent densissima saetis
corpora, turpe puta: turpis sine frondibus arbor,
turpis equus, nisi colla iubae flaventia velent;
pluma tegit volucres, ovibus sua lana decori est:
barba viros hirtaeque decent in corpore saetae. 850
unum est in media lumen mihi fronte, sed instar
ingentis clipei. quid? non haec omnia magnus
Sol videt e caelo? Soli tamen unicus orbis.
   Adde, quod in vestro genitor meus aequore regnat:
hunc tibi do socerum; tantum miserere precesque 855
supplicis exaudi! tibi enim succumbimus uni,
quique Iovem et caelum sperno et penetrabile fulmen,
Nerei, te vereor, tua fulmine saevior ira est.
atque ego contemptus essem patientior huius,
si fugeres omnes; sed cur Cyclope repulso 860
Acin amas praefersque meis conplexibus Acin?
ille tamen placeatque sibi placeatque licebit,
quod nollem, Galatea, tibi; modo copia detur:
sentiet esse mihi tanto pro corpore vires!
viscera viva traham divulsaque membra per agros 865
perque tuas spargam (sic se tibi misceat!) undas.
uror enim, laesusque exaestuat acrius ignis,
cumque suis videor translatam viribus Aetnam
pectore ferre meo, nec tu, Galatea, moveris.

.   .   .   .

DEDICATION OF A PARAPHRASE
UPON THE PSALMS TO THE KING

Our graver Muse from her long Dreame awakes,
Peneian Groves, and Cirrha's Caves forsakes:
Inspir'd with Zeale, she climbes th'Aethereall Hills
Of Solyma, where bleeding Balme distils;
Where Trees of Life unfading Youth assure,　　　　　　5
And Living Waters all Diseases cure:
Where the Sweet Singer, in coelestial Laies,
Sung to his solemne Harp Jehovah's Praise.
From that falne Temple, on her wings she beares
Those Heavenly Raptures to your sacred Eares:　　　　10
Not that her bare and humble Feet aspire
To mount the Threshold of th'harmonious Quire;
But that at once she might Oblations bring
To God: and Tribute to a god-like King.
And since no narrow Verse such Mysteries,　　　　　15
Deepe Sense, and high Expressions could comprise;
Her labouring Wings a larger compasse flie,
And Poesie resolves with Poesie;
Lest she, who in the Orient clearly rose,
Should in your Western World obscurely close.　　　　20

A PARAPHRASE UPON
ECCLESIASTES, IX

All under Heaven succeeds alike to all;
To good and bad, the same events befall;
To pure, impure; to those who Sacrifice,　　　　　15
To those who Pietie and God despise;
To th'innocent, the guiltie; such who feare
Flagitious Oathes, and those who fearelesse sweare.
What greater mischieef rules beneath the sunne
Than this; that all unto one period runne?　　　　20
Men, while they live are mad; profanely spend
Their flight of time; then to the dead descend.
Yet those have hope, who with the living dwell:
For living Dogs dead Lyons farre excell.

.　　.　　.　　.　　.　　.　　.　　.　　.　　.

A PARAPHASE UPON
ECCLESIASTES, XI

When thou shalt feare the roughnesse of the way;
When ev'ry peble shall thy passage stay: 50
When th' Almond-tree his boughs invests with white;
The Locust stoopes: then dead to all delight,
Man must at length to his long home descend:
Behold, the Mourners at his gates attend.
Advise; before the Silver Cord growes slacke;   55
Before the golden Boule asunder crack:
Before the Pitcher at the fountaine leake;
Or wasted Wheele besides the Cisterne breake.
Man, made of Earth, resolves into the same:
His Soule ascends to God, from whom it came.   60

.   .   .   .

DEO OPTIMO MAXIMO

O who hath tasted of thy Clemency
In greater measure, or more oft then I!   50
My gratefull Verse thy Goodnesse shall display.
O Thou who went'st along in all my way;
To Where the Morning with perfumed Wings
From the high Mountaines of Panchaea springs:
To that New-found-out World, where sober Night   55
Takes from th' Antipodes her silent flight;
To those darke Seas, where horrid Winter reignes,
And binds the stubborne Flouds in Icie chaines:
To Lybian Wasts, whose Thirst no showres asswage,
And where swolne Nilus cooles the Lions rage.   60
Thy Wonders in the Deepe have I beheld;
Yet all by those on Judah's Hils excell'd:
There where the Virgins Son his Doctrine taught,
His Miracles, and our Redemption wrought:
Where I by Thee inspir'd his Praises sung;   65
And on His Sepulchre my Offering hung.
Which way so e're I turne my Face, or Feet;
I see thy Glory, and thy Mercy meet.
Met on the Thracian Shoares; when in the strife

Of frantic Simoans thou preserv'dst my Life.   70
So when Arabian Thieves belaid us round,
And when by all abandon'd, Thee I found.
That false Sidonian Wolfe, whose craft put on
A Sheepe soft Fleece, and me Bellerophon
To Ruine by his cruell Letter sent,   75
Thou didst by thy protecting Hand prevent.
Thou sav'dst me from the bloudy Massacres
Of faithlesse Indians; from their treacherous Wars;
From raging Feavers, from the sultry breath
Of tainted Aire; which cloy'd the jawes of Death.   80
Preserv'd from swallowing Seas; when tow'ring Waves
Mixt with the Clouds, and opened their deep Graves.
From barbarous Pirats ransom'd: by those taught,
Successefully with Salian Moores we fought.
Then brought'st me Home in safety; that this Earth   85
Might bury me, which fed me from my Birth:
Blest with a healthfull Age; a quiet Mind,
Content with little; to this Worke design'd:
Which I at length have finisht by thy Aid;
And now my Vowes have at thy Altar paid.   90

XV

𝅏𝅏𝅏𝅏𝅏𝅏𝅏𝅏𝅏𝅏𝅏𝅏𝅏

SIR JOHN BEAUMONT
(1583-1627)

"Bosworth Field" shares a number of metrical qualities with the early English couplet of Chaucer and Spenser: it is, of course, a narrative, like their couplet poems. Its statements often come to rest at the ends of first lines (ll. 159, 163), its couplets are often enjambed (ll. 142, 160, 168), and, consequently, it unfolds in thought segments of various numbers of lines. The passage from lines 159–76, for instance, falls into one-, four-, one- two-, four-, four-, and two-line segments of thought. "Bosworth Field" does, however, sometimes settle into couplets (ll. 151–58), and it is pervaded with closed-couplet practices. One notices cases of metrically defined patterns of antithesis (ll. 150, 158, 164) and series (ll. 145–52). Still more modern, indeed, more prophetic, Beaumont has sometimes used periodic inversion to emphasize couplets and couplet elements. There are two cases in our brief excerpt (ll. 143, 173) of inversion's defining a first line, and one case (l. 171) in which it causes a dramatically enjambed first line. One also notices, by the way, periodic suspension in the four-line, noncouplet passage on the honor due to loyalty (ll. 160–63), a passage which might remind us of Chaucer's periodic handling of the Metellius anecdote in his "Wife of Bath's Prologue."

The "Two Feasts" and "True Form" poems are in the newer closed-couplet style. Among their sharply defined units one discovers well-balanced antithetical half-lines ("Feasts," ll. 16, 18), lines ("Feasts," ll. 4–5), and couplets ("Form," ll. 27–30); parallel half-lines ("Form," ll. 20–26), lines ("Form," ll. 44–45), and couplets ("Feasts," ll. 7–10; "Form," ll. 53–60) — and even two-couplet sets in rigid parallel ("Form," ll. 11–18). This last pattern with its breaks between every couplet is, admittedly, stiff. Indeed, Beaumont suffers from the oscillation between stiffness and laxity which plagued many of his near contemporaries. As an example of couplet laxity, actually of couplet breakdown, take lines 23–34 of "Two Feasts": Beaumont has not imposed the proper and necessary couplet emphasis on the two antithetical actions of descending and climbing; he has not even been able to work this elaborate pair of opposites, each one reinforced by symbolical flowers, into coherent English.

For the most part, however, Beaumont's individual couplets in these two poems are not only neatly but also dynamically articulated. Periodic inversion, which we found fairly common in "Bosworth Field," gives tension and force to many couplets and lines and makes both these poems, especially "True Form," move and live. Among the many periodically heightened couplets ("Feasts," ll. 9–10, 11–12, 21–22; "Form," ll. 3–4, 15–16), one finds this one, "Their forme surpassing farre the fetter'd staves, / Vaine care, and needlesse repetition saves," in which an inversion in each line has allowed Beaumont to begin this couplet-defined clause with its subject and close it with its verb. There are also period-heightened lines ("Form," ll. 2, 12, 31, 35) such as this, "But those that joyne most simply, run the best," in which the suspension by the subordinate clause of the main clause's predicate gives the correspondency between the two clauses a fine emphasis.

Beaumont did not generally weave his individual couplets together into significant larger systems of verse; we must wait on Falkland and Denham for that. He did, however, conclude "True Form" with a four-line pattern, binding its two couplets together not only with a periodic inversion, but with one which asserts a 'freezing–hotter' antithesis. Thus at the climax of this poem he created a dynamic imbalance, an imbalance he resolved with the line-defined antithesis between wonder and scorn on which the poem closes. Here the couplet and the stresses he placed on it allowed Beaumont briefly to give his poetry that combined luster and transparency he himself prescribed.

The Metamorphosis of Tobacco, a poem Beaumont published in 1602 when he was a very young man, shows none of the new dynamic tendencies of his later work. We may think of it as a forecast of Sandys's couplet translation of Ovid's *Metamorphoses* or as a sign of the conditions in which Sandys's translation would seem natural. But despite its obvious imitation of Ovidian mythology and Ovidian mellifluousness, Beaumont's poem strongly resembles early English couplet practice. He here presents the world with series of line-defined and couplet-defined items of general observation, catalogues of serious but completely unargued, completely unsupported, praises (ll. 477–508) and accusations (ll. 541–74). He makes little use of mid-line pause for internal rhetorical effects and little effort to organize significant larger systems. These couplets, despite their smoothness, jog along more like those in which William Baldwin made general observations on the state of England than like Sandys's prettily patterned lines and couplets.

THE METAMORPHOSIS OF TOBACCO

No publike bond of law, no private oth
Was needfull to the simple faith and troth:
Each had a censure in his owne consent
Without the feare of death or punishment: 480
Nor did the busie Client feare his cause,
Nor in strong brasse did they engrave their lawes,
Nor did the doubtfull parties faintly tremble,
While the brib'd Judge did dreadful looks dissemble:
Then safe from harm the vaunting Pine did stand,   485
And had no triall of the Shipwrights hand,
But stood upon the hill where first it grew,
Nor yet was forc'd another world to view:
Nor unto greedie Merchants yet were knowne
The shores of any land beyond their owne: 490
Ev'ry defencelesse Citie then was sure,
Nor could deepe ditches make it more secure:
The harmlesse thoughts of that blest age did beare
No warlike Trumpet, Cornet, Sword, or Speare:
No furious Souldier needed to defend   495
The carelesse folke, which quiet lives did spend,
Nor did ambitios Captaines know the way
To passe the cliffie shores of their owne sea:
The earth yet free from any forc'd abuse
Brought forth all things fit for each creatures use,   500
Without the helpe of any humane care,
Untoucht by harrow, and uncut by share,
And mortall men upon those meates did feede,
Which of themselves did from the earth proceede,
The mountaine Strawberie, the bitter Sloe,   505
And Mulberies which on rough boughs doe grow,

And homely Akornes, which did whilom fall
From the high trees, which *Jove* his owne doth call.

.   .   .   .

Now did the warie reaper with long bounds
Devide to portions the united grounds,
Which erst were common to each mortall wight,
As is the liquide ayre, or pleasant light:
Nor did they onely take the needfull corne,   545
And daily food, which from the earth was borne,
But to the bowels of their mother sought,
And cursed riches from the center brought,
Which the wise earth had cover'd unespide,
And neere unto the *Stygian* waves did hide.   550
First then began the phrases, Mine, and Thine:
Pure water turn'd to artificiall wine:
Pleasure unknowne, and more then simple mirth
Start up with gold from out the mangled earth:
Then bounds, then contracts at a racking price,   555
And from those bounds sprung boundlesse avarice:
Then hurtfull steele the workmans hand did feele,
And gold more hurtfull then the hurtfull steele:
And when both these were comen to perfect growth,
From thence came warre, that fights with help of both: 560
Then did the souldier, which in battell stands,
Shake glittring weapons with his bloodie hands:
All liv'd by wrong: each friend his friend did feare,
And brethren seldome linkt in friendship were:
The husband seekes the death of his owne wife,   565
And she againe grieves at her husbands life:
The angrie stepdames fearfull paysons make,
Which their new husbands hated child may take:
And the sonne wearie of his fathers stay,
Longs for his death before his fatall day.   570
White Pieties dispersed reliques lie
Conquer'd, and spoil'd of earthly dignitie,
And then *Astraea* last of heav'nly powers
Forsooke the earth reeking with bloodie showers.

.   .   .   .

Were my quaint polisht tongue my soules best hopes,
And grac't with figures, colours, schemes, and tropes,
This herbe would surpasse in excellence   775

The great'st Hyperboles of eloquence:
Yet this sweete simple by misordred use
Death or some dang'rous sicknesse may induce,
Should we not for our sustentation eate,
Because a surfet comes from too much meate?   780
Should we not thirst with mod'rate drinke represse,
Because a dropsie springs from such excesse?
Should we not take some holesome exercise
To chafe our vaines, and stretch our arteries,
Because abus'd in a laborious kind   785
It hurts the bodie, and amates the mind?
So our faire plant, that doth as needfull stand,
As heav'n, or fire, or aire, or sea, or land,
As Moone, or Starres, that rule the gloomie night,
Or *Tullies* friendship, or the Sunnie light,   790
Her sacred vertue in her selfe enroules,
And leaves the evill in vaine-glorious soules,
And yet who dyes cloid with celestiall breath,
Shall dye with joy a *Diagorian* death.

· · · · · · · · · ·

Who takes this med'cine need not greatly care,   855
Who *Galenist*, who *Paracelsians* are:
Nor need he seeke their *Rosaries*, their *Summes*,
Their *Secrets*, their *Dispensatoriums*:
Nor fill his pocket with their costly bils,
Nor stuffe his maw with their unsav'ry pils,   860
Nor make huge pitfals in his tender vaines,
With thousand other more then hellish paines,
But by this herbes celestiall qualitie
May keepe his health in mirth and jollitie:
It is the fountaine whence all pleasure springs,   865
A potion for imperiall crowned Kings.

· · · · · · · · · ·

BOSWORTH FIELD

Long since the *King* had thought it time to send
For trusty *Norfolke*, his undaunted friend,
Who hasting from the place of his abode,
Found at the doore, a world of papers strow'd;

Some would affright him from the Tyrants aide,   145
Affirming that his Master was betray'd;
Some laid before him all those bloody deeds,
From which a line of sharpe revenge proceeds
With much compassion, that so brave a Knight
Should serve a Lord, against whom Angels fight,   150
And others put suspicions in his minde,
That *Richard* most observ'd, was most unkind.
The *Duke* awhile these cautious words revolves
With serious thoughts, and thus at last resolves;
If all the Campe prove traytors to my Lord,   155
Shall spotlesse *Norfolke* falsifie his word;
Mine oath is past, I swore t'uphold his Crowne,
And that shall swim, or I with it will drowne.
It is too late now to dispute the right;
Dare any tongue, since *Yorke* spred forth his light,   160
Northumberland, or *Buckingham* defame,
Two valiant *Cliffords*, *Roos*, or *Beaumonts* name,
Because they in the weaker quarrell die?
They had the *King* with them, and so have I.
But ev'ry eye the face of *Richard* shunnes,   165
For that foule murder of his brothers sonnes:
Yet lawes of Knighthood gave me not a sword
To strike at him, whom all with joynt accord
Have made my Prince, to whom I tribute bring:
I hate his vices, but adore the King.   170
Victorious *Edward*, if thy soule can heare
Thy servant *Howard*, I devoutly sweare,
That to have sav'd thy children from that day,
My hopes on earth should willingly decay;
Would *Glouster* then, my perfect faith had tryed,   175
And made two graves, when noble *Hastings* died.
This said, his troopes he into order drawes,
Then doubled haste redeemes his former pause:
So stops the Sayler for a voyage bound,
When on the Sea he heares the tempests sound,   180
Till pressing hunger to remembrance sends,
That on his course his housholds life depends:
With this he cleares the doubts that vext his minde,
And puts his ship to mercy of the winde.

.   .   .   .

UPON THE TWO GREAT FEASTS OF THE ANNUNCIATION AND THE RESURRECTION FALLING ON THE SAME DAY, MARCH 25, 1627

Thrice happy day, which sweetly do'st combine
Two Hemispheres in th'Equinoctiall line:
The one debasing God to earthly paine,
The other raising man to endlesse raigne.
Christs humble steps declining to the wombe,   5
Touch heav'nly scales erected on his Tombe:
We first with *Gabriel* must this Prince convay
Into his chamber on the marriage day,
Then with the other Angels cloth'd in white,
We will adore him in this conqu'ring Night: 10
The Sonne of God assuming humane breath,
Becomes a subject to his vassall Death,
That Graves and Hell laid open by his strife,
May give us passage to a better life.
See for this worke how things are newly styl'd,   15
Man is declar'd, Almighty, God, a Child;
The Word made Flesh, is speechlesse, and the Light
Begins from Clouds, and sets in depth of night;
Behold the Sunne eclips'd for many yeeres,
And ev'ry day more dusky robes he weares,   20
Till after totall darknesse shining faire,
No Moone shall barre his splendor from the Aire.
Let faithful soules this double Feast attend
In two Processions: let the first descend
The Temples staires, and with a downe-cast eye   25
Upon the lowest pavement prostrate lie,
In creeping Violets, white Lillies shine
Their humble thoughts, and ev'ry pure designe;
The other troope shall climbe with sacred heate,
The rich degrees of *Salomons* bright seate,   30
In glowing Roses fervent zeale they beare,
And in the Azure Flowre de-lis appeare
Cellestiall contemplations, which aspire
Above the skie, up to th'immortall Quire.

TO HIS LATE MAJESTY, CONCERNING THE TRUE FORM OF ENGLISH POETRY

Great King, the Sov'raigne Ruler of this Land,
By whose grave care, our hopes securely stand:
Since you descending from that spacious reach,
Vouchsafe to be our Master, and to teach
Your English Poets to direct their lines,   5
To mixe their colours, and expresse their signes.
Forgive my boldnesse, that I here present
The life of Muses yeelding true content
In ponder'd numbers, which with ease I try'd,
When your judicious rules have been my guide.   10
   He makes sweet Musick, who in serious lines,
Light dancing tunes and heavy prose declines:
When verses like a milky torrent flow,
They equall temper in the Poet show,
He paints true formes, who with a modest heart,   15
Gives lustre to his worke, yet covers Art.
Uneven swelling is no way to fame,
But solid joyning of the perfect frame:
So that no curious finger there can find
The former chinkes, or nailes that fastly bind.   20
Yet most would have the knots of stiches seene,
And holes where men may thrust their hands between.
On halting feet the ragged Poem goes
With Accents, neither fitting Verse nor Prose.
The stile mine eare with more contentment fills   25
In Lawyers pleadings, or Phisicians bills.
For though in termes of Art their skill they close,
And joy in darksome words as well as those:
They yet have perfect sense more pure and cleare
Then envious Muses, which sad Garlands weare   30
Of dusky clouds, their strange conceits to hide
From humane eyes: and (lest they should be spi'd
By some sharpe *Oedipus*) the English Tongue
For this their poore ambition suffers wrong.
In ev'ry Language now in Europe spoke   35
By Nations which the Roman Empire broke,
The rellish of the Muse consists in rime,

One verse must meete another like a chime.
Our Saxon shortnesse hath peculiar grace
In choice of words, fit for the ending place,   40
Which leave impression in the mind as well
As closing sounds, of some delightfull bell:
These must not be with disproportion lame,
Nor should an Eccho still repeate the same.
In many changes these may be exprest: 45
But those that joyne most simply, run the best:
Their forme surpassing farre the fetter'd staves,
Vaine care, and needlesse repetition saves.
These outward ashes keepe those inward fires,
Whose heate the Greeke and Roman works inspires: 50
Pure phrase, fit Epithets, a sober care
Of Metaphors, descriptions cleare, yet rare,
Similitudes contracted smooth and round,
Not vext by learning, but with Nature crown'd.
Strong figures drawne from deepe inventions springs,   55
Consisting lesse in words, and more in things:
A language not affecting ancient times,
Nor Latine shreds, by which the Pedant climes
A noble subject which the mind may lift
To easie use of that peculiar gift,   60
Which Poets in their raptures hold most deare,
When actions by the lively sound appeare.
Give me such helpes, I never will despaire,
But that our heads which sucke the freezing aire,
As well as hotter braines, may verse adorne,   65
And be their wonder, as we were their scorne.

XVI

GEORGE WITHER (1588-1667)

Wither followed the medieval couplet style of Spenser more closely and more extensively than the modern, elegiac innovation, especially in his *Shepherd's Hunting* and *Prosopopoeia Britannica*. But he was, nevertheless, a willing imitator of Ovid and the English Ovidian adaptations in "An Elegiac Epistle from Fidelia to her Inconstant Friend" and of the English satirists and their Latin models in *Abuses Stript and Whipt*. He followed the enjambed romance couplet of Marlowe and Drayton, moreover, in his *Fair Virtue*.

Wither's facile imitations reveal to us, as well as anything, the variety of couplet practice open to poets and readers in the early years of the seventeenth century. This poet, however, has reduced the great variety of his models all to very nearly the same easy flowing verse. *Abuses Stript and Whipt*, for instance, recalls Spenser and Chaucer at least as much as Hall, Martial, and Juvenal. Wither's sense of the couplet, commonly, like his imagination, was abstract and general. None of his couplet practice reveals much of the couplet's literary dangers or opportunities — being neither stiff nor confused, neither pointed nor dynamic. It is just a neat, engagingly smooth way of providing sufferance for rather broadly and vaguely felt satiric or romantic, didactic or elegiac, pastoral or personal promptings.

One can find scattered through Wither's verse, even that which is most akin to Spenser and Chaucer, the rhetorical practices of the closed couplet: metrically defined parallels (*Hunting*, II, 46; *Prosopopoeia*, ll. 57–64), antitheses (*Hunting*, III, 48, 52–53), and inversions (*Hunting*, II, 41, 48–49; *Prosopopoeia*, ll. 54, 57–58). These practices are sparse, however, even in passages of sharply closed couplets, such as *Hunting*, III, 38–55, where they would seem to be most in order. It may be worth noting that this passage, although it moves in closed couplets, does not really seem to do so; it does not, in part, because the second lines often end on subordinate material so that the couplets seem to run downhill, to peter out. Thin as the rhetoric of this Spenserian poem is, it is nearly as rich as in those poems, like the "Elegiac Epistle" and *Abuses Stript and Whipt*, which cast at the closed-couplet style. It is, perhaps, less their rhetorical thinness, however, than their substantial diffuseness that makes Wither's verses run on with such tedious smoothness. Almost any set of two or three couplets in "An Elegiac Epistle," for example, could be cut to one: the meaning of lines 11–14 needs only such a couplet as "But since it must, pray flant you not nor scoff, / But read my pains before you cast them off" or such a line as "But ere you scoff at them, my sorrows read." The first two of the three couplets on remembrance (ll. 377–82), again, could simply be cut away without any loss of meaning.

The descriptive passage from *Fair Virtue* is, on the other hand, quite trenchant, especially when placed against the excesses of Drayton's romantic descriptions, and quite lovely; here Wither's poetic levelling has worked to advantage. But he is at his best, early and late in his career, when his sense of some opposing presence — courtiers, members of Parliament, or other great men — forces him, first, to be terse and pithy and pointed and, second, to qualify his miscellaneous metrical facility with a conversational bite, with an argumentatively tangy tone of voice. In his poems of this sort, "The Satire to Courtiers," "The Epilogue to Parliament," and "The Short Excuse," Wither moves toward the vital center of the closed-couplet world where Dryden and Pope ply their political and social arts.

ABUSES STRIPT AND WHIPT, I, i

Then to obtaine his Mistris, one man tries
How he can straine his wits to *Poetize*:
His *Passion* to relate, his skill he proves;
But in this blockish Age it little moves;   90
Nor doe I wonder much true meaning failes;
And wit so little in this case availes,
Sith Dunces can have Sonnets fram'd, and send them
As their inventions, when some others pend them.
    Another seekes by Valour to obtaine   95
His wished prize, but now that triall's vaine.

The third brings Wealth, and if he doe not speed,
The Woman's worth the suing for indeed.
   Then he that's neither valorous nor wise,
Comes ruffling in, with shameless brags and lies,   100
Making a stately, proud, vaine-glorious show
Of much good matter, when tis nothing so.
In steed of lands, to which he ne'er was heire,
He tells her tales of Castles in the ayre.
For martiall matters, he relates of frayes,   105
Where many drew their swords and ran their wayes:
His Poetry is such as he can cull
From Playes he heard at *Curtaine*, or at *Bull*;
And yet is fine coy Mistris-*Mary-Muffe*
The soonest taken with such broken stuffe.   110
   Another shallow braine hath no device,
But prates of some strange casts he had at Dice;
Brags of his play; yea sure it doth befall;
He vaunts oft-times of that which marreth all.

. . . .

ABUSES STRIPT AND WHIPT, I, vii

Thus doth it oftentimes with that man prove,
Who keepes not moderation in his love.
He having got a wife not onely fayre,
But modest, honest, wise and debonaire.   30
At first so wondrous meritorious deemes her;
As worthy all affection he esteemes her.
And waxeth so assur'd he dares be bold
Shee will not be allur'd to ill by gold,
Honour, nor beauty: but as she is chast,   35
So (is perswaded) will be to the last.
And to himselfe so well doth seeme to thrive,
He thinks his owne the happiest choise alive.
All which is good, and if no more I tell,
You cannot say wherein he doth not well: 40
But there he doth not his affection stay,
Further it tends, and further it will stray.
This man, not having learned to possesse

With temperance, so great a happinesse.
Oft his affections grow to that extreame,   45
As well he knowes not if he wake or dreame;
Then doth his *Love* (such love will ever doe it)
For a Companion take in *Feare* unto it.
A *Feare* of losing what he loves so much:
And then the nature of this *Feare* is such,   50
That it begets *Suspect*; which creeping in,
Doth by a little at the first begin
To make him doubt, his Spouse may loosly live.
But then her well knowne vertuous mind doth give
Such blamelesse testimonie of her good,   55
As that surmise is for a time withstood,
Till this disease upon him growes more strong,
Then he begins to thinke she doth him wrong:
Which if he doe, that one false thought's enough
To give all former truths the overthrowe.   60
And why? *Suspect* growes thereupon so great,
She thrusts *true judgment* quite beside her seat.
Which being done, then straight begins to wane
The good conceit he of his blisse had tane:
His only labour's how to bring't about,   65
To be assur'd of what he seeketh out.
A Cuckold he esteemes himselfe; and he
Were e'en as good indeed a Cuckold be:
Nay, rather then he'le be deceiv'd, the elfe
Will try to make a Cuckold of himselfe.   70

.   .   .   .

INTRODUCTORY SATIRE, TO
A SATIRE WRITTEN TO THE KING,
TO THE MERE COURTIERS

Sirs, I doe know your mindes; You looke for fees,
For more respect then needes, for caps and knees.
But be content, I have not for you now;
Nor will I have at all to doe with you.
For, though I seeme opprest, and you suppose   5
I must be faine to crouch to Vertues foes;

Yet know, your favours I doe sleight them more
In this distresse, then ere I did before.
Here to my *Liege* a message I must tell;
If you will let me passe, you shall doe well;   10
If you denie admittance, why then know,
I meane to have it where you will or no.
Your formall wisedome which hath never beene
In ought but in some fond invention seene,
And you that thinke men borne to no intent,   15
But to be train'd in Apish complement;
Doth now (perhaps) suppose mee indiscreet,
And such unused messages unmeet.
But what of that? Shall I goe sute my matter
Unto your wits, that have but wit to flatter?   20
Shall I, of your opinions so much prize
To lose my will that you may thinke me wise,
Who never yet to any liking had,
Unlesse he were a *Knave*, a *Foole*, or *mad*?
You *Mushroms* know, so much I weigh your powers,   25
I neither value *you*, nor what is yours.
Nay, though my crosses had me quite out-worne,
Spirit enough *I'de* finde your spight to scorne:
Of which resolv'd, to further my adventure,
Unto my *King*, without your leaves I enter.   30

THE SHEPHERD'S HUNTING, II

My first esteemed Dogge that I did finde,
Was by *descent* of olde *Acteons* kinde;
A *Brache*, which if I doe not aime amisse,
For all the world is just like one of his:
She's named *Love*, and scarce yet knowes her duty;   75
Her Damme's my Ladies pretty *Beagle, Beauty*.
I bred her up my selfe with wondrous charge,
Untill she grew to be exceeding large,
And waxt so wanton, that I did abhorre it,
And put her out amongst my neighbours for it.   80
The next is *Lust*, a Hound that's kept abroad
Mongst some of mine acquaintance, but a Toad
Is not more loathsome: 'tis a Curre will range

Extreamely, and is ever full of mange:
And cause it is infectious, she's not wunt   85
To come among the rest, but when they hunt.
Hate is the third, a Hound both deepe and long:
His *Sire* is *True*, or else supposed *Wrong*.
He'le have a snap at all that passe him by,
And yet pursues his game most eagerly.   90
With him goes *Envie* coupled, a leane Curre,
And yet she'le hold out, hunt we ne're so farre:
She pineth much, and feedeth little to,
Yet stands and snarleth at the rest that doe.

.   .   .   .

THE SHEPHERD'S HUNTING, III

Thou know'st that *Truth* and *Innocency* now,
If plac'd with meannesse, suffers more despight
Then *Villainies*, accompan'ed with might.   120
But thus it fell, while that my *Hounds* pursu'd
Their noysome prey, and every field laid strew'd
With *Monsters*, hurt and slaine; upon a beast,
More subtile, and more noysome then the rest,
My leane-flanckt Bitch, cald *Envy*, hapt to light: 125
And, as her wont is, did so surely bite,
That, though shee left behinde small outward smart,
The wounds were deepe, and rankled to the hart.
This, joyning to some other, that of late,
Were very eagerly pursu'd by *Hate*,   130
(To fit their purpose having taken leasure)
Did thus conspire to worke me a displeasure.
For imitation, farre surpassing *Apes*,
They laide aside their *Foxe* and *Wolvish shapes*,
And shrowded in the skinnes of harmlesse Sheepe   135
Into by-wayes, and open paths did creepe;
Where, they (as hardly drawing breath) did ly,
Shewing their wounds to every passer by;
To make them thinke that they were sheepe so foyl'd,
And by my Dogges, in their late hunting, spoyl'd.   140

.   .   .   .

AN ELEGIAC EPISTLE FROM FIDELIA
TO HER INCONSTANT FRIEND

Oft I have heard tel, and now for truth I finde,
Once out of sight, and quickly out of minde.
And that it hath been rightly said of old,
Love that's soon'st hot, is ever soonest cold.
Or else my teares at this time had not stain'd   5
The spotlesse paper, nor my lines complain'd.
I had not, now, been forced to have sent
These lines for *Nuncio's* of my discontent;
Nor thus, exchanged, so unhappily,
My songs of Mirth, to write an Elegie.   10
But, now I must; and, since I must doe so,
Let mee but crave, thou wilt not flout my woe:
Nor entertaine my sorrowes with a scoffe,
But, reade (at least) before thou cast them off.
And, though thy heart's too hard to have compassion,   15
Oh blame not, if thou pitty not my *Passion*,
For well thou know'st (alas, that er'e 'twas knowne)
There was a time (although that time be gone)
I, that for this, scarce dare a beggar bee,
Presum'd for more to have commanded thee.   20

.   .   .   .

Viewing againe those other walkes and Groves   365
That have beene witnesses of our chast loves;
When I beheld those Trees whose tender skin
Hath that cut out, which still cuts me within.
Or come, by chance, unto that pretty Rill
Where thou wouldst sit, and teach the neighbouring hill   370
To answere, in an Eccho, unto those
Rare *Problems* which thou often didst propose.
When I come there (thinke I) if these could take
That use of words and speech which we partake.
They might unfold a thousand pleasures then   375
Which I shall never live to taste agen.
And thereupon, *Remembrance* doth so racke
My thoughts, with representing what I lacke,
That in my minde those Clerkes doe argue well,

Which hold *Privation* the great'st plague of hell.   380
For there's no torment gripes mee halfe so bad,
As the *Remembrance* of those joyes I had.

.　.　.　.　.　.　.　.　.　.

I know, had I beene false, or my faith fail'd,
Thou wouldst at womens ficklenesse have rail'd;
And if in mee it had an error bin,
In thee shall the same fault be thought no sin?   480
Rather I hold that which is bad in mee,
Will be a greater blemish unto thee:
Because, by *Nature*, thou art made more strong,
And therefore abler to endure a wrong.
But 'tis our *Fortune*, you'le have all the power,   485
Onely the *Care* and *Burden* must be our.
Nor can you be content a wrong to do,
Unlesse you lay the blame upon us to.
Oh that there were some gentle-minded *Poet*
That knew my heart, as well as now I know it;   490
And would endeare me to his love so much,
To give the world (though but) a slender touch
Of that sad *Passion* which now clogs my heart,
And shew my truth, and thee how false thou art:
That all might know, what is beeleev'd by no man,   495
There's ficklenesse in men, and faith in woman.

.　.　.　.　.　.　.　.　.　.

FAIR VIRTUE, OR THE
MISTRESS OF PHILARETE

Two prettie *Rills* doe meet, and meeting make
Within one vally, a large silver lake:
About whose bankes the fertile mountaines stood,
In ages passed bravely crownd with wood;
Which lending Cold-sweet-shadowes, gave it grace,   5
To be accounted Cynthia's Bathing place.
And from her father *Neptunes* brackish Court,
Faire *Thetis* thither often would resort,
Attended by the Fishes of the *Sea*,
Which in those sweeter waters came to plea.   10

There, would the daughter of the *Sea-God* dive;
And thither came the Land-Nymphs every Eve,
To wait upon her: bringing for her browes,
Rich garlands of sweet flowres, and Beechy boughs.
    For, pleasant was that *Poole*; and neere it, then,   15
Was neither rotten Marsh, nor boggy Fen.
It was nor overgrowne with boystrous Sedge,
Nor grew there rudely then along the edge,
A bending Willow, nor a pricky Bush,
Nor broadleafd Flag, nor Reed, nor knotty Rush.   20
But here, wel order'd was a grove with Bowers:
There grassy-plots set round about with Flowers.
Here, you might (through the water) see the land,
Appeare, strowd o're with white or yellow sand.
Yonn, deeper was it; and the wind by whiffes.   25
Would make it rise, and wash the little cliffes,
On which, oft pluming sate (unfrighted than)
The gagling Wildgoose, and the snow-white Swan:
Withall those flockes of Fowles, which to this day,
Upon those quiet waters breed, and play.   30

.   .   .   .

PROSOPOPOEIA BRITANNICA, LECTURE I

When, in his might, the *Dogstar*, raigned, here,
And, when our *City*, and our *Armies,* were
Made jealous of each other, by their wiles,
Who, fought to nourish *Discord* in these *Iles*.
    Fill'd full of Thoughts, and sad, and sleeplesse lying   5
Upon my *Couch* there, silently, surveying
With *contemplations* eyes, the sick estate
Of these three *Kingdomes*, and, their likely Fate;
My rambling *Fancie* (which was newly come,
From whence I know not) brought into the room,   10
A *reverend Person*, who, upon him wore,
A Sea-green *mantle*, which was wrought all o're
With silver wavings (well resembled those
Which curle the *Ocean*, when a strong gale blowes)

And, had a Verge, or bordering imbost 15
Of Rock-work, like the *cliffs*, that guard our cost.
Rais'd with white *Saphirs*, looking o're a *strand*,
Bestrow'd with orient Pearls, and golden sand.
   In his left hand, he seem'd to bring with him
A *threefold*, but a broken *Diadem*, 20
Each *third* thereof contained counterfeits,
Of many differing shaped *Coronets*,
(Which had adorned it) most part of which
Seem'd also, broken, or defaced much;
And, not improperly, an *emblem* were 25
Of something, which this *Emperie* may feare.
With an heroick *look*, a Princely *pace*,
And awefull *presence*, entred he the place:
But, so, that *look*, and *pace*, and *presence*, had
A shadowing drawne over them, which made 30
Appearance, of a heart displeas'd, and sorry;
Yet, gave it, rather, excellence and glory
To his *demeanure*, then diminishment,
Of what, beseem'd a *Person* excellent.
Nor heeding me; nor seeming much to care 35
Who, then, was present, or, who was not there,
A turne or two, he walk'd; rais'd to the skies,
As one admiring, his majestick eyes;
And, with hands elevated, and display'd
Thus, like a much displeased *friend*, he said, 40
SEE, SEE! how MISCHIEF, like the *Learnean Snake*,
Renewes her heads, and still new life doth take!
The *fire* of WAR within our *fields* did flame,
A while agoe, and Gods hand quench'd the same.
The *match* and *powder* were together laid 45
In our chiefe *City*; and, he, also staid
Those probable effects, which could have shooke
These *Ilands*, if the project, then, had took.
As soone as that was past, another *Traine*
Was closely laid, to blow up all againe; 50
And, make these *Nations*, like the clod-borne brood
Of *Cadmus*, broachers of each others blood.
   Is there no end of *madnesse*? but, by fits,
Must they, who should be wisest, loose their wits?

And, still be forging new *Designes* and *Gins*,   55
To plague themselves, and others, for their *sins*?
Will not, the blind, *selfe-seeking parties*, leave,
Snares for themselvs, with their own hands to weave?
Will not the *Serpent* cease to bruise their heels,
Whom he pursues, though broken heads he feels?   60
Nor will the harmlesse *Doves*, become so wise
To know the *Birds of prey*, through their disguise,
Till they are all beguiled with their showes,
And, quite devour'd, by *Buzzard*, *Kites* and *Crowes*?
Shall wholsome counsell, alwaies, be withstood?   65
And, will you reinvolve your selves in blood,
What ever your best friends indeavour can,
And, as it were, in spight of GOD and *man*?

.   .   .   .

EPILOGUE TO PROSOPOPOEIA
BRITANNICA, TO THE PARLIAMENT

It is not *feare*, in me; nor is it shame,
Which makes me, at this time, conceal my *name*:
But, humble modestie, and consciousnesse,
Of that knowne frailty, and unworthinesse,
Wherewith my *Person*, outwardly is cloth'd,   5
Oft, makes my selfe, ev'n of my selfe so loth'd,
That (not without good reason,) I suspect
My purposes, may find the lesse effect,
If, ere you tast the fruit, I let you know,
In whose poor Garden, GOD, hath made it grow,   10
For, many times, the best wine pleaseth not,
Unlesse, we like the *Drawer*, and the *Pot*.
A homebred *Simples* vertue, few will owne;
A *Doctor* seemes best skil'd, that is unknowne:
Yea, miracles, by *Christ*, were seldome done,   15
Where, he reputed was, but *Josephs* son.
   How ere it please, or may be understood,
I dare aver, my purposes were good;
And, that, hereby, you have advantages
To do your *selves* an *honour*, if you please.   20

Therewith, you *profit*, likewise, may receive,
If, thereunto, but those respects you give,
Which are, in equity, to those things due,
That will both *profit*, and much *honour* you.
Gods *will be done*: and, if your *will* agree   25
With his, then, let your *will* be done on mee.

A SHORT EXCUSE WHY THIS PRISONER MAKES NO ADDRESS FOR HIS RELEASE TO GREAT PERSONS

I am inform'd, by men of good report,
That, there are Noble *Pers'nages* in *Court*
Who hate *Injustice*, and, are of their Tribe,
Who love not baseness, flattery, or a Bribe;
And, that, should I my self to these Adresse,   5
I might perhaps obtain a quick release.
'Tis possible; But, I may much indanger
Their *Quiet*; and, am now grown such a stranger
To Courtship, that I cannot Complement,
Or, act effectually, to that intent;   10
Nor think it prudence (were I mov'd that way)
To seek a Needle, in a Trusse of Hay.

.   .   .   .

XVII

✦✦✦✦✦✦✦✦✦✦✦✦✦✦✦

THOMAS CAREW
(1594-1640)

Carew's couplet practice derived in some measure from both the early English couplet and from the Latin elegiac distich. "Upon the King's Sickness" and, especially, "The Spring" show the English root; "My Mistress Commanding" and "Upon a Ribband" are clearly Ovidian. But there is one integrated mode of verse in all these poems, not the two strikingly different ones we observe in Marlowe or Beaumont, a mode whose major affinity is with Ben Jonson. Carew's couplets are, like Jonson's, almost never either loosely enjambed or stiffly closed.

"The Spring," for all its Chaucerian detail and atmosphere, is clearly Jonsonian. It presents, quite unlike Chaucer, a series of antitheses each item of which distinguishes either between the past winter and the present spring or between the spring's warmth and a mistress's coldness. Carew's material is such, in short, as could easily have been organized in closed couplets. But, despite several effects that depend on closure, such as line-defined parallels (ll. 4, 8)[1] and antitheses (l. 24), it has not been. Only two of its couplets, both tucked away in the middle of the poem (ll. 9–10, 11–12), are sharply defined; all the rest suffer some kind of enjambment. On the other hand, the poem's series of antitheses is articulated with perfect lucidity and grace. This is due, first, to the balance and clarity of the poem's substance and, second, to a variety of devices. One such device is the repeated use of "now" to introduce the separate elements of the winter-spring antithesis and the repeated use of "all . . . only" to punctuate the contrast between the spring and the mistress. A second device, one which both defines the thought and diffuses its utterance, is Carew's use of strong mid-line pause (ll. 2, 7, 19, 20, 22, 23). Still another, and one that naturally accompanies the de-

---

[1] My line references correspond to the line notations in *The Poems of Thomas Carew*, ed. Rhodes Dunlap (Oxford, 1957).

finitive use of mid-line pause, is the diffused correspondency in placing of rhetorically corresponding items: the "dead Swallow" and the "drowzie Cuckoo," for instance, are placed at the beginnings of succeeding lines; "The Oxe" and "Amyntas" are placed at the beginnings of couplets — although not succeeding ones; "open fields" and "cooler shade" are placed at opposite ends of the same couplet. In all these cases we find some metrical enforcement of parallel items, then, but not as pointed an enforcement as they would have normally received in closed-couplet deployment. Where the verse does give a strong metrical definition, in the case of the "fire side . . . cooler shade" antithesis, for instance, the fluency of the poem diffuses it. Even the poem's final June-January antithesis, because it is approached through enjambed lines and couplets, is less a striking formulation in itself than it is a normal and merely final rounding out of the whole poem's thought.

Carew has made the same kind of use of the couplet's narrower and more emphatic definition as this with which he closes "The Spring" throughout "My Mistress Commanding me to Return her Letters" (ll. 6, 14, 18, 26), using couplet balance and couplet closure to give climactic punctuation to the stages of that poem. Carew's couplets, however, are usually flexible even when they are closed and suggestive of balance even when they are enjambed. In lines 5–14 of "Upon a Ribband," for instance, we find five closed couplets every one of which contains an aspect of the contrast between the mistress's ribbon and her beauty, but every one of them has been differently formed, and three of the five are strikingly unbalanced. One can observe the same sort of flexibility in the series of closed couplets in lines 5–14 of "Upon the Kings Sickness," which describe death's power over the different stages of human life. One might, admittedly, describe these passages as irregular inside their couplets and stiff as systems of couplets — thus linking them to the medieval practice of poets like Baldwin and Breton. And the continuation of "Upon a Ribband" (ll. 13–22), which advances as a series of antitheses all but one of which are line-defined, that one being expanded to fill out a couplet (ll. 17–18), is undoubtedly stiff. It is, however, stiffly regular, and thus mannered — Ovidian in its neatness and cleverness, rather than medieval.

Such enjambed couplets as those which open the poem "To Ben Jonson," on the other hand, are inarguably Jonsonian. They allow Carew to give lucid utterance to his balanced judgments on Jonson's complaint against the age, a judgment that comprehends the justness and the limitations of Jonson's complaint, and on Jonson's plays, pointing out the difference in excellence between the earlier and the more recent ones. This whole poem, whose verse modulates in response to the complexity of its material but never to the point of confusion, exemplifies the style of Jonson and Carew at its best; the professions seem sincere, the criticism just, and the whole utterance is so variously and yet so precisely measured as to seem like a perfect manifestation of sense and reason.

After Carew, this form of couplet largely disappeared — to reappear with startling differences in Dryden. The age, it seems, required either the greater focus and intensity of the closed couplet with its chances, on the one hand, for more courtly and, on the other, for more satiric formulations, or the totally irrelevant and escapist wanderings of the enjambed romance couplet. That justness and detachment, that breadth of vision which radiates from the couplets of Jonson and Carew has no place in the neat and narrow compliments of Waller or in Cleveland's biting iambics.

XVIII

✠✠✠✠✠✠✠✠✠✠✠✠✠✠✠

SHAKERLEY MARMION
(1603-1639)

Although Marmion's verse often moves along in couplets (ll. 7–20, 33–36) and even makes use of metrically defined parallel (ll. 14, 18) and periodic (ll. 3, 5, 17, 37) arrangements, it nevertheless marks a stage between the romantic grace of Marlowe's *Hero and Leander* and the romantic perversity of William Chamberlayne's *Pharonnida*. For one thing, Marmion, with his couplet enjambment (ll. 2, 4, 26, 30, 46, 48) and his extensive use of heavy mid-line pause (ll. 4, 39, 41, 48), went beyond Marlowe in ignoring the couplet's powers of definition and emphasis. One discovers in Marmion's verse something of that oscillation between metrical stiffness (ll. 21–24, 31–36) and laxity (ll. 24–30, 43–50) which shows up in many of the minor couplet poets around this time; but the swing in Marmion goes from a crabbed, murky stiffness (ll. 21–24) to an extremely lax although graceful glide — as in the five and one-half lines describing Psyche's repast (ll. 43–48), which contain two parallel statements, the second of which suffers a three and one-half line diminution of rhetorical force.

More important than Marmion's weakening of the couplet is his abuse of it, that is, his use of its bounds and emphases to cloud rather than to clarify his utterance. One may notice, for one thing, his common practice of filling out second lines (ll. 8, 18, 26, 44, 46) and second halves of second lines (ll. 6, 12, 34) with syntactically and substantially minor material so that his couplets sink rather than rise to their rhyming closes. This impression is heightened by Marmion's commonly giving periodic strengthening to first lines (ll. 3, 5, 17, 37) and not to second lines. Marmion also abused his rhymes: he often used as rhyming syllables the secondary stresses of long words (ll. 2, 10, 12, 26) or words, such as "same" (l. 14) and "there" (l. 30), of negligible signification (ll. 6, 9, 46, 50). These practices of giving poetic emphasis to minor words and word systems and of slighting major ones naturally clouds Marmion's utterance, making it harder to understand than if he had written it down without rhyme or verse. One might make a case for these practices on the grounds of narrative fluency, but what surely drew Marmion to them was their very cloudiness — the specious atmosphere of mystery they lent to his otherwise simple and tedious romanticizing. At any rate, Marmion's romantic effect depends heavily on this metrically induced sense of visionary derangement — on the reader's being metrically assured, for instance, that his chief attention should go not to "Fountaine," "pillers," "bowle," or "spirit" but to "side," "same," "yet," and "in."

Comparing these couplets with Chaucer's in his romance "The Squire's Tale" will show, by the way, that there is no carryover — in verse or in verse-derived tone — from the great medieval poet to the seventeenth-century poets of romance. Marmion and Chamberlayne have lost the sense of a spoken voice that rang in virtually all of Chaucer's verses. The accents of normal speech would have ruined their efforts at mystery. So would that lively dynamics, first, between narrative fluency and narrative discrimination and, second, between a miscellaneous readiness of attention and a continuousness of critical intelligence which Chaucer achieved with his strong line, enjambed couplet, and flexibly measured movement. Their poetic pleasure was an easy, thoughtless flow, an uncritical drift on the tides of fancy, an escape from sense and judgment and everyday relevancy.

CUPID AND PYSCHE, I, ii

Thus *Psyche* on a grassy bed did lye,
Adorn'd with *Floraes* richest tapestry,
Where all her sences with soft slumber bound,
At last awakt, and rising from a swound
She spies a wood, with faire trees beautifi'd,   5
And a pure christall Fountaine by the side;
A Kingly Palace stood not farr apart,
Built not with humane hands, but devine *Art*;
For by the structure men might guesse it be
The habitation of some Deity: 10
The Roofe within was curiously o're spread
With *Ivory*, and Gold enamelled;
The Gold was burnisht, glistering like a flame,

And Golden pillers did support the same;
The walles were all with Silver wainscott lin'd,   15
With severall Beasts, and Pictures there inshrin'd,
The Floure, and Pavement with like glory shone,
Cut in rare figures, made of pretious Stone,
That though the Sun should hide his light away,
You might behold the house through its owne day.   20
Sure 'twas some wondrous power by *arts* extent
That fancied forth so great an argument:
And no lesse happy they, that did command,
And with their feet trod on so rich a land,
Psyche amaz'd, fixt her delighted eye,   25
On the magnificence, and treasury,
And wondred most, that such a masse of wealth
Was by no doore, nor guard, preserv'd from stealth:
For looking when some servant should appeare
She onely heard voices attending there,   30
That said, faire Mistresse why are you afraide?
All these are yours, and we to doe you ayd.
Come up into the roomes, where shall be showne
Chambers all ready furnisht, all your owne:
From thence descend, and take the spiced aire,   35
Or from your bath unto your bed repaire,
Whilst each of us, that *Eccho* represents,
Devoyd of all corporeall instruments,
Shall waite your Minister: no Princely fare
Shall wanting be, no dilligence, no care,   40
To doe you service. *Psyche* had the sence
To tast, and thanke the Gods beneficence:
When straight, a mighty golden dish was brought,
Repleat with all the dainties can be thought;
And next a bowle was on the table set,   45
Fraught with the richest Nectar, that ere yet
Faire *Hebe* fill'd to *Juno*, Heavens Queene,
Or *Ganimed* to *Jove*; yet none was seene,
Nor creature found to pledge, or to begin,
But some impulsive spirit brought it in.   50

.   .   .   .

XIX

✦✦✦✦✦✦✦✦✦✦✦✦✦✦✦

EDMUND WALLER
(1606-1687)

In passages of his later verse, Waller achieved unified systems of closed couplets. One can realize this most vividly by comparing, say, the poet's youthful disposition of a series of Bermudian charms (*Summer Islands*, I, 11–32) with his mature handling of a series of great English buildings ("On St. James's Park," ll. 85–108). The first three Bermudian items, cedars, smoke, and roofs, emerge one couplet at a time, and then, with a shifting of gears, come palmettos, figs, rocks, and tobacco, each one covering two couplets. The passage's one moment of metrical stress, and that a mild one, comes with the palmettos, which the reader expects to take up only one couplet and which he finds taking up two. The historic buildings, on the other hand, are handled flexibly throughout: Whitehall covering lines 85–90; Westminster Abbey, lines 91–104 (the Houses of Parliament being wedged into the Westminster Abbey passage at line 99); and Westminster Hall covering lines 105–8. The short shrift and the subordinate situation Waller has given the Houses of Parliament wonderfully suggest the Royalist tone he wants, and, indeed, the responsiveness of his verse to the different promptings of the halls throughout this passage gives a sense of the poet's living concern with his material. To further witness Waller's development, one might compare the spongy analogy between Aeneas and Charles I in his early "St. Andrews" poem (ll. 85–99) with the complex park-Europe, past-present comparison that he has perfectly defined in the last couplet of "On St. James's Park" (ll. 135–36). Waller was able to achieve so compressed and yet lucid a close to his later poem by tying this couplet-defined comparison into a syntactic unit he had worked out over the last ten lines (ll. 127–36). In Waller's later poetry there are many outcroppings of this couplet dynamics in which the poet has achieved at once both movement and stability, both complexity and clarity.

Waller was always a fallible poet, however, for all his famed smoothness. The Eden-Park (ll. 1–4) and the river-Town (ll. 9–12) antitheses at the beginning of "On St. James's Park," for instance, are terrible daubs. One can best bring out the failure of the first of these by comparing it with Pope's redaction of it in lines 7–10 of *Windsor Forest*. Between these two muddled antitheses, however, comes quite a good couplet (ll. 7–8) in which Waller has focussed an always-now opposition and achieved a metrical thrust with one stroke — by making "now" the last syllable of the couplet's first line. One finds the same mixture of bad and good in "The Last Verses" where a couplet which is badly marred by syntactic confusion (ll. 15–16) immediately follows one of the most memorable ones Waller ever wrote: "The soul's dark cottage, battered and decayed, / Lets in new light through chinks that time has made." And yet again, a vigorous two-couplet utterance of Cromwell's ability to focus his nation's martial instincts on foreign rather than domestic wars in "The Death of his Highness" (ll. 23–26) comes right after this stiff, ridiculously anticlimactic couplet: "Under the tropic is our language spoke; / And part of FLANDERS hath receiv'd our yoke."

Waller's tendency toward double-couplet systems has been pointed out in the preceding "Brief History." This four-line pattern, which adds a distinction between the pauses at the ends of odd and even couplets to the couplet hierarchy of pauses, Waller could settle into fairly comfortably throughout his career. Besides the famous "Panegyric," whose spacing declares its persistent commitment to this system of metrical order, one finds such organization both in early poems ("Phoebus and Daphne," ll. 11–18; *Summer Islands*, I, 17–32) and in the later ones ("On St. James's Park," ll. 1–12). But these, except for their consistent use in the "Panegyric," are meager and incidental expansions of a style that Waller, despite a long life and a long, excessively praised career, never brought to perfection.

As his short-windedness and his inevitable intermixture of poor couplets might suggest, Waller had a weak, a defective, poetic overview. Had he not lacked overview, he would surely have modified the tedious repetition of periodic inversion by which all but one of lines 11 through 16 of his *Summer Islands* have been defined. In five out of the possible six cases, Waller transposed a verb to the end of a line, and the continuation of the passage is not much better. This tedious narrowness of practice, this reduction of the diverse elements of his material to the same formula, reminds us that Waller was a friend of George Sandys. Every single line between lines 115 and 123 of "On St. James's Park," to give further evidence of Waller's narrow view of his poetry, maintains either a periodic shift, similar to those mentioned above, or a pair of items in parallel. The four couplets that give four strikingly different descriptions of a grove of trees in this same poem (ll. 67–74) give a different kind of evidence of Waller's narrowness of poetic view: in the separate couplets, the trees are described as "aged Trees," "Bold sons of earth," "green Palaces," and "old Counsellors." Only by reading this passage a couplet at a time — the way it must have been written — can we avoid a hopeless mixture of metaphor.

Waller devoted his couplets for the most part to the flattery of eminent men and women of his acquaintance. With the resources for neat and emphatic formulations which the closed couplet offered him, he could reduce the sighs of love and the tears of grief, tempests at sea and enduring trees, and even the great London fire to complimentary gestures. In "At Penshurst," for instance, Waller reduced, although with imperfect art, deer, beeches, and bowers to virtually identical flourishes in his public pose of hopeless love for Lady Dorothy Sidney. Nothing is real in this poem — neither the objects nor the emotion — nothing, that is, but the pose. We might remember, by way of contrast, Ben Jonson's "To Penshurst," whose grounds, animals, and folk were alive and, because they were alive, made Jonson's central assertion about Penshurst convincing and impressive. The difference between Jonson's compliment to Penshurst and Waller's to Lady Dorothy Sidney is rooted in each poet's couplet practice. Jonson's calculated enjambment reveals his intelligent responsiveness to his experiences of Penshurst; Waller's stiff closure reveals his determination to be polite.

OF THE DANGER HIS MAJESTY, BEING PRINCE, ESCAPED IN THE ROAD AT ST. ANDREWS

Now had his Highnes bid farewell to Spaine
And reach't the sphere of his owne power, the Main;
With Brittish bounty in his ship hee feasts
Th' Hesperian Princes, his amazed ghuests
To finde that watry wildernes exceed,   5
The entertainments of their great Madrid.
Healths to both Kings, attended with the rore
Of Canons, echo'd from th' affrighted shore.
With loud resemblance of his Thunder, prove

Bacchus the seed of cloud-compelling *Jove*;　　　　　　　10
While to his harp divine Arion sings
The loves and conquests of our *Albion* Kings.

.　　.　　.　　.　　.　　.　　.　　.

With the sweete sound of this harmonious lay
About the Keele delighted *Dolphins* play;
Too sure a signe of seas ensuing rage　　　　　　　　　35
Which must anon this Royall troup ingage.
To whom soft sleepe seemes more secure and sweete
Within the Towne commanded by our fleete.
These mighty Peeres plac'd in the guilded Barge,
Proud with the burden of so brave a charge,　　　　　　40
With painted Oares the youths begin to sweep
Neptunes smooth face, and cleave the yielding deep,
Which soone becomes the seate of sudden warre.
Betwixt the winde and tide, that fiercely jarre.

.　　.　　.　　.　　.　　.　　.　　.

The gentle vessell wont with state and pride
On the smooth back of silver Thames to ride,
Wanders astonisht through the angry Main,
As *Titans* Carre did, while the golden rein
Fil'd the young hand of his adventurous sonne,　　　　65
When the whole world an equall hazard runne.
To this of ours, the light of whose desire
Waves threaten now, as that was skard by fire.
　　Th' impatient Sea growes impotent and raves,
That (night assisting) his impetuous waves　　　　　　70
Should finde resistance from so light a thing,
These surges ruine, those our safety bring.
Th' oppressed vessell doth the charge abide,
Only because assail'd on every side.
So men with rage and passion set on fire,　　　　　　75
Trembling for haste, impeach their mad desire.
　　The pale *Iberians* had expir'd with feare,
But that their wonder did divert their care,
To see the Prince with danger mov'd no more,
Than with the pleasures of their Court before;　　　　80
God-like his courage seem'd, whom nor delight
Could soften, nor the face of death affright.
Next to the power of making tempests cease,
Was in that storme to have so calme a peace.

Great *Maro* could no greater tempest fain,   85
When the lowd winds usurping on the Main
For angry *Juno*, labour'd to destroy
The hated reliques of confounded *Troy*:
His bold *AEneas* on like billowes tost,
In a tall ship and all his countries lost,   90
Dissolves with fear, and both his hands upheld,
Proclaimes them happy whom the Greekes had quell'd
In honorable fight: Our Hero, set
In a small shallop, Fortune in his debt,
So neare a hope of crownes and scepters more   95
Than ever *Priam*, when he flourish'd, wore.
His loines yet full of ungot-Princes, all
His glory in the bud, lets nothing fall
That argues fear: if any thought annoyes
The gallant youth 'tis loves untasted joyes,   100
And deare remembrance of that fatal glance
For which he lately pawn'd his heart in *France*,
Where he had seen a brighter Nymph then shee
That sprung out of his present foe, the Sea.

.   .   .   .

AT PENSHURST

While in the Parke I sing, the listening Deere
Attend my passion, and forget to feare.
When to the Beeches I report my flame,
They bow their heads as if they felt the same.
To Gods appealing, when I reach their bowrs   5
With loud complaints, they answer mee in showrs.
To thee a wild and cruell soule is given,
More deafe then trees and prouder then the heaven,
Love's foe profest, why dost thou falsely faine
Thy selfe a *Sidney*, from which noble straine   10
Hee sprung, that could so far exalt the name
Of love, and warme our Nation with his flame,
That all we can of Love, or high desire
Seemes but the smoake of amorous *Sidneys* fire?
Nor call her Mother, who so well does prove   15
One brest may hold both Chastity and Love.

Never can shee that so exceeds the spring
In joy and bounty, be suppos'd to bring
One so destructive: to no humane stock
We owe this fierce unkindnes, but the rock: 20
That cloven rocke produc'd thee, by whose side
Nature to recompence the fatall pride
Of such sterne beauty, plac'd those healing springs,
Which not more helpe, then that destruction brings.
Thy heart no ruder than the rugged stone   25
I might, like *Orpheus* with my num'rous moane
Melt to compassion, now my trait'rous song
With thee conspires to do the singer wrong,
While thus I suffer not myselfe to lose
The memory of what augments my woes;   30
But with my owne breath still foment the fire
Which flames as high as phansy can aspire.
    This last complaint th' indulgent eares does pierce
Of just *Apollo* president of verse,
Highly concerned that the Muse should bring   35
Damage to one whom he had taught to sing.
Thus he advis'd me, On yon aged tree
Hang up thy Lute, and hie thee to the Sea,
That there with wonders thy diverted minde
Some truce, at least, may with this passion finde.   40
    Ah cruell Nymph, from whom her humble swaine
Flies for reliefe unto the raging maine!
And from the winds and tempests doth expect
A milder fate then from her cold neglect!
Yet there hee'l pray that the unkind may prove   45
Blest in her choyce, and vows this endlesse love
Springs from no hope of what shee can confer,
But from those gifts which heaven has heap'd on her.

THE BATTLE OF THE
SUMMER ISLANDS, I

Bermudas wall'd with rocks, who does not know,   5
That happy Island where huge Lemmons grow,
And Orange trees, which golden fruit doe beare,
Th' *Hesperian* garden boasts of none so faire.

There shining Pearl, Corall, and many a pound
On the rich shore of Amber-greece is found: 10
The lofty Cedar, which to heaven aspires,
The Prince of trees, is fuell for their fires:
The smoak by which their loaded spits doe turn,
For incense might on sacred Altars burn;
Their private roofs on odorous timber born,   15
Such as might Palaces for Kings adorn:
The sweet palmetta's a new *Bacchus* yield
With leaves as ample as the broadest shield;
Under the shadow of whose friendly boughs
They sit carousing where their liquor grows: 20
Figs there unplanted through the fields doe grow,
Such as fierce *Cato* did the Romans show,
With the rare fruit inviting them to spoil
Carthage, the Mistress of so rich a soil:
The naked rocks are not unfruitfull there,   25
But at some constant seasons every yeare
Their barren tops with luscious food abound,
And with the eggs of various fowles are crown'd:
Tobacco is the worst of things which they
To English landlords as their tribute pay: 30
Such is the mould, that the blessed tenant feeds
On pretious fruits, and payes his rent in weeds:
With candid Plantines, and the juicy Pine,
On choisest Melons, and sweete grapes they dine,
And with Potatoes fat their wanton swine.   35
Nature these Cates with such a lavish hand
Powres out among them that our courser land
Tasts of that bounty, and does cloth returne,
Which not for warmth, but ornament is worne:
For the kind spring, which but salutes us here,   40
Inhabits there, and courts them all the yeare:
Ripe fruits and blossomes on the same trees live.
At once they promise what at once they give.
So sweet the ayre, so moderate the clime.
None sickly lives or dyes before his time.   45
Heaven, sure, has kept this spot of earth uncurst,
To shew how all things were created first.

.   .   .   .

TO LORD FALKLAND

Brave Holland leads, and with him Falkland goes;
Who hears this told, and does not straight suppose
We send the Graces and the Muses forth
To civilize, and to instruct the North:
   Not that these ornaments make swords less sharp;   5
Apollo bears as well his Bow as Harp:
And though he be the patron of that Spring
Where in calm Peace the sacred Virgins sing,
He courage had to guard th' invaded throne
Of Jove, and cast th' ambitious Giants down.   10
   Ah! (noble Friend) with what impatience all
That know thy worth, and know how prodigall
Of thy great soul thou art, longing to twist
Bayes with that Ivy which so early kist
Thy youthful Temples, with what horrour wee   15
Think on the blind events of war, and thee
To Fate exposing that all-knowing brest
Among the throng as cheaply as the rest,
Where Oaks and brambles (if the Copse be burn'd)
Confounded lie to the same ashes turn'd!   20
   Some happy wind over the Ocean blow
This tempest yet, which frights our Island so,
Guarded with ships, and all the Sea our own,
From heaven this mischief on our heads is thrown.
   In a late Dream, the *Genius* of this Land   25
Amaz'd I saw like the fair *Hebrew* stand,
When first she felt the twins begin to jar,
And found her womb the seat of civill war:
Inclin'd to whose relief, and with presage
Of better fortune for the present Age,   30
Heaven sends, quoth I, this discord for our good,
To warm, perhaps, but not to waste our blood:
To raise our drooping spirits, grown the scorn
Of our proud Neighbors, who ere long shall mourn
(Though now they joy in our expected harms)   35
Wee had occasion to resume our Arms.
   A Lion so with self-provoking smart,
His rebell tail scourging his noble part,

Calls up his courage, then begins to roare,
And charge his foes, who thought him mad before.   40

A PANEGYRIC TO
MY LORD PROTECTOR

With such a Chief the meanest Nation blessed,
Might hope to lift her head above the rest;
What may be thought impossible to do
By Us, embraced by the sea, and you?   40

Lords of the world's great waste, the ocean, we
Whole forests send to reign upon the sea,
And ev'ry coast may trouble, or relieve:
But none can visit us without your leave.

Angels, and we, have this prerogative,   45
That none can at our happy seat arrive:
While we descend at pleasure, to invade
The bad with vengeance, and the good to aid.

Our little world, the image of the great,
Like that, amidst the boundless ocean set,   50
Of her own growth, hath all that Nature craves;
And all that's rare, as tribute from the waves.

As Egypt does not on the clouds rely,
But to her NILE owes more than to the sky;
So what our earth, and what our heav'n, denies,   55
Our ever-constant friend, the sea, supplies.

The taste of hot ARABIA's spice we know,
Free from the scorching sun, that makes it grow:
Without the worm, in PERSIAN silks we shine;
And, without planting, drink of ev'ry vine.   60

To dig for wealth we weary not our limbs;
Gold, tho' the heaviest metal, hither swims:
Ours is the harvest where the *Indians* mow,
We plough the Deep, and reap what others sow.

.   .   .   .

Your private life did a just pattern give,
How fathers, husbands, pious sons should live.

Born to command, your Princely virtues slept 135
Like humble *David's*, while the flock he kept.

But when your troubled country call'd you forth,
Your flaming courage, and your matchless worth,
Dazling the eyes of all that did pretend,
To fierce contention gave a prosp'rous end. 140

Still as you rise, the state, exalted too,
Finds no distemper while 'tis chang'd by you;
Chang'd like the world's great scene! when, without noise,
The rising sun night's vulgar lights destroys.

Had you, some ages past, this race of glory 145
Run, with amazement we should read your story:
But living virtue, all atchievements past,
Meets envy still, to grapple with at last.

.   .   .   .

UPON THE DEATH OF THE
LORD PROTECTOR

We must resign! Heav'n his great soul does claim
In storms, as loud as his immortal fame:
His dying groans, his last breath shakes our Isle;
And trees uncut fall for his fun'ral pile:
About his palace their broad roots are tost 5
Into the air, — So ROMULUS was lost!
New ROME in such a tempest miss'd her King;
And, from obeying, fell to worshipping.
On OETA's top thus HERCULES lay dead,
With ruin'd oaks, and pines, about him spread. 10
The poplar too, whose bough he wont to wear
On his victorious head, lay prostrate there.
Those his last fury from the mountain rent:
Our dying Hero, from the continent
Ravish'd whole towns; and Forts from SPANIARDS reft, 15
As his last legacy to BRITAIN left.
The ocean, which so long our hopes confin'd,
Could give no limits to his vaster mind,
Our bounds' enlargement was his latest toil;

Nor hath he left us pris'ners to our Isle: 20
Under the tropic is our language spoke;
And part of FLANDERS hath receiv'd our yoke.
From civil broils he did us dis-engage;
Found nobler objects for our martial rage:
And, with wise conduct, to his country show'd   25
Their antient way of conquering abroad.
Ungrateful then! if we no tears allow
To him that gave us peace, and empire too.
Princes that fear'd him, grieve; concern'd to see
No pitch of glory from the grave is free.   30
Nature herself took notice of his death,
And, sighing, swell'd the sea with such a breath,
That, to remotest shores her billows roul'd,
Th' approaching fate of her great ruler told.

ON ST. JAMES'S PARK AS LATELY IMPROVED BY HIS MAJESTY

Of the first Paradise there's nothing found,
Plants set by Heav'n are vanisht, and the ground;
Yet the description lasts; who knows the fate
Of lines that shall this Paradise relate?
　　Instead of Rivers rowling by the side   5
Of *Edens* Garden, here flows in the Tyde;
The Sea which always serv'd his Empire, now
Pays tribute to our Prince's pleasure too:
Of famous Cities we the founders know;
But Rivers old, as Seas, to which they go,   10
Are natures bounty; 'tis of more renown
To make a River than to build a Town.
For future shade young Trees upon the banks
Of the new stream appear in even ranks:
The voice of *Orpheus* or *Amphions* hand   15
In better order could not make them stand;
May they increase as fast, and spread their boughs,
As the high Fame of their great Owner grows!
May he live long enough to see them all
Dark shadows cast, and as his Pallace tall.   20
Me-thinks I see the love that shall be made,

The Lovers walking in that amorous shade,
The Gallants dancing by the Rivers side,
They bath in Summer, and in Winter slide.
Me-thinks I hear the Music in the Boats,   25
And the loud Eccho which returns the notes,
Whilst over head a flock of new sprung Fowl
Hangs in the air, and does the sun controul:
Darkening the skie they hover o're, and shrowd
The wanton Sailors with a feather'd cloud: 30
Beneath a shole of silver fishes glides,
And plays about the gilded Barges sides;
The Ladies angling in the Chrystal Lake,
Feast on the waters with the prey they take;
At once victorious with their Lines and Eyes   35
They make the Fishes and the men their prize.

.   .   .   .

Nere this my Muse, what most delights her, sees,
A living Gallery of aged Trees;
Bold sons of earth that thrust their arms so high,
As if once more they would invade the Sky;   70
In such green Palaces the first Kings reign'd,
Slept in their shades, and Angels entertain'd:
With such old Counsellors they did advise
And, by frequenting sacred Groves grew wise;
Free from th' impediments of light and noise   75
Man thus retir'd his nobler thoughts imploys:
Here Charles contrives the ordering of his States,
Here he resolves his neighb'ring Princes fates:
What Nation shall have peace, where War be made
Determin'd is in this oraculous shade;   80
The world, from India to the frozen North,
Concern'd in what this solitude brings forth.
His Fancy objects from his view receives,
The prospect thought and contemplation gives:
That seat of Empire here salutes his eye,   85
To which three Kingdoms do themselves apply,
The structure by a prelate rais'd, White-hall,
Built with the fortune of Romes Capitol;
Both disproportion'd to the present State
Of their proud founders, were approv'd by Fate;   90
From hence he does that Antique Pile behold,

Where Royal heads receive the sacred gold;
It gives them Crowns, and does their ashes keep;
There made like gods, like mortals there they sleep
Making the circle of their reign compleat,   95
Those Suns of Empire, where they rise they set:
When others fell, this standing did presage
The Crown should triumph over popular rage,
Hard by that House where all our ills were shap'd
Th' Auspicious Temple stood, and yet escap'd.   100
So snow on *Aetna* does unmelted lie,
Whence rowling flames and scatter'd cinders flie;
The distant Countrey in the ruine shares,
What falls from Heav'n the burning Mountain spares.
Next that capacious Hall, he sees, the room,   105
Where the whole Nation does for Justice come.
Under whose large roof flourishes the Gown,
And Judges grave on high Tribunals frown.
Here like the peoples Pastor he does go,
His flock subjected to his view below;   110
On which reflecting in his mighty mind,
No private passion does indulgence find;
The pleasures of his youth suspended are,
And made a sacrifice to publique care;
Here free from court-compliances He walks,   115
And with himself, his best adviser, talks;
How peaceful Olive may his Temples shade,
For mending Laws, and for restoring Trade;
Or how his Brows may be with Laurel charg'd,
For nations conquer'd and our bounds inlarg'd: 120
Of ancient Prudence here he ruminates,
Of rising Kingdoms and of falling States:
What ruling Arts gave Great *Augustus* Fame,
And how *Alcides* purchas'd such a name:
His eyes upon his native Palace bent   125
Close by, suggest a greater argument,
His thoughts rise higher when he does reflect
On what the world may from that Star expect
Which at his Birth appear'd to let us see
Day for his sake could with the Night agree;   130
A Prince on whom such different lights did smile,

Born, the divided world to reconcile:
Whatever Heaven or high extracted blood
Could promise or foretell, he will make good;
Reform these Nations, and improve them more,   135
Than this fair Park, from what it was before.

INSTRUCTIONS TO A PAINTER

First draw the Sea, That portion which between
The greater World, and this of ours is seen;
Here place the *Brittish*, there the *Holland* Fleet,
Vast floating armies, both prepared to meet:
    Draw the whole world, expecting who should Reign,   5
After this Combate, o're the conquer'd Main;
Make Heav'n concern'd and an unusual Star
Declare th' Importance of th' approaching War:
Make the Sea shine with Gallantry, and all
The *English* Youth flock to their Admiral,   10
The valiant Duke, whose early Deeds abroad,
Such Rage in Fight, and Art in conduct show'd;
His bright Sword now a dearer Int'rest draws,
His Brothers Glory, and his Countries Cause.
    Let thy bold Pencil, Hope, and Courage spread   15
Through the whole Navy, by that *Heroe* led;
Make all appear, where such a Prince is by
Resolv'd to Conquer, or resolv'd to Die:
    With His Extraction, and his Glorious mind
Make the proud Sails swell, more than with the wind;   20
Preventing Cannon, make His louder Fame
Check the *Batavians*, and their Fury tame:
So hungry Wolves, though greedy of their prey,
Stop when they find a Lion in their way.
Make him bestride the Ocean, and Mankind   25
Ask his consent, to use the Sea and Wind:
While his tall ships in the barr'd Channel stand,
He graspes the *Indies* in his Armed Hand.

. . . .

But who can always on the Billows lie:
The watry Wilderness yields no suplie;

Spreading our Sails, to *Harwich* we resort,
And meet the Beauties of the *Brittish* Court,   80
Th' Illustrious Dutchess, and her Glorious Train,
Like *Thetis* with her Nymphs adorn the Main.
The gazing Sea-gods, since the *Paphian* Queen
Sprung from among them no such sight had seen;
Charm'd with the Graces of a Troop so fair,   85
Those deathless Powers for us themselves declare,
Resolv'd the Aid of Neptunes Court to bring,
And help the Nation where such Beauties spring:
The Souldier here his wasted store supplies,
And takes new valour from the Ladies' eyes.   90

.   .   .   .

Against Him first Opdam his Squadron leads,
Proud of his late success against the Swedes,
Made by that Action, and his high Command,
Worthy to perish by a Princes hand: 140
   The tall Batavian in a vast ship rides,
Bearing an Army in her hollow sides,
Yet, not inclin'd the English ship to board,
More on his Guns relies, then on his Sword,
From whence a fatal Volly we receiv'd,   145
It miss'd the Duke, but His Great Heart it grieved,
Three worthy Persons from his side it tore,
And dy'd his Garment with their scatter'd Gore:
   Happy! to whom this glorious death arrives,
More to be valu'd then a thousand Lives!   150
On such a Theatre, as this, to dye,
For such a Cause, and such a Witness by!
Who would not thus a Sacrifice be made,
To have his Blood on such an Altar laid?

.   .   .   .

XX

JOHN MILTON
(1608-1674)

His couplet practice, like so many things in Milton's life and work, reveals him swimming against the current of his time. In early poems, especially in "Psalm CXIV" and "On the University Carrier," we find predominately closed couplets and a number of closed-couplet practices. The "Psalm" has line (ll. 17–18) and half-line (ll. 13, 16) parallels, line-defined antitheses (ll. 17, 18), and, more striking still, several line-defining inversions (ll. 2, 5, 6, 7, 15, 17, 18),[1] inversions which, like so many of Waller's in his *Summer Islands*, allow for the placing of verbs in rhyming positions. "On the University Carrier" has another aspect of common closed-couplet practice, a conversational tone. One notices, especially, the use of colloquial expressions like "twenty to one" and "if the truth were known" to fill out lines, and the explicit conversational exchange on which the poem closes.

If one turns to "Psalm I," which Milton versified rather late in his career, however, he finds neither the observance of the couplet stop, except at major breaks in thought (ll. 6, 10, 14), nor any hint of conversation. Right at the poem's beginning there are, curiously enough, parallel predicates, a couple of verb inversions, and a major antithesis, but none of these gives or receives couplet strengthening. Throughout this poem Milton has resisted what he called "the troublesome and modern bondage of rhyming," freely drawing his "sense . . . out from one verse into another"[2] and achieving that musical swelling of utterance, no doubt proper to a Psalm, which came naturally to this great verbal musician.

That Milton would pursue this kind of poetic effect, even while the rest of England was tuning its ear to more conversational strains, one

---

[1] My line references correspond to the line notations in "The Shorter English Poems," ed. F. A. Patterson, in *The Works of John Milton*, gen. ed. F. A. Patterson (New York, 1931), I, i.

[2] In the Preface to *Paradise Lost*.

might have predicted from the musical couplets in the early poems, "At a Vacation Exercise" and *Arcades*.

In these poems Milton made no use of the couplet's lines and half-lines to assert antitheses and little use of them to point parallels ("Vacation," l. 7; *Arcades*, ll. 43, 59). He seldom defined a line or couplet with inversion ("Vacation," ll. 7, 30; *Arcades*, ll. 52, 53, 71), and often allowed weak rhymes. There are not only such fuzzy rhymes as 'unto thee / do thee,' 'Pleasure / treasure,' 'Harmonie / captivitie,' 'comply / solemnity,' and 'ly / Necessity,' but one also finds modifiers like "before," "first," "upon," and "about" in rhyming places, and rhyming substantives are often objects of prepositions and, thus, parts of modifying phrases.

Moreover, as this weakening of the formal sinews of the couplet would suggest, the sense of these poems, while receiving incidental couplet punctuation, is largely unconfined. Consider, for instance, lines 32–43 of *Arcades*, a passage which is one segment of a longer sentence. The first couplet makes an address to figures who are worked into the main statement as its third predicate's direct object and as the possessor of its first predicate's direct object. This main statement, which contains a triply compounded predicate, covers six couplets, tapering off in the last of these with a subordinate clause. Although its three parallel predicates receive significant couplet definition and only one couplet is strongly enjambed, none is strongly closed or placed in any sharply defined relationship with any other; so the passage gives a flowing and enjambed effect. In another passage, one from "At a Vacation Exercise" (ll. 29–39), we can follow a process of couplet disintegration: the first couplet is neatly defined by an interruptive clause in its first line and a verb inversion in its second; the second and third couplets are parallel "such" clauses and the second is closed; but the third couplet, at its second line's midpoint, veers from the true topic, the mind's action, through the verbs "look" and "see" to a secondary topic, the mind's perceptions, which is presented without a major pause through the next five lines.

The impression of an unconfined musical flow, which comes primarily from the long drawn-out enjambment of the sense in these poems, is augmented by their pervasive assonantal and alliterative qualities. Take, for instance, the lines, "Not these new fangled toys, and trimming flight / Which takes our late fantastics with delight," with its various echoings of "a" and "i" or a longer passage from *Arcades* (ll. 54–60) which a texture of modulations through "o," "e," "a," and "u" harmonizes into one resounding lyrical wave. This re-echoing assonance not only underscores the impression in these poems of flow and glide, it also removes them from the realm of conversation to that of music — despite the fact that both are explicitly presented to us as spoken addresses.

No doubt the young Milton achieved this enjambed and ringing form of couplet, in part, by drawing on the tradition that gave us *Hero and Leander* and *Cupid and Psyche*, but even in these early couplet poems, we catch the beginnings of the mature Milton's blank-verse music.

XXI

꙳꙳꙳꙳꙳꙳꙳꙳꙳꙳꙳꙳꙳꙳

LUCIUS CARY,
LORD FALKLAND
(1610-1643)

What distinguishes Falkland from his immediate predecessors is his achievement of a pervasive closed-couplet dynamics — of that dynamics between closure and continuity, between poise and thrust, between definition and comprehensiveness which Sandys and Beaumont and Waller were all reaching toward. Our long quotation from Falkland's commendation "To Sandys on his *Psalms*" (ll. 85–148), for instance, suffers only one major break in thought, at line 110, in its whole course. The first thirty lines of the commendation "To Sandys on his *Divine Poems*," moving forward as they do in sets of two and three couplets, may seem a bit stiff to be called dynamic, but these sets are variously related in thought, and, after line 30, the poem sweeps to its close.

Falkland achieved the connections between his sharply individuated couplets in part by weaving them together in patterns of argument. In "*Psalms*," lines 111–48, for instance, he worked out a bipartite defense of Sandys's poetry, first, against the envious and, second, against the ignorant. He put down the envious by saying he merely hated them (ll. 113–14) since they secretly love the excellence they attack (ll. 115–16) and since they condemn their own actions in their hearts (l. 117), and he dismissed them with a rhetorically balanced and intellectually just imprecation (l. 118). The ignorant he treated more fully, first, giving their argument (ll. 119–26) and, then, opposing it with two arguments of his own (ll. 127–44). His first argument, which relates to all people, he based on an analogy (ll. 127–28), on authority (ll. 129–32), and on a logical inference (ll. 133–36); his second argument, which covers people who will be led to righteousness only by beauty, he based on logic (ll. 137–38, 143–44) and strengthened with analogy (ll. 139–42). As this outline may suggest, Falkland kept up the couplet throughout the development of his defense of Sandys and made persistent use of its pauses and segments to define and emphasize the stages of his argument.

On the other hand, he reinforced the impression of movement through his couplets with a number of formal devices, one of them being occasional couplet enjambment. This device augments Falkland's couplet dynamics, rather than merely destroying couplet closure, first, because it is only relative enjambment: every one of Falkland's couplets defines some unit of thought, if not a major unit, and every rhyme emphasizes a word of some importance. It augments couplet dynamics, secondly, because enjambments are rare, thus reminding us of the prevailing order even as they strain it, and because the couplets following enjambments reassert the order strongly. The couplet immediately following one enjambment (*"Poems,"* l. 22), for instance, holds two line-defined parallels, and that following another (*"Psalms,"* l. 90) has its first line integrated by an inversion and its second perfectly filled — with a predicate paralleling that defined in the first line and articulating its own antithesis — and strongly closed. Many couplets which do not seem enjambed share syntactically necessary terms with couplets adjoining and are thus yoked into larger unities. The subject of one couplet (*"Poems,"* ll. 19–20), for instance, resides in the second line of the preceding couplet and is shared by both. The substantive "eloquence" at the beginning of one couplet (*"Psalms,"* l. 95) is modified by the phrase, "Join'd to a Work so choice," at the beginning of the next couplet. Falkland often extended the major elements of a single sentence over several couplets, as in *"Poems,"* lines 31–44; the subject and verb of this passage, "I hope," stand at the beginning of the second couplet; its direct object, "That [etc.]," opens the sixth.

This intercouplet dynamics is also variously maintained within separate couplets. For one thing, Falkland composed many individual oblique couplets, that is, couplets which define rhetorical balances but give them a metrically unbalanced articulation. One of his couplets (*"Poems,"* ll. 35–36), for instance, confines half of the antithesis which fills it to just part of its first line; another (*"Psalms,"* ll. 115–16), contrariwise, extends and enjambs the first half of its antithesis and then compresses the second half. In *"Psalms,"* lines 1–2, again, Falkland gave oblique development to an antithesis, compressing its first half into six syllables and polishing off its second half by defining, in the couplet's second line, a subsidiary antithesis: "Had I no Blushes left, but were of Those, / Who Praise in Verse, what they Despise in Prose." Since, on the one hand, this couplet is syntactically incomplete and since, on the other, its second line stabilizes a complete antithesis, it is dynamically related to the couplet that follows. It thus reveals a texture of verse dynamics, being a dynamic element in a larger system of utterance as well as being dynamic within itself. Poetically it suggests that combination of intellectual responsiveness and intellectual firmness which is the special effect of the dynamically articulated closed couplet.

Another means by which Falkland achieved within his couplets the dynamics on which this effect is based was his combining first-line enjambment and first-line definitive inversion. Sometimes first-line enjambment accompanies a simple Wallerian verb inversion: "Or thinks it fit, we should not leave obtaine, / To learn with Pleasure, what we Act with Paine." But often the arrangement is more energetic, as in this couplet, "How e're I finish heere, my Muse her Daies / Ends in expressing thy deserved Praise," where the direct object is shifted to the end of the first line and the verb suspended until the beginning of the second. This couplet is also oblique, by the way, enduring an antithetical pivot at the midpoint of its first line.

Falkland was able to realize the dynamic stress between poise and thrust within the bounds of one closed line. He has achieved a texture of rhetorical balance and rhetorical climax in such lines as "Be rather to attaine, then to give Fame," in which antithetical infinitives join to govern the same rhyme-emphasized object; and "And Thou fresh Praise, and we fresh Good receive," in which parallel objects are governed by the same verb. Falkland endowed other individual lines with dynamic stress by playing slanted syntax against balanced rhetoric — against either antitheses ("*Poems*," l. 32; "*Psalms*," l. 8) or parallels ("*Poems*," l. 44; "*Psalms*," ll. 134, 148). Take, for instance, "Inspireth Prophecie, expelling Breath," whose complex rhetorical opposition (between breathing in and out and, further, between prophecy and mere breath) is not allowed to retard the syntactic slant from verb to participle — a downward slant with which Falkland tightened the necessary connection with the next couplet. Or take this line, "Would have the Way to that Way be so too," in which the syntax is so slanted, one member of this parallel being the object of a phrase that modifies the other, that verbal repetition was required to assert the parallel. This parallel, by the way, underscores the possibility that one weary way in life can lead to another equally weary; whereas, Falkland's syntactical discrimination underscores the divine willingness that he is arguing for to vary this series of ways and thus make life bearable.

To catch this significance of the poet's formal practice, however, one must follow the line in its context (*"Psalms,"* ll. 127–36). One must, indeed, always read through Falkland's couplets as well as in them to understand his poetic utterance and to realize the nature of his poetic achievement. To appreciate the conclusion to Falkland's commendation of Sandys's choice of a religious subject (*"Psalms,"* ll. 105–10), one must recognize: that the passage is one sentence whose subject, "Those," comes at its very opening, whose verb, "may . . . learne," comes in the first line of its third couplet, and whose object runs over that line and through the next; that the first couplet, although its first line emphasizes parallel suspensive clauses, is strikingly enjambed; that the second line of its second couplet defines two antithetical and further suspensive clauses; that the first line of its third couplet suspends the sentence's verb, although not to the line's end; and that this couplet's second line, the last of the passage, gives syntactically slanted utterance to a 'blest–blessed' parallel. One must also recognize, of course, that this passage concludes a much larger discursive segment that began, indeed, at line 85 of the poem. Then one will be able to get in touch, for instance, with the interlocking formal and verbal insistence, enunciated in the last line, of the propriety and the strain involved in a man's turning his blessed gifts to blessed account.

This passage is spectacularly dynamic, but even the first three quite steady couplets of *"Poems,"* whose second couplet both balances and slants away from its first, whose second couplet, again, is both closed and syntactically cemented to the third, require a breadth and refinement of poetic sensitivity new to the history of the heroic couplet.

TO MR. GEORGE SANDYS, ON HIS PARAPHRASE UPON THE PSALMS

Had I no Blushes left, but were of Those,
Who Praise in Verse, what they Despise in Prose:
Had I this Vice from Vanity or Youth;
Yet such a Subject would have taught me Truth:
Hence it were Banisht, where of Flattery 5
There is not Use, nor Possibility.
Else thou hadst cause to feare, lest some might Raise
An Argument against thee from my Praise.
I therefore know, Thou canst expect from me
But what I give, Historicke Poetry. 10

Friendship for more could not a Pardon win;
Nor thinke I Numbers make a Lie no Sinne.
And need I say more then my Thoughts indite,
Nothing were easier, then not to write.
Which now were hard; for wheresoere I Raise   15
My thoughts, thy severall Paines extort my Praise.

.   .   .   .

Yet, though we wonder at thy Charming Voice;   85
Perfection still was wanting in thy Choice;
And of a Soule, which so much Power Possest,
That Choice is hardly Good, which is not Best.
But though Thy Muse were Ethnically Chast,
When most Fault could be found; yet now Thou hast   90
Diverted to a Purer Path thy Quill;
And chang'd Parnassus Mount to Sions Hill:
So that blest David might almost Desire
To heare his Harp thus Echo'd by thy Lyre.
Such Eloquence, that though it were abus'd,   95
Could not but be (though not Allow'd) excus'd.
Join'd to a Work so choice, that though Ill-done,
So Pious an Attempt Praise could not shun.
How strangely doth it darkest Texts disclose,
In Verses of such sweetnesse; that even Those,   100
From whom the unknown Tongue conceales the Sense,
Even in the Sound, must finde an Eloquence.
For though the most bewitching Music could
Move men, no more than Rocks; thy Language would.
Those who make wit their Curse, who spend their Brain,   105
Their Time, and Art, in looser Verse, to gain
Damnation, and a Mistres; till they see
How Constant that is, how Inconstant she;
May from this great Example learne, to sway
The Parts th' are Blest-with, some more Blessed way.   110
Fate can against thee but two Foes advance;
Sharpe-sighted Envy, and Blind Ignorance:
The first (by Nature like a shadow, neare
To all great Acts) I rather Hate than feare:
For them, (since whatsoever most they Raise   115
In Private, That they most in Throngs Dispraise;
And know the Ill they Act Condemn'd within)

Who envies Thee, may no man envy Him.
The last I Feare not much, but Pity more:
For though they cannot the least Fault explore;   120
Yet, if they might the high Tribunall Clime,
To Them thy Excellence would be thy Crime:
For Eloquence with things Prophane they joine;
Nor count it fit to Mixe with what's Divine;
Like Art and Paintings laid upon a Face,   125
Of it self sweet; which more Deforme then Grace.
Yet, as the Church with Ornaments is Fraught,
Why may not That be too, which There is Taught?
And sure that Vessell of election, Paul,
Who Judais'd with Jewes, was All to All;   130
So, to Gaine some, would be (at least) Content,
Some for the Curious should be Eloquent:
For since the Way to Heaven is Rugged, who
Would have the Way to that Way be so too?
Or thinks it fit, we should not leave obtaine,   135
To learne with Pleasure, what we Act with Paine?
Since then Some stop, unlesse their Path be Even,
Nor will be led by Soloecismes to Heaven;
And (through a Habit scarce to be control'd)
Refuse a Cordial, when not brought in Gold;   140
Much like to them to that Disease Inur'd,
Which can be no way, but by Musick cur'd:
I Joy in Hope, that no small Piety
Will in their Colder Hearts be Warm'd by Thee.
For as none could more Harmony dispense;   145
So neither could thy flowing Eloquence
So well in any Task be us'd, as this:
To Sound His Praises forth, whose Gift it is.

TO MR. GEORGE SANDYS, ON HIS
PARAPHRASE UPON THE DIVINE POEMS

Such is the Verse thou Writ'st, that who reads Thine
Can never be content to suffer Mine:
Such is the Verse I Write, that reading Mine,
I hardly can beleeve I have read Thine:

And wonder, that their Excellence once knowne,   5
I nor correct, nor yet conceale mine owne.
Yet though I Danger feare then Censure lesse;
Nor apprehend a Breach, like to a Presse;
Thy Merits, now the second time, inflame
To sacrifice the Remnant of my Shame.   10
Nor yet (as first) Alone, but joyn'd with Those
Who make the loftiest Verse, seeme humblest Prose.
Thus did our Master, to His Praise, desire
That Babes should with Philosophers conspire:
And Infants their Hosanna's should unite   15
With the so Famous Areopagite.
Perhaps my stile too, is for Praise most fit;
Those shew their Judgment least, who shew their wit:
And are suspected, least their subtiller Aime
Be rather to attaine, then to give Fame.   20
Perhaps whil'st I my Earth doe interpose
Betwixt thy Sunne and Them, I may aid those
Who have but feebler Eyes and weaker Sight,
To beare thy Beames, and to support thy Light.
So thy Eclipse, by neighbouring Darkenesse made,   25
Were no injurious but a usefull Shade:
How e're I finish heere, my Muse her Daies
Ends in expressing thy deserved Praise:
Whose fate in this seemes fortunately cast,
To have so just an Action for her Last.   30
And since there are, who have been taught, that Death
Inspireth Prophecie, expelling Breath.
I hope, when these foretell, what happie Gaines
Posteritie shall reape from these thy Paines:
Nor yet from these alone, but how thy Pen,   35
Earth-like, shall yearely give new Gifts to Men;
And Thou fresh Praise, and we fresh Good receive
(For he who Thus can write can never Leave)
How Time in them shall never force a Breach;
But they shall alwayes Live and alwaies Teach: 40
That the sole likelihood which these present,
Will from the more rais'd Soules command Assent;
And the so taught, will not Beliefe refuse,
To the last Accents of a Dying Muse.

XXII

𝄢𝄢𝄢𝄢𝄢𝄢𝄢𝄢𝄢𝄢𝄢𝄢𝄢𝄢

JOHN CLEVELAND[1]
(1613-1658)

THE REBEL SCOT

How, Providence? and yet a Scottish crew?
Then Madame Nature wears black patches too!
What shall our nation be in bondage thus
Unto a land that truckles under us?
Ring the bells backward! I am all on fire.   5
Not all the buckets in a country quire
Shall quench my rage. A poet should be feared,
When angry, like a comet's flaming beard.
And where's the stoic can his wrath appease,
To see his country sick of *Pym*'s disease?   10
By Scotch invasion to be made a prey
To such pigwidgeon *Myrmidons* as they?
But that there's charm in verse, I would not quote
The name of *Scot* without an antidote;
Unless my head were red, that I might brew   15
Invention there that might be poison too.
Were I a drowsy judge whose dismal note
Disgorgeth halters as a juggler's throat
Doth ribbons; could I in Sir Empiric's tone
Speak pills in phrase and quack destruction;   20
Or roar like *Marshall*, that *Geneva* bull,
Hell and damnation a pulpit full;
Yet to express a *Scot*, to play that prize,
Not all those mouth-grenadoes can suffice.

---

[1] See pp. 92–96 on Cleveland's style and his historical importance.

Before a *Scot* can properly be curst,   25
I must like *Hocus* swallow daggers first.
   Come, keen *Iambics*, with your badger's feet
And badger-like bite until your teeth do meet.
Help, ye tart satirists, to imp my rage
With all the scorpions that should whip this age.   30
Scots are like witches; do but whet your pen,
Scratch till the blood comes, they'll not hurt you then.
Now, as the martyrs were enforced to take
The shape of beasts, like hypocrites at stake
I'll bait my *Scot* so, yet not cheat your eyes;   35
A *Scot* within a beast is no disguise.
   No more let *Ireland* brag; her harmless nation
Fosters no venom since the Scot's plantation:
Nor can our feigned antiquity obtain;
Since they came in, *England* hath wolves again.   40
The Scot that kept the Tower might have shown,
Within the grate of his own breast alone,
The leopard and the panther, and engrossed
What all those wild collegiates had cost
The honest high-shoes in their termly fees: 45
First to the savage lawyer, next to these.
Nature herself doth Scotchmen beasts confess,
Making their country such a wilderness:
A land that brings in question and suspense
God's omnipresence, but that CHARLES came thence,   50
But that *Montrose* and *Crawford*'s loyal band
Atoned their sin and christened half the land.
Nor is it all the nation hath these spots;
There is a Church as well as *Kirk* of Scots.
As in a picture where the squinting paint   55
Shows fiend on this side, and on that side saint.
He, that saw Hell in his melancholy dream
And in the twilight of his fancy's theme,
Scared from his sins, repented in a fright,
Had he viewed Scotland, had turned proselyte.   60
A land where one may pray with cursed intent,
O, may they never suffer banishment!
Had *Cain* been *Scot*, God would have changed his doom;
Not forced him wander but confined him home!

Like Jews they spread and as infection fly,   65
As if the Devil had ubiquity.
Hence 'tis they live at rovers and defy
This or that place, rags of geography.
They're citizens of the world; they're all in all;
Scotland's a nation epidemical.   70
And yet they ramble not to learn the mode,
How to be dressed, or how to lisp abroad;
To return knowing in the Spanish shrug,
Or which of the Dutch states a double jug
Resembles most in belly or in beard,   75
(The card by which the marineers are steered.)
No, the *Scots-errant* fight and fight to eat,
Their ostrich stomachs make their swords their meat.
Nature with Scots as tooth-drawers hath dealt
Who use to string their teeth upon their belt.   80
Yet wonder not at this their happy choice,
The serpent's fatal still to *Paradise*.
Sure, *England* hath the hemorrhoids, and these
On the north postern of the patient seize
Like leeches; thus they physically thirst   85
After our blood, but in the cure shall burst!
Let them not think to make us run of the score
To purchase villanage, as once before
When an act passed to stroke them on the head,
Call them good subjects, buy them gingerbread.   90
Not gold, nor acts of grace, 'tis steel must tame
The stubborn *Scot*; a Prince that would reclaim
Rebels by yielding, doth like him, or worse,
Who saddled his own back to shame his horse.
Was it for this you left your leaner soil,   95
Thus to lard Israel with Egypt's spoil?
They are the Gospel's life-guard; but for them,
The garrison of New Jerusalem,
What would the brethren do? The Cause! The Cause!
Sack-possets and the fundamental laws!   100
Lord! What a godly thing is want of shirts!
How a Scotch stomach and no meat converts!
They wanted food and raiment, so they took
Religion for their seamstress and their cook.

Unmask them well; their honours and estate,   105
As well as conscience, are sophisticate.
Shrive but their titles and their moneys poize,
A laird and twenty pence pronounced with noise,
When construed, but for a plain yeoman go,
And a good sober two-pence and well so.   110
Hence then, you proud impostors; get you gone,
You Picts in gentry and devotion;
You scandal to the stock of verse, a race
Able to bring the gibbet in disgrace.
Hyperbolus by suffering did traduce   115
The ostracism and shamed it out of use.
The Indian, that Heaven did forswear
Because he heard some Spaniards were there,
Had he but known what Scots in Hell had been,
He would *Erasmus*-like have hung between.   120
My Muse hath done. A voider for the nonce.
I wrong the Devil should I pick their bones;
That dish is his; for, when the Scots decease,
Hell, like their nation, feeds on barnacles.
    A Scot, when from the gallow-tree got loose,   125
    Drops into *Styx* and turns a Soland goose.

XXIII

✦✦✦✦✦✦✦✦✦✦✦✦✦✦✦

SIR JOHN DENHAM
(1615-1669)

In *Cooper's Hill*, Denham defined not only the couplet but, to their proper degrees, the couplet's elements as well, that is, each of the couplet's two lines and each line's two halves. Line and couplet patterns based on these definitions, especially balances and periods, are Denham's stock in trade. In single lines, for instance, one finds many parallel pairs (ll. 80, 178, 185) and many antitheses (ll. 76, 134, 168).[1] Denham has balanced nouns (ll. 76, 212), adjectives (ll. 140, 154), verbs (ll. 178, 185), phrases (l. 80), and complete predicates (ll. 134, 196) with remarkable variety. Many of his balances, such as the famous "Strong without rage, without oreflowing full," he has heightened, moreover, with inversion. Besides many single-line periods (ll. 26, 112, 134), there are many that cover, each of them, one whole couplet (ll. 39–40, 125–26, 161–62, 173–74). Consider, for example, this one, "*Thames, the most lov'd of all the Oceans sons, / By his old Sire, to his embraces runs,*" in which the subject and verb, which are set at the couplet's opposite extremes, are separated by a line and one-half of adjectival material and by a half-line adverbial phrase.

Periodic inversion, especially when, as in this couplet on the Thames, it spans a whole couplet, is obviously a means of both definition and thrust: it dramatizes the couplet's integrity while putting a tremendous strain on that of the couplet's individual lines. Periodic inversion within a line can have corresponding effects — on the line and on the caesurally defined half-lines. Take, for instance, "Betwixt their Frigid, and our Torrid Zone," where the suspension of the substantive strains the caesural break and thus tightens the 'Frigid–Torrid' antithesis. Denham's almost habitual practice of inversion thus allowed him to achieve an ex-

---

[1] My line references correspond to the line notations in *The Poetical Works of Sir John Denham*, ed. T. H. Banks (New Haven, 1928).

tensive couplet dynamics. He also employed, in this cause, a relative grammatical enjambment within many couplets, especially the line-end separation of a verb from the rest of its predicate, as in: "But such a Rise, as doth at once invite / A pleasure, and a reverence from the sight," or, better still, "No unexpected inundations spoyl / The mowers hopes, nor mock the plowmans toyl." In this couplet, Denham has given generalized material a poetic luster by playing the extensively balanced compound predicate against line and rhyme and meter, making the verb of the first member rhyme with the direct object of the second and alliterating the possessive noun of the first with the verb of the second. We discovered practices and effects like these, more functionally and less grandly employed, in the poetry of Lord Falkland.

Denham also shares with Falkland a verse dynamics that extends beyond the couplet to larger movements of verse. Some of his larger systems are imperfectly achieved, admittedly: among these are the introduction of the ruined abbey (ll. 111–20), a passage whose sense and movement are disturbed by a digressive line and one-half of general reflection, and the worse flawed passage on nature's variety (ll. 197–205), whose syntax is ruined and whose flow is quite blocked by two parenthetical couplets. But Denham's verse, by variously employing balances, inversions, and relative enjambment, often moves with the fullness and the strength he desired. We may notice, especially, the introduction of the Thames (ll. 159–65) with its line and couplet periods (ll. 159–60, 161–62) and its degrees of line and couplet enjambment; or the continuation of this passage (ll. 166–70) with its line balances and its syntactical flow; or the further continuation (ll. 169–74), which is one clause stretching over three couplets that unfolds as a system of actions (ll. 169–70) and nonactions (ll. 171–74); or the two couplets, immediately following this (ll. 175–78), which summarize the bounty of the river which the whole passage has been developing; or, finally, the measured and yet flowing movement of the whole description of the Thames (ll. 159–228).

Denham tried several common types of couplet poetry, such as the love elegy and the dramatic prologue, but *Cooper's Hill* is his one significant achievement. All the elements of the subject, scenic, historical, and philosophical, were so generalized, so lacking in inner necessity, that they left him free to realize his major poetic drive, which was to dramatize the couplet itself. He was able to select and manipulate his material arbitrarily and thus to work out as wide a variety of couplets and as strong a fabric of couplet dynamics as his metrical and rhetorical skills allowed. The result is an essentially abstract poem of fine patterns and excellently articulated verse movement whose best passages present nothing more pressing than a patriotic flourish about the Thames being the ocean's favorite river or a generalized observation of the seasonal extremes in farming, and one of whose most completely achieved lines is, "Wonder from thence results, from thence delight." It is easy to see why Denham's "strength" was so much more impressive to a time that was discovering the closed couplet and expanding its expressive powers than it is to ours.

XXIV

🕱🕱🕱🕱🕱🕱🕱🕱🕱🕱🕱🕱🕱🕱

ABRAHAM COWLEY
(1618-1667)

Although Cowley's complimentary address "To Lord Falkland" — which is not actually addressed to Falkland — lacks the persistent and flexible dynamics of Falkland's own poetry, it is a unified and, indeed, polished performance. Despite its several heavy pauses (ll. 4, 6, 10, 28, 32, 38), each of which retards the thought more than defining it, this poem makes a clear two-part argument of Falkland's intellectual power and his great value to his country. The first part proceeds chiefly by similes: likening, first, the harmonious variety in an army and, second, that among the species of things to the harmonious variety of Falkland's intelligence — each of these similes defined in well-controlled double couplets. The second part is developed in terms of a personal comparison, variously defined by formal couplet pauses, which spans sixteen lines (ll. 19–34). The eight-line conclusion, although neatly cast, might have been cut in half; lines 35–38 add little substance to Cowley's argument. But the last four lines of the poem, which describe the difference between mere soldiers and Lord Falkland, make a terse and proper climax.

Cowley's "Prologue to *The Adventures of Five Hours*" is also well composed. It develops one elaborate simile throughout its course, likening plagiarism to piracy. In the first half Cowley praises the author of the play for his piracy (and his new minting of the stolen treasure); in the second half he exhorts him to produce the treasure from his own mine which will assure his suffering the piracy of others. Cowley's use of the couplet allows him to assert the antithesis between these two parts of his address and to keep all its stages spruce and clear.

Neither these nor any of Cowley's couplet poems is either great or perfectly unique. The strains of Donne, Jonson, and Waller — among others — mingle in his usually competent but seldom distinguished couplet output. Cowley is more important for his contributions to the form, contributions which great poets, chiefly Dryden, would turn to wonderful and lasting effects.

The most striking of these contributions is Cowley's achievement, in well-defined couplets, of a heroic sweep. One thing Cowley did, especially in *Davideis*, was to work out series of major grammatical units. Take, for instance, the "Those" and "who" clauses in *Davideis*, I, 14–32; the "Beneath" phrases and the "where" clauses in *Davideis*, I, 71–81; the "He saw" and "He knew" clauses in *Davideis*, I, 110–25. Cowley also achieved the impression of sweep by the use of metrical imbalance: not only the oblique couplet ("Falkland," ll. 9–10, 35–36; *Davideis*, I, 84–85), which one finds more brilliantly produced in the poems of Falkland and Denham, but larger forms of obliqueness too, playing three lines against a fourth (*Davideis*, I, 9–12; "Falkland," ll. 38–42) and even a long set of lines against one balancing line ("Falkland, ll. 19–28). These heroic sweeps in Cowley commonly end in climactic utterance. In our brief passage from *Davideis*, for instance, such lines as "Their strength was *Armies*, his the *Lord of Hosts*" (l. 12), "I consecrate my *Magdalene* to Thee" (l. 32), and "There is a place deep, wondrous deep below" (l. 82) receive the emphases of great sweeps of verse. The heroic tone of *Davideis*, which depends on several things — among them the great events, the heroic language and references — is crucially augmented by this heroic metrical sweep. By thus transforming the closed couplet, Cowley opened the way to *MacFlecknoe* and, indeed, to the use of the couplet for all kinds of major poetic utterances.

Cowley's poem *On the Late Civil War* makes a more refined use of this grander employment of the couplet and applies it to a topic much closer to home. We might notice Cowley's use of the echoing "It was not so" (ll. 13, 21, 37) to define the great sweep of his heroic allusions and, on the other hand, his modulation to the quite sharp satiric formulation, "One makes false Devils, t'other makes false Gods" (l. 36). Such a range of couplet practices and effects puts us within reach of *Absalom and Achitophel*.

In another poem, *The Puritan and the Papist*, Cowley tried out the couplet much more extensively as a vehicle for political satire. His varied enunciation of Puritan "reservations," by which he undercuts their claims and pretensions, rings with the excess of discovery. By playing on this word in couplet after couplet (ll. 36, 38, 40, 42, 46), Cowley was able to articulate a series of pointedly refined satiric thrusts against the Puritans, opening one couplet after the other with an apparently sympathetic admission of Puritan views or conduct and then closing it with a ruinous "reservation." The stiffness and repetitiveness of Cowley's style reduced the force of this practice of satiric refinement, but in the varied and flexible style of Dryden, it would prove tremendously powerful. We can find a few examples of this use of the couplet to punctuate discursive refinements in Cowley's nonsatiric poetry: in this couplet from "Falkland," for instance, "Those *Men* alone (and those are useful too) / Whose *Valour* is the onely *Art* they know," where Cowley strengthens his assertion of the mere soldier's inferiority to Falkland by recognizing, in the first line's second half, that the soldier has, nevertheless, his own worth. But it is the satiric use of this device, as Cowley articulated it, extensively if imperfectly, in *The Puritan and the Papist*, that looks ahead to Dryden.

Cowley further augmented the closed couplet as a satiric instrument by using it in this poem to convey the impression of comprehensiveness. The balancing of religious extremes in half-lines (l. 62), lines (ll. 49–50, 59–60), and couplets (ll. 8–12) has this effect, thus giving to what is actually a satiric attack the rhetorical quality of detached judgment. Such a line as this — "Fooles understand not *them*, nor *Wise men you*" — and such a couplet as this — "They in a forraigne, and unknowne *tongue* pray, / You in an unknowne sence your prayers say" — for example, convey the impression of a fairly comprehended statement of extreme points of disagreement between Puritans and Papists while actually slamming the Puritans, that faction, significantly, at which the poet aims his address. Cowley also struck something like this note in other poems — in balancing Falkland and all other scholars, Falkland and all other soldiers, plagiarizing and creating, David and fate. Such efforts as these to achieve the impression of absolute intellectual command required large tracts of verse, but Cowley sometimes gives a taste of it in single lines like "All homebred Malice, and all forreign boasts." Such a line as this one, in which the poet suggests that he has exhausted international politics, brings us close to Dryden's "Without unspotted, innocent within," to his "In Friendship False, Implacable in Hate," and, indeed, to all his satirically comprehensive formulations.

The translations of Martial's epigrams here printed, which exemplify a favorite theme of Cowley's, look beyond the age of politics to the polite retirement of Pope and his age. They are, moreover, like Pope's essays and epistles, pointed and intimate in their address. And if they are not perfectly polite, as Walsh and Addison and Pope would always attempt to be, Cowley's poems of explicitly directed personal address, like that "To Lord Falkland," usually are. It is no wonder, then, that Cowley's reputation stood high well into the eighteenth century.

TO LORD FALKLAND, FOR HIS SAFE RETURN FROM THE NORTHERN EXPEDITION AGAINST THE SCOTS

Great is thy *Charge*, O *North*; be wise and just,
England commits her *Falkland* to thy trust;
Return him safe: *Learning* would rather choose
Her *Bodley*, or her *Vatican* to loose.
All things that are but *writ* or *printed* there,   5
In his unbounded Breast *engraven* are.
There all the *Sciences* together meet,
And every *Art* does all her *Kindred* greet,
Yet justle not, nor quarrel; but as well
Agree as in some *Common Principle*.   10
So in an *Army* govern'd right we see
(Though out of several Countrys rais'd it be)
That all their Order and their Place maintain,
The *English*, *Dutch*, the *Frenchmen* and the *Dane*.
So thousand diverse *Species* fill the aire,   15
Yet neither crowd nor mix confus'dly there,
Beasts, Houses, Trees, and Men together lye,
Yet enter *undisturb'd* into the Eye.
   And this great *Prince* of *Knowledge* is by Fate
Thrust into th' noise and business of a State,   20
All *Virtues*, and some *Customs* of the *Court*,
Other mens *Labour*, are at least his *Sport*.
Whilst we who can no action undertake,
Whom *Idleness* it self might *Learned* make,
Who hear of nothing, and as yet scarce know,   25
Whether the *Scots* in *England* be or no,
Pace dully on, oft tire, and often stay,
Yet see his nimble *Pegasus* fly away.
'Tis *Natures* fault who did thus partial grow,
And her *Estate* of *Wit* on *One* bestow.   30
Whilst we like *younger Brothers*, get at best
But a *small stock*, and must *work* out the rest.
How could he answer't, should the State think fit
To question a *Monopoly* of *Wit*?
   Such is the *Man* whom we require the same   35
We lent the *North*; untoucht as is his *Fame*.

He is too good for *War*, and ought to be
As far from *Danger*, as from *Fear* he's free.
Those *Men* alone (and those are useful too)
Whose *Valour* is the onely *Art* they know,   40
Were for sad *War* and Bloody *Battels* born;
Let *Them* the *State Defend*, and *He Adorn*.

THE PURITAN AND THE PAPIST

So two rude *waves*, by stormes together throwne,
Roare at each other, fight, and then grow *one*.
Religion is a *Circle*; men contend,
And runne the round in dispute without end.
Now in a *Circle* who goe contrary,   5
Must at the last *meet* of necessity.
The *Roman* to advance the *Catholicke cause*
Allows a *Lie*, and calls it *Pia Fraus*.
The *Puritan* approves and does the same,
Dislikes nought in it but the *Latin name*.   10
He flowes with these devises, and dares *ly*
In very *deed*, in *truth*, and *verity*.
He whines, and sighes out *Lies*, with so much ruth,
As if he griev'd, 'cause he could ne're speake truth.
Lies have possest the *Presse* so, as their due,   15
'Twill scarcely, 'I feare, henceforth print *Bibles* true.
Lies for their next strong Fort ha'th' *Pulpit* chose,
There throng out at the *Preachers mouth*, and *nose*.
And how e're grosse, are certaine to beguile
The poore *Booke-turners* of the *middle Isle*.   20
Nay to th' Almighty's selfe they have beene bold
To *ly*, and their blasphemous *Minister* told
They might say false to *God*, for if they were
Beaten, he knew't not, for he was not there.
But *God*, who their great *thankefulnesse* did see,   25
Rewards them straight with another *Victorie*,
Just such another at *Brainceford*; and san's doubt
Will *weary* er't be long their *gratitude* out.
Not all the *Legends* of the *Saints* of old,
Not vast *Baronius*, nor sly *Surius* hold   30
Such plenty of apparent *Lies*, as are

In your one *Author, Jo. Browne Cleric. Par.*
Besides what your small *Poets* have said, or writ,
Brookes, Strode, and the *Baron* of the *Saw-pit:*
With many a *Mentall Reservation,*   35
You'le maintaine *Liberty,* Reserv'd (your owne.)
For th' publique good the summes rais'd you'le disburse;
Reserv'd, (The greater part for your owne purse.)
You'le root the *Cavaliers* out, every man;
Faith, let it be *reserv'd* here; (*If yee can.*)   40
You'le make our gracious CHARLES, a *glorious King;*
Reserv'd (in *Heaven,*) for thither ye would bring
His Royall Head, the onely secure roome
For *glorious Kings,* whither you'le never come.
To keepe the estates o'th' Subjects you pretend;   45
Reserv'd (in your owne *Trunkes;*) you will defend
The *Church* of *England,* 'tis your *Protestation;*
But that's *New-England,* by'a small *Reservation.*
   Power of dispensing *Oaths* the *Papists* claime;
Case hath got leave *o' God,* to doe the same.   50
For you doe hate all *swearing* so, that when
You have sworne an *Oath,* ye *breake* it streight agen.
A Curse upon you! which hurts most these Nations,
Cavaliers swearing, or your *Protestations?*
Nay, though Oaths by you be so much abhorr'd,   55
Ye allow *God damne me* in the *Puritan Lord.*
   They keepe the *Bible* from *Lay-men,* but ye
Avoid this, for ye have no *Laytie.*
They in a forraigne, and unknowne *tongue* pray,
You in an unknowne *sence* your prayers say: 60
So that this difference 'twixt ye does ensue,
Fooles understand not *them,* nor *Wise men you.*

.   .   .   .

DAVIDEIS, I

I Sing the *Man* who *Judahs Scepter* bore
In that right hand which held the *Crook* before;
Who from best *Poet,* best of *Kings* did grow;
The two chief *gifts Heav'n* could on *Man* bestow.
Much danger first, much toil did he sustain,   5

Whilst *Saul* and *Hell* crost his strong fate in vain.
Nor did his *Crown* less painful work afford;
Less exercise his *Patience*, or his *Sword*;
So long her *Conque'ror Fortunes* spight pursu'd;
Till with unwearied *Virtue* he subdu'd   10
All homebred Malice, and all forreign boasts;
Their strength was *Armies*, his the *Lord of Hosts*.
     Thou, who didst *Davids* royal stem adorn,
And gav'st him *birth* from whom thy self was't *born*.
Who didst in *Triumph* at *Deaths Court* appear,   15
And slew'st him with thy *Nails*, thy *Cross* and *Spear*,
Whilst *Hells* black *Tyrant* trembled to behold,
The glorious light he forfeited of old,
Who Heav'ns *glad burden* now, and justest pride,
Sit'st high enthron'd next thy great *Fathers* side,   20
(Where hallowed Flames help to adorn that Head
Which once the *blushing Thorns* environed,
Till crimson drops of precious *blood* hung down
Like *Rubies* to enrich thine *humble Crown*.)
Ev'en *Thou* my breast with such blest rage inspire,   25
As mov'd the tuneful strings of *Davids Lyre*,
Guid my bold steps with thine old *trav'elling Flame*,
In these untrodden paths to *Sacred Fame*;
Lo, with *pure hands* thy heav'enly *Fires* to take,
My well-chang'd *Muse* I a chast *Vestal* make!   30
From earths vain joys, and loves soft witchcraft free,
I consecrate my *Magdalene* to Thee!
Lo, this great work, a *Temple* to thy praise,
On polisht *Pillars* of strong *Verse* I raise!
A *Temple*, where if *Thou* vouchsafe to dwell,   35
It *Solomons*, and *Herods* shall excel.
Too long the *Muses-Land* have *Heathen* bin;
Their *Gods* too long were *Dev'ils*, and *Vertues Sin*;
But *Thou, Eternal Word*, hast call'd forth *Me*
Th' *Apostle*, to convert that *World* to *Thee*;   40
T' unbind the charms that in slight *Fables* lie,
And teach that *Truth* is *truest Poesie*.

.   .   .   .

Beneath the silent chambers of the earth,
Where the *Suns* fruitful beams give *metals* birth,
Where he the growth of *fatal Gold* does see,

Gold which above more *Influence* has than *He*.
Beneath the dens where *unfletcht Tempests* lye,   75
And infant *Winds* their tender *Voyces* try,
Beneath the mighty *Oceans* wealthy Caves,
Beneath th' eternal *Fountain* of all Waves,
Where their vast *Court* the *Mother-waters* keep,
And undisturb'd by *Moons* in silence sleep,   80
There is a place deep, wondrous deep below,
Which genuine *Night* and *Horrour* does o'reflow;
No bound controls th' unwearied space, but *Hell*
Endless as those dire *pains* that in it dwell.
Here no dear glimpse of the *Suns* lovely face,   85
Strikes through the *Solid* darkness of the place;
No dawning *Morn* does her kind reds display;
One slight weak beam would here be thought the *Day*.
No gentle *stars* with their fair *Gems* of *Light*
Offend the tyr'anous and unquestion'd *Night*.   90
Here *Lucifer* the mighty *Captive* reigns;
Proud, 'midst his *Woes*, and *Tyrant* in his *Chains*.
Once *General* of a guilded *Host* of *Sprights*,
Like *Hesper*, leading forth the spangled *Nights*.
But down like *Lightning*, which him struck, he came;   95
And roar'd at his first plunge into the *Flame*.
Myriads of *Spirits* fell wounded round him there;
With dropping *Lights* thick shone the singed *Air*.
Since when the dismal *Solace* of their wo,
Has only been weak *Mankind* to undo;   100
Themselves at first against *themselves* they 'excite,
(Their dearest *Conquest*, and most proud delight)
And if those *Mines* of Secret *Treason* fail,
With open force mans *Vertue* they assail;
Unable to *corrupt*, seek to *destroy*;   105
And where their *Poysons* miss, the *Sword* employ.
Thus sought the *Tyrant Fiend* young *Davids* fall;
And 'gainst him arm'd the pow'erful rage of *Saul*.
He saw the beauties of his shape and face,
His female sweetness, and his manly grace,   110
He saw the nobler wonders of his *Mind*,
Great *Gifts*, which for Great *Works* he knew design'd.
He saw (t' ashame the strength of *Man* and *Hell*)
How by's young hands their *Gathite Champion* fell.

He saw the reverend *Prophet* boldly shed   115
The *Royal Drops* round his *Enlarged Head*.
And well he knew what *Legacy* did place,
The sacred *Scepter* in blest *Judahs* race,
From which th' *Eternal Shilo* was to spring;
A *Knowledge* which new *Hells* to *Hell* did bring!   120
And though no less he knew himself too weak
The smallest Link of strong-wrought *Fate* to break;
Yet would he rage, and struggle with the *Chain*;
Lov'd to *Rebel* though sure that 'twas in *vain*.
And now it broke his form'd design, to find   125
The gentle change of *Sauls* recov'ering *Mind*.
He trusted much in *Saul*, and rag'ed, and griev'd
(The great *Deceiver*) to be Himself *Deceiv'd*.

.   .   .   .

PROLOGUE TO
THE ADVENTURES OF FIVE HOURS

As when our Kings (Lords of the spacious Main)
Take in just wars a rich Plate Fleet of *Spain*;
The rude unshapen Ingots they reduce
Into a form of Beauty and of use;
On which the Conquerors Image now does shine,   5
Not His whom it belong'd to in the Mine;
So in the mild Contentions of the Muse
(The War which Peace it self loves and persues)
So have you home to us in triumph brought,
This Cargazon of *Spain* with Treasures fraught,   10
You have not basely gotten it by stealth,
Nor by Translation borrow'd all its wealth,
But by a pow'rful Spirit made it your own
Metal before, Money by you 'tis grown.
'Tis currant now, by your adorning it   15
With the fair stamp of your victorious wit:
   But though we praise this voyage of your Mind,
And though our selves enricht by it we find,
We're not contented yet, because we know
What greater stores at home within it grow;   20
We've seen how well you forrain Oars refine,

Produce the Gold of your own Nobler Mine.
The world shall then our Native plenty view,
And fetch materials for their wit from you,
They all shall watch the travails of your Pen,   25
And *Spain* on you shall make Reprisals then.

WOULD YOU BE FREE?

Would you be Free? 'Tis your chief wish, you say,
Come on; I'le shew thee, Friend, the certain way,
If to no Feasts abroad thou lov'st to go,
Whilst bounteous God does Bread at home bestow,
If thou the goodness of thy Cloaths dost prize   5
By thine own Use, and not by others Eyes.
(If onely safe from Weathers) thou can'st dwell,
In a small House, but a convenient Shell,
If thou without a Sigh, or Golden wish,
Canst look upon thy Beechen Bowl, and Dish;   10
If in thy Mind such power and greatness be,
The *Persian* King's a Slave compar'd with Thee.

MARTIAL, EPIGRAMMATON, II, liii

Vis liber fieri? mentiris, Maxime, non vis:
  sed fieri si vis, hac ratione potes.
liber eris, cenare foris si, Maxime, nolis,
  Veientana tuam si domat uva sitim,
si ridere potes miseri chrysendeta Cinnae,   5
  contentus nostra si potes esse toga,
si plebeia Venus gemino tibi iungitur asse,
  si tua non rectus tecta subire potes.
haec tibi si vis est, si mentis tanta potestas,
  liberior Partho vivere rege potes.   10

GIVE ME A COUNTRY

Me who have liv'd so long among the great,
You wonder to hear talk of a Retreat:
And a retreat so distant, as may show

No thoughts of a return when once I go.
Give me a Country, how remote so e're,   5
Where happiness a mod'rate rate does bear,
Where poverty it self in plenty flowes,
And all the solid use of Riches knowes.
The ground about the house maintains it there,
The House maintains the ground about it here.   10
Here even Hunger's dear, and a full board,
Devours the vital substance of the Lord.
The Land it self does there the feast bestow,
The Land it self must here to Market go.
Three or four suits one Winter here does wast,   15
One suit does there three or four winters last.
Here every frugal Man must oft be cold,
And little Luke-warm-fires are to you sold,
There Fire's an Element as cheap and free,
Almost as any of the other Three.   20
Stay you then here, and live among the Great,
Attend their sports, and at their tables eat.
When all the bounties here of Men you score:
The Places bounty there, shall give me more.

MARTIAL, EPIGRAMMATON, X, xcvi

Saepe loquar nimium gentes quod, Avite, remotas
  miraris, Latia factus in urbe senex,
auriferumque Tagum sitiam partriumque Salonem
  et repetam saturae sordida rura casae.
illa placet tellus in qua res parva beatum   5
  me facit et tenues luxuriantur opes:
pascitur hic, ibi pascit ager; tepet igne magligno
  hic focus, ingenti lumine lucet ibi;
hoc pretiosa fames conturbatorque macellus,
  mensa ibi divitiis ruris operta sui;   10
quattuor hic aestate togae pluresve teruntur,
  autumnis ibi me quattuor una tegit.
i, cole nunc reges, quidquid non praestat amicus
  cum praestare tibi possit, Avite, locus.

XXV

★★★★★★★★★★★★★★★★

WILLIAM CHAMBERLAYNE
(1619-1679)

The personification of the stream that encircled Pharonnida's island paradise, whose "wanton pride . . . Curld his proud Waves and stretcht them" (II, iv, 132–35), has an odd ring: curling and stretching are not actions one usually associates with masculine pride. It is strangely excessive, moreover, to have the stream's *pride* working on the *proud* stream. And turning this stream's proud, stretching, curling waves into a clear mirror (II, iv, 135–38), like turning "stately Hils" into a fence (II, iv, 163), is surely the kind of trick that can work only in a very mysterious poem. But that, of course, is what *Pharonnida* is.

Chamberlayne has achieved the air of mystery in this poem, first, by making what he is really talking about syntactically subordinate, time and again, to something abstract or figurative which he is not really talking about, thus commending not the city to our chief attention but the "Cities Pride" (II, iv, 150), not the stream but the "Armes of a . . . stream" (II, iv, 132), not the spring but the "Springs variety" (II, iv, 154), not the day itself but the "Dayes . . . Curtains" (II, iv, 175). The syntax itself adds to the mystification. One finds the "beauteous Fabrick," for instance, which began as the subject of a main clause, reduced in other terms ("That type of Paradice") to the object of an infinitive verb in an adjective clause *of the same sentence* — thus distantly and humbly modifying itself (II, iv, 130–38). That is, one finds this if he keeps on searching. The objects he is told in another sentence that he may "behold," namely, "herd" and "Lodge," he must hang on six and eight lines to get a glimpse of (II, iv, 173–81). And he will wait forever for the verb "Landskips" governs, or for the "There" item that might oppose and complete the "Here" with which these "Landskips" were introduced — if, as might well happen, he fails to see them as the indirect object of "yield" (II, iv, 171 ff.). The relevance of the modification

"Though from the Palace . . ." is never asserted, and the bits of phrases, like "If in Contention, shew to magnifie," that trail along behind it (II, iv, 155–60) seem to have no meaning. If ever poetry needed the clarification which the couplet with its emphases and its powers of definition can give, it is that of *Pharonnida.*

But Chamberlayne used his couplets not to clear up his poem, but to confound it further. He used rhyme, for instance, that force for emphasizing the important terms, the key substantives or necessary actions, to draw our attention to adjectives (II, iv, 131, 133, 161, 169), conjunctions (II, iv, 159), adverbs (II, iv, 145, 181), auxiliary verbs (II, iv, 134, 139, 153), and prepositions (II, iv, 146, 167, 179, 187): thus making us register with special force not "stream" but "wide," not "Prospect" or "City" but "unless," not "beauty" but "more," not "eye" or "Vale" but "o're," not "Deer" or "Grove" but "by."

As these rhymes suggest, Chamberlayne's verse, his lines and couplets, are terribly enjambed and his couplets' powers of definition, consequently, weakened. But Chamberlayne used what little force they had left, once again, not to clarify, but to confuse. Oddly enough, Chamberlayne's fancies, such as they were, would have often responded nicely to couplet ordering. The prospect from Pharonnida's palace, for instance, he conceived in two parts — more or less divided at line 162; and each of these parts he considered, at least to some extent, in the form of an antithesis. The first part, clearly, presents a contrast, an opposition, between plain nature and polished art, between the flowery vale and the splendid city. This antithesis runs right through the passage, but it is given metrical definition only once (II, iv, 156) and then in a largely incomprehensible segment of the passage. For the rest, bits and pieces of this antithetical matter, which give the otherwise abstract description its only substance, are tossed up helter-skelter with only the meagerest and cloudiest suggestion, besides that provided by the reiterated terms "nature" and "art" themselves, to indicate a coherent view — or, indeed, much of any view at all. The second part of the description, although more devoted to visual detail, feints at a general opposition of elements too — between the fair and the uncouth, the barren and the bountiful in nature. Its articulation is too diffuse to help, however, and it peters out somewhere after line 173 without a trace. The passage goes on to describe a scene which is, apparently, since it is beyond the almost invisible lodge and hidden in shadows, no part of the prospect at all.

It is not only these large poetic designs but virtually every expression in the poem that couplet ordering might have made clear. The opening of the palace's prospect (II, iv, 145–46), for instance, might easily have been straightened out: "Nor was she richer in domestic store / Than in the prospects her eyes wandered o're." This is not good verse, but it undoes the pointless misplacement of "rich" and conveys its sense easily to the mind. But that, of course, was not Chamberlayne's game. He was writing romantic, escapist poetry; the more confused, irrelevant, and strange it was, the more completely it freed the reader from his common sense, the better. Besides, Chamberlayne needed the disguise his metrical perversions gave to cover up the triteness, the tediousness of his story and the general skimpiness of his imagination.

It is fitting that the form best suited in English literature for discussing the practical affairs of life could become, when it was perverted, the most potent means of romantic escape. Chamberlayne was not the first or the last to use the couplet in this way, of course: Keats's *Endymion* lay ahead, and Drayton's *Man in the Moon*, behind. Drayton's description of Diana's clothing, moreover, probably overgoes anything in Chamberlayne in romantic haziness. But for sustaining the specious sense of mystery and strangeness over the long haul, Chamberlayne can hardly be matched.

PHARONNIDA, II, iv

Her thoughts clear calm, too smooth for th' turbulent
And busie City, wants that sweet content
The private pleasures of the Country did
Afford her Youth, but late attempts forbid   120
All places far remote, which to supply,
He unto one directs his choice, that by
Its scituation did participate
Of all those rural privacies, yet sate
Cloathd in that flowry Mantle, in the view   125
Oth' Castle Wals, which as plac'd neer it to
Delight, not trouble, in ful bulk presents,
Her publick Buildings various Ornaments.
    This beauteous Fabrick, where th' industrious hand
Of Art had Natures Midwife prov'd, did stand   130
Divided from the Continent, by th' wide
Armes of a spatious stream, whose wanton pride,
In Cataracts from th' Mountains broke, as glad
Of liberty to court the Valley, had

Curld his proud Waves, and stretcht them to inclose   135
That type of Paradice, whose Crown-top rose
From that clear Mirror, as the first dight saw,
Fair *Eden* 'mids the Springs of *Havilah*;
So fresh as if its verdant Garments had
Been in the first Creations beauties clad   140
Ere by mistaking of the fatal Tree,
That blooming type of blest Eternity,
Subjected was, by mans too easie Crime,
Unto the sick Vicissitudes of time.
   Nor was she in domestick beauty, more   145
Then Prospects rich, the wandring eye past o're
A flowry Vale, smooth, as it had been spred
By Nature, for the Rivers fragrant Bed.
At th' opening of that lovely Angle met
The Cities Pride, as costlier Art had set   150
That Master-piece of Wit and Wealth, to shew
Unpollisht Natures pleasures were below
Her splendid beauties, and unfit to be
Lookt on, less in the Springs variety:
Though from the Palace where in prospect stood   155
All that nice Art, or plainer Nature wood;
If in Contention, shew to magnifie,
Their power did stand, yet now appeard to vie
That Prospect, which the City lent, unless
Diverted from that civil Wilderness: 160
The pathless Woods, and ravenous Beasts within
Whose bulk were but the Metaphors for sin;
We turn to view the stately Hils, that fence
The other side oth' happy Isle, from whence
All that delight or profit could invent   165
For rural pleasures was for prospect sent.
   As Nature strove for something uncouth in
So fair a dress, the struggling streams are seen,
With a loud murmure rowling 'mongst the high
And rugged clefts, one place presents the eye   170
With barren rudeness, whilst a neighbouring field
Sits cloathd in all the bounteous spring could yield,
Here lovely Landskips, where thou mightst behold,
When first the Infant Morning did unfold

The Dayes bright Curtains, in a spacious Green, 175
Which Natures curious Art had spread between
Two bushy Thickets, that on either hand,
Did like the Fringe of the fair Mantle stand,
A timerous herd of grasing Deer, and by
Them in a shady Grove, through which the eye 180
Could hardly pierce, a wel-built Lodge, from whence
The watchful Keepers careful diligence,
Secures their private walks, from hence to look
On a deep Valley, where a silver Brook,
Doth in a soft and busie murmure slide 185
Betwixt two Hils, whose shadows strove to hide
The liquid wealth, they were made fruitful by,
From ful discoveries of the distant eye.

. . . .

PHARONNIDA, II, v

Look how a bright and glorious Morning, which
The youthful Brow of *April* doth enrich, 490
Smiles, till the rude Winds blow the troubl'd Clouds
Into her Eyes, then in a black Vail shrouds
Her self, and weeps for sorrow; so wept both
Our royal Lovers, each would, and yet was loath
To bid farwel, till stubborn time inforc'd 495
Them to that Task; first his warm Lips divorc'd
From the soft balmy touch of hers; next parts
Their hands, those frequent witnesses oth' heart's
Indissoluble Contracts: last, and worst,
Their eyes, — their weeping eyes, (oh Fate accurst, 500
That layes so hard a task upon my Pen,
To write the parting of poor Lovers) when
They had even lost their light in tears, were in
That shade, that dismal shade, forc'd to begin
The progress of their sorrow; he is gone, 505
Sweet, sad *Pharonnida* left — left alone,
To entertain grief in soft sighs, whilst he
'Mongst noise and tumult, oft finds time to be
Alone with sorrow, though encompast by
A numerous Army, whose brave Souls sweld high, 510

With hopes of Honour, least Fames Trump want breath,
Hast to supply't by Victory, or death.
   But ere calmd thoughts to prosecute our story,
Salute thy Ears with the deserved Glory
Our marshal Lovers purchast here, I must   515
Let my Pen rest awhile, and see the rust
Scour'd from my own Sword, for a fatal day
Draws on those gloomy hours, whose short steps may
In *Britains* blushing Chronicle write more
Of sanguine Guilt, then a whole Age before: 520
To tell our too neglected Troops that we
In a just Cause are slow, we ready see
Our rallied Foes, nor wil't our sloathful Crime
Expunge, to say, Guilt wakend them betime,
From every Quarter, the affrighted Scout   525
Brings swift Alarums in, hovering about
The clouded tops of the adjacent Hils,
Like ominous Vapours Lye their Troops, noise fils
Our yet unrallied Army, and we now
Grown legible, in the contracted Brow,   530
Discern whose heart looks pale with fear: If in
This rising storm of blood, which doth begin
To drop already, I'me not washt into
The Grave, my next safe Quarter shall renew
Acquaintance with *Pharonnida*, till then,   535
I leave the Muses to converse with men.

XXVI

𝔁𝔁𝔁𝔁𝔁𝔁𝔁𝔁𝔁𝔁𝔁𝔁𝔁

ANDREW MARVELL
(1621-1678)

Marvell's *Fleckno*, like Donne's "Satire I," describes in pithy but erratic couplets the poet's meeting with a presumptuous fool. Marvell, like Donne, made incidental use of the couplet — note lines 9–10 and 17–18, for instance — and, for the rest, practiced heavy mid-line pause (ll. 5, 6, 21, 32, 33), heavy odd-line pause (ll. 3, 11, 15), and couplet enjambment (ll. 6, 24, 32).[1] The impression of arrogance suggested by this treatment of couplet order, an impression, that is, of the poet's being indifferent to our understanding, Marvell augmented, again following Donne, with learned references (ll. 3, 6) and farfetched plays of wit (ll. 12, 18). One notices that the pun on "stanza," for instance, requires a ready knowledge of two languages. *Fleckno* thus projects the same snobbish exclusiveness, the same sense of clique, that one finds in Donne's satires.

Marvell's late poem "On *Paradise Lost*," with its witty play on "praise" and "commend" (ll. 51–52) and with its satiric swipes at the popular poet Dryden (ll. 17–22, 45–50), may also remind us of Donne. But its great movement from a skeptical meditation (ll. 1–22) to a public, complimentary address (ll. 23–54) and, within its first part, from doubt of Milton's intention (ll. 1–10) to fear of his success (ll. 11–16), to concern for the fate of his accomplished work (ll. 17–22) suggests, rather, the influence of Donne's great admirer, Ben Jonson — or better, perhaps, Jonson's influence modified by that of Waller. Marvell struck the Jonsonian note — the balanced but metrically unconfined progress of thought and the consequent impression of judgment and detachment — at the very start of this poem. The first four and one-half lines, stating the condition of his inquiry, balance the next five and one-half, which

---

[1] My line references correspond to the line notations in *The Poems and Letters of Andrew Marvell*, ed. H. M. Margoliouth (Oxford, 1927), I.

give Marvell's response. The catalogue of eight elements (ll. 3–5), again, by which Marvell defined the condition of his inquiry, is also Jonsonian in its handling: the four rather particular items of it are deployed, two and two, in a couplet; the four comprehensively general items of it are wedged into a half-line — thus giving the impression of order but not mechanical order. The poem is Jonsonian throughout: take the last, asymmetrical line, for instance, in which the irrelevancy of rhyme to Milton's poetry is indicated by Marvell's giving "*Rhime*" the emphasis of rhyme — an emphasis which does not overbalance that which Marvell gives with number, weight, and measure to "Number, Weight, and Measure." By thus using a wider range of poetic means than was unique and typical of the rhymed couplet, Marvell has defended this wider, this more Jonsonian, range.

Marvell's earlier poem "To Lovelace" also shows affinities with Jonson's sense and Waller's sweetness, but in a different proportion. Marvell wished to compliment Lovelace rather than to judge him, and his closed couplets, each one an elegantly turned item in the formulation of praise, reflect this more Wallerian intention. "To Lovelace" is most interesting, actually, as a prologue to the time when party would replace merit as the motive for poetic praise or blame. In recognizing the "tainted" air and the "infection of the times," Marvell implicitly prophesied the age of political upheaval and, of course, of political satire. His own poetry after 1650, which preceded the great achievements of Dryden, partially fulfilled this prophecy.

Marvell was not, however, really a political poet; he was, rather, a meditative poet. When he took up political subject matter and maintained his balance, as he did in composing his *First Anniversary*, the result can be described as historical poetry.

In *The First Anniversary*, Marvell has not balanced the political alternatives. He did not attempt to comprehend the side he opposed, namely, kingship; he presented it in his discussion (ll. 15–44), rather, as a foil for his praise of Cromwell. Marvell established his position at the opening of the poem by insisting on Cromwell's unique capacity for leadership. Other human beings are subject to the power of time; "*Cromwell alone*" keeps pace with time. There is no point throughout the poem at which Marvell indicates any room for argument — no bowing to the opinions and prejudices of a variously factious public, no politic attempt to point out the good points of opposing men or positions. He has reached the condition of reason which he hoped would come to prevail in all England, the sensible rule "where none withstand," and he will not play the political game. Quite simply and inarguably, "If these the Times, then this must be the Man."

Marvell had, then, no urge to be persuasive, no reason to account for contrary opinions, no need to comprehend in his utterance the feelings of the other party: his task was to celebrate the status quo. Such a monumental figure as that of the ocean, with which the poem opens, and such a noble figure as that of hunting (ll. 117–30), especially in the epic scope of Marvell's treatment, exactly suited this purpose. Eventually, as Marvell saw, he might be called on to cope with more complex conditions and engage in a more demanding and dynamic enterprise — the rousing of kings who had failed to make the human best of their responsibilities (ll. 117–24), but for the present, he was satisfied to celebrate "Angelique Cromwell," to "hollow far behind" this champion's heroic progress.

The poetic monument he has raised in this cause is, however, by no means simple-minded. The finest passage in the poem, for instance, distinguishes between the ideal of human government, which is present to Marvell's meditations, and Cromwell's actual reign (ll. 131–44): Cromwell must be the man, as Marvell saw, only because "these [are] the Times." The point for students of the couplet, however, is that Marvell arrived at this judgment on his own, that is, by private meditation. He did not conceive of the argument between kingly and Cromwellian rule as a political, but as a philosophical, argument; nor was he driven to focus it on the body politic, to project it into the arena where it would, in fact, be decided. Once he had tested it against his own sense of ideal truth, he was ready to describe and judge it. The couplet allows him to clarify his own thoughts, not to accommodate the thoughts of others: to compare the effective force of kings and Cromwell (l. 14), to enforce his own opinion of royal languor (l. 22), to punctuate the various aspects of royal tyranny (ll. 23–32), and to define the ideal political situation (l. 133). The closed couplet, thus, allowed Marvell to articulate the grounds of his firm but reasonable approval of the national status quo.

Marvell's chief failures as a political poet were, first, a refusal to focus his attention on the merely practical urgencies and, second, his unwillingness to comprehend in his political utterance the excellencies, the good grounds, for the faction he opposed. The second of these failures, although evident in *The First Anniversary*, comes out most clearly in *The Last Instructions to a Painter*, a poem Marvell wrote, essentially, as a member of the opposition. In this poem Marvell's hunger for clear-cut divisions, his desire, that is, to impose absolute judgments on the inevitable relativity of politics, is ruinously evident. His and his party's enemies were, according to Marvell, "Drunkards, Pimps and Fools"; their conduct was not a balance of good and bad, but a balance of "great debauch and little skill"; the king's chancellor, the Earl of Clarendon, a mean and petty creature to whom Parliament was poison, was chiefly motivated by greed and revenge. Marvell could not see what the king saw in Clarendon any more than he could see what the king saw in the Countess of Castlemaine. In short, he lacked political imagination. So the couplet, when he turned it toward political foes, became an essentially pejorative instrument.

Marvell's use of one partisan charge against the court — that the Duchess of York was involved in the alleged poisoning of Lady Denham — to develop another partisan charge — that Clarendon hated Parliament worse than poison — was an artful thrust, but only those who subscribed to these charges would be moved by it. His references to Clarendon's gout and to the Countess of Castlemaine's low tastes in love, once again, would delight those of Marvell's own party, but it would harden the lines between him and his foes, and it might repulse those who had been undecided. Marvell, then, who spoke only to a segment of the body politic, was practicing on a larger scale that exclusiveness, that cliquishness, that he had once copied from Donne. His use of esoteric imagery (ll. 13–14, 15–20, 345–46) and his learned references (ll. 337–40, 355–56, 360) augment this impression. The audience to which this poem addressed itself, the audience it projects, is not, then, the body politic at large but a radical and recalcitrant minority.

From this and other political poems of Marvell, nevertheless, Dryden could have drawn the heroic note that gave his poems their satiric grandeur: "*Cromwell* alone . . . *Cromwell* alone" may very well have begotten "Shadwell alone . . . Shadwell alone." Such are the tricks of literary history. And from a poem like *The First Anniversary*, if not from *The Last Instructions*, our great political satirist may have derived the necessary lessons of intellectual detachment and intellectual breadth.

XXVII
✥✥✥✥✥✥✥✥✥✥✥✥✥✥✥
JOHN CARYLL
(1625-1711)

Naboth's Vineyard, although its verse is not distinguished, is a valuable historical analogue to Dryden's *Absalom and Achitophel*. In both poems, a political situation is defined in terms of extensive biblical allegory, an allegory articulated chiefly in terms of narrative, portraiture, and dialogue. Both poets, correspondingly, infused their couplets with a heroically sweeping movement and employed heroic diction and heroic figures. One notices in *Naboth's Vineyard*, for instance, the falcon figure which Caryll has developed over six couplets (ll. 73–84).

It seems certain that Dryden knew this poem, which preceded *Absalom and Achitophel* by two years, when he came to write his great political poem. One notices several apparent echoes. Among them is Dryden's description of Achitophel as being "For close designs and crooked counsels fit," which follows Caryll's description of the similarly evil Arod as being "For bold attempts and deep intriguing fit." One might also compare, more broadly, of course, Caryll's sighing Ahab with the correspondent figure in Dryden's poem, the sighing Absalom. More important, however, Caryll's poem helps fill in our understanding of the political climate in which Dryden lived and wrote and our awareness of the political deployment of the couplet which his contemporaries would have expected. If we turn to *Absalom and Achitophel* from Caryll's poem, we can recapture something of Restoration England's first experience of that remarkable work.

NABOTH'S VINEYARD

Poor Naboth's vineyard next lies in his way,   55
His cov'tous eye had mark'd it for his prey;
He parley'd first — but what he could not worm
By treaty from him, he resolv'd to storm.

"How, Sir! can you think worthy your large soul
To crave my spot of land, my sleeping-hole?"   60
(Says Naboth) "I myself should prize it not,
Were it not sacred made by age and lot;
By lot consign'd to my forefather's hand
Who first with Joshua seiz'd this holy land.
'Twere sacrilege in me to give or sell   65
What to my name by Heav'n's appointment fell.
May Ahab his large kingdoms long possess;
Let Naboth his small vineyard hold in peace."
    Ahab was silent, but not satisfi'd;
The cov'tous poison through his veins did glide,   70
And what his greedy eye and heart devour
He will extort by an usurping pow'r.
    So have I seen the tow'ring falcon rise,
And next to nothing lessen to our eyes,
Beyond the call of any game or lure;   75
The tim'rous fowl such distance can endure,
But ill they measure by their own the sight
And sharpness of their tyrant's appetite;
She sports and plies her wings i'th' liquid air
As if she minded pleasure and not war.   80
But when the fowl, betray'd by flatt'ring hopes,
Takes wing, the watchful foe as lightning stoops;
What her eye mark'd her talons make her own,
As thunderstruck the quarry tumbles down.
    But ill did Ahab's eyes, with all their art,   85
Cover the secret rancor of his heart;
The wound did fester that his passion made,
Which soon his face unwillingly betray'd.
First Jezebel descri'd his secret pain:
"My Lord (she said) can your breast entertain   90
A grief or joy but what I must partake?
O, do not this unkind distinction make."
Shame to reveal, and greater shame to hide
His soul from her, his troubled thoughts divide.
At last he pour'd his grief into the ear   95
Of his too kind and fatal counsellor:
    "In vain, my dear, our scepter does command
From the North Sea to the Arabian sand;

In vain the kings of Aram are my slaves;
In vain my justice kills, my mercy saves,   100
If stubborn Naboth must his vineyard hold
In spite of all entreaty, pow'r, and gold;
If a poor worm of Israel proudly dares
Resist, not my commands, my very pray'rs."
    "Tread on that rebel worm," says Jezebel,   105
"The weight of a king's anger let him feel;
Crush him to nothing that your subjects may
Be taught by his example to obey."
    Then Ahab sigh'd, and said, "That must not be —
People and priests would rise in mutiny.   110
Too much we hazard for a thing so small;
The Tyrant Law, which monarchs does enthrall,
Controls the execution of my will
And makes the slave bold to resist me still."
    At this unmoveable stood Jezebel,   115
Like one fast bound by an enchanter's spell;
Her flaming cheeks had choler's deepest dye,
And like struck flints sparkl'd her furious eye;
Such heaving and such panting shook her breast,
As if some spirit had the place possess'd.   120
Then suddenly she starts with a loud cry:
    "If law must do the work, Naboth shall die.
Let not the Sanhedrim a monarch awe;
He that commands the judge commands the law.
Law is a poor dumb thing, which none can hear,   125
But by the mouth of an interpreter;
And in the people's mouth 'tis the old plea
For rebels, when their prince they disobey.
Fear not the law, but by the judge be fear'd;
Else, as the pedants gravely wag their beard,   130
Kings must of their prerogatives be stripp'd
As children are for breach of grammar whipp'd.
Then trust my skill — I'll bring you quick relief
To heal the wounds of your unseemly grief;
Both you and Naboth your just rights shall have: 135
You shall possess his vineyard, he his grave."
    Thus with her oily words she skins his sore,
But adds new poison to the ulc'rous core;

And that false comfort leaves in Ahab's mind
Which villains in their thriving mischiefs find.   140
She summons then her chosen instruments,
Always prepar'd to serve her black intents.
The chief was Arod, whose corrupted youth
Had made his soul an enemy to truth;
But nature furnish'd him with parts and wit,   145
For bold attempts and deep intriguing fit.
Small was his learning, and his eloquence
Did please the rabble, nauseate men of sense.
Bold was his spirit, nimble and loud his tongue,
Which more than law, or reason, takes the throng.   150
Him, part by money, partly by her grace,
The cov'tous Queen rais'd to a judge's place;
And, as he bought his place, he justice sold,
Weighing his causes not by law, but gold.
He made the justice seat a common mart;   155
Well skill'd he was in the mysterious art
Of finding varnish for an unsound cause,
And for the sound, imaginary flaws.
   With him fierce Jezebel consults the way
How she for harmless Naboth snares may lay.   160
"Madam," says he, "you rightly judge the course
Unsafe, to run him down by open force.
In great designs it is the greatest art
To make the common people take your part.
Some words there are which have a special charm   165
To wind their fancies up to an alarm:
Treason, Religion, Liberty are such;
Like clocks they strike when on those points you touch.
If some of these unto his charge you lay,
You hit the vein of their tarantula.   170
For, to say truth, the trick did never fail;
Loud calumny with them does still prevail.
I, Madam, of these means no scruple make;
Means from their end their good or badness take.
Naboth, a rebel to his sov'reign's will,   175
By any ways we lawfully may kill."
Whilst thus he pour'd his venom in her ear,
A spiteful joy did in her face appear:

She said, "Your faithful counsel I approve —
You have chalk'd out the way we are to move;   180
But still you leave untouch'd the hardest part,
Which most requires your industry and art:
Where is the crime? where are the witnesses?"
　　"It is my province, Madam, to find these
(Repli'd the Judge) and that our project may   185
Take faster hold, let there a solemn day
To seek the Lord by fasting and by pray'r
Be set apart. This will exactly square
With the whole model of our work design'd.
This will the people draw body and mind   190
To act their parts in Naboth's tragedy.
This builds the stage on which the wretch shall die.
As glasses, by the sun's reflected ray,
The silly lark into the net betray,
So will the people, by the dazzling thought   195
Of godliness, religiously be caught."
　　When the Queen saw that her design would take,
She with impatient haste the conf'rence brake;
Of av'rice and revenge such is the thirst
That with the least delay the patient's burst.   200
"Lose no more time (she cri'd) — with speedy care
Letters and orders for our seal prepare,
Such as the work requires. For 'till I gain
This point, each moment is an age of pain."
　　Since first for acting God proud angels fell,   205
Still to ape Heav'n has been the pride of Hell.
As the bright spir'ts always attend His throne,
And what He wills they execute as soon,
Our fury so could not conceive the fact
More nimbly than her agent-fiend did act.   210
　　Stay, hell hounds, stay! why with such rav'nous speed
Must the dear blood of innocence be shed?
Blind is your haste, and blinder is your rage;
Hell no successful war 'gainst Heav'n can wage.
You shoot at Naboth, but yourselves you wound   215
With poison'd darts, for which no cure is found;
The poison drawn from a remorseless heart
Baffles divine, much more all human art.

What will your rage effect, but lasting shame
In this, in the next world eternal flame?   220
With all your subtle arts of perjury,
And all the varnish of your bloody lie
To make him guilty, and you rightful seem,
Hell for yourselves you build, and Heav'n for him.
    Arod had always tools at his command   225
Of a fit temper for his work in hand;
But here no villains of a common size
In wickedness, or cunning would suffice.
Yet two he found, which did as much exceed
All common rogues as common facts this deed: 230
Malchus, a puny Levite, void of sense
And grace, but stuff'd with noise and impudence,
Was his prime tool — so venomous a brute
That every place he liv'd in spew'd him out.
Lies in his mouth and malice in his heart   235
By nature grew, and were improv'd by art.
Mischief his pleasure was, and all his joy
To see his thriving calumny destroy
Those whom his double heart and forked tongue,
Surer than viper's teeth, to death had stung.   240
Python his second was, and his alone;
For he in ills no other first would own.
A braver impudence did arm this wight —
He was a ruffian, and no hypocrite;
And with audacious and loud villainy   245
He did at once virtue and fame defy.
These two, though Malchus wore the longer cloak,
Were e'enly pair'd, and drew in the same yoke.
No foresters with keener appetite
In running down their hunted game delight   250
Than these the slaughter of the guiltless view,
Whom their malicious calumny pursue.
This goodly pair were, by their teacher's art,
Fully prepar'd and tun'd to play their part.

.   .   .   .

XXVIII

✯✯✯✯✯✯✯✯✯✯✯✯✯✯✯

JOHN DRYDEN
(1631-1700)

What T. S. Eliot said of another uneven major poet, Tennyson, is also true of Dryden: to appreciate his poetic accomplishment fully one must read widely in his work.[1] One can, however, follow Dryden's development as a practitioner of the couplet, which I have indicated in the "Brief History," in a fairly economical way by reading Dryden's first masterpiece, *Astraea Redux*; by reading along in the many dramatic prologues and epilogues which flowed forth in the period between this poem and *Absalom and Achitophel*;[2] and by reading that mature masterpiece and the two or three other great poems, especially *MacFlecknoe* and *The Medall*, which more or less accompanied it in time. Poems of Dryden's last decade, the decade of his political retirement, are also extremely valuable. Among the best of these are "The Prologue to *Don Sebastian*," the translations of Juvenal, "The Cock and the Fox," and "Theodore and Honoria."

---

[1] "*In Memoriam*," in *Selected Essays* (New York, 1950), p. 286.
[2] For convenience, see *The Poems and Fables of John Dryden*, ed. James Kinsley (London, 1962), which dates all the poems in its table of contents.

XXIX

JOHN WILMOT,
Earl of Rochester
(1647-1680)

Dryden's couplets define political issues and help him to call up a political atmosphere; whereas Rochester's present us with social discourse and a social atmosphere. His "Very Heroical Epistle," for instance, reveals a cynical gentleman cutting off his affair with his mistress. In "A Letter from Town," again, Artemisa tells her friend Cloe, who is stuck in the country, about the conduct of love affairs in London. And in "A Satire against Mankind," a cynically sensible gentleman discusses with an acquaintance of an enthusiastic turn of mind, who may be a Puritan clergyman, the nature and dignity of man — somewhat as Pope will discuss this question fifty years hence with Lord Bolingbroke in his *Essay on Man* — or, more nearly, perhaps, as Pope will discuss it with various personifications of pride. Rochester is as concerned as Dryden with the eminent people of his time, but to him they are, at the most, eminent ladies and gentlemen; King Charles is merely a "Great Sir" — more the ruler of love's empire than of England's. Rochester's couplets are thus conversational, rather than oratorical.

His couplet poetry is full of conversational practices. In "A Satire," for instance, he makes a pointed address to an individual gentleman, by referring to "Sir" and "you," by making extensive use of the imperative mood, and by employing such conversational expressions as "what's a clock," "I'le bring it to the test," "You'le be undone," and "as far as I can see"; Rochester has even entertained his respondent's objections (ll. 48–71),[1] as Pope will do so often in his later poems. Rochester's "Very Heroical Epistle" is similarly colloquial, using, for instance, such expressions as "my Cheat," "Us'd 'em well," and "My *Mrs.*"

---

[1] My line references correspond to the line notations in *Poems*, ed. V. de Sola Pinto (Cambridge, Mass., 1953).

These poetic conversations are directed at two circles of respondents, the first, an intimate circle containing only the speaker's immediate addressee and himself, and, the second, a broad one which includes the whole polite world. The indications of this double conversational circle are most clear and obvious in the "Heroical Epistle." Rochester begins it by addressing his mistress (ll. 1–29); then, with an epigrammatic generalization on women (ll. 30–31), he turns to the polite world at large and continues to the end developing an elegant, widely scandalous pose. This double circle of social appeal appears, defined in rather the same way, in the "Prologue Spoken at Court." The speaker, Lady Elizabeth Howard, opens with an address to all the fine gentlemen present and then turns, with a single couplet of explanation (ll. 21–22), to direct a pointed appeal at the king. Pope will create a similar double circle, unlike Donne, who confined himself to a witty intimate, but Pope will articulate it with a much finer grain, coming toward the end of his career to implicate both his immediate respondent and the world at large in virtually every couplet and, indeed, every word of his discourse. It is, however, crucially important as an element of Rochester's poetry. "A Satire against Mankind" is most effective when it is understood as an address both against and to mankind, when it evokes the impression of the speaker forcing both his immediate conversational opposite and his proud, elegant acquaintance in general to face their own smallness and absurdity.

Rochester's couplet practice corresponds with his prevailingly social intention. The couplet and its elements are, for him, ways of achieving pointed wit, of sharpening bon mots: ". . . all Men would be *Cowards* if they durst"; "The *Knaves,* will all agree to call you *Knave*"; ". . . Women, Beggar-like, still haunt the Door, / Where they've received *Charity* before." His couplets, as a result of this emphasis on point and wit, are often very stiff. Only two of the first nine lines of the "Heroical Epistle" are even relatively enjambed, and only three or four in the first fourteen lines of "All-Pride." Even when Rochester is working out an extended figure of speech, such as the sun figure in the "Heroical Epistle" (ll. 18–23), or an extended system of argument, like that on human reason in the "Satire" (ll. 98–111), his discourse moves stiffly — a couplet and even a line at a time. Of course, these couplets are richly textured: almost every line of the passage on human reason, for instance, defines an opposition or a distinction, and there are, moreover, various relationships asserted between the individual lines of single couplets and between separate couplets. Ideally speaking, however, each couplet has its own life and force and makes its own point.

There is, of course, despite the epigrammatic nature of these couplets, some movement between them, some intracouplet dynamics. In "A Letter from Town," for instance, Rochester has yoked together a set of couplets in apposition, "Love," "Refuge," "Director," "drop," and "blessing," each of which governs a line, a couplet, or two couplets, and all of which join to form the subject of "is grown [etc.]" (ll. 40–51). One notices, however, the same need to cope with this series of figures one at a time as in reading the series of figures Waller used in describing a grove of old trees in his poem "On St. James's Park." A subtler system of connections comes a little further on in "A Letter from Town" (ll. 54–61), in which "Our Silly sex," in some cases represented by "who" and "that" and in some cases being merely understood, governs the series of verbs, 'born–turn–hate–call–Forsake.' This achievement of so clear a relationship and so sharp a definition of elements that basic syntactic parts can be sloughed and, thus, that greater and greater trenchancy becomes possible to the poet looks ahead to Pope, especially to the mature Pope. Rochester has achieved something of the same confined, highly self-conscious movement between couplet and couplet in his comparison of man and beast in "A Satire" (ll. 115–26), in his likening of All-Pride to Harlequin ("All-Pride," ll. 15–22), and in his conclusion to "A Satire" (ll. 179–224).

The sharp definition of couplets that we have found in Waller and now in Rochester makes the problem of discursive transition a persistent, crucial, and — as Pope was to show — poetically valuable one. Waller recognized the problem only fitfully; Rochester more extensively. In this couplet from "A Satire," which joins the section on man's reason to that on man in general, "Thus I think Reason righted, but for Man / I'le nere recant defend him if you can," we see Rochester consciously at work on it. Pope, in his early poem, *Windsor Forest*, would take up the problem abstractly and achieve a number of elegant large-scale transitions. In his later work, he would make transition a persistent sinew, an important expressive element of his poetry. It was Rochester, who deployed the closed couplet for the purposes of social satire, and Waller, who deployed it for those of social compliment, who passed this poetic problem, this opportunity, on to Pope. To reckon Pope's advance in the handling of couplet transitions, one might compare the close of Rochester's "Satire" (ll. 179–224), an extensive description of a just man the development of which contains two imperfectly digested contrasts — the vain prelate (ll. 193–208) and the senile councillor (ll. 209–14) — with Pope's extensive portrait of Atticus, or, in the same connection, Rochester's use of metaphor in his portrait of All-Pride with Pope's in his portrait of Sporus.

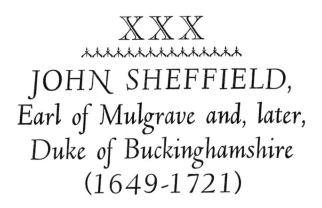

XXX

JOHN SHEFFIELD,
Earl of Mulgrave and, later,
Duke of Buckinghamshire
(1649-1721)

Sheffield employed the closed couplet as a social, rather than a political, instrument. This is as true of his practice in *An Essay upon Satire*, which Dryden is supposed to have helped him write, as it is of his other poems.

All these closed-couplet poems reveal, first of all, that closely defined lucidity of thought which our measure in its most narrow disposition allows — that lucidity which we have described as persistently within the reach of epigram. In *An Essay upon Satire*, for instance, one finds formulations such as "Learn to write well, or not to write at all" serving especially to mark climaxes in the discourse. This line is, of course, similar to that which concludes the opening couplet of *An Essay on Poetry*: "Nature's chief Master-piece is writing well." Both of these lines and the whole works they ornament — both, significantly, called essays — naturally look forward to Pope's *Essay on Criticism*. Pope quoted the second of these lines in the *Essay*, we may remember. The epigrammatic tendency of this pre-Popian social poet is also evident in the "Elegy" we have printed. The second and sixth lines of its first paragraph and the last couplet all reveal the epigrammatic impression that naturally accompanies the close combination of meter, rhetoric, and wit.

The social flavor of Sheffield's poetry — the impression it gives, that is, of broadly polite conversation — is augmented by its figures. We may notice, for example, the wittily satiric dog and cat analogies with which this poet has punctuated his portraits of Buckingham and Shaftesbury in *An Essay upon Satire* and the showy but still broadly accessible figures of the sun (ll. 9–14) and the eagle (ll. 155–70) in *An Essay on Poetry*. Both kinds of figures, that indicative of social contempt and that which makes an elegant show, once again, crop up over and over in Pope: Sporus was likened to a spaniel, for instance; knowledge to an ocean's shore and, more splendid still, to the Alps.

Sheffield, finally, was devoted to the correct, the polite, the elegant, that is, to the social graces. In his satiric contemplation of human conduct, he took up the little specks, as he said (*Satire*, 1. 35), not the great and dangerous vices; in formulating his suggestions on the polite art of writing, correspondingly, he turned his attention chiefly to its "nicer faults" (*Poetry*, 1. 179). The epigrammatic line in which he focusses his feelings about satire, "A Satyr's Smile is sharper than his Frown," epitomizes the profoundly social style and substance of Sheffield's closed-couplet poetry.

AN ESSAY UPON SATIRE

How vain and how insensible a Beast
Is man! who yet would lord it o'er the rest!
Philosophers and Poets vainly strove
In every age the lumpish Mass to move:
But those were Pedants, if compar'd with these,   5
Who know not only to instruct, but please:
Poets alone found the delightful Way,
Mysterious Morals gently to convey
In charming Numbers, that when once Men grew
Pleas'd with their Poems, they grew wiser too.   10
Satire has always shin'd among the rest,
And is the boldest Way, perhaps the best,
To shew Men freely all their foulest Faults;
To laugh at their vain Deeds and vainer Thoughts.
    In this great work the wise took diff'rent ways,   15
Tho' each deserving its peculiar Praise:
Some did our Folly with just Sharpness blame;
Whilst others laugh'd, and scorn'd us into Shame.
But, of these two, the last succeeded best;
As Men hit rightest, when they shoot in jest.   20
    Yet, if we may presume to blame our Guides,
And censure those who censur'd all besides:
In all things else they justly are preferr'd;

In this alone methinks the Ancients err'd:
Against the grossest Follies they declaim,   25
Hard they pursue, but hunt ignoble Game.
Nothing is easier than such Blots to hit,
And but the Talent of a vulgar Wit.
Besides 'tis Labour lost; for who would teach
W———sly to write, or *Te———* to preach?   30
'Tis being devout at Play, wise at a Ball,
Or bringing Wit and Friendship to *Whitehall.*
   But, with sharp Eyes those nicer Faults to find,
Which lie obscurely in the wisest Mind,
That little Speck, which all the rest will spoil;   35
To wash off this, would be a noble Toil;
Beyond the loose-writ Libels of this Age,
Or the forc'd Scenes of our declining Stage.

.   .   .   .

Nor should the royal Mistresses be nam'd;
Too ugly, or too easy to be blam'd;
With whom each rhiming Fool keeps such a pother,
They are as common that way, as the other:
While sauntring *Charles* betwixt so mean a Brace,   65
Meets with dissembling still in either place,
Affected Humour, or a painted Face.
In loyal Libels we have often told him
How one has jilted him, the other sold him,
How that affects to laugh, how this to weep;   70
But who so long can rail, as he can keep?
Was ever prince by two at once misled,
Foolish, and False, Ill-natur'd and Ill-bred?

.   .   .   .

And first behold the merriest Man alive
Against his careless Genius vainly strive;   85
Quit his dear Ease some deep Design to lay,
Appoint the Hour, and then forget the Day.
Yet he will laugh, ev'n at his Friends, and be
Just as good Company as *Nokes,* or *Lee*;
But when he would the Court, or Nation rule,   90
He turns himself the best to Ridicule.
When serious, few for great Affairs more fit;
But shew him Mirth, and bait that Mirth with Wit,

That Shadow of a Jest shall be enjoy'd,
Tho' he left all Mankind to be destroy'd.   95
   So Puss, transform'd, sat like a mumping Bride,
Pensive, and prudent, till the Mouse she spy'd;
But soon the Lady had him in her Eye,
And from the board did just as oddly fly.
   Straining above our Nature does no good;   100
We must sink back to our old Flesh and Blood.
   As by our little Matchiavel we find,
That nimblest Creature of the busy kind:
His Legs are crippled, and his Body shakes,
Yet his bold Mind, that all this Bustle makes,   105
No Pity of its poor Companion takes;
What Gravity can hold from laughing out,
To see that lug his feeble Limbs about?
Like Hounds ill coupled, *Jowler* is so strong,
He jades poor *Trip*, and drags him all along.   110
'Tis such a Cruelty as ne'r was known,
To use a Body thus, tho' 'tis ones own.
Yet this vain Comfort in his Mind he keeps;
His Soul is soaring, while his Body creeps.
Alas! that soaring, to those few who know,   115
Is but a busy Flutt'ring here below.
So visionary Brains ascend the Sky,
While on the Ground entranc'd the Wretches lie;
And so late Fops have fancy'd they can fly.
   Next, our new Earl, with Parts deserving Praise,   120
And Wit enough to laugh at his own Ways;
Yet loses all soft Days and sensual Nights,
Kind Nature checks, and kinder Fortune slights,
Striving against his Quiet all he can,
For the fine Notion of a busy Man: 125
And what is that at best, but one whose Mind
Is made to vex himself, and all Mankind?
Drudging for Wealth, a Courtier let him live;
For, if some odd fantastick lord will drive
A Hackney Coach, and meaner Business do,   130
We should both pay him, and admire him too
But is there any other Beast alive,
Can his own Harm so wittily contrive?

Will any Dog, that has his Teeth and Stones,
Refin'dly leave his Bitches and his Bones,   135
To turn a Wheel, and bark to be employ'd;
While *Venus* is by Rival Dogs enjoy'd?
Yet this vain Man, to get a Statesman's Name,
Forfeits his Friends, his Freedom, and his Fame.

.   .   .   .

AN ESSAY ON POETRY

Of all those arts in which the Wise excell,
Nature's chief Master-piece is writing well:
No writing lifts exalted man so high,
As sacred and Soul-moving Poesy:
No kind of Work requires so nice a Touch,   5
And if well finish'd, nothing shines so much.
But Heav'n forbid we should be so profane,
To grace the Vulgar with that noble Name.
'Tis not a Flash of Fancy, which sometimes
Dazling our Minds, sets off the slightest Rhimes;   10
Bright as a Blaze, but in a Moment done:
True Wit is everlasting, like the Sun;
Which, tho' sometimes behind a Cloud retir'd,
Breaks out again, and is by all admir'd.
Number and Rhime, and that harmonious Sound,   15
Which not the nicest Ear with Harshness wound,
Are necessary, yet but vulgar Arts;
And all in vain these superficial Parts
Contribute to the Structure of the Whole,
Without a genius too; for that's the Soul.   20

.   .   .   .

As all is Dulness, when the Fancy's bad;   35
So, without Judgment, Fancy is but mad:
And Judgment has a boundless Influence
Not only in the choice of Words, or Sense,
But on the World, on Manners, and on Men;
Fancy is but the Feather of the Pen;   40
Reason is that substantial, useful part,
Which gains the Head, while t'other wins the Heart.

.   .   .   .

Of all the ways that wisest Men could find
To mend the Age and mortify Mankind,
SATYR well writ has most successful prov'd,
And cures, because the Remedy is lov'd.
'Tis hard to write on such a Subject more,   135
Without repeating things said oft' before:
Some vulgar Errors only we'll remove,
That stain a Beauty which we so much love.
Of chosen Words some take not care enough,
And think they should be, as the Subject rough;   140
This Poem must be more exactly made,
And sharpest Thoughts in smoothest Words convey'd.
Some think, if sharp enough, they cannot fail,
As if their only Business was to rail:
But human Frailty nicely to unfold,   145
Distinguishes a Satyr from a Scold.
Rage you must hide, and Prejudice lay down;
A Satyr's Smile is sharper than his Frown;
So while you seem to slight some Rival Youth,
Malice itself may pass sometimes for Truth.   150
The *Laureat* here may justly claim our Praise,
Crown'd by *Mac-Fleckno* with immortal Bays;
Yet once his *Pegasus* has borne dead Weight,
Rid by some lumpish Minister of State.
    Here rest my Muse, suspend thy cares a while,   155
A more important Task attends thy Toil.
As some young Eagle, that designs to fly
A long unwonted Journey through the sky,
Weighs all the dang'rous Enterprise before,
O'er what wide Lands and Seas she is to soar,   160
Doubts her own Strength so far, and justly fears
That lofty Road of airy Travellers;
But yet incited by some bold Design
That does her Hopes beyond her Fears incline,
Prunes every Feather, views her self with Care,   165
At last, resolv'd, she cleaves the yielding Air;
Away she flies, so strong, so high, so fast,
She lessens to us, and is lost at last.
So (tho' too weak for such a weighty thing)
The Muse inspires a sharper Note to sing.   170

And why should Truth offend, when only told
To guide the ignorant and warn the bold?
On then, my Muse, adventrously engage
To give Instructions that concern the *Stage.*
    The Unities of Action, Time, and Place, 175
Which, if observ'd, give Plays so great a Grace,
Are, tho' but little practis'd, too well known
To be taught here, where we pretend alone
From nicer faults to purge the present Age,
Less obvious Errors of the *English* Stage. 180

.   .   .   .

Yet to our selves we justice must allow,
Shakespear and *Fletcher* are the Wonders now:
Consider Them, and read them o'er and o'er; 220
Go see them play'd; then read them as before;
For tho' in many things they grosly fail,
Over our Passions still they so prevail,
That our own Grief by theirs is rock'd asleep,
The Dull are forc'd to feel, the Wise to weep. 225
Their Beauties imitate, avoid their Faults;
First, on a Plot employ thy careful Thoughts;
Turn it, with time, a thousand several ways,
This oft alone has given Success to Plays.

.   .   .   .

ELEGY TO THE DUCHESS OF R———

Thou lovely Slave to a rude Husband's Will,
By Nature us'd so well, by him so ill!
For all that Grief we see your Mind endure
Your glass presents you with a pleasing Cure.
Those Maids you envy for their happier State, 5
To have your Form would gladly have your Fate;
And of like Slavery each Wife complains,
Without such Beauty's Help to bear her Chains.
Husbands like Him we evrywhere may see,
But where can we behold a Wife like Thee? 10
    While to a Tyrant you by Fate are ty'd,
By love you tyrannize o'er all beside:
Those Eyes, tho' weeping, can no Pity move;

Worthy our Grief! More worthy of our Love!
You while so fair (do Fortune what she please)   15
Can be no more in Pain than we at Ease:
Unless unsatisfied with all our Vows,
Your vain Ambition so unbounded grows,
That you repine a Husband should escape
Th' united force of such a Face and Shape.   20
If so, alas! for all those charming Pow'rs,
Your case is just as desperate as ours.
Expect that Birds should only sing to you,
And, as you walk, that every Tree should bow;
Expect those Statues as you pass should burn;   25
And that with Wonder Men should Statues turn;
Such Beauty is enough to give things Life,
But not to make a Husband love his Wife:
A Husband, worse than Statues, or than Trees;
Colder than those, less sensible than these.   30
Then from so dull a Care your Thoughts remove,
And waste not Sighs you only owe to Love.
'Tis pity, Sighs from such a Breast should part,
Unless to ease some doubtful Lover's Heart;
Who dies because he must too justly prize   35
What yet the dull Possessor does despise.
Thus precious jewels among *Indians* grow,
Who, nor their Use, nor wondrous Value know;
But we for those bright Treasures tempt the Main,
And hazard Life for what the Fools disdain.   40

XXXI

𐀀𐀀𐀀𐀀𐀀𐀀𐀀𐀀𐀀𐀀𐀀𐀀𐀀𐀀𐀀

JOHN OLDHAM
(1653-1683)

Oldham achieved a movement, a great sweep, in his couplets which is reminiscent of Cowley's *Davideis*. Notice, for instance, the interweaving of "you" and "who" elements in one passage (*Jesuits*, I, 30–40) and the extremely flexible deployment of imperative verbs in another (*Jesuits*, I, 44–65). Oldham has not used this heroic movement like Dryden, however, to encompass divisive issues in a comprehensive and refined political utterance; he is strictly a partisan. He has described Loyola, for instance, as "the fam'd *Impostor* . . . by Fiend possest" who gives out "Hellish Oracles" with "impious Breath." He presents Loyola describing himself and his followers as Moslems and as pagan Carthaginians. Loyola's followers, likewise, he likens to "Vassal Fiends," and he presents them offering their leader "an Hecatomb / Of *Huguenots*." The heroic sweep of the verse underscores Loyola's dynastic pretensions, his vast ambition and power, and thus heightens the poet's warning to all good Protestants. It is also useful, incidentally, in piling high Jesuitical hypocrisy, allowing Oldham, for instance, to make an accumulative distinction between the Pope's probable nature — "a Punk, a Witch, [etc.]" — and the Jesuits' descriptions of him — "Holy, Vertuous [etc.]" — (ll. 80–100). Chiefly by using "altho" clauses, Oldham has set nineteen lines (eight couplets and a triplet) of the truth against one couplet of Jesuitical profession — thus asserting the enormity of Jesuit hypocrisy. The effect is dramatic and impressive, but it completely lacks the refinement and the balance which such poetry as this must achieve to rise above factional rant.

Oldham's great sweeps of verse are, moreover, rhetorically crude and imperfect. Take, for instance, the passage (*Jesuits*, I, 44–65) which is made up of a series of commands. Only its second, third, and fifth couplets, each of which defines one complete command, maintain the couplet as a metrical norm. The crucial first couplet gives a stiff articulation to three short-winded commands — a bad start for a long, sweeping system; the fourth and sixth each holds two — although in excessively unbalanced fashion; and the seventh, "Plot, Enterprize, contrive, endeavour: spare / No toil, nor Pains: no Death, nor Danger fear," seethes with nine syllables of seriatim commands and then eleven that hold a pair in complex inversion. We have here a belated case of the mixture of confusion and excessive patterning that troubled the closed couplet in its beginnings. This passage, in general, regularly acknowledges only one formal pause, the couplet pause, and it adheres to that too stiffly: the informing satiric spirit seems, thus, ritualistic in its principles and ineffective in its coping with details.

Other great verse movements have different flaws. The "who" digression in one of them (*Jesuits*, I, 30–43) is confusing in its reference: this "who," which governs lines 36–39, can refer either to you, "Whose Conqu'ring Troops" correspond to it in metrical placing, or to "all Opposers," who stand in close but not perfectly close proximity to it. A subtler failure comes up in the ghostly Spenser's extended distinction between poetry and other forms of business ("Spenser," ll. 226–38). Oldham's plan was to present a five-couplet description of successful lines of work and a one-couplet description of poetical unsuccess. But the five couplets break down into two two-couplet units on medicine and trade — both of these units stiffly closed — and then one couplet on prostitution. The one couplet on poetry balances, at most, only that on prostitution, which it immediately follows, and the first four couplets are left dangling. Actually the oblique form of the climactic couplet smudges this minimum satiric balance, even though it is tied to the prostitution couplet by a similar political reference — a reference, by the way, that Oldham did not make in treating medicine or trade.

We might describe the crudity of Oldham's verse movement another way — by looking at one of his devices. Quite often he has asserted a stronger tie between succeeding noncouplet lines than between his couplets: by making a heavy pause after a first line (*Jesuits*, I, 3, 22, 84, 86) or by making the last line of one couplet and the first line of the next rhetorically parallel (*Jesuits*, I, 61–62, 87–88; "To a Friend," ll. 57–58; "Spenser," ll. 22–23, 94–95, 98–99). This practice, which naturally weakens the couplet as a poetic norm, is effective in achieving a climax like that in *Jesuits*, I, 61–62 where closely related "Till" clauses strengthen the impression of the speaker's goal and of his ambition. But elsewhere it causes a metrical cloudiness, an uneasy rocking (see esp. *Jesuits*, I, 1–13, and "Spenser," ll. 93–102), weakening a reader's confidence in the poet's aesthetic grasp and, by extension, in his probity and intelligence.

The youthful Oldham no doubt looked back to the Elizabethan couplet satirists, especially Marston, and beyond them to the Latin satirists, especially Juvenal, to find sanction for his fierce, frothing productions. But Dryden's insistence on Oldham's "rugged . . . / force," like his description of Charles's lechery as "vigorous warmth," surely makes the best of this poet's unrefined and imperfectly realized powers.

SATIRES UPON THE JESUITS, III, LOYOLA'S WILL

Long had the fam'd *Impostor* found Success,
Long seen his damn'd Fraterniti's increase,
In Wealth, and Power, Mischief, and Guilde improv'd.
By Popes, and Pope-rid Kings upheld, and lov'd:
Laden with Years, and Sins, and num'rous Scars,   5
Got some i' th' Field, but most in other Wars,
Now finding Life decay, and Fate draw near,
Grown ripe for Hell, and *Roman* Calendar,
He thinks it worth his Holy Thoughts, and Care,
Some hidden Rules, and Secrets to Impart,   10
The Proofs of long Experience, and deep Art,
Which to his Successors may useful be
In conduct of their future Villany.
Summon'd together, all th' Officious Band
The Orders of their Bedrid-Chief attend;   15
Doubtful, what Legacy he will bequeath,
And wait with greedy Ears his dying Breath:
With such quick Duty Vassal Fiends below
To meet commands of their Dread Monarch go.
    On Pillow rais'd, he do's their entrance greet,   20
And joys to see the wish'd Assembly meet:
They in glad Murmurs tell their Joy aloud,
Then a deep silence stills th' expecting Croud,
Like *Delphick* Hag of old, by Fiend possest,
He swells, wild Frenzy, heaves his panting Brest,   25
His bristling Hairs stick up, his Eye-Balls glow,
And from his Mouth long strakes of Drivel flow:

Thrice with due Rev'rence he himself doth cross,
Then thus his Hellish Oracles disclose.

    Ye firm Associates of my great Design,   30
Whom the same Vows, and Oaths, and Order joyn,
The faithful Band, whom I, and *Rome* have chose,
The last Support of our declining Cause:
Whose Conqu'ring Troops I with Success have led
'Gainst all Opposers of our Church, and Head;   35
Who e're to the mad *German* owe their Rise,
Geneva's Rebels, or the hot-brain'd *Swiss*;
Revolted Hereticks, who late have broke
And durst throw off the long-worn Sacred Yoke:
You, by whose happy Influence *Rome can* boast   40
A greater Empire, than by *Luther* lost:
By whom wide Nature's far-stretch'd Limits now,
And utmost *Indies* to its Crosier Bow:

    Go on, ye mighty Champions of our Cause,
Maintain our Party, and subdue our Foes: 45
Kill Heresie, that rank, and pois'nous Weed,
Which threatens now the Church to overspread:
Fire *Calvin*, and his Nest of Upstarts out,
Who tread our Sacred Mitre under Foot;
Stray'd *Germany* reduce; let it no more   50
Th' Incestuous *Monk* of *Wittenberg* adore:
Make stubborn *Engl.* once more stoop its Crown,
And Fealty to our Priestly Sovereign own:
Regain our Church's Rights, and the *Island* clear
From all remaining Dregs of *Wickliff* there.   55
Plot, Enterprize, contrive, endeavour: spare
No toil, nor Pains: no Death, nor Danger fear:
Restless your Aims pursue: let no defeat
Your sprightly Courage, and Attempts rebate,
But urge to fresh, and bolder, ne're to end   60
Till the whole World to our great *Caliph* bend:
Till he thro' every Nation every where
Bear Sway, and Reign as absolute, as here:
Till *Rome* without controul, and Contest be
The Universal Ghostly Monarchy.   65

    Oh! that kind Heaven a longer Thread would give,
And let me to that happy Juncture live:

But 'tis decreed! — at this he paus'd, and wept,
The rest alike time with his Sorrow kept:
Then thus continued he — Since unjust Fate   70
Envies my Race of Glory longer date;
Yet, as a wounded General, e're he dies,
To his sad Troops, sighs out his last Advice,
(Who, tho' they must his fatal Absence moan,
By those great Lessons conquer, when he's gone)   75
So I to you my last Instructions give,
And breath out Counsel with my parting Life:
Let each to my important words give Ear,
Worth your attention, and my dying Care.
    First, and the chiefest thing by me enjoyn'd.   80
The Solemn'st tie, that must your Order bind,
Let each without demur, or scruple pay
A strict Obedience to the *Roman* Sway:
To the unerring Chair all Homage Swear,
Altho a Punk, a Witch, a Fiend sit there: 85
Who e're is to the Sacred Mitre rear'd,
Believe all Vertues with the place conferr'd:
Think him establish'd there by Heav'n, tho he
Has Altars rob'd for bribes the choice to buy,
Or pawn'd his Soul to Hell for Simony: 90
Tho he be Atheist, Heathen, *Turk*, or *Jew*,
Blasphemer, Sacrilegious, Perjur'd too:
Tho Pander, Bawd, Pimp, Pathick, Buggerer,
What e're old *Sodom's* Nest of Lechers were:
Tho Tyrant, Traitor, Pois'oner, Parracide,   95
Magician, Monster, all, that's bad beside:
Fouler than Infamy; the very Lees,
The Sink, the Jakes, the Common-shore of Vice:
Strait count him Holy, Vertuous, Good, Devout,
Chast, Gentle, Meek, a Saint, a God, who not?   100

.   .   .   .

But one thing more, and then with joy I go,
Nor ask a longer stay of Fate below:
Give me again once more your plighted Faith,   655
And let each seal it with his dying breath:
As the great *Carthaginian* heretofore
The bloody reeking Altar touch'd, and swore

Eternal Enmity to th' *Roman* Pow'r:
Swear you (and let the Fates confirm the same)   660
An endless Hatred to the *Luth'ran* Name:
Vow never to admit, or League, or Peace,
Or Truce, or Commerse with the cursed Race:
Now, through all Age, when Time, or Place soe're
Shall give you pow'r, wage an immortal War: 665
Like *Theban* Feuds, let yours your selves survive,
And in your very Dust, and Ashes live.
Like mine, be your last Gasp their Curse. — At this
They kneel, and all the Sacred Volumn kiss;
Vowing to send each year an Hecatomb   670
Of *Huguenots*, an Off'ring to his Tomb.
    In vain he would continue; — Abrupt Death
A Period puts, and stops his impious Breath:
In broken Accents he is scarce allow'd
To faulter out his Blessing on the Crowd,   675
    Amen is eccho'd by Infernal Howl,
    And scrambing Spirits seize his parting Soul.

OVID'S ELEGY II, iv, IMITATED

'Tis not one Face alone subdues my Heart,
But each wears Charms, and every Eye a Dart:
And wheresoe'er I cast my Looks abroad,
In every place I find Temptations strow'd.
The modest kills me with her down-cast Eyes,   15
And Love his ambush lays in that disguise.
The brisk allures me with her gaity,
And shews how Active she in Bed will be:
If Coy, like Cloyster'd Virgins, she appears,
She but dissembles, what she most desires: 20
If she be vers'd in Arts, and deeply read,
I long to get a Learned Maidenhead:
Or if untaught, and Ignorant she be,
She takes me then with her simplicity:
One likes my Verses, and commends each Line,   25
And swears that *Cowley's* are but dull to mine:
Here in mere Gratitude I must approve,
For who, but would his kind Applauder love?

Another damns my Poetry, and me,
And plays the Critick most judiciously: 30
And she too fires my Heart, and she too charms,
And I'm agog to have her in my arms.
One with her soft and wanton Trip does please,
And prints in every step, she sets, a Grace:
Another walks with stiff ungainly tread;   35
But she may learn more pliantness abed,
This sweetly sings, her Voice does Love inspire,
And ev'ry Breath kindles, and blows the fire:
Who can forbear to kiss those Lips, whose sound
The ravish'd Ears does with such softness wound?   40
That sweetly plays: and while her Fingers move,
While o'er the bounding Strings their Touches rove,
My Heart leaps too, and every Pulse beats Love:
What Reason is so pow'rful to withstand
The magick force of that resistless Hand?   45

.   .   .   .

A SATIRE ADDRESSED TO A
FRIEND THAT IS ABOUT TO
LEAVE THE UNIVERSITY

If you for Orders, and a Gown design,
Consider only this, dear Friend of mine,   40
The Church is grown so overstock'd of late,
That if you walk abroad, you'll hardly meet
More Porters now than Parsons in the street.
At every Corner they are forc'd to ply
For Jobs of hawkering Divinity: 45
And half the number of the Sacred Herd
Are fain to strowl, and wander unpreferr'd:
    If this, or thoughts of such a weighty Charge
Make you resolve to keep your self at large;
For want of better opportunity,   50
A School must your next Sanctuary be:
Go, wed some Grammar-Bridewel, and a Wife,
And there be at *Greek*, and *Latin* for your life:
With birchen Scepter there command at will,
Greater than *Busby's* self or Doctor *Gill*:   55

But who would be to the vile Drudg'ry bound
Where there so small encouragement is found?
Where you for recompence of all your pains
Shall hardly reach a common Fidler's gains?
For when you've toil'd, and labour'd all you can,   60
To dung, and cultivate a barren Brain:
A Dancing-Master shall be better paid,
Tho he instructs the Heels, and you the Head:
To such Indulgence are kind Parents grown,
That nought costs less in breeding than a Son: 65
Nor is it hard to find a Father now,
Shall more upon a Setting-dog allow:
And with a freer hand reward the Care
Of training up his Spaniel, than his Heir.

.   .   .   .

'Thas ever been the top of my Desires,   115
The utmost height to which my wish aspires,
That Heav'n would bless me with a small Estate,
Where I might find a close obscure retreat;
There, free from Noise, and all ambitious ends,
Enjoy a few choice Books, and fewer Friends,   120
Lord of my self, accountable to none,
But to my Conscience, and my God alone:
There live unthought of, and unheard of, die,
And grudg Mankind my very memory.
But since the Blessing is (I find) too great   125
For me to wish for, or expect of Fate:
Yet maugre all the spight of Destiny,
My Thoughts, and Actions are, and shall be free.

.   .   .   .

A SATIRE IN WHICH THE PERSON OF SPENSER ATTEMPTS TO DISSUADE THE AUTHOR FROM STUDYING POETRY

One night, as I was pondering of late
On all the mis'ries of my hapless Fate,
Cursing my rhiming Stars, raving in vain
At all the Pow'rs, which over Poets reign:

In came a ghastly Shape, all pale, and thin,   5
As some poor Sinner, who by Priest had been
Under a long Lent's Penance, starv'd, and whip'd,
Or par'boil'd Lecher, late from Hot-house crept:
Famish'd his Looks appear'd, his Eyes sunk in,
Like Morning-Gown about him hung his Skin,   10
A Wreath of Lawrel on his Head he wore,
A Book, inscrib'd the *Fairy Queen*, he bore.
   By this I knew him, rose, and bow'd, and said,
Hail reverend Ghost: all hail most sacred Shade!
Why this great Visit? why vouchsaf'd to me,   15
The meanest of thy British Progeny?
Com'st thou in my uncall'd, unhallow'd Muse,
Some of thy mighty Spirit to infuse;
If so; lay on thy Hands, ordain me fit
For the high Cure, and Ministry of Wit: 20
Let me (I beg) thy great Instructions claim,
Teach me to tread the glorious paths of Fame.
Teach me (for none does better know than thou)
How, like thy self, I may immortal grow.
   Thus did I speak, and spoke it in a strain,   25
Above my common rate, and usual vein;
As if inspir'd by presence of the Bard,
Who with a Frown thus to reply was heard,
In stile of Satyr, such wherein of old
He the fam'd Tale of *Mother Hubberd* told.   30

.   .   .   .

Perhaps, fond Fool, thou sooth'st thy self in dream,   85
With hopes of purchasing a lasting Name?
Thou think'st perhaps thy Trifles shall remain,
Like sacred *Cowley*, and immortal *Ben*?
But who of all the bold Adventurers,
Who now drive on the trade of Fame in Verse   90
Can be ensur'd in this unfaithful Sea,
Where there so many lost and shipwrack'd be?
How many Poems writ in ancient time,
Which thy Fore-fathers had in great esteem,
Which in the crowded Shops bore any rate,   95
And sold like News-Books, and Affairs of State,
Have grown contemptible, and slighted since,

As *Pordage*, *Fleckno*, or the *British Prince*?
Quarles, *Chapman*, *Heywood*, *Withers* had Applause,
And *Wild*, and *Ogilby* in former days;   100
But now are damn'd to wrapping Drugs, and Wares,
And curst by all their broken Stationers:
And so may'st thou perchance pass up and down,
And please a while th' admiring Court, and Town,
Who after shalt in *Duck-lane* Shops be thrown,   105
To mould with *Silvester*, and *Shirley* there,
And truck for pots of Ale next *Stourbridg* Fair,
Then who'll not laugh to see th' immortal Name
To vile *Mundungus* made a Martyr flame?
And all thy deathless Monuments of Wit   110
Wipe Porters Tails, or mount in Paper-Kite?

.   .   .   .

My own hard Usage here I need not press,   165
Where you have every day before your face
Plenty of fresh resembling Instances:
Great *Cowley's* Muse the same ill Treatment had,
Whose Verse shall live for ever to upbraid
Th' ungrateful World, that left such Worth unpaid.   170
Waller himself may thank Inheritance
For what he else had never got by Sense.
On *Butler* who can think without just Rage,
The Glory, and the Scandal of the Age?
Fair stood his hopes, when first he came to Town,   175
Met every where with welcomes of Renown,
Courted, and lov'd by all, with wonder read,
And promises of Princely Favour fed:
But what Reward for all had he at last,
After a Life in dull expectance pass'd?   180
The Wretch at summing up his mis-spent days
Found nothing left, but Poverty, and Praise:
Of all his Gains by Verse he could not save
Enough to purchase Flannel, and a Grave:
Reduc'd to want, he in due time fell sick,   185
Was fain to die, and be interr'd on tick:
And well might bless the Fever that was sent,
To rid him hence, and his worse Fate prevent.

.   .   .   .

All Trades, and all Professions here abound,   225
And yet Encouragement for all is found:
Here a vile Emp'rick, who by Licence kills,
Who every week helps to increase the Bills,
Wears Velvet, keeps his Coach, and Whore beside,
For what less Villains must to *Tyburn* ride.   230
There a dull trading Sot, in Wealth o'ergrown
By thriving Knavery, can call his own
A dozen Mannors, and if Fate still bless,
Expects as many Counties to possess.
Punks, Panders, Bawds, all their due Pensions gain,   235
And every day the Great Mens Bounty drain:
Lavish expence on Wit, has never yet
Been tax'd amongst the Grievances of State.
The *Turky*, *Guinny*, *India* Gainers be,
And all but the Poetick Company: 240
Each place of Traffick, *Bantam*, *Smyrna*, *Zant*,
Greenland, *Virginia*, *Sevil*, *Alicant*,
And *France*, that sends us Dildoes, Lace, and Wine,
Vast profit all, and large Returns bring in:
Parnassus only is that barren Coast,   245
Where the whole Voyage, and Adventure's lost.

.   .   .   .

XXXII

DANIEL DEFOE
(1660-1731)

Dryden's political impulse and a number of devices by which he articulated political poetry persist in Defoe's *True-Born Englishman*, but the balance, the breadth, and the grandeur by which Dryden's verse transcended the issues it treated are gone.

Such echoes from Dryden as "Amphibious Ill-born Mob" are mere incidents in Defoe's design. This one, for instance, is an artful mosaic of Dryden's feeling for the London mob, that headstrong, moody, murmuring race, and his description of Achitophel's amphibious, two-legged son which Defoe has composed to fit his own satire of the true-born Englishman. The whole passage of which this allusion is a part (I, 120–39) has a freshness, a rude vigor of movement, that makes its accumulation of incompatible racial strains quite effective. Its last line, in which Defoe insists on the higgledy-piggledy nature of the English by a higgledy-piggledy catalogue, "Your *Roman-Saxon-Danish-Norman* English," owes something of its cumulative force to Dryden, no doubt, but it has still its own special flavor.

Oddly enough this flavor comes in large part from the catalogue's obvious incompleteness: Welsh, Irish, and others, who were touched in the passage at large, simply could not fit into the final composite description. And that shows, Defoe would say, how various, how totally lacking in integrity, the English composite is: its description simply cannot be comprehended in the normal measures of utterance. The arbitrary system of selection and omission on which this stroke is based, however, like Defoe's chance lore about Hengist and Sueno, makes an incomplete, a journalistic, effect: *The True-Born Englishman* is just one editorial which is subject to answer by another, and so on.

Defoe's poem is rough-and-ready journalism throughout. His usage is erratic; his rhymes are often imperfect; his meter is sometimes rugged and sometimes flabby. One notices, for instance, the unlucky 'Graham–name' chime in one line (I, 347), and the combination of alexandrine looseness and equivocally stressed line end which weakens the force of another (II, 30). Nevertheless, by variously employing couplet emphases and by applying something of Restoration couplet dynamics, Defoe has savaged a political view he opposed with good effect.

THE TRUE-BORN ENGLISHMAN, I

The *Romans* first with *Julius Caesar* came,	120
Including all the Nations of that Name,	
Gauls, *Greeks*, and *Lombards*; and by Computations,	
Auxiliaries, or Slaves of ev'ry Nation.	
With *Hengist*, *Saxons*; *Danes* with *Sueno* came,	
In search of Plunder, not in search of Fame.	125
Scots, *Picts*, and *Irish* from th' *Hibernian* Shore;	
And Conqu'ring *William* brought the *Normans* o'er.	

All these their Barb'rous Off-spring left behind
The Dregs of Armies, they of all Mankind;
Blended with *Britains* who before were here, 130
Of whom the *Welsh* ha' blest the Character.
  From this Amphibious Ill-born Mob began
That vain ill natur'd thing, an Englishman.
The Customs, Sirnames, Languages, and Manners,
Of all these Nations are their own Explainers: 135
Whose Relicks are so lasting and so strong,
They ha' left a *Shiboleth* upon our Tongue;
By which with easie search you may distinguish
Your *Roman-Saxon-Danish-Norman* English.

.   .   .   .

France justly boasts the Ancient Noble Line
Of *Bourbon*, *Mommorency*, and *Lorrain*. 340
The *Germans* too their House of *Austria* show,
And *Holland* their Invincible *Nassau*.
Lines which in Heraldry were ancient grown,
Before the Name of *Englishman* was known.
Even *Scotland* too, her Elder Glory shows, 345
Her *Gourdons*, *Hamiltons*, and her *Monroes*;
Douglas, *Mackays*, and *Grahams*, Names well known,
Long before Ancient *England* knew her own.

But *England*, Modern to the last degree,
Borrows or makes her own Nobility,   350
And yet she boldly boasts of Pedigree:
Repines that Foreigners are put upon her,
And talks of her Antiquity and Honour:
Her S————lls, S————ls, C————ls, De-la-M————s,
M————ns, and M————ues, D————s and V————s,   355
Not one have *English* Names, yet all are *English* Peers.
Your *Houblons*, *Papillons*, and *Lethuliers*,
Pass now for *True-born English* Knights and Squires,
And make good Senate Members, or Lord-Mayors.
Wealth, howsoever got, in *England* makes   360
Lords of Mechanicks, Gentlemen of Rakes:
Antiquity and Birth are needless here;
'Tis Impudence and Money makes a *P————r*.
    Innumerable City-Knights we know,
From *Blewcoat-Hospitals* and *Bridewell* flow.   365
Draymen and Porters fill the City Chair,
And Foot-Boys Magisterial Purple wear.
Fate has but very small Distinction set
Betwixt the *Counter* and the Coronet.
Tarpaulin Lords, Pages of high Renown,   370
Rise up by Poor Mens Valour, not their own.
Great Families of yesterday we show,
And Lords, whose Parents were *the Lord knows who*.

THE TRUE-BORN ENGLISHMAN, II

The Breed's describ'd: Now, *Satyr*, if you can,
Their Temper show, for *Manners make the Man*.
Fierce as the *Britain*; as the *Roman* Brave;
And less inclin'd to Conquer than to Save:
Eager to Fight, and lavish of their Blood;   5
And equally of *Fear and Forecast* void.
The *Pict* has made 'em Sowre, the *Dane* Morose,
False from the *Scot*, and from the *Norman* worse.
What Honesty they have, the *Saxons* gave them.
And That, now they grow old, begins to leave them.   10
The Climate makes them Terrible and Bold;
The *English* Beef their Courage does uphold:

No Danger can their Daring Spirit pall,
Always provided that their Belly's full.
   In close Intrigues their Faculty's but weak,   15
For gen'rally whate'er they know, they speak:
And often their own Councils undermine,
By their Infirmity, and not Design;
From whence the Learned say it does proceed,
That *English* Treasons never can succeed,   20
For they're so open-hearted, you may know
Their own most secret Thoughts, and others too.
   The Lab'ring Poor, in spight of Double Pay,
Are Sawcy, Mutinous, and *Beggarly*:
So lavish of their Money and their Time,   25
That want of Forecast is the Nation's Crime.
Good Drunken Company is their Delight;
And what they get by Day, they spend by Night.
Dull Thinking seldom does their Heads engage,
But Drink their Youth away, and Hurry on Old Age.   30
Empty of all good Husbandry and Sense;
And void of Manners most, when void of Pence.
Their strong aversion to Behaviour's such,
They always talk too little, or too much.
So dull, they never take the pains to think: 35
And seldom are good natur'd, *but in Drink.*
   In *English* Ale their dear Enjoyment lies,
For which they'll starve themselves and Families.
An *Englishman* will fairly Drink as much
As will maintain two Families of *Dutch*:   40
Subjecting all their Labour to the Pots;
The greatest Artists are the greatest Sots.

.   .   .   .

XXXIII

WILLIAM WALSH

(1663-1709)

The derivation of Pope's verses from those of Walsh is evident in many echoes: grave Clarissa (*Rape*, V, 9–34) echoes the end of Walsh's "To his Book"; the poetically embalmed beauties of Walsh ("Elegy," ll. 11–12) turn up as poetically embalmed critics of Pope (*Arbuthnot*, ll. 169–72); Belinda's mourning of her lock (*Rape*, IV, 147–76) Pope derived from Walsh's mourning of Delia (ll. 29–40); and Belinda herself (*Rape*, II, 1–18) is a reflection of the miscellaneously flirtatious Delia (ll. 61–64). The discipleship suggested by these echoes is evident in the elegant but languid closure of Pope's early verses.

Almost every couplet in our selection from Walsh's poetry is sharply closed; indeed, there are many closed first lines ("Book," l. 19; "Elegy," l. 3; "Epistle," ll. 13, 17, 27). Walsh virtually always observed the couplet's normal scale of pauses: that is, in their ascending order, the midline, the line, the couplet. And he has, naturally, achieved a wide variety of couplet patterning: antitheses in couplet ("Book," ll. 19–20; "Epistle," ll. 5–6, 15–16) and line ("Book," l. 10; "Elegy," l. 15; "Epistle," l. 24; "Delia," ll. 60, 61), for instance; parallels in couplet ("Elegy," ll. 3–4; "Epistle," ll. 33–34) and line ("Book," l. 16; "Delia," ll. 67, 68); and various periodic emphases of line ("Book," ll. 3, 5; "Elegy," l. 19; "Epistle," ll. 9, 19; "Delia," ll. 50, 51) and couplet ("Book," ll. 17–18; "Elegy," ll. 21–22, 31–32; "Delia," ll. 47–48). One also finds line and couplet definition of common syntactic elements such as if-then ("Elegy," ll. 17–18), and other main and subordinate clauses ("Epistle," ll. 7–8; "Delia," ll. 55–56). Walsh's couplets are, in short, intensely polished. The studied elegance and grace of this couplet — "Those who Love's dear, deluding Pains have known, / May, in my fatal Stories, read their own" — can hardly be found outside the poetry of Walsh, except in that of the youthful Pope.

[344]

Walsh also worked out systems of couplets on which Pope would build. One notices the series of couplet-defined comparisons in "Delia" (ll. 45–54), for instance, the three-couplet system of opposition and climax in "An Elegy" (ll. 7–12), and the strict balance, later in the same poem (ll. 17–24), of a good woman who suffered from a bad poetic report (two couplets) with a bad woman who benefitted from a good one (two couplets). There are also more flowing systems than these. There is the three-couplet unit ("Book," ll. 5–10) whose first and last couplets oppose one another and whose middle couplet expands the thought of the first — although one might argue, admittedly, that cutting this middle couplet would actually sharpen and improve the poem. Or there is the better system ("Epistle," ll. 7–12) whose first two couplets define an if-then relationship and whose third couplet expands on the figure, enunciated in the second, of a labyrinth. Walsh also achieved occasional compressions. In "An Elegy," lines 29–36, a two-couplet figure of the sun, which breeds different things in a marsh and in good soil, is focussed in the single couplet following, each of whose lines mirrors a whole couplet above. This compression freed Walsh to fill a fourth couplet with purely descriptive or otherwise enriching material — thus packing into the four-couplet measure more than its normal measure of sense. Unfortunately, Walsh's realization of this chance is lame: the noun that governs the last couplet's verbs is unclear, and the couplet is pretty empty besides. Still, Walsh's achievement of this kind of metrical compression is portentous. Pope will articulate such patterns of compression with good discursive effect as early as *An Essay on Criticism* — in distinguishing between two kinds of pedant, for instance (ll. 112–17) — and improve on them as his career advances. Consider, say, the Atticus portrait from *An Epistle to Dr. Arbuthnot* (ll. 191–214), whose last couplet — "Who would not laugh if such a man there be? / Who would not weep if Atticus were he?" — represents all the prior description in general in the last half of its first line and focusses it all on Atticus in the last half of its second line.

All of Walsh's larger systems of verse, it will be noticed, are composed, as Pope's will be, of tightly defined couplets: nothing was allowed to weaken that essential poetic measure. Its definitive tyranny is heightened by Walsh's difficulty, a difficulty he shared with Waller, in making firm, clear connections between his couplets: Walsh often gave insufficient metrical emphasis, for instance, to intercouplet pronominal ("Elegy," ll. 9–12, 25–28; "Epistle," ll. 21–24) and adjectival ("Epistle," l. 29; "Delia," l. 59) antecedents. However, this seldom weakens the couplet-by-couplet clarity and grace of his poetry. A greater flaw than its stiffness of measure and languor of flow is this poetry's lack of particularity in its figures, in its substantial reference, or in its address. Walsh directed conventional, generalized emotions to conventional and generalized correspondents. No particularity of feeling or perception reveals itself by any metrical crabbedness, by any stress on the couplet's formal requirements. Walsh's love, annoyance, hope, and grief all resolved themselves in nicely rounded statements of elegant generality.

In inheriting Walsh's elegance, Pope also inherited his metrical languor and his poetic vagueness. By comparing "Delia," which was Walsh's memorial to Mrs. Tempest, with Pope's "Fourth Pastoral," which the youthful prodigy, at Walsh's request, also turned into a memorial to Mrs. Tempest (a comparison Pope himself suggested),[1] one can assess Pope's indebtedness and the scope of his poetic problem.

TO HIS BOOK

Go, little Book, and to the World impart
The faithful Image of an Am'rous Heart;
Those who Love's dear, deluding Pains have known,
May, in my fatal Stories, read their own.
Those who have liv'd from all its Torments free,   5
May find the Thing they never felt, by Me:
Perhaps, advis'd, avoid the gilded Bait,
And, warn'd by my Example, shun my Fate.
While with calm Joy, safe landed on the Coast,
I view the Waves on which I once was tost.   10
Love is a Medley of Endearments, Jars,
Suspicions, Quarrels, Reconcilements, Wars;
Then Peace again. O wou'd it not be best,
To chace the fatal Poison from our Breast?
But, since so few can live from Passion free,   15
Happy the Man, and only happy he,
Who with such lucky Stars begins his Love,
That his cool Judgment does his Choice approve.
Ill grounded Passions quickly wear away;
What's built upon Esteem can ne'er decay.   20

---

[1] See the dedication to Pope's pastoral, "Winter," and the footnote to the dedication in *The Poems of Alexander Pope*, ed. John Butt (New Haven, 1963), p. 135.

AN ELEGY, THE POWER OF VERSE, TO HIS MISTRESS

While those bright Eyes subdue where-e'er you will,
And, as you please, can either save or kill;
What Youth so bold the Conquest to design?
What Wealth so great to purchase Hearts like thine?
None but the Muse that Privilege can claim,   5
And what you give in Love, return in Fame.
Riches and Titles with your Life must end;
Nay, cannot ev'n in Life your Fame defend:
Verse can give Fame, can fading Beauties save,
And after Death redeem them from the Grave;   10
Embalm'd in Verse, thro distant Times they come,
Preserv'd, like Bees, within an Amber Tomb.
Poets, (like Monarchs, on an Eastern Throne,
Restrain'd by nothing but their Will alone)
Here can cry up, and there as boldly blame,   15
And, as they please, give Infamy or Fame.
In vain the Tyrian Queen resigns her Life,
For the Bright Glory of a spotless Wife,
If lying Bards may false Amours rehearse,
And blast her Name with Arbitrary Verse.   20
While One, who all the Absence of her Lord,
Had her wide Courts with pressing Lovers stor'd;
Yet, by a Poet grac'd, in deathless Rimes,
Stands a chaste Pattern to succeeding Times.
With Pity then the Muses Friends survey,   25
Nor think your Favours there, are thrown away,
Wisely like Seed on fruitful Soil they're thrown,
To bring large Crops of Glory and Renown.
For, as the Sun that in the Marshes breeds
Nothing but nauseous and unwholesome Weeds;   30
With the same Rays on rich and pregnant Earth,
To pleasant Flow'rs, and useful Fruits gives Birth:
So Favours cast on Fools, get only Shame;
On Poets shed, produce eternal Fame:
Their gen'rous Breasts warm with a genial Fire,   35
And more than all the Muses can inspire.

AN ELEGY UPON QUITTING HIS MISTRESS

I know, CELINDA, I have borne too long,
And by forgiving, have increas'd my Wrong:
Yet if there be a Power in Verse to slack
Thy Course in Vice, or bring fled Virtue back,
I'll undertake the Task; howe'er so hard,   5
A gen'rous Action is its own Reward.
O! were thy Virtues equal to thy Charms,
I'd fly from Crowns to live within those Arms:
But who, O! who, can e'er believe thee just,
When such known Falsehoods have destroy'd all Trust?   10
    Farewell, false fair! nor shall I longer stay;
Since we must part, why should we thus delay?
Your Love alone, was what my Soul could prize,
And missing that, can all the rest despise.
Yet should I not repent my Follies past,   15
Could you take up, and grow reserv'd at last;
'Twould please me, parted from your fatal Charms,
To see you happy in another's Arms.
Whatever Threatenings Fury might extort,
O! fear not I should ever do you hurt;   20
For tho my former Passion is remov'd,
I would not injure one I once had lov'd.
Adieu! while thus I waste my Time in vain,
Sure there are Maids I might intirely gain:
I'll search for such, and to the first that's true,   25
Resign the Heart so hardly freed from you.

AN EPISTLE TO A LADY WHO HAD RESOLVED AGAINST MARRIAGE

Madam, I cannot but congratulate
Your resolution for a single state;
Ladies, who would live undisturb'd and free,
Must never put on Hymen's livery;
Perhaps its outside seems to promise fair,   5
But underneath is nothing else but care.
If once you let the gordian knot be ty'd,

Which turns the name of virgin into bride,
That one fond act your life's best scene foregoes,
And leads you in a labyrinth of woes,   10
Whose strange meanders you may search about,
But never find the clue to let you out.
The married life affords you little ease,
The best of husbands is so hard to please:
This in wives' careful faces you may spell,   15
Though they dissemble their misfortunes well.
No plague's so great as an ill-ruling head,
Yet 'tis a fate which few young ladies dread:
For Love's insinuating fire they fan,
With sweet ideas of a godlike man.   20
Chloris and Phyllis glory'd in their swains,
And sung their praises on the neighbouring plains;
Oh! they were brave, accomplish'd, charming men,
Angels till marry'd, but proud devils then.
Sure some resistless power with Cupid sides,   25
Or we should have more virgins, fewer brides;
For single lives afford the most content,
Secure and happy, as they're innocent:
Bright as Olympus, crown'd with endless ease,
And calm as Neptune on the Halcyon seas: 30
Your sleep is broke with no domestic cares,
No bawling children to disturb your prayers;
No parting sorrows to extort your tears,
No blustering husband to renew your fears!
Therefore, dear madam, let a friend advise,   35
Love and its idle deity despise:
Suppress wild Nature, if it dares rebel;
There's no such thing as "leading apes in Hell."

DELIA, LAMENTING THE DEATH OF MRS. TEMPEST, WHO DIED UPON THE DAY OF THE GREAT STORM

What living Nymph is bless'd with equal Grace?
All may dispute, but who can fill thy Place?
What Lover in his Mistress hopes to find
A Form so lovely, with so bright a Mind?

DORIS may boast a Face divinely Fair,   45
But wants thy Shape, thy Motions, and thy Air.
LUCINDA has thy Shape, but not those Eyes,
That while they did th' admiring World surprize,
Disclos'd the secret Lustre of the Mind,
And seem'd each Lover's inmost Thoughts to find.   50
Others, whose beauty yielding Swains confess,
By Indiscretion make their Conquest less,
And want thy Conduct and obliging Wit
To fix those Slaves who to their Chains submit.
As some Rich Tyrant hoards an useless Store,   55
That would, well plac'd, inrich a Thousand more:
So did'st thou keep a Croud of Charms retir'd
Would make a Thousand other Nymphs admir'd.
Gay, Modest, Artless, Beautiful and Young,
Slow to Resolve; in Resolution Strong;   60
To All obliging; yet reserv'd to All;
None could Himself the favour'd Lover call:
That which alone could make his Hopes endure,
Was, that he saw no other Swain secure.
Whither, ah! whither are those Graces fled?   65
Down to the Dark, the Melancholy Shade?
Now, Shepherds, now lament! and now deplore!
DELIA *is Dead, and Beauty is no more!*

.   .   .   .

XXXIV

✦✦✦✦✦✦✦✦✦✦✦✦✦✦✦✦

MATTHEW PRIOR
(1664-1721)

Prior's early "Advice to the Painter" strongly resembles Dryden in both its political subject matter and in its use of such stylistic devices as the hemistich (ll. 19, 28), the triplet (ll. 3–5, 12–14, 36–38), and the whip-lash effect (l. 51).[1] This poem has something of Dryden's movement too: its opening paragraph, for instance, is one sentence five lines long whose first couplet defines a "since" clause and whose next three lines, a triplet, define the three commands composing the main clause; its second paragraph (ll. 6–23), a continuation of this series of commands, runs its whole course with hardly one full stop — although it obviously benefits throughout from line and couplet definition. When we read such a line as, "From the *Duke's* ashes raise the KING of LYME," we see that Prior has also caught something of Dryden's complex heroical-satiric tone. With his reference to Achitophel (l. 16), the young poet admitted his discipleship.

But "Advice to the Painter" is really quite different from *Absalom and Achitophel*. Nor is it merely in the crudity of his style — in his over-dependence on the triplet, in his augmenting one triplet with a hemistich (ll. 26–29), in his lapsing into a fourteener (l. 55) — that Prior differs from his model. For one thing, he presents his political event, Mon-mouth's rebellion, not at the time of decision, but after the outcome is assured. For another, he presents, not the illusion of intellectual engage-ment, but a partisan avowal. "Advice to the Painter" lacks, then, the sense of urgency and the sense of dynamic comprehension which charac-terize *Absalom and Achitophel*; it is a poem of political celebration.

Its unifying formal principle, advice to a painter, which accords with its narrow and static intention, derives, significantly, from Edmund Wal-

---

[1] My line references correspond to the line notations in *The Literary Works of Matthew Prior*, ed. H. Bunker Wright and Monroe K. Spears (Oxford, 1959), I.

ler's "Instructions to a Painter," a poem in flattery of the Duke of York. Prior's "Advice" is, in large part, Wallerian flattery turned upside down. The line which has been characterized as a Drydenesque whiplash, "Resolv'd to conquer or resolv'd to — fly," is, in fact, a parody of the line from Waller's "Instructions," "Resolv'd to Conquer, or resolv'd to Die."

There are virtually no traces of Dryden — or of politics — in the poem "To King William," which Prior wrote about ten years after his "Advice to the Painter." This later poem does have a kind of movement — its first sentence runs sixteen lines, for instance — but this is the movement of national pomp, not of national decision. "To King William" not only celebrates a past event — as "Advice" did — but it copes with it in an entirely ceremonial fashion. Prior did not address the body politic in this poem, nor did he describe actual events. Rather, he presented to guardian deities a set of generalized professions and gestures. Personifications of Britain, the Law, and Justice, for instance, bow at altars, wrest traitorous daggers, and manipulate balances and swords, Britain taking two couplets to express herself, the Law and Justice, one couplet each (ll. 9–16). We are closer here to Pope's social sylphs than to Dryden's national heroes. The age of national upheaval and ferment has passed, and the poet shifts the center of his attention from the political to the polite.

Prior's couplet verse after 1700 had many forms, but his best couplet poems, like the best of Pope and Gay and Young, focussed on society and projected the impression of polite social address. The inferiority of Prior's *Solomon*, especially its inferiority to *An Essay on Man*, derives in large part from its indecisiveness of tone and address. Prior could not decide whether he wished to suggest the conversation of gentlemen, which is the clear foundation of Pope's *Essay*, or the discourse of a preacher or the lyrical lament of a meditative bard. The second line of *Solomon* reveals Prior's desire to play both the gentleman and the clergyman; its thirteenth line, a melodically but not conversationally defensible utterance, shows his lyrical susceptibility. The "Epilogue to *Phaedra*," with its gossipy balancing of social ethic and social hypocrisy, is a more coherent and a more satisfactory couplet exercise. So is the "Epistle to Mr. Harley." Although this poem describes an obviously political condition, that of patronage, its address, that of friend to friend, and its basic appeals to the principles of friendship and reputation are social. In this age even statesmen are gentlemen first.

XXXV

GEORGE GRANVILLE,
Lord Lansdowne
(1667-1735)

The verse of "Granville, the polite," is chiefly useful as a sign of the new age in English poetry, the age of elegant retirement which began after the Glorious Revolution.

Granville's poetic address to Mrs. Higgons makes a vivid if extreme definition of the new age, a definition which the poet articulates by way of a contrast between the political business which had characterized the past age and his own present choice, the groves of retirement. Granville's description of the vicious life in courts and cities is so flat and humorless that it recalls the universal complaints of Baldwin and Spenser. His advice to the courtier to "smile when you devour" has a figurative flavor which makes it pass, but the suggestion which precedes it in the very same line, "Hug when you stab," is excessive and hence crude as poetic statement. Granville's insistence that honesty cannot possibly dwell in courts and cities (ll. 75–78) goes along with this.

His description of retirement goes wrong in a subtler but equally ruinous way. It is not so much that these "flowery Vales, where Nymphs and Shepherds meet" sound unreal, phony — mere cliché — as that the wish to burrow in such an absolute retreat, in a situation so perfectly removed from the haunts and habitations of men, contradicts the pervasive style of the poem. On the one hand, Granville bids, "Farewell then Cities, Courts, and Camps, farewell, / Welcome, ye Groves, here let me ever dwell, / From Cares, from Business, and Mankind remove"; on the other hand, throughout the poem he addresses not only a lady who obviously inhabits these places to which she has called him back but, through her, all courtiers and men of business. Granville apparently felt this discrepancy between his pose and his address, or so his allowance of one exception, "inspiring LOVE," seems to suggest, but neither this admission, which seems hardly to apply to the speaker's relationship with Mrs. Higgons, nor anything else in the poem redeems it.

This persistent discrepancy between the speaker's pose and his action, oddly enough, instills a pervasive insult in the polite Granville's poetic discourse. Anyone who listens to his talk about the evil of the courts, anyone, that is, who still attends the world of human activity — and this obviously includes the lady whose entreaty that he return the speaker is answering —must endure the implication that he is a fool or a knave, since nobody commits himself to human activity but fools and knaves. Only the speaker himself, Wycherly, and Cato are wrenched from this insulting implication. Before Pope could make this pose of polite retirement the focus of great poetry he had to redefine "retirement," tactfully bringing it into line with the pervasive social solicitations of the couplet as he and Walsh and Granville, all looking back to Waller, were employing it.

Despite his poetic crudities and confusions, Granville gives us the clearest and most explicit signal that this social mode of couplet has become the predominate one. In his address of 1690 to Mrs. Higgons, he announces the new age, the age whose essential situation was that of polite retirement and whose essential concerns were those less urgent but more universal ones Pope would consider in his essays and epistles. In his own "Essay upon unnatural Flights in Poetry," which, of course, treats one of these topics — that of literature, which Sheffield treated before him and which Pope would soon come to — Granville has recognized the emergence of the new age even more explicitly (ll. 109–20). But he made the definitive click into its characteristic pose, a pose whose varieties Pope would enunciate, in this 1690 address to Mrs. Higgons.

The verse by which Granville realized this pose of polite and elegant ease is broadly suitable to it. But it is, as Dr. Johnson insisted, verse without any special distinction.[1] Granville took it over chiefly from Waller, as he gratefully acknowledged: he wrote a long poem, for instance, avowedly "in imitation of the style of Mr. Waller," and in his poem on Waller's death he called that inaugurator of the polite in English literature "the god of verse, who was the king." I have described this style in sufficient detail in my essays on Waller and Walsh. Granville's incidental faults — the patches of poor English, the occasionally dull couplets ("Higgons," ll. 95–96) and the occasionally shapeless ones ("To Mira," ll. 3–6) — hardly need close attention.

---

[1] "George Granville, Lord Lansdowne," in *Lives of the Poets*, in *Works* (Troy, N.Y., 1903), IX, 319.

AN ADDRESS TO MRS. ELIZABETH HIGGONS, OCCASIONED BY HER VERSES TO THE POET, INTREATING HIM TO RETURN TO PUBLIC LIFE, WRITTEN IN THE YEAR 1690

CEASE, tempting SIREN, cease thy flatt'ring Strain,
Sweet is thy charming song, but sung in vain:
When the Winds blow, and loud the Tempests roar,
What Fool would trust the Waves, and quit the Shore?
Early, and vain, into the World I came, 5
Big with false Hopes, and eager after Fame;
Till looking round me, ere the Race began,
Madmen, and giddy Fools, were all that ran;
Reclaim'd betimes, I from the Lists retire,
And thank the Gods, who my Retreat inspire. 10
In happier Times our Ancestors were bred,
When Virtue was the only Path to tread:
Give me, ye Gods! but the same Road to Fame,
Whate'er my Fathers dar'd, I dare the same.
Chang'd is the Scene, some baneful planet rules 15
An impious World, contriv'd for Knaves and Fools.
Look now around, and with impartial Eyes
Consider, and examine all who rise;
Weigh well their Actions, and their treach'rous Ends,
How Greatness grows, and by what Steps ascends; 20
What Murders, Treasons, Perjuries, Deceit;
How many crush'd, to make one Monster great.
Would you command? Have FORTUNE in your Pow'r?
Hug when you stab, and smile when you devour;
Be bloody, false, flatter, forswear, and lie, 25
Turn Pander, Pathick, Parasite, or Spy;
Such thriving Arts may your wish'd Purpose bring,
A Minister at least, perhaps a KING.
   FORTUNE, we most unjustly partial call,
A Mistress free, who bids alike to all; 30
But on such Terms as only suit the Base,
Honour denies and shuns the foul Embrace.
The honest Man, who starves and is undone,
Not FORTUNE, but his Virtue keeps him down.

Had CATO bent beneath the conqu'ring Cause,   35
He might have liv'd to give new Senates Laws;
But on vile Terms disdaining to be great,
He perish'd by his Choice, and not his Fate.
Honours and Life, th' usurper bids, and all
That vain mistaken Men GOOD-FORTUNE call,   40
Virtue forbids, and sets before his Eyes
An honest Death, which he accepts, and dies:
O glorious Resolution! Noble Pride!
More honour'd, than the Tyrant liv'd he dy'd;
More lov'd, more prais'd, more envy'd in his Doom,   45
Than CAESAR trampling on the Rights of Rome.
The Virtuous Nothing fear, but Life with Shame,
And Death's a pleasant Road that leads to Fame.
      On Bones, and Scraps of Dogs, let me be fed,
My Limbs uncover'd and expos'd my Head   50
To bleakest Colds, a Kennel be my Bed.
This, and all other Martyrdom for thee,
Seems glorious, all, thrice beauteous Honesty!
Judge me, ye Pow'rs! let FORTUNE tempt or frown,
I stand prepar'd, my Honour is my own.   55
      Ye great Disturbers, who in endless Noise,
In Blood and Rapine seek unnatural Joys;
For what is all this Bustle, but to shun
Those Thoughts with which you dare not be alone?
As Men in Misery, opprest with Care,   60
Seek in the Rage of Wine to drown Despair.
Let others fight, and eat their Bread in Blood,
Regardless if the Cause be bad or good;
Or cringe in Courts, depending on the Nods
Of strutting Pigmies who would pass for Gods.   65
For me, unpractis'd in the Courtiers School,
Who loathe a Knave, and tremble at a Fool;
Who honour generous WYCHERLEY opprest,
Possest of little, worthy of the best,
Rich in himself, in Virtue, that outshines   70
All but the fame of his immortal Lines,
More than the wealthiest Lord, who helps to drain
The famish'd Land, and rouls in impious Gain;
What can I hope in Courts? Or how succeed?

Tygers and Wolves shall in the Ocean breed,   75
The Whale and Dolphin fatten on the Mead;
And every Element exchange its Kind,
Ere thriving Honesty in Courts we find.
   Happy the Man, of Mortals happiest He,
Whose quiet Mind from vain Desires is free;   80
Whom neither Hopes deceive, nor Fears torment,
But lives at Peace, within himself content,
In Thought, or Act, accountable to none,
But to himself, and to the Gods alone:
O Sweetness of Content! Seraphick Joy!   85
Which nothing wants and nothing can destroy.
   Where dwells this Peace, this Freedom of the Mind?
Where, but in Shades remote from Human kind;
In flowery Vales, where Nymphs and Shepherds meet,
But never comes within the Palace Gate.   90
Farewell then Cities, Courts, and Camps, farewell,
Welcome, ye Groves, here let me ever dwell,
From Cares, from Business, and Mankind remove,
All but the MUSES, and inspiring LOVE:
How sweet the Morn! How gentle is the Night!   95
How calm the Evening! And the Day how bright!
   FROM hence, as from a Hill, I view below
The crowded World, a mighty Wood in show,
Where several Wanderers travel Day and Night,
By different Paths, and none are in the Right.   100

TO MIRA

NATURE, indulgent, provident and kind,
In all things that excel, some Use design'd;
The radiant Sun, of every heavenly Light
The first, (did MIRA not dispute that Right)
Sends from above ten thousand Blessings down;   5
Nor is he set so high for Show alone,
His Beams reviving with auspicious Fire,
Freely we all enjoy what all admire:
The Moon and Stars, those faithful Guides of Night,
Are plac'd to help, not entertain the Sight: 10
Plants, Fruits, and Flow'rs the fertile Fields produce,

Not for vain Ornament, but wholesome Use;
Health they restore, and Nourishment they give,
We see with Pleasure, but we taste to live.
   Then think not, MIRA, that thy Form was meant   15
More to create Desire, than to content;
Would the just Gods so many Charms provide
Only to gratify a Mortal's Pride?
Would they have form'd thee so above thy Sex,
Only to play the Tyrant, and to vex?   20
'Tis impious Pleasure to delight in Harm,
And Beauty should be kind, as well as charm.

TO THE COUNTESS OF NEWBOURG, INSISTING EARNESTLY TO BE TOLD WHO I MEANT BY MIRA

With MIRA's Charms, and my extreme Despair,
Long had my Muse amaz'd the Reader's Ear,
My Friends, with pity, heard the mournful Sound,
And all enquir'd from whence the fatal Wound;
Th' astonish'd World beheld an endless Flame,   5
Ne'er to be quench'd, unknowing whence it came:
So scatter'd Fire from scorch'd VESUVIUS flies,
Unknown the Source from whence those Flames arise:
ÆGYPTIAN NILE so spreads its Waters round,
O'erflowing far and near, its Head unfound.   10
   MIRA herself, touch'd with the moving Song,
Would needs be told to whom those Plaints belong;
My timorous Tongue, not daring to confess,
Trembling to name, would fain have had her guess;
Impatient of Excuse, she urges still,   15
Persists in her Demand, she must, she will;
If silent, I am threaten'd with her Hate;
If I obey — Ah! what may be my Fate?
Uncertain to conceal, or to unfold;
She smiles — the Goddess smiles — and I grow bold.   20
My vows to MIRA, all were meant to thee,
The Praise, the Love, the matchless Constancy.
'Twas thus of old, when all th' immortal Dames
Were grac'd by Poets, each with several Names;

For VENUS, CYTHEREA was invok'd;   25
Altars for PALLAS, to TRITONIA smok'd.
Such names were theirs; and thou the most divine,
Most lov'd of heav'nly Beauties — MIRA's thine.

ESSAY UPON UNNATURAL
FLIGHTS IN POETRY

As when some Image of a charming Face
In living Paint, an Artist tries to trace,
He carefully consults each beauteous Line,
Adjusting to his Object, his Design,
We praise the Piece, and give the Painter Fame,   5
But as the just Resemblance speaks the Dame.
Poets are Limners of another kind,
To copy out Ideas in the Mind;
Words are the Paint by which their Thoughts are shown,
And Nature sits, the Object to be drawn;   10
The written Picture we applaud, or blame,
But as the due Proportions are the same.
    Who driven with ungovernable Fire,
Or void of Art, beyond these Bounds aspire,
Gigantick Forms, and monstrous Births alone   15
Produce, which Nature, shockt disdains to own.
By true Reflexion I would see my Face,
Why brings the Fool a Magnifying-Glass?
    "But Poetry in Fiction takes delight,
    "And mounting in bold Figures out of sight,   20
    "Leaves Truth behind, in her audacious Flight:
    "Fables and Metaphors, that always lye,
    "And rash Hyperboles that soar so high,
    "And every Ornament of Verse must die.
Mistake me not: No Figures I exclude,   25
And but forbid Intemperance, not Food.
Who would with care some happy Fiction frame,
So mimicks Truth, it looks the very same;
Not rais'd to force, or feign'd in Nature's Scorn,
But meant to grace, illustrate, and adorn.   30
Important Truths still let your Fables hold,
And moral Mysteries with Art unfold.

Ladies and Beaux to please, is all the Task,
But the sharp Critik will Instruction ask.
   As Veils transparent cover, but not hide,   35
Such Metaphors appear when right apply'd;
When thro' the Phrase we plainly see the Sense,
Truth, where the Meaning's obvious, will dispense;
The Reader what in Reason's due, believes,
Nor can we call that false, which not deceives.   40

.   .   .   .

Our King return'd, and banish'd Peace restor'd,
The Muse ran mad to see her exil'd Lord;
On the crack'd Stage the Bedlam Heroes roar'd,
And scarce could speak one reasonable Word;   100
DRYDEN himself, to please a frantick Age,
Was forc'd to let his Judgment stoop to Rage,
To a wild Audience he conform'd his Voice,
Comply'd to Custom, but not err'd by Choice:
Deem then the People's, not the Writer's Sin,   105
ALMANSOR's Rage, and Rants of MAXIMIN;
That Fury spent in each elaborate Piece,
He vies for Fame with ancient ROME, and GREECE.
   First MULGRAVE rose, ROSCOMMON next, like Light,
To clear our Darkness, and to guide our Flight;   110
With steady Judgment, and in lofty Sounds,
They gave us Patterns, and they set us Bounds;
The STAGIRITE and HORACE laid aside,
Inform'd by them, we need no foreign Guide:
Who seek from Poetry a lasting Name,   115
May in their Lessons learn the Road to Fame;
But let the bold Adventurer be sure
That every Line the Test of Truth endure;
On this Foundation may the Fabrick rise,
Firm and unshaken, till it touch the Skies.   120
   From Pulpits banish'd, from the Court, from Love,
Forsaken Truth seeks Shelter in the Grove;
Cherish, ye Muses! the neglected Fair,
And take into your Train th' abandon'd Wanderer.

XXXVI

JONATHAN SWIFT
(1667-1745)

In his couplet writing, as in much of his work, Swift wished to reduce, to humble, to deflate the objects of his satiric address. We can see this intention in his figures of speech. He likened critics, in his address "To Mr. Congreve," not merely to city butterflies but to country worms, and he compared them, again, to mushrooms — although unfavorably. He reduced great ministers, in "To Mr. Gay," to stewards, false stewards, and to cooks who are either impossibly careless or disgustingly greedy. The Trojans and Greeks, whom he alluded to by way of giving a mock-heroic description of the boxed-in beau ("Shower," ll. 43–52),[1] are themselves reduced at the very moment of their introduction to "Troy Chair-men" and "Bully *Greeks*." Notice that the Trojans are also degraded in syntax — reduced to the adjectival condition.

Swift's metrical practices fit this design of reducing everything to that most meager and absurd condition — that is, of course, its true nature — which is evident in these figures of speech. In this couplet from "Description of a City Shower," for example, "Here various Kinds by various Fortune led, / Commence Acquaintance underneath a Shed," the last half-line, a modification of the Dryden whiplash, undoes the heroic ring of the first line and the elegant geniality of the first half of the second, leaving us with the sense of mankind's absurd dependence. Or consider the couplet following: "Triumphant Tories, and desponding Whigs, / Forget their Feuds, and join to save their wigs." Again, a heroic first line is exploded in the second, this time by a balance which reduces the statesmen's grounds of agreement and disagreement to feuds and wigs. The shower itself, although it is enough to reveal the smallness and helplessness of mankind, is submitted to the same kind of treatment. The

---

[1] My line references correspond to the line notations in *The Poems of Jonathan Swift*, ed. Harold Williams (Oxford, 1958), 3 vols.

noble antiquity of "sable cloud" and "Welkin," which concludes the first couplet of its introduction, is overturned in the next one, in which the cloud is likened in a neat parenthesis to a drunkard and the shower, by obvious extension, to vomit (ll. 13–16). The beginning of the shower is likened to a mop but — again with a whiplash modification — to a dirty one (ll. 19–20). The reduction of the shower to its proper size with such figures and such metrical emphases naturally strengthens Swift's degradation of man.

In "Toland's Invitation," we find the same metrical practices: there is, for instance, the whiplash by which Toland equates the soul's enlivenment to drunkenness (ll. 17–18) and the line obliquely balancing honesty and stink (l. 38). Likewise in "The Author," Swift reveals the shallowness of his critics in the line, "Nor shew'd the Parson in his Gait or Face." The balance of "Parson" by "Gait or Face" suggests the nature and validity of their judgments.

Swift also reduced the couplet itself, turning it into a flat, talky, completely unelevated medium of communication: "In every Mouth the question most in Vogue / Was; *When will* THEY *turn out this odious Rogue?*" Swift sometimes lowered the couplet's symmetry and power, moreover, with expletives ("Congreve," ll. 95–96; "Author," ll. 9–10) and, more often, with flatly oblique couplets ("Congreve," ll. 103–4; "Shower," ll. 3–4; 45–46). Take this couplet, for instance, about the girl shaking out her dirty mop: "You fly, invoke the Gods; then turning, stop / To rail; she singing, still whirls on her mop." Its obliqueness, first of all, puts tremendous emphasis on the undignified action, "To rail." The whole couplet, moreover, is shapelessly fragmentary; railing is only one of the five actions "You" perform — clearly more than can be defined by the couplet's formal pauses, and the two actions of "she" are, in consequence of so much business by "You," inadequately defined in the part of a line they are confined to. Such flooding of the couplet, by which its proper bounds are abused and its aesthetic dignity ignored, is characteristic of Swift ("Toland," ll. 33–36; "Author," ll. 21–22). In the triplet which concludes "A Description," to further exemplify it, Swift spreads out eight separate items:

> Sweepings from Butcher's Stall, Dung, Guts, and Blood,
> Drown'd Puppies, stinking Sprats, all drench'd in Mud,
> Dead Cats, and Turnip-Tops come tumbling down the Flood.

Mid-line pause may be seen in the first line to define the general "Sweepings" from three particularizations, but the two items in the second line, since both are stuffed into one half of the line, enjoy no such metrical definition, and neither do the two items in the third. The series is, of course, vividly clear, both in its muddy embellishment and in its tumbling action, but its members have been carefully deprived of the emphasis, the exaltation, which series of all kinds had enjoyed in couplet verse since the time of Sandys.

Dryden and Pope gave a splendor to the objects of their satire — to Achitophel and Sporus, say — even as they attacked them. More important still, with the symmetry, the dynamics, and the grandeur of their verse, they always conveyed their own brilliance, their own intelligence and power. But Swift, who explicitly included himself ("The Author") and his efforts ("Congreve," ll. 93–94) in his satiric focus, spares nothing. In reducing both the objects of his satiric attention and his satiric medium itself — that medium which asserts and, indeed, symbolizes the comprehension and the detachment of such satirists as Dryden and Pope — Swift has composed several compelling degradations of human actions and the human intelligence.

XXXVII

🦋🦋🦋🦋🦋🦋🦋🦋🦋🦋🦋🦋🦋🦋

JOSEPH ADDISON
(1672-1719)

The press of an audience that Addison felt and tried to convey in his "Prologue to *The Drummer*" forced him to modify his natural impulse toward neatness. Indeed, the variety of the couplets in the passage by which he reconciled the ladies to the play's ghost (ll. 29–38) [1] and its multicouplet coherence remind us of Dryden's prologues. But the passage just above this one is more regular, more normally Addisonian. We find one couplet in it given to the censure of this play in general followed by three more, each of which defines one particular kind of censure (ll. 17–24). This passage is an example of the "correct," the "polite," form of couplet practice which Addison helped to establish.

Even his complimentary address to Dryden, that master of an earlier practice, is an example of the new correctness. One notices many verse-defined parallels in this poem — of lines (ll. 9–10, 13–14, 19–20, 21–22) and half-lines (ll. 2, 4, 16, 18, 30, 32, 33). The half-line parallels, moreover, commonly fill the second, the metrically climactic, lines so that one finds himself drawn from one complimentary resolution to the next. There are, significantly, almost no antitheses in this poem whose aim is not judgment but applause. It is, of course, neat and polished throughout, as effective compliment must be. Take, for example, Addison's handling of the Latin poets whose work Dryden had translated (ll. 9–10): one couplet describes them in general; then Vergil and Horace are given one line each and Persius and Juvenal one couplet each; then follows one couplet of summary. No couplet in this passage is enjambed, and no first line overflows except for the one in the Persius couplet.

This passage, which details Dryden's accomplishments, is concluded with a two-couplet system (ll. 23–26) which shows significant move-

---

[1] My line references correspond to the line notations in *The Miscellaneous Works of Joseph Addison*, ed. A. C. Guthkelch (London, 1914), I.

ment; the "how" clause, which makes up its second couplet, parallels the second line of the first couplet and is governed by the first couplet's verb; moreover, the second half of the second couplet's first line and the first half of its second line, which contain parallel adjective phrases, suspend its predicate. However, its modest dynamics, which is resolved in its fourth line, a mechanically balanced alexandrine, serves merely to bring this central part of the poem to a resounding close. The rest of the poem is quite narrowly confined.

The subject matter of the "Letter from Italy," which gave Addison a topic he could praise and blame with insouciance and suggested a natural opposition, that between Italy and his own land, by which the poet could illuminate his judgments, allowed him to employ his neat, polished style with more telling effect. Indeed, his sharp contrast between Italy's bounty and the misery of her people (ll. 113–18) and his more flowing relinquishment of this enslaved land's riches (ll. 131–40) can bear comparison with similar passages in the youthful Pope's *Windsor Forest* (ll. 51–60, 29–36).

"To the King" and *The Campaign*, in which Addison tried to strike a heroic note with his polite couplets, are neat in formulation but crude in effect. The elegance of "Their Swords they brandish and require the Fight" (l. 66) depends on our mistaking a real battle for a martial parade. The line "The Cries of Orphans, and the Widow's Tears" (l. 86), unfortunately, cannot be so mistaken. Its cold-blooded neatness hardly ennobles the warfare which, no doubt, begot these cries and tears. Even if one ignores the widows and orphans, he will find the heroic compliment in such lines as "They break through all, for *William* leads the way" or "And nations bless the Labours of his sword" unconvincing and, indeed, inane. This Addisonian heroic, this attempt to describe warfare with the forms of social compliment, was the right vehicle, as Pope understood, for describing a polite game of cards. The reduction of war's horrors to a social activity is frightful, but the elevation of a social activity to war's glory can be amusing and instructive. One may compare in this connection lines 149–54 of *The Campaign* with the game of Ombre in Pope's *Rape of the Lock* (III, 75–86).

XXXVIII

AMBROSE PHILIPS
(1675-1749)

EPISTLE TO THE EARL OF DORSET

From frozen climes, and endless tracts of snow,
From streams which northern winds forbid to flow,
What present shall the muse to *Dorset* bring,
Or how, so near the pole, attempt to sing?
The hoary winter here conceals from sight   5
All pleasing objects which to verse invite.
The hills and dales, and the delightful woods,
The flow'ry plains, and silver-streaming floods,
By snow disguis'd, in bright confusion ly,
And with one dazzling waste fatigue the eye.   10
    No gentle breathing breez prepares the spring,
No birds within the desert region sing.
The ships, unmov'd, the boist'rous winds defy,
While rattling chariots o'er the ocean fly.
The vast *Leviathan* wants room to play,   15
And spout his waters in the face of day.
The starving wolves along the main sea prowl,
And to the moon in icy valleys howl.
O'er many a shining league the level main
Here spreads itself into a glassy plain: 20
There solid billows of enormous size,
Alps of green ice, in wild disorder rise.
    And yet but lately have I seen, ev'n here,
The winter in a lovely dress appear.
'E're yet the clouds let fall the treasur'd snow,   25
Or winds begun through hazy skies to blow,

At ev'ning a keen eastern breez arose,
And the descending rain unsully'd froze.
Soon as the silent shades of night withdrew,
The ruddy morn disclos'd at once to view   30
The face of nature in a rich disguise,
And brighten'd ev'ry object to my eyes:
For ev'ry shrub, and ev'ry blade of grass,
And ev'ry pointed thorn, seem'd wrought in glass;
In pearls and rubies rich the hawthorns show,   35
While through the ice the crimson berries glow.
The thick-sprung reeds, which watry marshes yield,
Seem'd polish'd lances in a hostile field.
The stag in limpid currents, with surprise,
Sees crystal branches on his forehead rise: 40
The spreading oak, the beech, and tow'ring pine,
Glaz'd over, in the freezing aether shine.
The frighted birds the rattling branches shun,
Which wave and glitter in the distant sun.
    When if a sudden gust of wind arise,   45
The brittle forest into atoms flies,
The crackling wood beneath the tempest bends,
And in a spangled show'r the prospect ends:
Or, if a southern gale the region warm,
And by degrees unbind the wintry charm,   50
The traveller a miry country sees,
And journies sad beneath the dropping trees:
Like some deluded peasant, *Merlin* leads
Through fragrant bow'rs, and thro' delicious meads,
While here inchanted gardens to him rise,   55
And airy fabricks there attract his eyes,
His wandring feet the magick paths pursue,
And while he thinks the fair illusion true,
The trackless scenes disperse in fluid air,
And woods, and wilds, and thorny ways appear,   60
A tedious road the weary wretch returns,
And, as he goes, the transient vision mourns.

XXXIX

ᛉᛉᛉᛉᛉᛉᛉᛉᛉᛉᛉᛉᛉ

EDWARD YOUNG

(1683-1765)

There are many crudities in Young's couplet style. His syntax is often hazy, for one thing: in *Love of Fame*, VI, for instance, the antecedent of "Important" (l. 190), the reference of "He" (l. 516), and the governance of "lays" (l. 510) are all unclear. Young's rhetoric is often imperfect: in one case, for instance, he lumped absolutes and objects helter-skelter in a single series (ll. 211–15); in another, he paralleled an unaddressed remark with a sharply pointed one (ll. 221–22). His meter is sometimes bad: "And would draw on jack-boots, as soon as gloves." His verse also suffers many sudden shifts, especially sudden drops in tone: there is the baldly didactic couplet, for instance, that closes the sharply particularized portrait of the slovenly Alicea (ll. 224–25), and the flat "There are" which answers the purely rhetorical question about truly serious feminine faults (ll. 373–75). Young's irony, again, is sometimes obvious (l. 379) and sometimes unclear (ll. 503–4).

Of course, Young was a fallible, a minor, poet. But his crudities stem not only from this but from his effort to apply the political manner of Dryden to the social concerns and the social milieu of Pope. *Love of Fame*, by the way, was composed between the time of Pope's *Rape of the Lock* and his *Moral Essays*.

Young often employed the whiplash effect (ll. 276, 380, 390, 434, 492, 528), a device by which Dryden, following Cowley, had distinguished between sharply divided opinions in the body politic. "And never broke the sabbath," gives us the Whig, the Puritan, view of Corah; "but for gain" turns it into the Tory view. Such a sharp reversal of sentiment naturally offends against the decorum of social poetry, whose basic mode lies in defining particular deviations from generally held principles of conduct. The last line of this couplet, "Is there whom you detest, and seek his life? / Trust no soul with the secret — but his wife," defines not a deviation from the rule of loyalty which all ladies and gentlemen can accept; rather, it articulates an opinion, that all wives are false, over which these two great social groups must split. Here is a whiplash enunciation of the same kind of general opinion: "Men sigh in vain, for *none*, but for their *wives*." Dryden might well have hoped to unify the enfranchised gentlemen of England, who disagreed about king and commons, on such a point as this. But such an opinion, especially when it is given this dramatic kind of expression, will divide polite society into warring camps.

The whiplash line, "And what is still more dreadful — spoils your face," disturbs the social address of Young's poetry in rather a different way. Its first half is directed, as the whole passage (ll. 487–92) has been, at the world in general, but the second half focusses sharply on the ladies. The reversal is, then, not in sentiment but in the speaker's sense of his audience. This unsteady sense of audience plagues *Love of Fame* throughout. Dryden's audience was both too crude and too masculine for Young's explicitly embraced social concerns and social milieu. But Young continually oscillates between it and the smaller, partially feminine audience, that of the drawing room, which properly belongs to him. We have just noticed instances of Young's turning to a masculine audience and reminding this social segment of its antagonism to the other. One might also study, in this connection, the discussion of women's notion of the backward fall (ll. 249–80). It opens with the unqualified expression of masculine prejudice which excludes the ladies — except possibly as angry eavesdroppers — but shifts suddenly to an elegantly polite, if sardonic, conversation with Clio. This conversation runs on for some time. But at the end of it, the speaker turns away from Clio and discusses her and all women in the same high and mighty tone as that with which the passage opened. Indeed, the speaker's report of one more opinion of Clio, a report that is concluded with a whiplash explanation, is really quite unpleasant if one recalls the speaker's polite talk with Clio in the couplets immediately preceding. Young, like Waller, no doubt counted heavily on couplet closure to encapsulate the jarring elements of his poetry.

Young's handling of the couplet reflects this veering unsteadiness in his address. The conversation with Clio, which we have just mentioned in another connection, presents us with a series of very strongly closed couplets: in each one, Clio describes, first, a general excellence and, then, a particular flaw in one of her friends. And we have noticed the importance to Young's maintenance of anything like the tone of politeness of this series's being closed off from the immediately following comments of Young's primary speaker. Other passages, on the other hand, must be read in one great sweep of attention to carry their full weight of meaning. The description of female gambling (ll. 493–528), especially its last segment, furnishes us a case in point. This passage, many of whose details are badly smudged (see esp. ll. 495–504), may remind us of the Elizabethan satirists or draw us ahead to the early work of Charles Churchill. Unfortunately, like all of Young's verse, it lacks the great thrust of Churchill and even the rough impetus of Marston. The persistent closure and integrity of Young's individual couplets distracts the reader from the vast connections on which his sense of this poetry's larger unities depends. Even the suspensive paragraph on family ruin (ll. 517–28), whose meaning is only asserted in its last line, struggles along from one sharply closed couplet, and even from one closed line, to the next.

The description of Julia (ll. 179–90) reveals a similarly unlucky compromise between the sweeping movement of Dryden and the pointed definition of Pope. It describes a large this-but-that course, but the strong closure of every single couplet disjoints this large design and damages its total effect. One couplet in this passage, "For her own breakfast she'll *project a scheme*, / Nor *take* her *Tea* without a *stratagem*," furnishes an especially neat case of Young's falling between the two stools. This pair of items, breakfast and tea, completely misses Dryden's comprehensiveness — since a span between early and late eating is hardly the point here; on the other hand, neither of these items approaches the sharpness of a Popean example. Still, this couplet and much of Young's satire would seem like pretty sharp social satire if we lacked *The Rape of the Lock* and the *Moral Essays*.

LOVE OF FAME, SATIRE VI

Julia's a manager, she's born for rule,
And knows her *wiser* husband is a *fool*;   180
Assemblies holds, and spins the *subtle thread*
That guides the lover to his fair one's bed;
For difficult amours can smooth the way,
And tender letters *dictate*, or *convey*.
But if depriv'd of such important cares,   185
Her wisdom condescends to less affairs.

For her own breakfast she'll *project a scheme*,
Nor *take* her *Tea* without a *stratagem*;
Presides o'er *trifles* with a *serious* face,
Important by the virtue of *grimace*.   190

.   .   .   .

Go breakfast with *Alicea*, there you'll see
Simplex munditiis, to the last degree.   210
Unlac'd her stays, her night-gown is unty'd,
And what she has of head-dress is aside.
She drawls her words, and waddles in her pace;
Unwash't her hands, and much besnuff'd her face.
A nail uncut, and head uncomb'd she loves;   215
And would draw on jack-boots, as soon as gloves.
Gloves by queen *Bess*'s maidens might be mist,
Her blessed eyes ne'er saw a female *fist*.
Lovers beware! to wound how can she fail
With scarlet finger, and long jetty nail?   220
For *Hervey* the first *wit* she cannot be,
Nor cruel *Richard* the first *toast* for thee;
Since full each other station of *renown*,
Who would not be the greatest *Trapes* in town?
Women were made to give our eyes delight,   225
A *female sloven* is an odious sight.

.   .   .   .

Ladies there are who think *one* crime is *all*;
Can women then, no way but *backward* fall?   250
So sweet is *that one* crime they don't pursue,
To pay its loss, they think all others *few*.
Who hold that crime so dear, must never claim
Of *injur'd modesty* the sacred name.
  But *Clio* thus. "What, railing without end?   255
"Mean task! how much more generous to commend?"
Yes, to commend as you are wont to do,
My kind *instructor*, and *example* too.
  "*Daphnis*, says *Clio*, has a charming eye:
"What pity 'tis her shoulder is awry?   260
"*Aspasia*'s shape indeed — but then her air —
"The man has parts who finds destruction, there.
"*Almeria*'s wit has something that's divine;
"And wit's enough — how few in all things shine?

"*Selina* serves her friends, relieves the poor —   265
"Who was it said *Selina*'s near threescore?
"At *Lucia*'s match I from my soul rejoice,
"The world congratulates so wise a choice;
"His lordship's rent-roll is exceeding great —
"But mortgages will sap the best estate.   270
"In *Sherley*'s form might cherubims appear,
"But then — she has a *freckle* on her *ear*."
Without a *but*, *Hortensia* she commends,
The first of women, and the best of friends;
Owns her in person, wit, fame, virtue bright;   275
But how comes this to pass? — she dy'd last night.
     Thus nymphs commend, who yet at Satire rail;
Indeed *that*'s needless, if *such* praise prevail;
And whence such praise? our virulence is thrown
On *others* fame, thro' fondness for our *own*.   280

.   .   .   .

O *Juvenal*! for thy severer rage!
To lash the ranker follies of our age.
Are there among the females of our isle
Such faults, at which it is a fault to *smile*?
There are. Vice, once by *modest nature* chain'd,   375
And *legal ties*, expatiates unrestrain'd,
Without thin *decency* held up to view,
Naked she stalks o'er *law*, and *gospel* too.
Our matrons lead such exemplary lives,
Men sigh in vain, for *none*, but for their *wives*;   380
Who *marry* to be *free*, to range the more,
And wed one man, to wanton with a score.
Abroad too kind, at home 'tis stedfast hate,
And one eternal tempest of debate.
What foul eruptions from a look most meek?   385
What thunders bursting from a dimpled cheek?
Their *passions* bear it with a lofty hand;
But then, their *reason* is at due command.
Is there whom you detest, and seek his life?
Trust no soul with the secret — but his wife.   390
Wives wonder that their conduct I condemn.
And ask, what kindred is a *spouse* to them?

.   .   .   .

Atheists are few; most nymphs a godhead own,
And nothing but his *attributes* dethrone.
From Atheists far, they stedfastly believe
God is, and is almighty — to *forgive.*
His other excellence they'll not dispute;   435
But *mercy,* sure, is his chief attribute.
Shall pleasures of a short duration chain
A *lady*'s soul in everlasting pain?
Will the great author us poor worms destroy,
For now and then a *sip* of transient joy?   440
No, he's for ever in a smiling mood,
He's like themselves; or how cou'd he be good?
And they blaspheme who blacker schemes suppose —
Devoutly, thus, *Jehovah* they depose
The *pure*! the *Just*! and set up in his stead   445
A Deity, that's perfectly *well bred.*

.   .   .   .

The love of gaming is the worst of ills,
With ceaseless storms the blacken'd soul it fills,
Inveighs at heav'n, neglects the ties of blood,
Destroys the pow'r, and will of doing good,   490
Kills health, pawns honour, plunges in disgrace,
And what is still more dreadful — spoils your face.
   See yonder set of thieves that live on spoil,
The *scandal,* and *the ruin* of our isle!
And, see, (strange sight!) amid that ruffian band,   495
A form divine high wave her snowy hand;
That rattles loud a small enchanted box,
Which loud as thunder on the board she knocks.
And as fierce storms, which earths foundation shook,
From *Æolus*'s cave impetuous broke,   500
From this small cavern a mixt tempest flies,
Fear, rage, convulsion, tears, oaths, blasphemies!
For men, I mean, the Fair discharges none;
She (guiltless creature!) swears to heav'n alone.
   See her eyes start! cheeks glow! and muscles swell!   505
Like the mad maid in the *Cumean* cell.
Thus that divine one her *soft* nights employs!
Thus tunes her soul to tender nuptial joys!
And when the cruel morning calls to bed,

And on her pillow lays her aking head,   510
With the dire images her dreams are crown'd.
The *die* spins lovely, or the *cards* go round:
Imaginary ruin charms her still,
Her happy lord is cuckol'd by *Spadil*:
And if she's brought to bed, 'tis ten to one,   515
He marks the forehead of her *darling* son.
    O scene of horror, and of wild despair!
Why is the rich *Atrides*' splendid heir
Constrain'd to quit his ancient lordly seat,
And hide his glories in a mean retreat?   520
Why that drawn sword? and whence that dismal cry?
Why pale distraction thro' the family?
See my lord threatens, and my lady weep,
And trembling servants from the tempest creep.
Why that gay *son* to distant regions sent?   525
What fiends that *daughter*'s destin'd match prevent?
Why the whole house in sudden ruin laid?
O nothing but last night — my Lady play'd.

.   .   .   .

XL

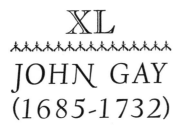

JOHN GAY
(1685-1732)

The short-windedness of Waller's couplet practice, a short-windedness obviously prompted by the nature of the couplet, presented an aesthetic challenge to Pope, a challenge to which he responded throughout his career. But this short-windedness presented John Gay, rather, with an opportunity to define the stops and starts of his own various but short-winded curiosity. Gay was not like Pope but, rather, like Pope's Belinda: his sprightly intelligence, quick and unfixed, could sympathize with the fisherman and with the fish, with the chimney sweep and the man whose coat he daubs, with the thief and with his victim. The couplet, with its many points of definitive closure, provided him with the perfect literary means to punctuate and clarify such mercurial sympathies as these.[1]

The opening lines of *The Fan* are typical of Gay's couplet practice and of his literary effect. We have here, after one couplet introduces "that graceful toy," which is the poet's avowed topic, a comical slippage of concentration. Not in the second or third couplets, however. Each of these defines a type of fan which he will *not* take up in this poem. The strictness with which each is subordinated to "that graceful toy" and paralleled to one another — "Not . . . / Which . . . / / Nor . . . / Which . . ." — projects the impression of perfect control. The third item in this series of ineligible fans, however, the wide-spreading fan of Indostan, leads the poet out of his path on a five-couplet digression. We note, first of all, that this item has its own governing subject, not the

---

[1] Dr. Johnson described *Trivia*, which he recognized to be the happiest and most characteristic example of Gay's style, as "sprightly, various and pleasant," in "John Gay," in *Lives of the Poets*, in *Works* (Troy, N. Y., 1903), IX, 309. Wallace Cable Brown, similarly, describes Gay as the "Mr. Spectator of his time," and acknowledges his "mixture of wit, satire and sympathy," in "Gay's Mastery of the Heroic Couplet," *PMLA*, LXI (1946), 121–25.

poet but the poet's muse; second, that this wide-spreading fan, as things develop, is not even the direct object of the muse's action but only one detail in a luxurious scene; and, finally, that Gay has been led into a description of this scene, the spicy Asian grove, by the very fact of denying that he would be led there. In handling the next item in this series, the palmetto fan, Gay wanders even farther afield, this time on an eight-couplet digression. The scene in which this fan appears, namely, Bermuda, is the subject of the sentence by which he proclaims its indifference to him, and the "muse," who governed the preceding digression, is reduced to the direct object in this one and thus totally sacrificed as a governing influence. For two couplets Gay insists on his unconcern with this seductive scene — not even mentioning the type of fan one might find there; and then in the third couplet, "Yet let me in some od'rous shade repose, / Whilst in my verse the fair *Palmetto* grows," he abandons himself to it. Then follow five leisurely couplets on Bermuda's production of the palmetto fan. Couplet form and closure have allowed Gay to define the steps of his "wand'ring Muse" in this passage and thus to maintain lucidity of detail while engaging in a generally chaotic digression — a digression whose effect is the trivialization of his avowed topic. The lucidity of these details which obstruct it, indeed, augment its comical degradation. Unfortunately for the total poetic effect of this passage, "that graceful toy" was already quite trivial enough before Gay subjected it to his art. One might compare the tact and balance with which Pope preserved the dignity of another item of trivia in the opening lines of *The Rape of the Lock* with Gay's practice here.

Gay's readiness to shift his gaze is also apparent in our selection from *Rural Sports* in which one can discover the poet turning rapidly back and forth between the fisherman and the fish. His shifts are so abrupt, indeed, that the full power of the couplet stop is required to keep the pronominal references clear — especially at line 247. The charm of this passage comes from this shiftiness of the poet's sympathy to whose rapidity only the couplet could give a lucid utterance. There is a similar shifting of attitude in the lament for Blouzelinda in "Friday" of *The Shepherd's Week*: the speaker comes to forget about his beloved's being dead, as it were, in the course of describing her habits when she was alive. This tragicomic diversion of sentiment is especially evident in lines 55–62. Here the speaker becomes so absorbed in describing the happy past that he slips briefly into the present tense: "Sometimes, like wax, she rolls the butter round, / Or with the wooden lilly prints the pound." We find another large-scale example of this shift and slide in Gay's poetic address — a shift by which he has often counterpoised contradictory feelings or actions — in the "Epistle to Pulteney." In this poem, Gay has introduced the style he has chosen as proper for describing the follies of Paris by giving a five-couplet example of the style he is rejecting as improper (ll. 31–42).

In *Trivia* Gay's couplet projection of his ready but giddy curiosity found its happiest employment. The giddiness of the London scene, the shifting round of its trivial interests and dangers, was perfect grist for his poetic mill. One notices, for example, the poem's oscillations between imperative and indicative moods, most of them defined by couplets, in the discussion of the dirty and sullying trades (II, 25–44). This shifting of mood marks a shifting of the speaker's concern between warnings and descriptions, between an interest in the walker as a possible victim of London's current of people and an interest in the current.

There is a more complex set of shiftings in Gay's extensive treatment of pickpockets (III, 51–86). Its first couplets jump back and forth between walkers and thieves much like the passage above on the sullying trades. But at line 63, with the introduction of a third party, the honest tradesman who spies the pickpocket at his work, the passage quickens. In this and the next three lines, by using line rather than couplet definition, Gay describes the tradesman (one line), the thief (two noncouplet lines), and the group of victims (one line) — achieving an almost Chaucerian flavor. In the first couplet following, the fleeing thief is likened to a fox; in the second, without the poet's asserting an analogy between the chase of the fox and the chase of the thief, he gives himself to the fox chase. Gay has been lured into giving his full attention to this rural scene much as he was lured into the spicy grove and into an obliviousness to Blouzelinda's death in earlier poems. He jumps back to the thief in the next couplet, however, and follows the thief's apprehension and punishment through the next two couplets. Even these couplets reveal Gay's variety of address, however; the first of them — all but the first half of its first line, anyway — addresses the thief with great compassion (and just a touch of epic grandeur); the last two describe his mundane punishment with perfect detachment.

The aesthetic rule which allowed Gay to achieve such effects as these was, quite simply, that he should maintain the syntactic integrity and the sharp closure of his individual couplets. He commonly maintained the integrity of his separate couplets even in those multicouplet passages which were connected by their substance. Each of the five couplets on the confederacy between pickpockets and ballad singers (*Trivia*, III,

77–86), for instance, is a separate, sharply closed syntactic unit: there is both a change in verb mood and one in the focus of attention between the second and the third of these, and a sharp change in the tone between the fourth and fifth. A two-couplet passage on one of the lewd French ladies, again, is simply a pair of sharply separated couplets ("Pulteney," ll. 163–66), and so is another such passage on another such lady a bit farther on (ll. 173–76). The example of the plain style in the same poem is composed, again, of five sharply individuated couplet units (ll. 31–40). The five couplets on the Asian grove in *The Fan* (I, 7–16) are somewhat more unified, making up, as they do, only two syntactically independent statements, but this passage suffers a complete break after its third couplet. There is no couplet in it, moreover, that requires an enjambed reading to complete its sense: a "Where" couplet, a "While" couplet, and a "But" couplet are simply snapped on to utterances that would have been complete without them.

There are almost no tightly woven passages of verse — such as one finds more and more brilliantly composed in the later poetry of Pope — in Gay's couplet production. A mere two-couplet system, such as the one which is yoked by the division of the verb "shall . . . Refuse" ("Pulteney," ll. 11–14), is rather unusual. Even so lightly enjambed a couplet system as the 'When // Then' pair is rare in Gay ("Friday," ll. 69–72; *Trivia* III, 9–12); and such combined couplets come most often at those atypical parts of poems, their openings (*Sports* I, 1–4, 5–8; *Trivia*, I, 1–6). Otherwise, Gay proceeded from one sharply individuated couplet to the next, enjoying in this way a wonderful freedom of mobility. The most engaging of his poems, *Trivia*, is that one in which he made the most extensive use of this freedom.

The incidental irregularities in Gay's metric, primarily the sharp breaks he sometimes makes at the ends of first lines and at mid-lines, augment the impression of his poetic shiftiness. Sometimes we find breaks at first lines which are roughly equal in weight to the breaks at adjoining couplet ends (*Sports*, I, 239; "Friday," l. 79). In the "Epistle to Pulteney," especially, one finds patches of this line by closed-line movement of verse (ll. 61–64, 167–70, 179–84). There are also a few cases of the line break's being heavier than that at the close of the adjoining couplet (*Sports*, I, 238; *Trivia*, III, 53). With one of these extra-heavy line divisions (*Trivia*, III, 63), Gay has wonderfully suggested the excitement, the sudden wrench in his attention, caused by the flight of the pickpocket. The heavy mid-line pause, sometimes following a couplet enjambment, is almost exclusively confined to *Trivia* (I, 5; II, 27,

41, 61; III, 11, 57, 71, 283). Its use heightens the impression, which Gay wished to give, that the current of London life requires sudden shifts and adjustments of attention.

Although Gay was Pope's exact contemporary and died first, he used the couplet, like the form's later masters, as an assertive rather than a conversational device. Gay's poems are, of course, colloquial and often ingratiating, but none of them, not even the epistles, creates a precise or responsive audience — as Pope's poetry came more and more forcefully to do. Gay addressed a quite generally conceived audience on whose polite forbearance, on whose comfortable diffidence, indeed, he depended for his hearing. The persistent triviality of his subject matter perfectly suits such an attitude. Pope took up more and more socially controversial issues as his career advanced, and his poetry, correspondingly, describes a more and more profoundly drawn social controversy, finally reaching the virtual breakdown of communication between Pope's speaker and society in *Epilogue to the Satires*. But Gay took topics toward which he could expect society to be, if not always indifferent, at least always detached. Thus the persistent colloquial style of his poems, on the one hand, and their almost perfect unconcern for society's responses, on the other, do not produce an incoherency — although this condition does, of course, produce minor poetic utterance. Gay's careful selection of topics which would suggest no social division and little social response allowed him to use the closed couplet as he wished, that is, to express his own giddy but vivid sensitivity to various passing parades. In his less good poems, like *The Fan*, his giddiness seems arbitrary and self-willed — merely a hobbyhorsical predilection of his own; in his best poem, *Trivia*, it seems to be the necessary and unavoidable reflection of his material, of the shifting and variously interesting current of city life.

RURAL SPORTS, I

When a brisk gale against the current blows,
And all the watry plain in wrinkles flows,
Then let the fisherman his art repeat,
Where bubbling eddys favour the deceit.
If an enormous salmon chance to spy   225
The wanton errours of the floating fly,
He lifts his silver gills above the flood,
And greedily sucks in th' unfaithful food;

Then downward plunges with the fraudful prey,
And bears with joy the little spoil away.   230
Soon in smart pain he feels the dire mistake,
Lashes the wave, and beats the foamy lake,
With sudden rage he now aloft appears,
And in his eye convulsive anguish bears;
And now again, impatient of the wound,   235
He rolls and wreaths his shining body round;
Then headlong shoots beneath the dashing tide,
The trembling fins the boiling wave divide;
Now hope exalts the fisher's beating heart,
Now he turns pale, and fears his dubious art;   240
He views the tumbling Fish with longing eyes,
While the line stretches with th' unwieldy prize;
Each motion humours with his steady hands,
And one slight hair the mighty bulk commands;
Till tir'd at last, despoiled of all his strength,   245
The game athwart the stream unfolds his length.
He now, with pleasure, views the gasping prize
Gnash his sharp teeth, and roll his blood-shot eyes;
Then draws him to the shore, with artful care,
And lifts his nostrils in the sick'ning air: 250
Upon the burthen'd stream he floating lies,
Stretches his quivering fins, and gasping dies.

.   .   .   .

THE FAN, I

I sing that graceful toy, whose waving play
With gentle gales relieves the sultry day.
Not the wide fan by *Persian* dames display'd,
Which o'er their beauty casts a grateful shade;
Nor that long known in *China*'s artful land,   5
Which, while it cools the face, fatigues the hand:
Nor shall the muse in *Asian* climates rove,
To seek in *Indostan* some spicy grove,
Where stretch'd at ease the panting lady lies,
To shun the fervor of meridian skies,   10
While sweating slaves catch ev'ry breeze of air,
And with wide-spreading fans refresh the fair;

No busie gnats her pleasing dreams molest,
Inflame her cheek, or ravage o'er her breast,
But artifical Zephyrs round her fly,   15
And mitigate the feaver of the sky.
 Nor shall *Bermudas* long the Muse detain,
Whose fragrant forests bloom in *Waller*'s strain,
Where breathing sweets from ev'ry field ascend,
And the wild woods with golden apples bend;   20
Yet let me in some od'rous shade repose,
Whilst in my verse the fair *Palmetto* grows:
Like the tall pine it shoots its stately head,
From the broad top depending branches spread;
No knotty limbs the taper body bears,   25
Hung on each bough a single leaf appears,
Which shrivell'd in its infancy remains,
Like a clos'd fan, nor stretches wide its veins,
But as the seasons in their circle run,
Opes its ribb'd surface to the nearer sun: 30
Beneath this shade the weary peasant lies,
Plucks the broad leaf, and bids the breezes rise.
 Stay, wand'ring Muse, nor rove in foreign climes;
To thy own native shore confine thy rhimes.
Assist, ye Nine, your loftiest notes employ,   35
Say what celestial skill contriv'd the toy;
Say how this instrument of love began,
And in immortal strains display the fan.

. . . .

THE SHEPHERD'S WEEK, FRIDAY

Is *Blouzelinda* dead? farewel my glee!
No happiness is now reserv'd for me.
As the wood pigeon cooes without his mate,
So shall my doleful dirge bewail her fate.   30
Of *Blouzelinda* fair I mean to tell,
The peerless maid that did all maids excel.
 Henceforth the morn shall dewy sorrow shed,
And ev'ning tears upon the grass be spread;
The rolling streams with watry grief shall flow,   35
And winds shall moan aloud — when loud they blow.

Henceforth, as oft as autumn shall return,
The drooping trees, whene'er it rains, shall mourn;
This season quite shall strip the country's pride,
For 'twas in autumn *Blouzelinda* dy'd.   40
    Where-e'er I gad, I *Blouzelind* shall view,
Woods, dairy, barn and mows our passion knew.
When I direct my eyes to yonder wood,
Fresh rising sorrow curdles in my blood.
Thither I've often been the damsel's guide,   45
When rotten sticks our fuel have supply'd;
There I remember how her faggots large,
Were frequently these happy shoulders charge.
Sometimes this crook drew hazel boughs adown,
And stuff'd her apron wide with nuts so brown;   50
Or when her feeding hogs had miss'd their way,
Or wallowing 'mid a feast of acorns lay;
Th' untoward creatures to the stye I drove,
And whistled all the way — or told my love.
    If by the dairy's hatch I chance to hie,   55
I shall her goodly countenance espie,
For there her goodly countenance I've seen,
Set off with kerchief starch'd and pinners clean.
Sometimes, like wax, she rolls the butter round,
Or with the wooden lilly prints the pound.   60
Whilome I've seen her skim the clouted cream,
And press from spungy curds the milky stream.
But now, alas! these ears shall hear no more
The whining swine surround the dairy door,
No more her care shall fill the hollow tray,   65
To fat the guzzling hogs with floods of whey.
Lament, ye swine, in gruntings spend your grief,
For you, like me, have lost your sole relief.
    When in the barn the sounding flail I ply,
Where from her sieve the chaff was wont to fly,   70
The poultry there will seem around to stand,
Waiting upon her charitable hand.
No succour meet the poultry now can find,
For they, like me, have lost their *Blouzelind*.
    Whenever by yon barley mow I pass,   75
Before my eyes will trip the tidy lass.

I pitch'd the sheaves (oh could I do so now)
Which she in rows pil'd on the growing mow.
There ev'ry deale my heart by love was gain'd,
There the sweet kiss my courtship has explain'd.   80
Ah! *Blouzelind*! that mow I ne'er shall see,
But thy memorial will revive in me.

    Lament, ye fields, and rueful symptoms show,
Henceforth let not the smelling primrose grow;
Let weeds instead of butter-flow'rs appear,
And meads, instead of daisies, hemlock bear;
For cowslips sweet let dandelions spread;
For *Blouzelinda*, blithsome maid, is dead!
Lament ye swains, and o'er her grave bemoan,
And spell ye right this verse upon her stone.   90
Here Blouzelinda *lyes — Alas, alas*!
Weep shepherds — and remember flesh is grass.

.   .   .   .

TRIVIA, I

Through winter streets to steer your course aright,
How to walk clean by day, and safe by night,
How jostling crouds, with prudence to decline,
When to assert the wall, and when resign,
I sing: Thou, *Trivia*, Goddess, aid my song,   5
Thro' spacious streets conduct thy bard along;
By thee transported, I securely stray
Where winding alleys lead the doubtful way,
The silent court, and op'ning square explore,
And long perplexing lanes untrod before.   10
To pave thy realm, and smooth the broken ways,
Earth from her womb a flinty tribute pays;
For thee, the sturdy paver thumps the ground,
Whilst ev'ry stroke his lab'ring lungs resound;
For thee the scavinger bids kennels glide   15
Within their bounds, and heaps of dirt subside.
My youthful bosom burns with thirst of fame,
From the great theme to build a glorious name,
To tread in paths to ancient bards unknown,

And bind my temples with a Civic crown;   20
But more, my country's love demands the lays,
My country's be the profit, mine the praise.

.   .   .   .

TRIVIA, II

If cloath'd in black, you tread the busy town,   25
Or if distinguish'd by the rev'rend gown,
Three trades avoid; oft in the mingling press,
The barber's apron soils the sable dress;
Shun the perfumer's touch with cautious eye,
Nor let the baker's step advance too nigh: 30
Ye walkers too that youthful colours wear,
Three sullying trades avoid with equal care;
The little chimney-sweeper skulks along,
And marks with sooty stains the heedless throng;
When small-coal murmurs in the hoarser throat,   35
From smutty dangers guard thy threaten'd coat:
The dust-man's cart offends thy cloaths and eyes,
When through the street a cloud of ashes flies;
But, whether black or lighter dyes are worn,
The chandler's basket, on his shoulder born,   40
With tallow spots thy coat; resign the way,
To shun the surly butcher's greasy tray,
Butchers, whose hands are dy'd with blood's foul stain,
And always foremost in the hangman's train.
     Let due civilities be strictly paid.   45
The wall surrender to the hooded maid;
Nor let thy sturdy elbow's hasty rage
Jostle the feeble steps of trembling age:
And when the porter bends beneath his load,
And pants for breath; clear thou the crouded road.   50
But, above all, the groping blind direct,
And from the pressing throng the lame protect.
You'll sometimes meet a fop, of nicest tread,
Whose mantling peruke veils his empty head,
At ev'ry step he dreads the wall to lose,   55
And risques, to save a coach, his red-heel'd shoes,
Him, like the miller, pass with caution by,

Lest from his shoulder clouds of powder fly.
But when the bully, with assuming pace,
Cocks his broad hat, edg'd round with tarnish'd lace,   60
Yield not the way; defie his strutting pride,
And thrust him to the muddy kennel's side;
He never turns again, nor dares oppose,
But mutters coward curses as he goes.

.   .   .   .

TRIVIA, III

Trivia Goddess, leave these low abodes,
And traverse o'er the wide ethereal roads,
Celestial Queen, put on thy robes of light,
Now *Cynthia* nam'd, fair regent of the night.
At sight of thee the villain sheaths his sword,   5
Nor scales the wall, to steal the wealthy hoard.
O may thy silver lamp from heav'n's high pow'r
Direct my footsteps in the midnight hour!
    When night first bids the twinkling stars appear,
Or with her cloudy vest inwraps the air,   10
Then swarms the busie street; with caution tread,
Where the shop-windows falling threat thy head;
Now lab'rers home return, and join their strength
To bear the tott'ring plank, or ladder's length;
Still fix thy eyes intent upon the throng,   15
And as the passes open, wind along.
.   .   .   .

Where the mob gathers, swiftly shoot along,
Nor idly mingle in the noisy throng.
Lur'd by the silver hilt, amid the swarm,
The subtil artist will thy side disarm.
Nor is the flaxen wigg with safety worn;   55
High on the shoulder, in a basket born
Lurks the sly boy; whose hand to rapine bred,
Plucks off the curling honours of thy head.
Here dives the skulking thief, with practis'd slight,
And unfelt fingers make thy pocket light.   60
Where's now thy watch, with all its trinkets, flown?
And thy late snuff-box is no more thy own.

But lo! his bolder thefts some tradesman spies,
Swift from his prey the scudding lurcher flies;
Dext'rous he 'scapes the coach with nimble bounds,　　　65
Whilst ev'ry honest tongue *stop thief*! resounds.
So speeds the wily fox, alarm'd by fear,
Who lately filch'd the turkey's callow care;
Hounds following hounds, grow louder as he flies,
And injur'd tenants joyn the hunter's cries.　　　70
Breathless he stumbling falls: Ill-fated boy!
Why did not honest work thy youth employ?
Seiz'd by rough hands, he's dragg'd amid the rout,
And stretch'd beneath the pump's incessant spout:
Or plung'd in miry ponds, he gasping lies,　　　75
Mud choaks his mouth, and plaisters o'er his eyes.
　　Let not the ballad-singer's shrilling strain
Amid the swarm thy list'ning ear detain:
Guard well thy pocket; for these *Syrens* stand,
To aid the labours of the diving hand;　　　80
Confed'rate in the cheat, they draw the throng,
And cambric handkerchiefs reward the song.
But soon as coach or cart drives rattling on,
The rabble part, in shoals they backward run.
So *Jove*'s loud bolts the mingled war divide,　　　85
And *Greece* and *Troy* retreat on either side.

.　　.　　.　　.　　.　　.　　.　　.　　.

Who can the various city frauds recite,
With all the petty rapines of the night?
Who now the Guinea-dropper's bait regards,
Trick'd by the sharper's dice, or juggler's cards?　　　250
Why should I warn thee ne'er to join the fray,
Where the sham-quarrel interrupts the way?
Lives there in these our days so soft a clown,
Brav'd by the bully's oaths, or threat'ning frown?
I need not strict enjoyn the pocket's care,　　　255
When from the crouded play thou lead'st the fair;
Who has not here, or watch, or snuff-box lost,
Or handkerchiefs that *India*'s shuttle boast?
　　O! may thy virtue guard thee through the roads
Of *Drury*'s mazy courts, and dark abodes,　　　260
The harlot's guileful paths, who nightly stand,

Where *Katherine-street* descends into the *Strand*.
Say, vagrant Muse, their wiles and subtil arts,
To lure the stranger's unsuspecting hearts;
So shall our youth on healthful sinews tread,   265
And city cheeks grow warm with rural red.
   'Tis she who nightly strowls with saunt'ring pace,
No stubborn stays her yielding shape embrace;
Beneath the lamp her tawdry ribbons glare,
The new-scower'd manteau, and the slattern air;   270
High-draggled petticoats her travels show,
And hollow cheeks with artful blushes glow;
With flatt'ring sounds she sooths the cred'lous ear,
My noble captain! charmer! love! my dear!
In riding-hood near tavern-doors she plies,   275
Or muffled pinners hide her livid eyes.
With empty bandbox she delights to range,
And feigns a distant errand from the *'Change*;
Nay, she wil oft the Quaker's hood prophane,
And trudge demure the rounds of *Drury-lane*.   280
She darts from sarsnet ambush wily leers,
Twitches thy sleeve, or with familiar airs
Her fan will pat thy cheek; these snares disdain,
Nor gaze behind thee, when she turns again.
   I knew a yeoman, who for thirst of gain,   285
To the great city drove from *Devon*'s plain
His num-rous lowing herd; his herds he sold,
And his deep leathern pocket bagg'd with gold;
Drawn by a fraudful nymph, he gaz'd, he sigh'd;
Unmindful of his home, and distant bride,   290
She leads the willing victim to his doom,
Through winding alleys to her cobweb room.
Thence thro' the street he reels, from post to post,
Valiant with wine, nor knows his treasure lost.
The vagrant wretch th' assembled watchmen spies,   295
He waves his hanger, and their poles defies;
Deep in the Round-house pent, all night he snores,
And the next morn in vain his fate deplores.
   Ah hapless swain, unus'd to pains and ills!
Canst thou forgo roast-beef for nauseous pills?   300
How wilt thou lift to Heav'n thy eyes and hands,

When the long scroll the surgeon's fees demands!
Or else (ye Gods avert that worst disgrace)
Thy ruin'd nose falls level with thy face,
Then shall thy wife thy loathsome kiss disdain,   305
And wholesome neighbours from thy mug refrain.

. . . .

Consider, reader, what fatigues I've known,
The toils, the perils of the wintry town;
What riots seen, what bustling crouds I bor'd,   395
How oft I cross'd where carts and coaches roar'd;
Yet shall I bless my labours, if mankind
Their future safety from my dangers find.
Thus the bold traveller, (inur'd to toil,
Whose steps have printed *Asia*'s desert soil,   400
The barb'rous *Arabs* haunt; or shiv'ring crost
Dark *Greenland*'s mountains of eternal frost;
Whom providence in length of years restores
To the wish'd harbour of his native shores;)
Sets forth his journals to the publick view,   405
To caution, by his woes, the wandring crew.
    And now compleat my gen'rous labours lye,
Finish'd, and ripe for immortality.
Death shall entomb in dust this mould'ring frame,
But never reach th' eternal part, my fame.   410
When *W*——— and *G*———, mighty names, are dead;
Or but at *Chelsea* under custards read;
When Criticks crazy bandboxes repair,
And Tragedies, turn'd rockets, bounce in air;
High-rais'd on *Fleet-street* posts, consign'd to fame,   415
This work shall shine, and walkers bless my name.

EPISTLE III, TO
WILLIAM PULTENEY, ESQUIRE

Pult'ney, methinks you blame my breach of word;
What, cannot *Paris* one poor page afford?
Yes, I can sagely, when the times are past,
Laugh at those follys which I strove to taste,
And each amusement, which we shar'd, review,   5

Pleas'd with meer talking, since I talk to you.
But how shall I describe in humble prose,
Their Balls, Assemblies, Operas and Beaus?
In prose, you cry! Oh no, the Muse must aid,
And leave *Parnassus* for the *Tuillerie*'s shade;　　　　10
Shall he (who late *Britannia*'s city trod,
And led the draggled Muse, with pattens shod,
Through dirty lanes, and alley's doubtful ways)
Refuse to write, when *Paris* asks his lays!
　　Well, then, I'll try. Descend, ye beauteous Nine,　　15
In all the colours of the rainbow shine,
Let sparkling stars your neck and ear adorn,
Lay on the blushes of the crimson morn,
So may ye Balls and gay Assemblies grace,
And at the Opera claim the foremost Place.　　　　20
　　Trav'lers should ever fit expression chuse,
Nor with low phrase the lofty theme abuse.
When they describe the state of eastern Lords,
Pomp and magnificence should swell their words;
And when they paint the serpent's scaly pride,　　25
Their lines should hiss, their numbers smoothly slide;
But they, unmindful of Poetic rules,
Describe alike Mockaws, and Great *Moguls*.
Dampier would thus, without ill-meaning satyr,
Dress forth in simple style the *Petit-maitre*.　　　　30
　　In Paris, *there's a race of animals,*
(I've seen them at their Operas and Balls)
They stand erect, they dance when-e'er they walk,
Monkeys in action, perroquets in talk;
They're crown'd with feathers, like the cockatoo,　　35
And, like camelions, daily change their hue;
From patches justly plac'd they borrow graces,
And with vermilion lacker o'er their faces,
This custom, as we visibly discern,
They, by frequenting Ladies toilettes, learn.　　40
Thus might the trav'ler easy truth impart.
Into the subject let me nobly start.
　　How happy lives the man, how sure to charm,
Whose knot embroider'd flutters down his arm!
On him the Ladies cast the yielding glance,　　　　45

Sigh in his songs, and languish in his dance;
While wretched is the Wit, contemn'd, forlorn,
Whose gummy hat no scarlet plumes adorn;
No broider'd flowers his worsted ankle grace,
Nor cane emboss'd with gold directs his pace;   50
No Lady's favour on his sword is hung.
What, though *Apollo* dictate from his tongue,
His wit is spiritless and void of grace,
Who wants th' assurance of brocade and lace.
While the gay fop genteelly talks of weather,   55
The fair in raptures doat upon his feather;
Like a Court Lady though he write and spell,
His minuet step was fashion'd by *Marcell*;
He dresses, fences. What avails to know?
For women chuse their men, like silks, for show.   60
Is this the thing, you cry, that *Paris* boasts?
Is this the thing renown'd among our Toasts?
For such a flutt'ring sight we need not roam;
Our own Assemblys shine with these at home.

.   .   .   .

Sometimes the *Tuillerie's* gawdy walk I love,
Where I through crouds of rustling manteau's rove;
As here from side to side my eyes I cast,   135
And gaz'd on all the glitt'ring train that past,
Sudden a fop steps forth before the rest;
I knew the bold embroidery of his vest.
He thus accosts me with familiar air,
Parbleu! on a fait cet habit en Angleterre!   140
Quelle manche! ce galon est grossierement range;
Viola quelque chose de fort beau et degage!
This said: On his red heel he turns, and then
Humms a soft minuet, and proceeds agen.
Well; now you've Paris *seen, you'll frankly own*   145
Your boasted London *seems a country town;*
Has Christianity yet reach'd your nation?
Are churches built? Are Masquerades in fashion?
Do daily Soupes your dinners introduce?
Are musick, snuff, and coaches yet in use?   150
Pardon me, Sir; we know the *Paris* mode,
And gather *Politesse* from Courts abroad.

Like you, our Courtiers keep a num'rous train
To load their coach; and tradesmen dun in vain.
Nor has Religion left us in the lurch,   155
And, as in *France*, our vulgar croud the Church;
Our Ladys too support the Masquerade,
The sex by nature love th' intriguing trade.
Strait the vain fop in ign'rant raptures crys,
Paris *the barbarous world will civilize*!   160
Pray, sir, point out among the passing band
The present Beauties who the town command.
See yonder dame; strict virtue chills her breast,
Mark in her eye demure the Prude profest;
That frozen bosom native fire must want,   165
Which boasts of constancy to one Gallant!
This next the spoils of fifty lovers wears,
Rich Dandin's *brilliant favours grace her ears;*
The necklace Florio's *gen'rous flame bestow'd,*
Clitander's *sparkling gems her finger load;*   170
But now, her charms grown cheap by constant use,
She sins for scarfs, clock'd stockings, knots, and *shoes.*
This next, with sober gait and serious leer,
Wearies her knees with morn and ev'ning prayer;
She scorns th' ignoble love of feeble pages,   175
But with three Abbots in one night engages.
This with the Cardinal her nights employs,
Where holy sinews consecrate her joys.
Why have I promis'd things beyond my power!
Five assignations wait me at this hour,   180
The sprightly Countess first my visit claims,
To morrow shall indulge inferior dames.
Pardon me, Sir; that thus I take my leave;
Gay Florimella *slily twitch'd my sleeve.*

.   .   .   .

AN ELEGY ON A LAP DOG

Shock's *fate I mourn; poor* Shock *is now no more,*
Ye Muses mourn, ye chamber-maids deplore.
Unhappy *Shock!* yet more unhappy Fair,
Doom'd to survive thy joy and only care!

Thy wretched fingers now no more shall deck,   5
And tye the fav'rite ribband round his neck;
No more thy hand shall smooth his glossy hair,
And comb the wavings of his pendent ear.
Yet cease thy flowing grief, forsaken maid;
All mortal pleasures in a moment fade: 10
Our surest hope is in an hour destroy'd,
And love, best gift of heav'n, not long enjoy'd.
    Methinks I see her frantick with despair,
Her streaming eyes, wrung hands, and flowing hair;
Her *Mechlen* pinners rent the floor bestrow,   15
And her torn fan gives real signs of woe.
Hence Superstition, that tormenting guest,
That haunts with fancy'd fears the coward breast;
No dread events upon this fate attend,
Stream eyes no more, no more thy tresses rend.   20
Tho' certain omens oft' forewarn a state,
And dying lyons show the monarch's fate;
Why should such fears bid *Celia*'s sorrow rise?
For when a Lap-dog falls, no lover dyes,
    Cease, *Celia*, cease; restrain thy flowing tears,   25
Some warmer passion will dispell thy cares.
In man you'll find a more substantial bliss,
More grateful toying, and a sweeter kiss.
    He's dead. Oh lay him gently in the ground!
And may his tomb be by this verse renown'd.   30
Here Shock, *the pride of all his kind, is laid;*
Who fawn'd like man, but ne'er like man betray'd.

XLI

꙳꙳꙳꙳꙳꙳꙳꙳꙳꙳꙳꙳꙳꙳

ALEXANDER POPE
(1688-1744)

To follow the development of Pope's style, which I have discussed in the "Brief History," one should read three early poems and a number of later ones. The three early poems, each of which is a masterpiece in its way, are *Windsor Forest, An Essay on Criticism*, and *The Rape of the Lock*. The first of these is a virtuoso performance which reveals Pope's debt to the tradition of Waller and Denham, and his remarkable superiority to that tradition; the second is Pope's first significant accomplishment of his most typical and most valuable poetic mode, the polite essay; and the third is the youthful poet's first effort to cope with subject matter both important to his world and at least potentially disagreeable. In his later poetry he came to focus the great social style of the *Essay* on the great social concerns which he had touched — if in a rather trivial form — in the *Rape*.

The first, the earliest, of these mature achievements is *An Essay on Man*, which follows Pope's three early masterpieces by nearly twenty years. Its first epistle reveals Pope's growth as a metrist, the new sufficiency of his couplets to define the most interesting, complex, and controversial problems he and his age confronted. Its fourth epistle furnishes the first example — or one of the first examples — of his extended poetic range. In this epistle the speaker discovers himself and his correspondent, with whom he has hitherto been in such perfect harmony that their discourse seemed to have but one voice, to be at serious and troublesome odds. In considering happiness, the subject of this epistle, he recognizes that his philosophic friend is not happy, that he cannot perfectly reconcile himself, as the speaker argues that one should, to the part he has been forced to play in the great scene of human life. The interruptions of the speaker, which were a merely rhetorical countenancing of pride and folly in the first three epistles — and hardly attributable to the speaker's guide, philosopher, and friend — suddenly acquire a personal ring and the force of a living intelligence: " 'What differ more (you cry) than crown and cowl?' / I'll tell you, friend, A Wise man and a Fool"; "Look next on Greatness; say where Greatness lies? / 'Where, but among the Heroes and the Wise?' " The unreconciled, the unhappy correspondent is enunciating feelings here very much like those Pope himself will utter on later occasions. But in this case, he argues for happiness based on resignation, and the poem ends with him trying to console his strangely unphilosophical friend:

> When statesmen, heroes, kings, in dust repose,
> Whose sons shall blush their fathers were thy foes,
> Shall then this verse to future age pretend
> Thou wert my guide, philosopher and friend?

Whether or not we call this speaker Pope and the imperfectly resigned statesman he is addressing Bolingbroke, their voices and their attitudes present us in the fourth epistle of the *Essay* with a conversational stress, a social dynamics which is new and, indeed, revolutionary in Pope's practice.[1] The extended use of his conversational style which this epistle suggests — the applying of its elements and qualities not only to complexities in the discourse but also to discordancies between the different parties engaged in it — is the rule in the great discursive poems that followed *An Essay on Man*.

The greatest of these poems, those in which this extended range of Pope's style has been most fully and dynamically employed, are: the second epistle of the *Moral Essays*, *An Epistle to Dr. Arbuthnot*, and the second dialogue of the *Epilogue to the Satires*. In the second *Moral Essay*, Pope shares a profoundly searching satire of women with one of their number, Mrs. Martha Blount as it seems, and manages in the process to address her in the most courtly, complimentary, and, indeed, personally ingratiating manner; in the *Epistle*, he and his friend, who per-

---

[1] This extension of Pope's awareness of the possibilities and the implications of his style is also evident in "The First Satire of the Second Book of Horace Imitated," a poem Pope seems to have composed between the time he first drafted and the time he completed the fourth epistle of the *Essay*. Here also, in following Horace, he reveals his speaker in partial disagreement with a discursive correspondent and thus, as in the fourth epistle, faced with the dual problem of achieving harmony in his conversation and bringing order to his subject matter. It is fitting that Pope should have come into an understanding of the full range of his conversational style of poetry, on the one hand, by engaging in serious and no doubt troubling conversations with a friend and, on the other hand, by imitating a poem of the greatest classical master of the conversational style.

sistently represents to him the likelihood and the danger of his offending society, discuss his difficult and precarious social situation as a famous satiric poet, finally reaching a statement on his life and nature which, as the friend acknowledges, will surely be socially acceptable; in the *Epilogue*, Pope retains his politeness and the appearance of a hope for social accord throughout a conversation with a representative member of society, a conversation whose every exchange reveals a dreadful failure of actual communication between Pope and this gentleman and demonstrates the virtual impossibility of Pope's reaching any real agreement with his society. There are several other great conversations in Pope's mature poetic practice, but these three reveal his style at its greatest stretch: each of them being throughout its course pointedly devoted to a formulation of social agreement on some complex and important public topic, and to an agreement achieved under the most testing social conditions.

Finally, there is *Dunciad IV*, in which Pope, following the logic of the *Epilogue*, comes to a tragic abnegation of his style, a tragic dissociation of the closed couplet from its conversational commitments and its conversational implications, a tragic diminution of this great symbol of common sense to a vehicle for solipsistic declamation.

XLII

SAMUEL JOHNSON
(1709-1784)

Johnson composed in closed couplets like the other poets of his age. But he organized his thoughts primarily in groups of couplets, in couplet paragraphs.

One great passage of *The Vanity of Human Wishes*, for instance, is organized of a section on typical old age (ll. 255–90),[1] a section on atypically fortunate old age (ll. 291–311), and a brief conclusion. Its two large sections are subdivided as well: that on fortunate old age presents a paragraph of its possible graces (ll. 291–98) — a paragraph, by the way, which Johnson has set in general contrast with the graceless actions of typical old age just above it — and a paragraph on the sorrows which even the most fortunate old age must endure (ll. 299–310). The "Prologue in Drury Lane" is composed of two major sections, one of dramatic history (ll. 1–38) and one of dramatic prophecy. These two major sections, like those on old age described above, are subdivided — each one in its own special way. Even the little birthday address "To a Young Lady" reveals this kind of massive arrangement: there is a section of good wishes (ll. 1–8) and a section of good advice (ll. 9–19).

The impression of command Johnson achieved with these large, variously related, and variously subdivided segments of poetic thought allowed him to practice a looser couplet order than Pope had done and still project the eighteenth-century effect of polish and control. One notices in the section of good wishes in "To a Young Lady," mentioned just above, for instance, that the repeated use of "may" as a clause and couplet governor is clouded by the fact that Johnson, although he commenced the first and third couplets with this term, tucked it away inside

---

[1] My line references correspond to the line notations in *The Poems of Samuel Johnson*, ed. D. Nichol Smith and Edward L. McAdam (Oxford, 1941).

the second. His disposition of parallel imperative verbs in the advice section of this same poem is even more irregular.

The different subdivisions of Johnson's description of typical old age are also loosely articulated. Johnson describes the failure of three senses: seeing (ll. 263–64), taste (ll. 265–66), and hearing (ll. 267–72). Each of them is differently formed, and the third runs for four couplets as opposed to one couplet each for the first two. This impression of their obliqueness is exaggerated because of the couplet that introduces them: "In vain their gifts the bounteous seasons pour, / The fruit autumnal, and the vernal flower." This couplet does not lead into questions of either sight or taste very precisely, or into that of hearing at all. The extended section on hearing is also equivocated in its connections. While parallel in substance to the couplets above, it is actually set in a kind of contrast with a two-couplet section below, one on the talking of old age: if the old man cannot hear with pleasure, still he can talk. This section on talking, to follow the passage a little further, is set at its conclusion into a different relationship still: a contrast between the old man's talking and the attention he gets from his heirs (ll. 277–78). Then follows something on *their* talking (ll. 279–82). The shifts in this material are fairly sharply defined with couplet breaks, and the parts sufficiently related with logical terms, but each new segment is developed in its own fashion, and each one commonly is related to the material following it in a way that sets it in a somewhat different light from that in which it was introduced. This variety in their forms and their relationships augments the weight, the relevance, of each segment and gives the passage as a whole a thickness of discursive texture.

To study the looseness of Johnson's couplets and couplet systems in a smaller compass, we may turn to his production of the three-couplet if-then system in his "Prologue to *Irene*":

> If Truths like these with pleasing Language join;
> Ennobled, yet unchang'd, if Nature shine:
> If no wild Draught depart from Reason's Rules,
> Nor Gods his Heroes, nor his Lovers Fools:
> Intriguing Wits! his artless Plot forgive;
> And spare him, Beauties! tho' his Lovers live.

The first two couplets state the condition, the third, the inference — so far, so good. But the repetition of the term "if," not only at the opening of each of the first two couplets, but also halfway through the first couplet's second line, reveals an inner irregularity. The appearance of perfect order in the third couplet, that is, the appearance of its two lines' being parallel, is also partially disappointed. They are parallel in substance, the first being an appeal to the wits, the second an appeal to the beauties, but the first line closes with its appeal, "forgive," whereas the second line opens with its appeal, "spare." And then the couplet naturally tails off. Those lines in "The Prologue to *The Good-Natur'd Man*" in which Johnson develops the likenesses of playwrights to politicians (ll. 11–24) are similarly loose in production. Each of the first three couplets defines something common to both professions; the term "both," which insists on their similarity, is absent from the first couplet, present in the second as the subject of its clause, and in the third as the object of a preposition. Thus, once again, we find substantial parallels presented in rhetorically irregular fashion.

Right after these three couplets come two sets of two couplets each which appear at first glance to be almost as precisely ordered as the verse of Pope: the first couplet in each set describes something about the politician, the second, a corresponding thing about the playwright. But neither in the two pairs nor in the couplets that make them up has Johnson achieved parallel utterance. One notes, as a sign of this, that "Th' offended burgess" opens the first line of the first couplet; that its mate, "the poet's foes" (notice also the shift to plural number), comes near the end of the second couplet's first line; that "swelling Crispin," again, begins the second line of the third couplet; and that its mate, "the pert apprentice" (notice also the shift from a name to a term), comes near the end of the fourth couplet's first line. Each of these couplets is different from the others throughout. Each of three successive couplets in the "Prologue to *Irene*," again, although every one of them opens with the imperative "Learn" (ll. 9–14), is different in form from the others.

Perhaps the best sign of Johnson's relaxation of the couplet is his common practice of allowing an anticlimactic second line. Sometimes this practice is disguised by the second line's being grand in language or sound (*London*, ll. 121–22; *Vanity*, ll. 311–12). But one finds second lines again and again in Johnson's verse filled with quite obviously expansive matter (*Vanity*, ll. 315–16; "Comus," ll. 7–8) or — even more frequently — with matter of modification (*Vanity*, ll. 273–74, 313–14; "Lady," ll. 1–2, 5–6, 15–16; "Irene," ll. 9–10, 31–32). Such couplets can be floated effectively because Johnson has always conveyed a sense of command and discursive purpose in the larger segments of his verse.

Johnson's large-scale poetic movement has another major effect besides that of loosening the individual couplets: namely, that of diminishing the impression of conversation and of social awareness. His great patterns of discourse have an *ex cathedra* solemnity, a weighty roll to them, which makes interruption futile and, as it were, unnecessary. Johnson speaks in his couplet poems from a position of accumulated experience — like Imlac in *Rasselas* — and achieved wisdom. In *London* he describes this great sweep of utterance as a 'transport' (1. 97); in *The Vanity of Human Wishes* it modulates between public lecture and public musing, but in both cases, Johnson speaks on, and his audience can merely attend. In these long satiric poems, Johnson was, of course, following Juvenal — hence the rather un-Johnsonian 'transport.' But then, Johnson chose Juvenal as his model. The massive blocks of uninterruptible poetic order, moreover, characterize the poem "To a Young Lady" and the theatrical prologues.

The prologues, nevertheless, show more public responsiveness than any other of Johnson's couplet poetry: that is to say, they come closer to the heart of the closed-couplet tradition. It is because of this, I believe, that Yvor Winters singled them out of Johnson's poetry for special praise.[2] "The Prologue to *The Good-Natur'd Man*," more than any other of the prologues, recreates for us the living conditions for which it was written. The "poet's foes" (ll. 17–20), "the pert apprentice" (ll. 21–24), and the broad group of auditors who were capable of being fair or, at least, of being flattered (ll. 25–30) all live in this poem as the necessary counterparts to its explicit statement, as a vital penumbra. But even the prologues reveal a stiffness of mind, an overwhelming sense of absolute intelligence and judgment to which the interruptions of society are irrelevant. The speaker of Johnson's poems brooks no peer, no useful social acquaintance. Every one of the prologues ends, for instance, on appeals not to people, but to principles: to "Truth" ("Drury Lane," 1. 62), to justice (*"Irene,"* ll. 33–34), and to "Desert" (*"Comus,"* 1. 38). The "Prologue to *Irene*" does not really end on an appeal at all, but on a command: "In Reason, Nature, Truth he dares to trust: / Ye Fops be silent; and ye Wits be just." The "Prologue to *The Good-Natur'd Man*" ends with more ceremony, but the equation it draws between merit and praise similarly squeezes out the varieties, the prejudices, and the follies from its audience — those qualities which characterize every human assembly and which, as Dryden and Pope knew, must be solicited. In both these cases, of course, Johnson's speaker is turning his back on fops and

---

[2] "The Heroic Couplet and Its Recent Rivals," in *In Defense of Reason* (Denver, 1943), pp. 136–37. I am deeply indebted to this essay for my understanding of the couplet.

wits, certain that he has nothing to learn from them, nothing useful to gain from confronting their feelings or opinions.

This poetry does, of course, have its own ponderous force, the force of deeply held and deeply tested opinion — of opinion squared with evidences of human life gathered from China to Peru. But the loosened couplet organization in which Johnson articulates this opinion and its diminished impression of social awareness — with the correspondingly diminished impression of an intelligent social milieu — mark a decline in the couplet's evocative power from the practice of Pope, a loss in its expressive density.

XLIII

᚛᚛᚛᚛᚛᚛᚛᚛᚛᚛᚛᚛᚛᚛

OLIVER GOLDSMITH
(1730-1774)

Goldsmith presents us with an extremely facile embodiment of that stress between definition and movement which we have found to be central to closed-couplet poetry.

First, for the definition. Goldsmith often used half-lines (*Village*, ll. 10, 22, 292, 298)[1] and lines (*Village*, ll. 61–62, 83–84) to define pairs in parallel, and whole couplets (*Village*, ll. 25–30, 41–48, 273–76; "Epilogue to *Stoops*," ll. 48–57) to define the separate parallel items of series. Some of the elegiac catalogues in *The Deserted Village*, such as the village's vanished charms (ll. 9–14), the different elements of note in the now ruined inn (ll. 225–36), and the inn's long departed inhabitants (ll. 241–50), are textures of parallel half-lines, lines, and couplets. Goldsmith also made use of the couplet and its elements, although less frequently, to define antitheses (*Village*, ll. 3–4, 14, 20, 34, 53–56, 266; "Epilogue to *Man*," l. 28). He sometimes practiced a form of the comprehensive pattern of antithesis which we found in Dryden: "The young contending as the old surveyed," for instance; again, "A Bed by night, a chest of drawers by day"; and, yet again, "The men have tails, the women paint the face." In the contrast between the nobles and the peasantry (*Village*, ll. 53–56), by which he asserts the tragedy of the peasants' departure from the land, Goldsmith has approximated Dryden's argumentative and political use of this pattern.

Goldsmith achieved movement as well as definition in his couplet production. He often varied his normal, square couplets with oblique ones (*Village*, ll. 31–32, 63–64, 201–2, 299–300; "*Zobeide*," ll. 25–26; "*Stoops*," ll. 72–73) and often modified their flow with periodic inver-

---

[1] My line references correspond to the line notations in *The Collected Works of Oliver Goldsmith*, ed. Arthur Friedman (Oxford, 1966), IV and V.

sions (*Village*, ll. 24, 35–36, 55–56, 67, 85, 86, 91). There is a remarkable case of Goldsmith's balancing an antithesis between two oblique couplets, both of them oblique to exactly the same degree (*Village*, ll. 273–76)— quite an odd way of his composing verse both lucid and flexible. Goldsmith also articulated single sentences, single movements of syntax and thought, over numbers of couplets. The first sentence of *The Deserted Village*, for instance, covers fifteen couplets. It is not a tightly woven statement like Pope's great attack on Atticus or a sinewy and wide-ranging one like Dryden's opening thrust at Achitophel: it is composed of a three-couplet address to Auburn; then a catalogue of Auburn's charms, which enjoys many definitive pauses (to l. 14); and, finally, a syntactically diminishing set of "when" and "while" clauses, these also metrically defined, on Auburn's sports. A tighter system of couplets, also essentially one sentence, is the elegiac "I still had hopes" passage (*Village*, ll. 83–96). Sentence systems which cover several couplets are fairly common in Goldsmith (*Village*, ll. 287–302; "*Zobeide*," ll. 1–14). None of them reveals Pope's compression or Dryden's comprehensiveness, but all are fluent — all showing that combination of order and movement which is this form's essential property.

Goldsmith also followed the closed-couplet tradition by infusing his poems with the impression of conversation. We find a hint of colloquial zest and flow, for instance, in the portrait of the village schoolmaster (ll. 193–216) and much more than a hint in the prologues and epilogues. The poet's friends' refusal to write him an epilogue, as described in "The Epilogue to *The Good-Natur'd Man*" (ll. 11–20), approaches Pope in raciness and compression. The old poet's refusal runs two couplets, holding in its last line a counterproposal, that "Your brother Doctor" might write one; in the next two couplets are given the Doctor's refusal; and within the following couplet Goldsmith has wedged, first, the Doctor's counterproposal, that the theater manager should write the epilogue, then, the manager's refusal, and, finally, the manager's reason for refusing. There are, again, in "The Epilogue to *She Stoops to Conquer*" (ll. 50–55), three couplets, each one addressed to a different segment of the audience, the gamblers, the lawyers, and the doctors, whose second lines define in every case some typical talk of that profession: for instance, "Doctors, who cough and answer every misfortuner, / 'I wish I'd been call'd in a little sooner.' " The colloquial flavor is so strong in this couplet, indeed, that it virtually obliterates the meter.

What distinguishes Goldsmith's couplet poetry, however, is its tremendous variety of incidental lyrical practices and its pervasively lyrical appeal.[2]

This lyricism is extremely pronounced in *The Deserted Village*. First, there is the poet's extensive use of assonance and alliteration throughout this poem. Assonance is especially potent in such lines as "Led up their sports beneath the spreading tree," "Amazed the gazing rustics ranged around," and "The robe that wraps his limbs in silken sloth," but one finds line after line qualified with its presence (ll. 2, 4, 6, 13, 23, 27, etc.). The lines quoted just above are, of course, alliterative as well as assonantal. And there are many more alliterative lines in *The Deserted Village* (ll. 8, 24, 25, 50, etc.). Some of them, like this one — "And rural mirth and manners are no more" — are overwhelmingly musical. Indeed, the effect of such sounding combinations is to erode the normal accentual movement of the poem, a movement which naturally goes along with a conversational, a discursive, effect, and to suggest in its place a quantitative, a flowing and musical form of utterance. Such an impression is augmented by Goldsmith's fairly common practice of elision, that is, of slurring eleventh syllables in his ten-syllable lines. Each of the first five lines of the poem, significantly, reveals such a slurred syllable; this asserts the poem's musical tendency, that is, its tendency to flow, and establishes the strong lyrical undercurrent on which its effect heavily depends. Such elision continues fairly frequently, although less frequently, throughout the poem (ll. 12, 14, 33, 35, 37, etc.).

Various kinds of verbal echoes reinforce this poem's musical quality. One notices, for example, many reflective phrases: "loveliest village" in the first line suggests a quantitative equivalency with the alliterating and similarly elided "earliest visit" in the third; "labouring swain" in the second line is echoed in the fourth line's "lingering blooms," and that, although in rather a different way, in the fifth line's "lovely bowers." This practice seems less common in the body of the poem, but the sense of at least one crucial passage is heightened by a subliminal effect of this kind. In this couplet, "But a bold peasantry, their country's pride, / When once destroyed, can never be supplied," the poet has yoked his subject and predicate, which he separated from one another for dramatic emphasis, by the 'peasantry–never be' chime. More obvious and more significant than such subtle syllabic reflections are Goldsmith's many re-

---

[2] I am generally indebted throughout this essay to Wallace C. Brown, "Goldsmith: The Didactic-Lyric," in *The Triumph of Form* (Chapel Hill, 1948), pp. 142–60. In composing several of the essays on the later masters of the couplet, indeed, I have built on foundations laid down by Professor Brown in this book.

frain-like echoes: "Sweet Auburn" and "sweet village" (ll. 1, 31, 35, 75), for example, and "How often have I" (ll. 7, 9, 15), and "I still had hopes" (ll. 85, 89, 95). Such quasi refrains ring variously throughout *The Deserted Village.*

Goldsmith's most persistent verbal echo, however, is his repetition of individual words. Such words as "round" (ll. 22, 28, 33, 77, 83, 203, 214, 248, 272, 283), "charm" (ll. 9, 31, 34, 36, 289, 291, 296), "sweet" (ll. 1, 31, 32, 35, 75, 242), "bower" (ll. 5, 33, 37, 47, 86), "lovely" (ll. 1, 5, 35), and "sport" (ll. 6, 18, 24, 31, 36, 71, 281), each of them incidentally endowed now and again with such emphases as rhyme, assonance, and alliteration can give, echo and re-echo through the poem. It should be noted, first, that these words are rather vague; Goldsmith has, of course, used "sweet," the one sharply definable term in my list, only in a figurative sense. It should be noted, second, that most of these terms have an emotional rather than a substantial value; "sport" suggests any kind of free and happy activity, and "bower" calls up visions of sylvan comfort, of unfettered and innocent ease. Goldsmith's various repetitions of these terms fill them with all the vaguely associative, unfocussed emotional power they can bear. Some of his poem's most emphatic moments derive their quality from a clustering of them:

> These were thy charms sweet village: sports like these
> With sweet succession, taught even toil to please:
> These round thy bowers their chearful influence shed,
> These were thy charms — But all these charms are fled.

We must recognize, however, in addition to the lyrical aura Goldsmith derives from "charms" and "sports" in these lines, a more solid rhetorical impression; since both these terms have been extensively particularized in the preceding lines, the "charms" and "sports" now fled from Auburn should be clear in our minds as well as dear to our hearts.

The Deserted Village is a didactic, a forensic, poem whose chief mode of argument is that of elegiac appeal. The poem shifts in its address quite appropriately between the ruined and lamented town and "Ye friends to truth, ye statesmen." The town is, however, the primary addressee and the poem's tone is, correspondingly, primarily lyrical. Even the appeals to the statesmen (ll. 51–62, 265–86) are shot through with lyrical suggestions and make as much of an appeal to their sensibility as to their sense. In general the poem strikes a varying balance between the discursive and the lyrical. In the portrait of the schoolmaster, for instance, the discursive, the conversational, element seems predominant. Goldsmith has conveyed the anxious whispers of the students (ll. 197–204), the credulous reports of the villagers (ll. 207–10), and the amused comment of the parson (ll. 211–12) as one might have heard them spoken. But even these evocations of village talk show the lyrical tinge, the quantitative flow: notice the "village . . . little" (l. 196), "day's . . . faces" (l. 200), and "write . . . cypher" (l. 208) cases of assonance; the "severe . . . view" (l. 197), "tremblers . . . trace" (l. 199), and "love . . . learning" (l. 206) cases of alliteration; the intralinear repetitions of "knew" (l. 198) and "jokes" (l. 202); and the extralinear, extracouplet repetitions of "well" (ll. 199, 200, 201, 203), "still" (ll. 212, 215), and "knew" (ll. 198, 207, 216). The last two couplets of the passage, in which Goldsmith employed all these musical practices (ll. 213–16), gives the passage a profoundly lyrical close. This persistent lyricism is, of course, the means by which Goldsmith makes his elegiac argument, his appeal to nostalgia. The lyrical flavor which permeates this comic portrait of the schoolmaster, for instance, keeps continually before us the painful awareness that his time is past. Goldsmith is not reporting village talk, but, rather, mourning the loss of this kind of talk which he can now only remember and never hear again.

The peculiar dynamics in *The Deserted Village*, then, is one the poet has struck between the traditional discursive and argumentative mode of the closed couplet and a lyrically flowing and emotional mode of his own. One can study a different example of this same dynamics, a very nearly burlesque production of it, in "The Epilogue to *She Stoops to Conquer*." Observing this achievement in serious causes and comic ones, we may credit Goldsmith with a kind of couplet creativity, a kind of couplet extension. But his work, like Johnson's and Crabbe's and Cowper's, gives us a diminished version of the form. No one is eligible to interrupt *The Deserted Village*, no response is to be considered, no interested audience can engage the speaker in the stresses of argumentative exchange and thus work with him toward a more refined awareness, toward a more common sense. The public listens passive and virtually ignored as the speaker modulates his Orphic address, achieving a poetic resolution merely between his own two expressive urges — to lecture and to sing.

XLIV

✠✠✠✠✠✠✠✠✠✠✠✠✠✠✠✠

CHARLES CHURCHILL
(1731-1764)

It is easy to point out elements of movement in Churchill's couplet pro-
duction: enjambed couplets (*Hogarth*, ll. 14, 32; *Author*, ll. 76, 88,
166, 338; *Gloster*, ll. 4, 38, 42);[1] enjambed first lines (*Apology*, ll. 7,
146; *Hogarth*, ll. 3, 11, 25); and, on the other hand, heavy pauses at the
ends of first lines (*Hogarth*, l. 51; *Author*, ll. 85, 315, 363, 365; *Gloster*,
ll. 19, 21, 55, 157, 175); and even a few heavy mid-line pauses (*Au-
thor*, l. 365; *Gloster*, ll. 4, 5, 23, 39). One finds several examples, more-
over, of Churchill's tying two couplets together by paralleling the last
line of one rhetorically with the first line of the next (*Hogarth*, ll. 36–37;
Author, ll. 2–3, 182–83, 328–29; *Gloster*, ll. 30–31) — a practice
which reminds us of John Oldham. Indeed, Churchill often seems like a
better bred and a more talented Oldham.

Churchill, however, made much more persistent use of the couplet's
definitive resources than Oldham had done. He balanced and defined
many antitheses, for example, with lines (*Apology*, l. 147; *Hogarth*,
l. 35; *Author*, ll. 66, 92, 167, 334), with couplets (*Apology*, ll. 150–51,
152–53), and with pairs of couplets (*Apology*, ll. 166–69; *Author*,
ll. 377–80). He also composed many large measures of his verse in
accordance with antithetical promptings — between noble and ignoble be-
havior in an eleven-couplet passage of *The Author* (ll. 163–84), and be-
tween vicious and virtuous behavior in a twenty-three-couplet sweep of
the *Epistle to Hogarth* (ll. 7–52). Churchill has also defined pairs of
parallels with individual lines (*Apology*, ll. 2, 162, 163), couplets
(*Hogarth*, ll. 17–18, 43–44; *Author*, ll. 313–14), and pairs of cou-
plets (*Hogarth*, ll. 3–6). He has, moreover, used combinations of lines and
couplets to define series of parallel items — the series of problems one

---

[1] My line references correspond to the line notations in *The Poetical Works of
Charles Churchill*, ed. Douglas Grant (Oxford, 1956).

might take to Guthrie (*Author*, ll. 307–14), for instance, and the series of miraculous genealogical tricks by which Guthrie would solve these problems (*Author*, ll. 317–42). And, finally, he has composed many of the great movements of his poetry by enunciating series of parallels — such as the series of "Is this the land?" questions in a long passage of *The Author* (ll. 51–92). Such elements of close-grained order and lucidity, which pervade Churchill's poetic practice, add the flavor of Pope's conversational couplets, with their implications of social intimacy and politeness, to the oratorical flow of Oldham, already noticed, with its suggestions of a broader and more universally public address. The resulting impression from these two concurrent modes, from this compromise between the two major forms of closed couplet, is naturally one of equivocation. Is Churchill's speaker addressing Smollett or Gloster or some other gentleman of his immediate acquaintance, as he often explicitly asserts, or is he addressing the English nation, as his resounding utterance seems commonly to imply?

This equivocation of his address, whose application we will describe a little later, is maintained by Churchill's most characteristic stylistic device, his use of periodic inversion. One finds, on the one hand, many intraline (*Apology*, ll. 1, 5, 11, 66; *Hogarth*, ll. 4, 9; *Author*, ll. 3, 83) and intracouplet (*Hogarth*, ll. 5–6, 49–50; *Author*, ll. 57–58, 63–64, 331–32) inversions, by which the line and couplet are naturally dramatized and strengthened. But, on the other hand, Churchill's periods often draw us beyond the couplet's bounds, thus weakening its dignity and its powers of definition. Typical of Churchill is such a couplet as this: "Should Love of Fame, in every noble mind / A brave disease, with love of Virtue join'd." In this couplet, first of all, a suspensive modification overflows the first line and holds off to the couplet's end the proper rhetorical companion of "Love of Fame," that is, of course, "love of Virtue"; second, the term "join'd" in the suspended element is also periodically transposed; finally, the whole couplet, despite this periodic binding, thrusts into the next couplet before revealing the action of these two kinds of love.

As this example suggests, Churchill also used inversions, as he did antitheses and parallels, in forming the larger measures of his verse. But this device, which promotes both movement and stability within the couplet, is essentially a cue for movement, for climactic thrust, indeed, in its larger forms. The suspension of the giant's victim in the opening lines of *The Apology* (ll. 1–6), for instance, and then the suspension of the analogous critic's victim (ll. 7–14) impel us to make first one and then a second extended intellectual thrust through this seven-couplet system. The beginning of the *Epistle to Hogarth* and a passage from *The Author* (ll. 307–27) furnish us with similar, if less dramatic, cues for extended spans of attention. In the first of these, Churchill has suspended, first, the results of vicious action and then, in an antithetical passage, the results of virtuous action; in the second, he has suspended the name and ability of a man who could solve certain problems and then, in a parallel passage, the profession and nature of a man who could solve more dreadful problems. In yet another long passage from *The Author* (ll. 51–92), Churchill held up, with a long "when" digression (ll. 74–86), one of the parallel "where" clauses by which he was composing the passage in general. Looking back here, we may notice that all these passages of extended suspension actually present us with a texture of stylistic modes — a texture of stability and movement, of steadiness and thrust. They thus furnish large-scale versions of the dynamics we have analyzed — in Churchill and in the tradition of closed-couplet poetry generally — within and between individual couplets.

Churchill also expanded the closed-couplet tradition by using oblique compositional blocks of discourse. We find, first, many examples of intracouplet obliqueness (*Hogarth*, ll. 11–12, 33–34; *Author*, ll. 89–90, 163–64, 307–8; *Gloster*, ll. 24–25). Then there are the oblique patterns a few couplets in length. One notices, for instance, that the material on the saint, in this two-couplet parallel of the saint and the wit —

> The rigid Saint, by whom no mercy's shewn
> To Saints whose lives are better than his own,
> Shall spare thy crimes, and WIT, who never once
> Forgave a Brother, shall forgive a Dunce —

ends only with the third line's midpoint and that the wit and his exactly correspondent action are wedged into a line and one-half. More brilliant, although no more perfectly articulated, is the balancing of three lines on the speaker of *The Dedication of the Sermons* with three lines on his satiric target:

> I, like an idle Truant, fond of play,
> Doting on toys, and throwing gems away,
> Grasping at shadows, let the substance slip;
> But you, *my Lord*, renounc'd Attorneyship
> With better purpose, and more noble aim,
> And wisely played a more substantial game.

This passage is not only metrically but rhetorically oblique, since the speaker describes himself as merely laying down the ministry while the Bishop of Gloster has both laid down the law and taken up the ministry. This obliqueness is emphasized by the striking difference in verb placing in the two sections of the passage. Churchill nevertheless gives an impression of extremely refined balance and one that is, even though it pivots at the end of its second couplet's first line, crucially dependent on couplet ordering and definition.

Churchill also imposed such rhetorical obliqueness on the large measures of his verse. We might notice in this connection the section of general opinion on public show (ll. 37–44) by which he canted the long " 'Tis not" series in *Gloster* (ll. 33–60), or, to pick a more obvious case, the parallel between Guthrie and the evil parson in *The Author*:

With rude unnat'ral jargon to support,
Half *Scotch*, half *English*, a declining Court,
To make most glaring contraries unite,
And prove, beyond dispute, that black is white,   310
To make firm Honour tamely league with shame,
Make Vice and Virtue differ but in name,
To prove that Chains and Freedom are but one,
That to be sav'd must mean to be undone,
Is there not GUTHRIE? Who, like him, can call   315
All Opposites to proof, and conquer all?
He calls forth living waters from the rock;
He calls forth children from the barren stock;
He, far beyond the springs of Nature led,
Makes Women bring forth after they are dead;   320
He, on a curious, new and happy plan,
In *Wedlock*'s sacred bands joins Man to Man;
And, to complete the whole, most strange, but true,
By some rare magic, makes them fruitful too,
Whilst from their loins, in the due course of years,   325
Flows the rich blood of GUTHRIE's *English Peers*.
Dost Thou contrive some blacker deed of shame,
Something which Nature shudders but to name,
Something which makes the Soul of man retreat,
And the life-blood run backward to her seat?   330
Dost Thou contrive, for some base private end,
Some selfish view, to hang a trusting friend,

To lure him on, e'en to his parting breath,
And promise life, to work him surer death?
Grown old in villainy, and dead to grace,   335
Hell in his heart, and TYBURNE in his face;
Behold, a Parson at thy Elbow stands,
Low'ring damnation, and with open hands
Ripe to betray his Saviour for reward;
The Atheist Chaplain of an Atheist Lord.   340

Substantially, this passage reads as follows: if you desire a minor crime to help you advance yourself, get Guthrie, if a major crime, get the evil parson. But the terms of these parallel sections, although their relationship is clear, differ tremendously. "Guthrie," the subject of its verb, is suspended by a long series of infinitive phrases; "Parson," the direct object of its verb, is suspended by two long questions — these questions, by the way, being parallel in substance and oblique in form. In general, although Churchill always composed in rhetorical systems whose principles are evident, he characteristically composed these systems obliquely. Once again, then, we find the interpenetration of the conversational and the oratorical styles of the closed couplet or, better perhaps, the stretching, the expanding of a conversational mode into an oratorical one.

One final point on Churchill's couplet production. Every one of the great systems we have been studying is reinforced in its movement by syntactic interconnections. The passage beginning "Is this the land" (*Author*, ll. 51–92), that making the contrast between the rewards paid to vicious and to virtuous actions (*Hogarth*, ll. 7–52), and that on the evil parson (*Author*, ll. 327–40), for instance, each takes up essentially a single sentence, a single syntactic sweep.

Several poetic effects of Churchill's style can now be pointed out. First, when the great sweeps of his verse are suspensive, as in the opening lines of *The Apology* and in the passage on the evil parson in *The Author*, Churchill achieves wonderful climactic effects, wonderfully striking crystallizations of his meaning. Second, the great sweeps of Churchill's verse, whether suspensive or not, assimilate great wealths of evidence and give the impression, which comes from this, of extremely weighty utterance. The great introduction of the *Epistle to Hogarth* (ll. 1–52), for instance, opens and closes with general statements about virtuous public action to which the great sweep of material between them gives powerful evidence, evidence whose chief weight naturally falls on the significantly isolated closing line: "No crime's so great as daring to excel." The "Is this the land?" passage in a later poem, *The Author* (ll. 51–92), also achieves this impression of an overwhelmingly argued position, but in a subtler way. Its theme, that England has declined tragically since the time of Spenser, Jonson, and Shakespeare, is not stated; it simply emerges as the argument's inescapable inference. This inference seems so absolute or, rather, the great sweep of evidence by which Churchill has implied it seems so absolute that it need not be stated. Such effects as these of climax and overwhelming persuasiveness are central to Churchill's poetry until his late and unfinished poem, *The Dedication of the Sermons.*

In this poem, Churchill essentially avoids the flashy but fragmentary effect of climax, rather as he did in the "Is this the land?" passage from *The Author*, which is stylistically his penultimate work. But he also avoids defining such a sharply derogatory, rather simple-minded theme as that passage evoked. We have, instead, an uninterrupted web of satiric equivocation: [2] an explicit utterance, a surface, of praise for William Warburton, and a pervasive undercurrent of furious, implacable blame — the two woven together in an utterance of unfailing if exaggerated good breeding. This equivocation of effect depends, in great part, on the equivocation of address whose elements we have been describing. We may relate them in general: the Popean, the pointedly conversational, address to Gloster, with its accompaniment of neatly flattering formulations which had belonged to the closed couplet since Waller, carries the surface impression, that of polite flattery; the Oldhamesque oratorical sweep, with its incidental, flickering incongruities and its resounding appeal to a wider audience and a more universal standard of judgment than that on which the flattery is based, carries the undercurrent of fury. We may describe this poem as a great stream of hideously dissolving honors, thus recalling Dryden's dissolving praise of Achitophel. But it must be noticed immediately that Dryden *discussed* Achitophel whereas Churchill *addresses* Gloster. The eighteenth-century poet, unlike his great predecessor, must remain on polite terms with his satiric target all the while he is destroying him. This combination of explicit flattery and

---

2 Throughout this essay I am in close agreement with the few extremely perceptive remarks Yvor Winters made on Churchill in "The Heroic Couplet and Its Recent Rivals," in *In Defense of Reason* (Denver, 1943), pp. 138–43, in which he speaks of the *Dedication* as inhabiting the "ambiguous territory between irony and eulogy," and, again, of Churchill's poetry in general as "one of profound and bitter innuendo," but I am not in perfect agreement with Winters's more extensive but less profound appreciation of Churchill in his essay "The Poetry of Charles Churchill," in *Forms of Discovery* (Chicago, 1967), pp. 121–45.

latent insult, then, is Churchill's special achievement in *The Dedication of the Sermons.*

There are, of course, many signs of it in Churchill's earlier poems, the clearest of them coming, oddly enough, in these poems' patches of incoherence and confusion. At one pivotal point after another in the early poems, Churchill practiced or fell into anywhere from a line to a few couplets of imperfectly defined and related matter. At the pivot of the analogy which opens *The Apology* (ll. 7–8), for example, one cannot tell who the "giant names" are — that is, one cannot ascertain the poet's satiric focus. Again, when Churchill shifts from his display of virtue to virtue's reward, in the *Epistle to Hogarth*, he presents us with almost two full couplets of unattached description:

> Rage in her eye, and Malice in her breast,
> Redoubled Horror grinning on her crest,
> Fiercer each snake, and sharper ev'ry dart,
> Quick from her cell shall madd'ning ENVY start.

It is not until the end of the second couplet that we are told that this raging, malicious, and horrible figure is Envy. The first couplet on the evil parson in *The Author* (ll. 335–36) presents us with the same kind of frightful but unattached impression. *The Dedication* is a sort of extended and highly refined rhetorical pivot: a persistently unresolved articulation of the poet's attitude toward the correspondent of his address.

The brief passages of unattached satiric matter we have just discussed are all quickly and simply resolved, so that they allow a brief climax, a little click from haziness to assurance. A full passage with a similar click in the early poems is that in which Churchill develops his feelings about Smollett (*Apology*, ll. 146–69). One may naturally compare this passage with the whole of *The Dedication*, in which Churchill develops his feelings about William Warburton, the Bishop of Gloster. The first four couplets of the Smollett passage express an almost unalloyed adulation of Smollett; only the most alert reader would grow suspicious of the 'wantoning tongue' in which it is declaimed. Then, with a reversal of his explicit preference of Smollett over Fielding, Churchill reverses the whole passage, and his concluding couplets assert an unalloyed attack on Smollett.

There is no crude click of intention in *The Dedication* and no unalloyed statement. The combination of movement and definition Churchill had acquired in his brief but prolific career allowed him to heap praise on Warburton and, at the same time, to salt it with ruinous modifications. These modifications get swept along in the torrent of flattery without hindering its flow, but, at the same time, they receive the half-line, line, and couplet emphases which strengthen them to resist and spoil its explicit meanings. Consider the beginning of this poem:

HEALTH to great GLOSTER — from a man unknown,
Who holds thy health as dearly as his own,
Accept this greeting — nor let modest fear
Call up one maiden blush — I mean not here
To wound with flatt'ry — 'tis a Villain's art,   5
And suits not with the frankness of my heart.
Truth best becomes an *Orthodox* Divine,
And, spite of hell, that Character is mine;
To speak e'en bitter truths I cannot fear,
But truth, *my Lord*, is panegyric here.   10

The significance of balancing "great GLOSTER" with a "man unknown" (1. 1) remains undetermined owing to its oblique presentation and to the poem's forward impetus. This impetus also frees us from considering whether a "maiden blush" (1. 4) is the right kind of blush for a dignified man of the church; and, again, from pausing over "*Orthodox* Divine" (1. 7) to wonder, say, how one differs from an unorthodox divine. We will learn in passing, by the way, that orthodox divines love ease (1. 11) and, again in passing, wealth (1. 22). Everything in this poem can be said, in a sense, to be conveyed to us in passing.

Its great sweep spares us, once again, from studying the ambiguity of reference of the innocent aside, "I mean not here" (1. 4). If stabilized as part of the couplet it actually concludes, it might indict Warburton for the worst of all sins to socially oriented man, hypocrisy. If taken with the counterrunning syntax, it makes a much less harmful suggestion, that the speaker may wound Warburton with flattery some other time, but even this hint of dislike is diminished by its metrically de-emphatic point of conclusion — at the midpoint of a first line (ll. 4–5). We might pause over another ambiguously related phrase, "by mistaken kings" (1. 38), remembering that Warburton has both degrees, whose purchase is mentioned in the half-line preceding it, and titles, whose misplacing is mentioned in that which follows. Actually, the great movement of the poem, which is partly responsible for these ambiguities, disallows or, at least, discourages our explicit formulation of them. It carries the reader on: maintaining elements in its course which it does not give him the time or the clear indication to fit together; emphasizing the mixed elements of evidence with metrical points of definition, but variously avoiding any absolute order of these elements, any absolute formulation of their relevance.

What Churchill has achieved in *The Dedication of the Sermons*, as has been suggested, is the social counterpart of Dryden's political poetry. Dryden, of course, took a stand in *Absalom and Achitophel*; he gathered, he comprehended, the diverse elements of evidence and then marshalled them into patterns of dissolving blame (in discussing Charles's lechery) or dissolving praise (in discussing Shaftesbury's conduct as a judge), patterns, that is, whose intentions, even if tactfully introduced, were clear — Charles was God's chosen ruler; Shaftesbury was as evil as Lucifer. Dryden's political poetry presented judgments and decisions; that is, of course, what politics requires. But Churchill resided in and responded to, not political, but social conditions, conditions, that is, that neither require nor allow absolute judgments. Churchill's couplet movement allowed him, however, to achieve society's equivalent of Dryden's seemingly unbiased political rejection, the unacknowledged insult. He engaged explicitly in the most acceptable form of social address, flattery, and was able, while engaging in it, to undermine it, to suggest its falsity and hollowness, to suggest the truth about the eminent man his own humble station and society's laws of politeness forced him to flatter. The texture of flattery and insult he has achieved is the social version of that satire which Dryden most highly prized,[3] the cutting off of a man's head without disturbing its position on his shoulders.

---

[3] *Essays*, ed. W. P. Ker (Oxford, 1900), II, 93.

XLV

𝟀𝟀𝟀𝟀𝟀𝟀𝟀𝟀𝟀𝟀𝟀𝟀𝟀𝟀𝟀

WILLIAM COWPER
(1731-1800)

Cowper fell into the conventional parallel ordering of lines ("Retirement," ll. 398, 406, 412; "Epistle to Mrs. Newton," ll. 1, 36),[1] couplets ("Retirement," ll. 413–14, 423–24), and pairs of couplets ("Mrs. Newton," ll. 11–14; "Epistle to Hill," ll. 36–39) with perfect ease. Antitheses defined in lines ("Mrs. Newton," ll. 14, 22, 34; "Hill," l. 19) and couplets ("Hill," ll. 10–11) came easily too — although he found less use for this dramatic opposing of things than for the neatness of parallels. Cowper also made facile use of conventional line ("Conversation," ll. 116, 117; "Retirement," l. 409) and couplet ("Mrs. Newton," ll. 15–16; "Retirement," ll. 415–16) inversions.

He articulated these standard elements of couplet integration and stability, furthermore, in keeping with the tradition, as polite conversation. The "Epistle to Mrs. Newton" is so colloquial, indeed, that so definitive and intellectual a device as the parallel "In consequence" couplets (ll. 13–16) and such a satiric one as the whiplash suspension, "to be wet through" (l. 32), have become purely laughing matters. Cowper maintained the flexibility and flow proper to such conversational productions, in large part, by his use of the conventional oblique couplet. He employed every degree of obliqueness from the most moderate, which parallels two items in one line of a couplet with one item in the other ("Conversation," ll. 115–16), to such strongly oblique couplets as this — "But, not to moralize too much, nor strain / To prove an evil of which all complain" — whose rhetorical pivot comes after the first line's eighth syllable. Cowper also made use of syntactic thrust. In his mailing directions to Mrs. Newton (ll. 15–26), for instance, one sentence spans six couplets. His story of the Chinese or Japanese emperor ("Hill,"

---

[1] My line references correspond to the line notations in *The Poetical Works of William Cowper*, ed. H. S. Milford (Oxford, 1905).

[415]

ll. 42–53), again, takes six couplets but only three sentences. And we can read lines 395–415 of "Retirement" as one sentence or, if we follow the sense and not the punctuation and thus pause at lines 405 and 406, as four. Cowper's original verse, at any rate, never simply clicks along a couplet at a time.

Despite his easy absorption of traditional couplet practices, however, Cowper's own verse is hardly traditionally dynamic. He has relaxed the form inside the couplet and out, persistently sacrificing energy to ease, intensity to coziness. Notice, for instance, the rejection of couplet definition in his ordering of these three parallel substantives: "Green balks and furrow'd lands, the stream that spreads / Its cooling vapour o'er the dewy meads." The third substantive is separated from the first two by the caesura of the first line, but the first two are not defined, the one from the other, by any metrical means, and the first-line break is quite useless. This does not enrich or destroy the form — this carrying of obliqueness just one step too far; it merely softens it. Or take this projection of a conversational exchange between a man servant and his employer:

> Go, fellow! — whither? — turning short about —
> Nay — stay at home — you're always going out.
> 'Tis but a step, sir, just at the street's end. —
> For what? — An please you, sir, to see a friend.

In the last line of this quotation, the employer's two syllables are so wedged into the servant's request, so imperfectly accommodated to the metrical properties of the form, that one really needs the dashes Cowper or his editor has supplied to be sure that the employer has spoken at all. Or consider, finally, these lines from the same poem: "With frequent intercourse, and always sweet, / And always friendly, we were wont to cheat / A tedious hour — and now we never meet." This oblique *triplet*, in which the last half-line balances the first two and one-half lines, is another case of pushing obliqueness one step further than one can do and, at the same time, maintain that tension between definition and movement which we mean by couplet dynamics.

Cowper has also relaxed the form in producing his extracouplet patterns. One notices in these lines from "Retirement," for instance —

> Ask not the boy, who when the breeze of morn
> First shakes the glitt'ring drops from every thorn
> Unfolds his flock, then under bank or bush
> Sits linking cherry stones, or platting rush,
> How fair is freedom? — he was always free —

that the first four and one-half lines are balanced by the last half of the fifth line — without this half-line's getting couplet emphasis. Again, one notices that the very next four lines on the rural boy's "prime pleasures" are paralleled by one line on his "chief concern":

> To carve his rustic name upon a tree,
> To snare the mole, or with ill-fashion'd hook,
> To draw th' incautious minnow from the brook,
> Are life's prime pleasures in his simple view,
> His flock the chief concern he ever knew.

There are more exaggerated cases of Cowper's unbalanced composition in the burlesque "Epistle to Mrs. Newton": one line on the good aspect of Mrs. Newton's gift, for instance, balances eleven lines on the bad (ll. 3–14), and one line on the lack of news in general gives way to five lines on an exception (ll. 27–32).

Cowper's couplet poetry seems undynamic and spongy also because it is wordy and diffuse. Cowper often takes two or three times as many words or couplets to say a thing as Pope would have done. Notice, for instance, in his "Epistle to Hill" (ll. 54–58) the two couplets on the consequences of a proposition with which he has opposed one couplet on the proposition itself. They could easily have been worked into one couplet such as, say, "Could such a law as this be made to hold / In England, we'd find many catching cold." The whole paragraph in which he explains to his friend the relevance and validity of a little story he has just told him ("Hill," ll. 32–41) could surely be cut without much loss. Perhaps the best way to realize Cowper's diffuseness is to compare this little story itself (ll. 20–32) — with its two couplets of almost irrelevant background, its expletives, and its stage directions — to Pope's three-couplet account of the conversation between old Euclio and his lawyer (*Moral Essays*, I, 256–61).

Cowper's couplet verse in general is as conversational as Pope's was, but Cowper's conversation is little more than friendly chatter. Society is not for Cowper, as it was for Pope, the arena in which the great issues of life can be determined, nor is conversation the medium in which man can face his central concerns. No doubt for the troubled Cowper, as for the romantic poets, the inner life of each man was the vital center of his attention, and his own almost inarticulate feelings the determinant of his life's vital issues. And so the couplet, with its insistence on definition, on public articulation, and on social scrutiny, must dwindle in relevance. We can see this dwindling of the couplet in Cowper's verse, which, although both pointed and conversational, is narrow and even trifling in its achievements.

Cowper's translation of Milton's Latin elegies is quite different from his original couplet poetry; it is an elegant anachronism. A comparison between the catalogues of poets in the Cowper-Milton elegy (VI, 19–28) and the Marlowe-Ovid elegy (I, xv, 9–20) reveals the same stiff and mannered couplet ordering in both. Cowper, like Marlowe, has followed his model closely, producing, that is, a couplet-for-distich equivalency, and he thus ticks off his catalogue a couplet and a poet at a time with almost clockwork regularity. Cowper, again like Marlowe, has reproduced some of his model's balances and parallels (ll. 10, 25–26, 28), lost some (ll. 14, 20, 30), and added some of his own (ll. 32, 34). Cowper was no more able than Marlowe to duplicate the balances that the conjugated Latin agreements allow, and Milton loved this kind of balance (ll. 12, 16, 19, 22, 24). But Cowper's couplets, especially when he was improving on his model, have a polish and a grace Marlowe could hardly have imagined. Notice, for instance, the inversion and the slanted parallel in line 22 of Cowper's translation, the comprehensive balance of food and drink in line 29, and the combination of effects in this line: "And casks not wine alone, but verse, bestow." The intracouplet grace and variety of this old-fashioned, elegiac transcription was only possible at the end of a great tradition.

MILTON'S ELEGY VI, TO CHARLES DIODATI, TRANSLATED

How pleasant, in thy lines describ'd, appear
December's harmless sports, and rural cheer!   10
French spirits kindling with caerulean fires,
And all such gambols, as the time inspires!
　　Think not that wine against good verse offends;
The Muse and Bacchus have been always friends,
Nor Phoebus blushes sometimes to be found   15
With ivy, rather than with laurel, crown'd.
The Nine themselves ofttimes have join'd the song,
And revels of the Bacchanalian throng;
Not even Ovid could in Scythian air
Sing sweetly — why? no vine would flourish there.   20
What in brief numbers sung Anacreon's muse?

Wine, and the rose, that sparkling wine bedews.
Pindar with Bacchus glows — his every line
Breathes the rich fragrance of inspiring wine,
While, with loud crash o'erturn'd, the chariot lies   25
And brown with dust the fiery courser flies.
The Roman lyrist steep'd in wine his lays
So sweet in Glycera's, and Chloe's praise.
Now too the plenteous feast, and mantling bowl
Nourish the vigour of thy sprightly soul;   30
The flowing goblet makes thy numbers flow,
And casks not wine alone, but verse, bestow.
Thus Phoebus favors, and the arts attend,
Whom Bacchus, and whom Ceres, both befriend.
What wonder then, thy verses are so sweet,   35
In which these triple powers so kindly meet.

.   .   .   .

MILTON, ELEGIA SEXTA, AD CAROLUM DIODATUM RURI COMMORANTEM

Quàm bene solennes epulas, hilaremque Decembrim
    Festaque coelifugam quaecoluere Deum,   10
Deliciasque refers, hyberni guadia ruris,
    Haustaque per lepidos Gallica musta focos.
Quid quereris refugam vino dapibusque poesin?
    Carmen amat Bacchum, Carmina Bacchus amat.
Nec puduit Phoebum virdes gestasse corymbos,   15
    Atque hederam lauro praeposuisse suae.
Saepius Aoniis clamavit collibus Euoe
    Mista Thyonêo turba novena choro.
Naso Corallaeis mala carmina misit ab agris:
    Non illic epulae non sata vitis erat.   20
Quid nisi vina, rosasque racemiferumque Lyaeum
    Cantavit brevibus Tëia Musa modis?
Pindaricosque inflat numeros Teumesius Evan,
    Et redolet sumptum pagina quaeque merum,
Dum gravis everso currus crepat axe supinus,   25
    Et volat Eléo pulvere fuscus eques.
Quadrimoque madens Lyricen Romanus Iaccho

Dulce canit Glyceran, flavicomamque Chloen.
Jam quoque lauta tibi generoso mensa paratu,
    Mentis alit vires, ingeniumque fovet.   *30*
Massica foecundam despumant pocula venam,
    Fundis & ex ipso condita metra cado.
Addimus his artes, fusumque per intima Phoebum
    Corda, favent uni Bacchus, Apollo, Ceres.
Scilicet haud mirum tam dulcia carmina per te   *35*
    Numine composito tres peperisse Deos.

.   .   .   .

XLVI

⚶⚶⚶⚶⚶⚶⚶⚶⚶⚶⚶⚶⚶

GEORGE CRABBE
(1754-1832)

Crabbe was able to turn the closed couplet to narrative use without seriously undermining its form or integrity. The only obvious irregularities in his long story "Procrastination," for instance, are three triplets (ll. 19–21, 313–15, 331–33); three alexandrine lines, each one concluding one of these triplets; and three or four enjambed couplets (ll. 191, 240, 288).

His persistent composition in oblique couplets is the one significant adjustment of the form his narrative intentions required. The oblique couplet, examples of which we found in *Cooper's Hill,* is that couplet which modifies the regular rule that the caesural pauses are subordinate to the pause at the end of the couplet's first line; its most obvious and common sign is an enjambed first line. "Procrastination," like Crabbe's other mature narrative poetry, is a texture, a mingling, of regularly formed and obliquely formed couplets. Its first six couplets, for instance, reveal a perfect alternation of them, the first being oblique, the second regular, and so on.

The poem's first couplet — "Love will expire, the gay, the happy dream / Will turn to scorn, indiff'rence, or esteem" — whose first half-line is rhetorically parallel, rhetorically equivalent, to its concluding line and one-half — exemplifies one type of oblique couplet which is common in Crabbe's poetry. Here is another couplet of the same kind: " 'Here you may live, my Dinah! here the boy / And you together my estate enjoy.' " Somewhat less common than this oblique form which contains two parallel segments, one of them longer than the other, is one such as this — "Loth were the lovers; but the aunt declared / 'Twas fortune's call, and they must be prepared" — which contains two antithetically balanced segments of utterance which are metrically inequivalent.

Just as common as this two-part obliqueness, and much more versatile, is that of three parts. Take this couplet, for instance: "Talk'd of departing, and again her breath / Drew hard, and cough'd, and talk'd again of death." It is one case among several (ll. 34–35, 152–53, 251–52) in which the first of three segments in a couplet is especially tied to the third segment. Equally common are couplets whose second or middle segment — the one, that is, which spans the line break — is closely linked to its third segment: "Others, ill match'd, with minds unpair'd, repent / At once the deed, and know no more content," for instance, and, "Then bade her see how her poor aunt sustain'd / The ills of life, nor murmur'd nor complain'd." Crabbe has also patterned the middle segment of his tripartite couplets sometimes. There are several cases in which it defines a rhetorical parallel, such as "with his tawny cheek, / And pitted face" and "the widow smiled; / And bade her wait," and there are a few cases in which it defines antitheses: "what was once her pride / And now her shame."

As some of these examples should suggest, Crabbe's oblique patterns are often quite complex. In this three-part couplet, for instance, "Rupert was call'd in other clime, t'increase / Another's wealth, and toil for future peace," the middle segment makes a syntactically slanted parallel with the first — since "Another's" reflects "other" — and a syntactically exact parallel with the third — "increase" and "toil" being parallel verbs. The tension thus drawn suggests the miserable difference between what Rupert hoped to do and what he would have to do. Consider this couplet: "We parted bless'd with health, and I am now / Age-struck and feeble, so I find art thou." Its second and third segments of thought, which run parallel to one another, stand in contrast with the first. Their bipartite nature, their specificity — that is, their treating the present condition of the two lovers one lover at a time — and their combined metrical weight project the tone and the implication of Dinah's hypocritical resignation. This oblique pattern, " 'Thou too perhaps art wealthy; but our fate / Still mocks our wishes, wealth is come too late,' " also has allowed Crabbe to accommodate Dinah's complex motives to the closed couplet. The direct opposition of its extremes — "Thou . . . art wealthy . . . [but] wealth has come too late" — is reinforced by a syntactically slanted opposition — between "fate" and "wishes" — in the middle segment. How can we avoid the ruin of our wishes, Dinah asks, when mocking fate joins time in opposing them, and all we have to support them is wealth? On the other hand, the 'wealthy–wealth' repetition, showing as it does that the prudent Dinah's thoughts begin and end with wealth, makes it clear that time and fate can never be anything but subordinate powers in her world.

Now and then Crabbe slipped from the three-part couplet into one, like this, of four parts: " 'What must I answer?' — Trembling and distress'd / Sank the pale Dinah by her fears oppress'd." The parallel here between the last half of the first line and the last half of the second, especially as it has been reinforced by rhyme and by the inversion of its second member, fragments the couplet. Crabbe, however, could make even this choppy pattern work sometimes, as in this couplet — "Thine eye is sunken, furrow'd is thy face, / And downward look'st thou — so we run our race," whose first three segments give particular evidence which is brought to bear in the general statement which is its fourth segment.

Both this choppy four-part couplet and the oblique three-part couplet exemplify another general modification in closed-couplet structure which Crabbe's narrative intentions seem to have forced upon him: that is, the practice of cramming. A storyteller must deal in details; he must point out many things and yet get on with his tale. Crabbe apparently found it impossibly binding, first, to confine his couplets and couplet lines to pairs of things and, second, to work every single thing into a pattern of implied judgment. At any rate, he has resorted to lines such as these — "Time lost, youth fled, hope wearied, and at last" and "Proud and indignant, suffering, sick, and poor" — to give his story the necessary wealth of detail and yet keep it moving along. The oblique line, which wedges in an extra item of information (ll. 1, 5, 7, 33) or which crams two items on one side of a caesural pause and puts only one on the other side (ll. 2, 23, 27, 37), is common in Crabbe's poetry. Unfortunately, it cannot be defended as the oblique couplet can, not, at least, as a regular practice. The individual line has only one formal interior pause; to force a second weakens the line's integrity and retards its flow. One extra intralinear pause or even two can be used for incidental effects, as Pope's couplet poetry shows, but to make it a regular part, a persistent part, of one's practice must compromise the form. Of course, many of Crabbe's fragmentary lines are redeemed in some measure by being parts of regular or dynamically oblique couplets, that is, by being woven into the generally strong texture of his couplet production.

But what is the narrative use of weaving the oblique couplet as a normal strand into one's couplet texture? There are, first, the mechanical benefits. Crabbe used oblique couplets to facilitate many necessary narrative shifts — between the different people of his story (ll. 24, 34, 54, 106, 180, 291), between its different places (ll. 306, 323), and between many of its chronological steps (ll. 142, 212, 217, 220, 291, 336).

More important than this, Crabbe's making the oblique couplet a normal element of his style allowed him to cope unobtrusively with the complexities of his characters. We have already noticed something of this use of the oblique couplet. It is more evident still, perhaps, in the following passages: first, that on the aunt's sickness (ll. 31–34); second, that in which Rupert offers himself to Dinah (ll. 263–86); third, that which describes Rupert's disillusionment (ll. 291–99). I have listed these in an ascending scale of couplet obliqueness and, correspondingly, of narrative intensity. In the first of these examples, three oblique, sharply closed couplets describe Rupert's request of Dinah and her aunt's hypocritical response to it; the fourth couplet, a regular one, which closes the passage, projects her obstinacy and the lovers' resignation: "Thus to the lovers was her mind express'd, / Till they forbore to urge the fond request." The last of these three passages, that which discloses Rupert's disillusionment, is composed of three oblique couplets and an equally oblique triplet, all of which have been tightly woven together: the last half-line of the second couplet, for instance, runs parallel rhetorically with the first half-line of the third; and the first half-line of the triplet stands in sharp antithesis to the last line and one-half of the third couplet, which immediately precedes it. Thus Crabbe has conveyed the intensity of this moment, with its revelations and with its contradictions and reversals of feeling, by composing a whole texture of obliqueness, by putting the couplets' ends as well as the ends of their first lines under a tremendous formal strain. Only in its last line, a metrically balanced alexandrine, does this passage reach stability — a stability which asserts the total ruin of Rupert's hopes and the desolation of his future.

The regular couplet Crabbe used commonly as a staple of his narrative and exposition — always gaining from it the natural impression of detachment and clarity of vision. The second, fourth, and sixth couplets of "Procrastination" exemplify this common use. But the persistent presence of oblique couplets allowed Crabbe, now and again, to turn regular couplets to special expressive account. The harshness of the lovers' fate, for instance, emerges from the stiffness of this couplet: "He for uncertain duties doom'd to steer, / While hers remain'd too certain and severe." Elsewhere couplet regularity underscores the essential emptiness of Rupert's prospects as revealed in the simple-minded shiftings of his letters between good hopes and bad (ll. 66–71); and the inanity of the conversation of Dinah's social callers (ll. 182–89).

The reduction of epistles and conversation exemplified by Rupert's letters and Dinah's society may remind us that with Crabbe we are rapidly slipping from the age of Pope, from the age in which conversational epistles and conversation itself were deemed the proper conduits for man's most profound concerns. Pope used the couplet, we remember, to create a forum as well as a subject matter, but Crabbe's couplets, like those of Johnson and Goldsmith, are only relevant to their subject matter. The sense of a community, the sense of a speaker who is responsive to his audience as well as to his topic, has withered away. Crabbe's couplets, regular and oblique, have relevance only to the story he is telling; they never indicate his concern for the varieties of social response or his willingness to attend to social promptings. By his extensive use of the oblique couplet, Crabbe was able to accommodate, first, the narrative shifts and progressions of his material and, second, the shifting complexities of narrative characters — but not society's shifting responses to these things. By maintaining couplet closure and by texturing his composition with regular couplets, Crabbe retained the irreducible minimum public effect of this form — its lucidity and its impression of intellectual detachment. The narrative voice of Crabbe's tales always enjoys this standard couplet benefit; its details seem to be the products of a clear vision and its judgments the determinations of a sensible, balanced mind.

We can see Crabbe's desire for these standard couplet qualities in his introduction to "Procrastination" (ll. 1–12), which sets the story in a broad general framework. This story, the introduction implies, is not merely a tale, a romance; it is an example of vital and generally relevant truth; we should see it as one element in the great scheme of our experience, as one more evidence of human nature. Crabbe has renewed this implication of his introduction with other general pronouncements throughout the story (ll. 84–87, 267–68, 333), the last two of these being presented, significantly, as the thoughts of the disillusioned Rupert, of one, that is, who has learned from experience and reached the point of vantage from which he can generalize his learning. Crabbe's closed couplets also give a telescopic sharpness to everything. Thus metrically emphasized, terms like "pleasure" (ll. 76, 88), "prudent" (ll. 15, 218), and "wealth" (ll. 234, 235) strike us with the full force of their irony. And thus metrically defined, the movements and the elements of the action reveal with perfect clarity their course and their relationships: the aunt's hypocrisies, her calculated misinterpretations, and her self-pity; the niece's step-by-step change from loving to loving things.

PROCRASTINATION

Love will expire, the gay, the happy dream
Will turn to scorn, indiff'rence, or esteem:

Some favour'd pairs, in this exchange, are bless'd,
Nor sigh for raptures in a state of rest;
Others, ill match'd, with minds unpair'd, repent   5
At once the deed, and know no more content;
From joy to anguish they, in haste, decline,
And with their fondness, their esteem resign:
More luckless still their fate, who are the prey
Of long-protracted hope and dull delay: 10
'Mid plans of bliss the heavy hours pass on,
Till love is wither'd, and till joy is gone.
    This gentle flame two youthful hearts possess'd,
The sweet disturber of unenvied rest:
The prudent Dinah was the maid beloved,   15
And the kind Rupert was the swain approved:
A wealthy aunt her gentle niece sustain'd,
He, with a father, at his desk remain'd;
The youthful couple, to their vows sincere,
Thus loved expectant; year succeeding year,   20
With pleasant views and hopes, but not a prospect near.
Rupert some comfort in his station saw,
But the poor virgin lived in dread and awe;
Upon her anxious looks the widow smiled,
And bade her wait, 'for she was yet a child.'   25
She for her neighbour had a due respect,
Nor would his son encourage or reject;
And thus the pair, with expectations vain,
Beheld the seasons change and change again:
Meantime the nymph her tender tales perused,   30
Where cruel aunts impatient girls refused;
While hers, though teasing, boasted to be kind,
And she, resenting, to be all resign'd.
    The dame was sick, and when the youth applied
For her consent, she groan'd, and cough'd, and cried: 35
Talk'd of departing, and again her breath
Drew hard, and cough'd, and talk'd again of death:
'Here you may live, my Dinah! here the boy
And you together my estate enjoy;'
Thus to the lovers was her mind express'd,   40
Till they forbore to urge the fond request.
    Servant, and nurse, and comforter, and friend,

Dinah had still some duty to attend;
But yet their walk, when Rupert's evening call
Obtain'd an hour, made sweet amends for all;   45
So long they now each other's thoughts had known,
That nothing seem'd exclusively their own;
But with the common wish, the mutual fear,
They now had travell'd to their thirtieth year.
    At length a prospect open'd — but, alas!   50
Long time must yet, before the union, pass;
Rupert was call'd in other clime, t' increase
Another's wealth, and toil for future peace;
Loth were the lovers; but the aunt declared
'Twas fortune's call, and they must be prepared;   55
'You now are young, and for this brief delay,
And Dinah's care, what I bequeath will pay;
All will be yours; nay, love, suppress that sigh;
The kind must suffer, and the best must die:'
Then came the cough, and strong the signs it gave   60
Of holding long contention with the grave.
    The lovers parted with a gloomy view,
And little comfort but that both were true;
He for uncertain duties doom'd to steer,
While hers remain'd too certain and severe.   65
    Letters arrived, and Rupert fairly told
'His cares were many, and his hopes were cold;
The view more clouded, that was never fair,
And love alone preserved him from despair:'
In other letters brighter hopes he drew,   70
'His friends were kind, and he believed them true.'
    When the sage widow Dinah's grief descried,
She wonder'd much why one so happy sigh'd:
Then bade her see how her poor aunt sustain'd
The ills of life, nor murmur'd nor complain'd.   75
To vary pleasures, from the lady's chest
Were drawn the pearly string and tabby vest;
Beads, jewels, laces, all their value shown,
With the kind notice — 'They will be your own.'
    This hope, these comforts cherish'd day by day,   80
To Dinah's bosom made a gradual way;
Till love of treasure had as large a part

As love of Rupert, in the virgin's heart.
Whether it be that tender passions fail
From their own nature, while the strong prevail;   85
Or whether av'rice, like the poison-tree,
Kills all beside it, and alone will be;
Whatever cause prevail'd, the pleasure grew
In Dinah's soul, — she loved the hoards to view;
With lively joy those comforts she survey'd,   90
And love grew languid in the careful maid.
   Now the grave niece partook the widow's cares,
Look'd to the great and ruled the small affairs;
Saw clean'd the plate, arranged the china show,
And felt her passion for a shilling grow: 95
Th' indulgent aunt increased the maid's delight,
By placing tokens of her wealth in sight;
She loved the value of her bonds to tell,
And spake of stocks, and how they rose and fell.
   This passion grew, and gain'd at length such sway,   100
That other passions shrank to make it way;
Romantic notions now the heart forsook,
She read but seldom, and she changed her book;
And for the verses she was wont to send
Short was her prose, and she was Rupert's friend.   105
Seldom she wrote, and then the widow's cough,
And constant call, excused her breaking off;
Who, now oppress'd, no longer took the air,
But sate and dozed upon an easy chair.
The cautious doctor saw the case was clear,   110
But judged it best to have companions near;
They came, they reason'd, they prescribed — at last,
Like honest men, they said their hopes were past;
Then came a priest — 'tis comfort to reflect,
When all is over, there was no neglect;   115
And all was over — by her husband's bones,
The widow rests beneath the sculptured stones,
That yet record their fondness and their fame,
While all they left the virgin's care became;
Stock, bonds, and buildings; — it disturb'd her rest,   120
To think what load of troubles she possess'd:
Yet, if a trouble, she resolved to take

Th' important duty, for the donor's sake;
She too was heiress to the widow's taste,
Her love of hoarding, and her dread of waste.   125
  Sometimes the past would on her mind intrude,
And then a conflict full of care ensued;
The thoughts of Rupert on her mind would press,
His worth she knew, but doubted his success;
Of old she saw him heedless; what the boy   130
Forbore to save, the man would not enjoy;
Oft had he lost the chance that care would seize,
Willing to live, but more to live at ease:
Yet could she not a broken vow defend,
And Heav'n, perhaps, might yet enrich her friend.   135
  Month after month was pass'd, and all were spent
In quiet comfort and in rich content:
Miseries there were, and woes the world around,
But these had not her pleasant dwelling found;
She knew that mothers grieved, and widows wept,   140
And she was sorry, said her prayers, and slept:
Thus pass'd the seasons, and to Dinah's board
Gave what the seasons to the rich afford;
For she indulged, nor was her heart so small,
That one strong passion should engross it all.   145
  A love of splendour now with av'rice strove,
And oft appear'd to be the stronger love:
A secret pleasure fill'd the widow's breast,
When she reflected on the hoards possess'd;
But livelier joy inspired th' ambitious maid,   150
When she the purchase of those hoards display'd:
In small but splendid room she loved to see
That all was placed in view and harmony;
There, as with eager glance she look'd around,
She much delight in every object found,   155
While books devout were near her — to destroy,
Should it arise, an overflow of joy.
  Within that fair apartment, guests might see
The comforts cull'd for wealth by vanity:
Around the room an Indian paper blazed,   160
With lively tint and figures boldly raised;
Silky and soft upon the floor below,

Th' elastic carpet rose with crimson glow;
All things around implied both cost and care,
What met the eye was elegant or rare: 165
Some curious trifles round the room were laid,
By hope presented to the wealthy maid:
Within a costly case of varnish'd wood,
In level rows, her polish'd volumes stood;
Shown as a favour to a chosen few,   170
To prove what beauty for a book could do:
A silver urn with curious work was fraught;
A silver lamp from Grecian pattern wrought:
Above her head, all gorgeous to behold,
A time-piece stood on feet of burnish'd gold;   175
A stag's head crest adorned the pictured case,
Through the pure crystal shone th' enamell'd face;
And while on brilliants moved the hands of steel,
It click'd from pray'r to pray'r, from meal to meal.
    Here as the lady sate, a friendly pair   180
Stept in t'admire the view, and took their chair:
They then related how the young and gay
Were thoughtless wandering in the broad highway;
How tender damsels sail'd in tilted boats,
And laugh'd with wicked men in scarlet coats;   185
And how we live in such degen'rate times,
That men conceal their wants, and show their crimes;
While vicious deeds are screen'd by fashion's name,
And what was once our pride is now our shame.
    Dinah was musing, as her friends discoursed,   190
When these last words a sudden entrance forced
Upon her mind, and what was once her pride
And now her shame, some painful views supplied;
Thoughts of the past within her bosom press'd,
And there a change was felt, and was confess'd: 195
While thus the virgin strove with secret pain,
Her mind was wandering o'er the troubled main;
Still she was silent, nothing seem'd to see,
But sate and sigh'd in pensive reverie.
    The friends prepared new subjects to begin,   200
When tall Susannah, maiden starch, stalk'd in;
Not in her ancient mode, sedate and slow,

As when she came, the mind she knew, to know;
Nor as, when list'ning half an hour before,
She twice or thrice tapp'd gently at the door;   205
But, all decorum cast in wrath aside,
'I think the devil's in the man!' she cried;
'A huge tall sailor, with his tawny cheek,
And pitted face, will with my lady speak;
He grinn'd an ugly smile, and said he knew,   210
Please you, my lady, 'twould be joy to you;
What must I answer?' — Trembling and distress'd
Sank the pale Dinah by her fears oppress'd;
When thus alarm'd, and brooking no delay,
Swift to her room the stranger made his way.   215
     'Revive, my love!' said he, 'I've done thee harm,
Give me thy pardon,' and he look'd alarm:
Meantime the prudent Dinah had contrived
Her soul to question, and she then revived.
     'See! my good friend,' and then she raised her head,   220
'The bloom of life, the strength of youth is fled;
Living we die; to us the world is dead;
We parted bless'd with health, and I am now
Age-struck and feeble, so I find art thou;
Thine eye is sunken, furrow'd is thy face,   225
And downward look'st thou — so we run our race;
And happier they, whose race is nearly run,
Their troubles over, and their duties done.'
     'True, lady, true, we are not girl and boy;
But time has left us something to enjoy.'   230
     'What! thou hast learn'd my fortune? — yes, I live
To feel how poor the comforts wealth can give;
Thou too perhaps art wealthy; but our fate
Still mocks our wishes, wealth is come too late.'
     'To me nor late nor early; I am come   235
Poor as I left thee to my native home:
Nor yet,' said Rupert, 'will I grieve; 'tis mine
To share thy comforts, and the glory thine;
For thou wilt gladly take that generous part
That both exalts and gratifies the heart;   240
While mine rejoices.' — 'Heavens!' return'd the maid,
'This talk to one so wither'd and decay'd?

No! all my care is now to fit my mind
For other spousal, and to die resign'd:
As friend and neighbour, I shall hope to see,   245
These noble views, this pious love in thee;
That we together may the change await,
Guides and spectators in each other's fate;
When fellow-pilgrims, we shall daily crave
The mutual prayer that arms us for the grave.'   250
    Half angry, half in doubt, the lover gazed
On the meek maiden, by her speech amazed;
'Dinah,' said he, 'dost thou respect thy vows?
What spousal mean'st thou? — thou art Rupert's spouse;
The chance is mine to take, and thine to give;   255
But, trifling this, if we together live:
Can I believe, that, after all the past,
Our vows, our loves, thou wilt be false at last?
Something thou hast — I know not what — in view;
I find thee pious — let me find thee true.'   260
    'Ah! cruel this; but do, my friend, depart;
And to its feelings leave my wounded heart.'
    'Nay, speak at once; and Dinah, let me know,
Mean'st thou to take me, now I'm wreck'd, in tow?
Be fair; nor longer keep me in the dark;   265
Am I forsaken for a trimmer spark?
Heav'n's spouse thou art not; nor can I believe
That God accepts her who will man deceive:
True I am shatter'd, I have service seen,
And service done, and have in trouble been;   270
My cheek (it shames me not) has lost its red,
And the brown buff is o'er my features spread;
Perchance my speech is rude; for I among
Th' untamed have been, in temper and in tongue;
Have been trepann'd, have lived in toil and care,   275
And wrought for wealth I was not doom'd to share;
It touch'd me deeply, for I felt a pride
In gaining riches for my destined bride:
Speak then my fate; for these my sorrows past,
Time lost, youth fled, hope wearied, and at last   280
This doubt of thee — a childish thing to tell,
But certain truth — my very throat they swell;

They stop the breath, and but for shame could I
Give way to weakness, and with passion cry;
These are unmanly struggles, but I feel   285
This hour must end them, and perhaps will heal.' —
    Here Dinah sigh'd as if afraid to speak —
And then repeated — 'They were frail and weak;
His soul she loved, and hoped he had the grace
To fix his thoughts upon a better place.'   290
    She ceased; — with steady glance, as if to see
The very root of this hypocrisy, —
He her small fingers moulded in his hard
And bronzed broad hand; then told her his regard,
His best respect were gone, but love had still   295
Hold in his heart, and govern'd yet the will —
Or he would curse her: — saying this, he threw
The hand in scorn away, and bade adieu
To every lingering hope, with every care in view.
    Proud and indignant, suffering, sick, and poor,   300
He grieved unseen; and spoke of love no more —
Till all he felt in indignation died,
As hers had sunk in avarice and pride.
    In health declining, as in mind distress'd,
To some in power his troubles he confess'd,   305
And shares a parish-gift; — at prayers he sees
The pious Dinah dropped upon her knees;
Thence as she walks the street with stately air,
As chance directs, oft meet the parted pair:
When he, with thickset coat of badge-man's blue,   310
Moves near her shaded silk of changeful hue;
When his thin locks of grey approach her braid,
A costly purchase made in beauty's aid;
When his frank air, and his unstudied pace,
Are seen with her soft manner, air, and grace,   315
And his plain artless look with her sharp meaning face;
It might some wonder in a stranger move,
How these together could have talk'd of love.
    Behold them now! — see there a tradesman stands,
And humbly hearkens to some fresh commands;   320
He moves to speak, she interrupts him — 'Stay,'
Her air expresses — 'Hark! to what I say:'

Ten paces off, poor Rupert on a seat
Has taken refuge from the noon-day heat,
His eyes on her intent, as if to find   325
What were the movements of that subtle mind:
How still! — how earnest is he! — it appears
His thoughts are wand'ring through his earlier years;
Through years of fruitless labour, to the day
When all his earthly prospects died away: 330
'Had I,' he thinks, 'been wealthier of the two,
Would she have found me so unkind, untrue?
Or knows not man when poor, what man when rich will do?
Yes, yes! I feel that I had faithful proved,
And should have soothed and raised her, bless'd and loved.'   335
    But Dinah moves — she had observed before
The pensive Rupert at an humble door:
Some thoughts of pity raised by his distress,
Some feeling touch of ancient tenderness;
Religion, duty urged the maid to speak   340
In terms of kindness to a man so weak:
But pride forbad, and to return would prove
She felt the shame of his neglected love;
Nor wrapp'd in silence could she pass, afraid
Each eye should see her, and each heart upbraid;   345
One way remain'd — the way the Levite took,
Who without mercy could on misery look;
(A way perceived by craft, approved by pride),
She cross'd, and pass'd him on the other side.

XLVII

****

GEORGE GORDON,
Lord Byron
(1788-1824)

The Corsair, although a romantic tale, shows Byron's considerable responsiveness to the couplet's promptings toward order and lucidity. The lines describing Conrad, for example, unfold as a three-couplet statement of Conrad's seeming ordinariness (I, 193–98),[1] a two-couplet modification of this statement (I, 199–202), and a catalogue of Conrad's features, presented as supporting evidence (I, 203–12). Byron made some use of couplet definition in showing how each item of this catalogue suggests some hidden power in Conrad which close scrutiny would allow one to recognize. It is true that the first item, Conrad's cheek, takes up only half a line and fails to hint at any hidden quality, and that the second, Conrad's hair, a description of which fills out the first couplet of the catalogue, merely hides his fine forehead, but the third item, Conrad's "rising lip," fills the whole second couplet with its sinister suggestions. It was, of course, not Byron's intention to display the character of Conrad as George Crabbe would have done, precisely laying before us all its relevant qualities for our detached and clear-sighted consideration; rather, he wished to sweep us into the vortex of Conrad's strange and powerful nature. But he has marked out at least the geography of its outskirts.

Even so obviously self-indulgent a subject as "Childish Recollections" was modified by the couplet's promptings toward intellectual control and public articulation. In lines 55–76, for example, Byron describes a contrast between the natural honesty of the child and the adult's learned hy-

---

[1] My line references correspond to the line notations in *The Complete Poetical Works of Lord Byron*, ed. P. E. More (Cambridge, Mass., 1933).

pocrisy. A couplet break has allowed him to make its central transition to "Hypocrisy, the gift of lengthen'd years," with perfect precision and clarity. A bit later in the poem we find a more elaborate system of composition than this of simple contrast. There is a general statement, that his "fancy soars not on detraction's wing," which covers two couplets (ll. 77–80); a series of three exceptions, the first of which takes up four couplets (ll. 81–88) and the next two, two couplets each (ll. 89–92, 93–96); and a one-couplet summary. Throughout "Childish Recollections," moreover, we come upon formulations which depend on couplet closure, patterns that reveal something of a closed-couplet sensibility. There is the line-defined antithesis, "And he who wields must sometimes feel the rod," which benefits from an inverted disposition, and such straightforward antithetical lines as "And all may rail while I shall rest in peace" and "In love to friends, in open hate to foes." It is only just, however, to recognize a confusion in the passage of which this last line is a part (ll. 55–76), a confusion between two overlapping contrasts, that between friend and foe and that between honesty and hypocrisy. In the quoted line, for instance, only the adjective "open" suggests the contrast between openness and hypocrisy although that seems to be the dominant one in the passage at large. But Byron has slid back and forth between these two contrasts all the way along.

Byron made imperfect or, at least, incomplete use of the couplet even in those poems whose matter was most susceptible to its dictates. One notices how in the most famous of these, *English Bards and Scotch Reviewers*, he labored the equation between Wordsworth and the idiot boy (ll. 247–54), never quite getting the two in the satiric focus which the couplet provides, and how he smudged the 'Coleridge–ass' equivalency (ll. 261–64). Equally important, Byron has lost the conversational responsiveness, the politeness of address, which gave Pope's satiric statements their immediacy and their strength. The exclamations, the oratorical swell that overflows the form now and again, the repetitions of merely assertive or merely sounding terms make Byron's satire a form of self-indulgence. It seems, as Professor Leavis has suggested, like the unrestrained fulmination of a rude, arrogant schoolboy,[2] and the force of its judgments is, consequently, terribly weakened.

The Age of Bronze, whose obviously didactic intent should have made it fit very securely into couplets, often moves more like blank verse. There are, for instance, the fluent lines on the grave's power (ll. 21–26);

---

[2] "Byron's Satire," in *Revaluation* (London, 1949), p. 150. I owe more to this book than I have been able to acknowledge in my notes.

since their decisive breaks commonly occur at mid-lines (ll. 22, 23, 25, 26), the one strong couplet pause (l. 24) seems almost like a formal flaw, an abrupt and improper stiffness in the flow of the thought. There is, moreover, a lyrical — that is, for our purposes, an anticonversational — impulse in this poem. Such an impulse runs through all Byron's couplets, indeed, including those of *English Bards*. We might notice, for instance, that poem's echoing "turgid ode and tumid stanza" and "tells the tale"; the assonantal "framer of a lay"; the sibilant "Southey! Southey! cease thy varied song"; and the variously musical "The babe unborn thy dread intent may rue." In *The Age of Bronze* we may notice the close-grained repetition, "How vain, how worse than vain," and the refrain, "He wept for worlds" — both of which may remind us of *The Deserted Village*.

This persistent tendency of Byron's couplets away from the impression of polite conversation that dwelled in those of Pope and suggested a speaker of intelligent responsiveness, this tendency toward a monolithic lyrical flow, stands out most clearly in *The Island*. The "songs of Toobonai" (II, i) make use of assonance, of lyrical expressions like "islet's softest shade," "forest depth," "warrior's head," and "ruffled mane," and of melodious proper names, blurring the couplet's indications of a well-punctuated discursive progress into one fluent sweep of seductive and, indeed, virtually mindless melody.

XLVIII

ᛉᛉᛉᛉᛉᛉᛉᛉᛉᛉᛉᛉᛉ

JOHN KEATS
(1795-1821)

The antecedents of Byron's *English Bards and Scotch Reviewers* are the satires of Dryden and Pope and the closed-couplet tradition in general; the antecedents of Keats's *Endymion* are Marlowe's *Hero and Leander*, Drayton's *Man in the Moon*, Chamberlayne's *Pharonnida*, and the enjambed romance couplet tradition in general. But Byron produced a coarsened version of his form of couplet, whereas Keats refined upon his.

Unlike Drayton and Chamberlayne, Keats had a basic sense of discursive order which guided him in developing ideas (I, 1–24), in describing scenery (I, 63–88), and in narrating events (I, 578–632).[1] In the opening five lines of *Endymion*, he asserted the persistence of beauty by making what amounts to four parallel statements, the third of which, a "never" statement, gives this assertion a little antithetical texture; these four statements, although each one is metrically different from the others, all receive some formal punctuation — the first of them probably too much. Then Keats discussed the consequence of this persistence. This consequence, namely, that "Some shape of beauty moves away the pall / From our dark spirits," he argued in two complex sentences which are parallel syntactically although inverse in order: beauty has this consequence in spite of certain hindrances; yes, in spite of them it does have this consequnce (I, 6–13). He concluded with a catalogue of those forms of beauty whose persistence has this consequence (I, 13–24). The relationships between the items in this catalogue are, admittedly, not perfectly defined. Is the "endless fountain," with which it concludes, for instance, an expansion of the immediately preceding "lovely tales," or does it include all the forms of beauty, sun, moon, daffodils, and the

---

[1] My line references correspond to the line notations in *The Poetical Works of John Keats*, ed. H. W. Garrod (London, 1956).

rest? Except for such uncertainties in detail, however, the movement of the passage is clear.

The scenic description in *Endymion*, I, 63–88, which one can compare with a corresponding passage of *Pharonnida*, also makes good sense: the forest "had" dangerous shades, in which lambs but not men became lost (I, 63–79); the paths, which were safe for men, led to lawns, from which one could get a mingled view of foliage and sky (I, 79–88). The articulation of these elements of the scene is, of course, imperfect; the lawn, which turns out to be Keats's central interest, is syntactically subordinated to the paths — whose only value was their leading to this lawn; it is introduced, indeed, as the object of an adverbial phrase. Even the relationship between the paths and the other leading syntactical item in the passage, namely, the forest, is hazy. But one can still imagine these paths all leading through some other parts of the forest than its gloomy shades and carrying one surely and inevitably to a beautiful lawn somewhere in the leafy heart of it.

The organization of Endymion's dream (I, 578–632) is, if anything, easier to follow than these other two passages. The first half of it, which leads up to the dream vision, is a texture of sequence — "presently," "lo!" "again" — and response — "so," "At which," "To commune"; the second half of it gives a variously embellished list of the vision's feminine charms, a list which Keats ordered in three parts: the vision's hair, its first part, left naked her ears, neck, and brow, its second part; these, in turn, blended in with the items which made up the third part, her lips, eyes, cheeks, smiles, and sighs. This catalogue of visionary charms closes, naturally, with a statement of Endymion's response to their combined force. One can usefully compare this passage with a corresponding one in *The Man in the Moon*, that passage in which Drayton's Phoebe first appears to her adorer (ll. 122–256).

It is to their syntactical and logical coherence that these passages owe their clarity, for Keats has made almost as little use of couplet definition in composing them as Chamberlayne and Drayton did in composing their less clear thoughts and sentences. There is, however, a kind of rule to Keats's metrical practice, even if it is not a couplet rule: generally speaking, he used the caesural break and the odd-line break to define his material and avoided the couplet break. The general statement with which *Endymion* opens, for instance, has no strong couplet pause until that at its next-to-last couplet and nothing like a couplet unit any place except for its last two lines; whereas it suffers heavy pauses at the ends of odd lines 1, 5, 19, and 21 and in the middles of lines 2, 3, 11, 13, 15,

16, and 18. There are only two heavy couplet pauses in the description of the forest (I, 66, 72) and only four in the long description of Endymion's dream (I, 597, 599, 609, 619) — with many heavy odd-line and mid-line pauses in both passages.

One can hardly speak of couplet dynamics in this verse, which is organized according to a sort of controlled metrical perversity, but the pulse of the rhymes does seem to me to have an expressive value. These persistent if unobserved stops give the poem what Coleridge would call "fast thick pants," conveying the adolescent breathlessness and feverishness of which Keats himself spoke in the poem's "Preface." One imagines that the adolescent Keats wanted this quality, this impression of his gasping after immortally passionate breath, even though, as he himself admitted, he could not look back on its accomplishment with approval.

The more defined and lucid movement of *Lamia* marks a reversion toward the more obvious and conventional uses of the couplet. The opening of Part II, for instance, uses two couplets to define and to contrast two situations of love, "Love in a hut" and "Love in a palace." The third couplet defines a general statement on "the moral" apparently implicit in this contrast; and the next couplets go on to tie this moral, as well as Keats could do, into his present story. In the conclusion of *Lamia*, again, Keats enclosed his tripartite question on Lamia, Lycius, and Apollonius in a moderately oblique couplet, "What wreath for Lamia? What for Lycius? / What for the sage, old Apollonius?" He also used the couplet to sharpen his three-part answer to this question and to clarify the attack on philosophy which his consideration of Apollonius allowed him to raise. But even in handling materials so abstract and schematic as these on love and philosophy, Keats could not quite make the couplet work — could not quite commit himself to its strictures. The question about Lamia's wreath he did wind up in a couplet, a precariously oblique and inverted one, but the unhappy Lycius required an extra half-line; and then sage, old Apollonius had to be drawn out over a half-line, a line — that is, an enjambed couplet, be it noticed — and another half-line. The discourse on philosophy which follows shifts erratically for six lines or so, settles briefly into a stiff line-by-line movement, and finally is lopped off with a line-and-one-half reference back to the story of Lamia.

With Keats's untimely death, the chance for a revival of the closed couplet, the chance, that is, for an application to romantic urges and ambitions of the public articulation, public scrutiny, and public judgment which the closed couplet induces, was lost.

Index of Authors and Critics

Index of Poems

Subject Index